Critical *Issues in* CRIME AND JUSTICE

*Mary Maguire: I would like to dedicate this
book to Joan and Bruce Maguire, who taught me what I needed
to know about justice, and to Melinda, who makes the words jump off the page.*

*Dan Okada: To the four people who mean the
most to me in life: Sharon, Erin, Anny, and Greg Okada.
I am grateful for all you give, all you do, and all you are. Namaste.*

Critical
Issues in
CRIME
AND
JUSTICE

Thought, Policy, and Practice

Mary Maguire | Dan Okada

California State University, Sacramento

EDITORS

Los Angeles | London | New Delhi
Singapore | Washington DC

For information:

SAGE Publications, Inc.
2455 Teller Road
Thousand Oaks,
   California 91320
E-mail: order@sagepub.com

SAGE Publications Ltd.
1 Oliver's Yard
55 City Road
London EC1Y 1SP
United Kingdom

SAGE Publications India Pvt. Ltd.
B 1/I 1 Mohan Cooperative
   Industrial Area
Mathura Road, New Delhi 110 044
India

SAGE Publications
   Asia-Pacific Pte. Ltd.
33 Pekin Street #02-01
Far East Square
Singapore 048763

Printed in the United States of America

Library of Congress Cataloging-in-Publication Data

Critical issues in crime and justice : thought, policy, and practice / editors, Mary Maguire, Dan Okada.
      p. cm.
Includes bibliographical references and index.
ISBN 978-1-4129-7057-0 (pbk.)
   1. Criminal justice, Administration of. 2. Criminology. I. Maguire, Mary (Mary Helen) II. Okada, Dan.

HV7419.C758 2011
364—dc22   2010001773

This book is printed on acid-free paper.

10   11   12   13   14   10   9   8   7   6   5   4   3   2   1

Acquisitions Editor:	Jerry Westby
Editorial Assistant:	Eve Oettinger
Production Editor:	Karen Wiley
Copy Editor:	April Wells-Hayes
Typesetter:	C&M Digitals (P) Ltd.
Proofreader:	Jeff Bryant
Indexer:	Molly Hall
Cover Designer:	Candice Harman
Marketing Manager:	Helen Salmon
Cover artwork:	Olga Storms, www.olgastorms.com

Brief Contents _____

Detailed Contents_____

PART III. Policing and Law Enforcement

PART IV. Policy and Jurisprudence

PART V. Corrections and Societal Response   295

Preface _____

The creation of a single volume that spans the breadth of information contained in any institution's criminal justice major curriculum offers a bold challenge. A certain level of arrogance goes into conceiving a project such as this: In an academic endeavor that has become so popular, the presumption that one volume can capture the spirit, breadth, and vigor of this field is indeed daunting. We have considered direction and content, ideology and relevance, and we believe this work is a worthwhile addition to the world of academic criminal justice and criminology.

A growing number of capstone courses are required throughout virtually every academic discipline offering a major. Because of the ideology, perspective, direction, and vision of both the department housing the course and the professor delivering it, different philosophies and pedagogies guide their direction.

However, perhaps unique is the fundamental belief that soon-to-be college graduates should be able to demonstrate the knowledge they have acquired through an integration and synthesis of their course work. A highlight of the capstone experience might be the creation of a final project, an individual illustration of the synthesis of their undergraduate curriculum. Another might be, very simply, a curriculum-based opportunity to juxtapose, correlate, and integrate the perspectives and information learned in all courses taken by any one student—in short, the major's final examination. This collection aims to support a variety of capstone iterations.

Topics included span the gamut of a traditional criminal justice or criminology curriculum. Most major curricula include components of crime theory, law enforcement, jurisprudence, corrections, and organizations. The essays included here broadly represent those areas.

Students have been known to declare a major after having been influenced by popular culture and the media. The "If it bleeds, it leads" ethos of modern information dissemination routinely highlights the exploits of criminal justice practitioners and the need to conquer those who would cause them harm. These depictions, while often titillating and perhaps noteworthy, are just as often extraordinary and atypical. They overly dramatize or sensationalize human misery and suffering. Our students become fascinated with the possibility of engaging a world glamorized as violent or confrontational so that their attitudes must likewise be aggressive and decisive rather than thoughtful or reflective. Some will see the social complexities more clearly. Students are torn by the perception that practitioners take action but academics regard and wait. What is the right approach? This is the yin/yang of academic criminal justice.

This is also the real world that academic criminal justice seeks to understand, contextualize, examine, and consider. While the work of the academic must be general and uncertain, the events we examine are specific, even personal. We hope the journey you take with us is informative, provocative, even exciting—for criminal justice is all these things, both inside the classroom and out.

Acknowledgments _____

Our heartfelt gratitude goes to our executive editor, Jerry Westby. Not only is Jerry a pleasure to work with, his publishing wisdom and guidance made this a much better book than it would have been otherwise. Many thanks also to the tireless efforts of his assistant, Eve Oettinger, who possesses the unique skill of moving mountains with a whisper. We also thank our copy editor, April Wells-Hayes, for her stellar attention to detail. Another note of thanks goes to the very talented Olga Storms, who generously donated her art to the cover. Lastly, we thank the reviewers, whose efforts and expertise provided insight and feedback that helped to shape this book into its current form: Barbara Sims, Pennsylvania State University, Harrisburg; Richard M. Hough, University of West Florida; Robert M. Baggett, University of North Florida; and Michael Leiber, Virginia Commonwealth University. Obviously, any errors in judgment, analysis, or interpretation are ours alone.

1

Introduction

The Many Voices in Justice

Mary Maguire

Dan Okada

American culture is fascinated by crime. College and university criminology and criminal justice departments continue to multiply, and classes are packed with students eager to learn. The *CSI* and *Law and Order* franchises are among the most popular of all mainstream and cable network television programs; both are regularly programmed to fill time slots virtually every day and night. Even though society places crime and deviance outside of accepted and expected social frameworks, their prohibition makes them inherently interesting. The media adage "If it bleeds, it leads" suggests a fascination with misery and human suffering. Network newscasters refer to "slow" news days as those without homicides or with few crimes. Airplane crashes and instances of homicide do not happen very often, but when they do, viewing audiences are riveted to their chairs.

How has this allure with human failing and despair served the criminal justice system and the study of criminology over the years? For some, this attraction with what might be called deviance (but in many cases should be referred to simply as difference) fosters curiosity and motivates questions that call for deeper understanding. For others, it creates discomfort with the status quo and fosters a need for moral entrepreneurship. Some are comfortable with the stretching of social boundaries, while others believe that stasis is maintained by holding firmly to traditional social norms. Those with different philosophical and cultural persuasions bring competing pressures to bear on elected officials to reform or to maintain an accepted standard. Because criminological concerns are often third-rail issues for policymakers (gun control, legalization of marijuana, prison sentencing, funding for law enforcement as well as for inmate programs), the louder voice among constituents is often what guides policy development. In other words, it is not necessarily clear evidence or even the consequences to individuals or communities that motivates criminal justice policy; rather, it is the policymaker's allegiance to the ideology of his or her constituents, however well- or ill-informed they may be.

A historical perspective illustrates these sometimes conflicting ideologies as they have alternately become the dominant way of thinking and the driving force of criminal justice policy. Legal scholar Michael Tonry (1996, 1998, 2001, 2004) has written at length about paradigm shifts in criminological and justice thinking and action. He notes that the proverbial criminal justice pendulum, which is often based on a "moral panic" (2004), swung from the reform-minded due process/offender's rights policy initiatives of the 1960s to the crime control model's "tough on crime" mandatory minimums of the 1980s. The reform ideology evaporated when multiple forces converged to shift policy to accord with the crime control model.

A catalyst of this shift was Martinson's (1974) "What Works" article, which reported that prison programs were not effectively rehabilitating prisoners. Martinson's findings, although they were later revised, were used to justify a change from indeterminate to determinate sentencing. If inmates could not be rehabilitated, imprisoning them for a determined amount of time seemed to be a reasonable option. Almost simultaneously, in May 1973, what became known as the Rockefeller drug laws went into effect in New York. These draconian measures stipulated that a prison sentence for selling 2 ounces or more of heroin, morphine, cocaine, or marijuana would carry the same prison term as second-degree murder: a sentence of 15 to 25 years to life. This new, punitive framework paved the way for the development of a "tough on crime" mentality across the nation, with the resulting adoption of mandatory minimums and harsher sentences across a broader range of offenses.

The paradigm shift that occurred in the United States from reform to retribution resulted in the largest prison system in the world. With more than 7 million people on probation, in jail or prison, or on parole at the end of 2007 (Bureau of Justice Statistics, 2009), 1 in every 100 Americans was under some form of correctional supervision (Pew Charitable Trusts, 2009). Clear and Cadora (2003) highlight the unintended consequences to some communities that were inhabited by more residents who had been in prison than not. Disadvantaged communities with high numbers of residents returning from prison are more likely to accept and take on the prison culture, thus exacerbating problems in those already vulnerable neighborhoods. In essence, with the ideological shift to retribution, we have created our own tautological social problem. With our get-tough crime policies, we have created a system impervious to attempts at outside intervention. By increasing the number of convictions and the terms of prison sentences, we have weakened community structures and created a prison system that is almost too large to be sustained, even in the best of economic times.

Just as a number of factors converged in the 1970s to create the shift to retribution, a number of factors are converging today to swing the pendulum back, an unsustainable prison system being one of them. Prison systems across the country were nearly at maximum capacity in the previous century, and overcrowding has continued into this century with state resources further co-opted and diverted to fight the War on Terror. This has placed untenable pressure on an already strained system. With the housing market collapse of 2008, economic conditions mandated that most states cut public funding for many governmental services, including law enforcement and corrections. With fewer state and federal resources available, conversations about the legalization of marijuana began in California (in direct contrast to the thinking that brought about the Rockefeller drug laws), as have negotiations for early inmate release. Sentences for crack and for cocaine, which were historically disparate, have been equalized and now stand simply as guidelines, not mandates, in most states. Retributive policies are under closer assessment in the light of worsening economic conditions.

With a cursory inspection, it is clear that the drift of criminal justice practice and policy has been barely affected by empirical evidence, by cost-effectiveness, or by beneficial or even fair practices. Evidence-based program assessments have been few. The fate of individuals who engage in deviant and sometimes criminal behavior is the result of the choices they make and the political winds of the time. In many cases, sanctions are not based on what is best for the individual, for the victim, or for the long-term health and safety of American communities. The waning of the "tough on crime" position is a consequence of the economic conditions of the time. Its passing is accompanied by no acknowledgment of ideological or practical failure, by no plan for effecting positive change in disadvantaged neighborhoods anywhere. Simply put, the ideological changes that in turn change laws and lives are not proactive. Criminal justice legislation is reactive and, as such, debilitating to many communities and cultures.

How should we, as criminal justice and criminology professionals, respond to the conundrums of the justice system as it interfaces with the changing social, political, and economic times? Clearly, our fascination with crime and deviance alone is not enough to develop and/or sustain improvement in our justice system. Historically, we have been guided by the vocal families of victims of rare, albeit heinous, crimes. We have also been guided by various stakeholders, such as labor unions, victims' rights and other political action groups, academics, and enterprising political leaders. Although each group has a point of view worthy of attention, beneficial contributions through non-collaborative action are not enough. One could speculate that what is missing is the appropriate dose of interdisciplinary study and research, thoughtful and articulate reflection, and reasonable action, leading to effective social policies in the service of that responsible evidence.

This text, *Critical Issues in Crime and Justice: Thought, Policy, and Practice*, brings multiple and varied voices together to discuss the contemporary issues facing criminal justice. One goal of this volume is to contribute to the educational conversation about issues of crime and justice so that fear and sensationalism will lose their influence on justice policy. The chapters in this volume are meant to stimulate critical thinking and dialogue about substantive justice issues as well as the justice process.

REFERENCES

Bureau of Justice Statistics (BJS). (2009). *Corrections statistics.* Retrieved June 15, 2009, from http://www.ojp.usdoj.gov/bjs/correct.htm

Clear, T., & Cadora, E. (2003). *Community justice.* Belmont, CA: Wadsworth.

Martinson, R. (1974). What works? Questions and answers about prison reform. *Public Interest, 35,* 22–54.

Pew Charitable Trusts. (2009). *One in 31: The long reach of American corrections.* Retrieved from http://www.pewcenteronthestates.org/uploadedFiles/PSPP_1in31_report_FINAL_WEB_3-26-09.pdf

Tonry, M. (1996). *Sentencing matters.* New York: Oxford University Press.

Tonry, M. (2001). *Penal reform in overcrowded times.* New York: Oxford University Press.

Tonry, M. (2004). *Thinking about crime: Sense and sensibility in American penal culture.* New York: Oxford University Press.

Tonry, M., & Moore, M. (Eds.). (1998). *Youth violence.* New York: Oxford University Press.

PART I

Criminal Justice and Criminological Paradigms

2 The Importance of Ethics in Criminal Justice

Cyndi Banks

In criminal justice systems, the application of ethical norms has come to be recognized as a crucial part of the process of doing justice. Whether an action is performed by law enforcement, corrections, judges, lawyers, or justice policymakers, we expect that decision making will be ethical, and when it is not, we anticipate that those who violate ethical norms will be held accountable. The field of *normative ethics* sets standards of conduct to assist in determining how to act, and it draws on such sources as religions, natural law, and written law in shaping ethical standards. *Applied ethics* is concerned with resolving issues that raise questions about what is right or wrong and what is good or bad. Criminal justice professionals, who often possess the right to control others through the application of force and coercion, must understand how to act in situations in which ethical dilemmas arise, if they are to avoid accusations of abuse of their powers. Ethical theories about how to act and the rightness or wrongness of acts provide a foundation from which to analyze ethical dilemmas and arrive at a correct conclusion or resolution.

This chapter discusses ethical issues within the justice sector, as well as the theoretical basis from which to make determinations about ethical issues and dilemmas. The aim is to draw attention to the principal normative and applied ethical questions that arise within the sector, to briefly indicate the range and scope of perspectives concerning such questions, and to highlight how disregard for ethical issues and arguments can result in incoherent and irrational policymaking and improper and unprincipled conduct.

Police Ethics

Of all the elements in criminal justice systems, policing is the most likely to provoke ethical dilemmas. In the early days of law enforcement in the United States, the police relied unhesitatingly on physical force and coercion to maintain control of the streets and paid little attention to ethical standards. An institutional culture comprising the values, attitudes, and norms of law enforcement developed within policing and this culture has encouraged and condoned corruption and the use of force, including lethal force, within the community. Research studies of policing began to identify the nature of policing and developed models of the crime fighter, the emergency operator, the social enforcer, and the social peacekeeper (Kleinig, 1996). Above all, commentators suggested that police developed the notion that the cause of crime fighting was noble, and therefore sometimes justified unethical conduct. Police culture supported corruption, the excessive use of force, a cynical and suspicious approach to the community, and the notion that police were themselves victims. Codes of ethics were devised, published, and promoted but were often flouted in favor of the noble cause (Crank & Caldero 2000). Frequently, police managers reason that police abuse and corruption are caused by the individual acts of "rotten apples" and reject explanations that these acts are indicative of systemic abuse. However, studies have shown that corruption and racism in particular are systemic within law enforcement—particularly the tendency of police to stereotype people in a form known as "racial profiling" (Reiner, 1985; Skolnick, 1966; Walker, Spohn, & DeLone 2000, p. 95). How do we explain this incidence of noble-cause corruption within law enforcement? To a great extent, it can be linked to the extensive discretionary powers possessed by law enforcement, which can be employed for good or bad ends and purposes. While opponents of broad police discretionary powers contend that the police should be limited by laws and internal rules, regulations, and codes of ethics, others argue that curtailing discretion will impede crime fighting and endanger the community.

Generally, public opinion seems accepting of broad discretionary powers as long as those powers are not directed at the opinion holders themselves. Police misuse of force is a major issue in the exercise of police discretion, and despite codes and rules of ethics that regulate its use, many situations place law enforcement in the position of having to make a determination about the degree and application of force and coercion. Of course, police may be held accountable subsequently for rule violations, but by that time innocent people may have fatally suffered at their hands. Police culture and the influence of past histories of violence play an important part in determining the level of violence that law enforcement considers acceptable in any given policing situation. As well as force and coercion on the streets, police have powers over individual citizens during interrogation and investigation, and here questions may arise about entrapment, the rights of persons apprehended by police, and such practices as police lying and deception, which tend to be accepted modes of policing. Indeed, some argue that the public has no choice but to accept a certain level of police corruption and abuse in the interests of public safety and in serving the noble cause. Of course, people apprehended by police are normally treated with respect for their dignity and rights; however, sometimes detainees are flagrantly abused, as the following case illustrates.

Case Study: "Cop Gets 15 Years in Torture Case"

In one of the worst cases of police abuse of power and brutality in recent times, two patrolmen who were involved in the 1997 New York attack on Haitian immigrant Abner Louima in the police station bathroom of the 70th Precinct in the Flatbush section of Brooklyn were sentenced to 15 years and 8 months and 30 years imprisonment. One patrolman, Charles Schwarz, was found to have held down Louima as he was tortured by fellow officer Justin Volpe, who sodomized Louima with a broomstick, tearing a one-inch hole in Louima's rectum and bladder. According to Volpe, who admitted the attack and was sentenced to 30 years imprisonment, he initially assaulted Louima in a patrol car and then punished him at the police station because he believed Louima had assaulted him during a fight outside a Brooklyn nightclub. Volpe afterward boasted of his actions to fellow officers and, walking through the stationhouse with the broomstick in his hand, claimed to have "broken a man down."

In 2001, Louima settled an $8.7 million lawsuit against the City of New York. City officials characterized the incident as an aberration and denied that any systemic brutality existed within the police force. In February 2002, the U.S. federal court of appeals reversed the conviction of Schwartz, finding insufficient evidence that he had assisted in the assault. Schwartz had always claimed that he was not the officer who assisted Volpe. His account was supported by Volpe himself, but Louima identified Schwartz as the second man involved in the assault.

Source: From "Cop Gets 15 Years in Torture Case," by Tom Hays, June 27, 2000, Associated Press. Used with permission of The Associated Press. Copyright © 2009. All rights reserved.

Discrimination

There is a consistent belief among minorities that racism exists in multiple forms within the justice system at certain decision-making points, for example, in police decisions about arrest, in granting alleged offenders bail, in jury selection, and in conviction and sentencing. Numerous studies have shown that, although there may be no systemic racism, individual acts of discrimination do take place at certain points within the criminal justice system where decisions are made, and also that racism may be present in complex forms hidden from obvious view (Georges-Abeyie in Russell, 1998, p. 32; Pope & Feyerherm, 1990). This means that all those who exercise decision-making powers within the system should always act ethically and must deliver decisions that are free from explicit or implicit racial bias and discrimination. The following case demonstrates how police can target and scapegoat minorities.

Case Study: "Looking Mexican"

In July 1997, the city of Chandler, a suburb of Phoenix, Arizona, with a population of 143,000, began Operation Restoration, which was intended to construct a new civic center, including police headquarters, municipal court, and library, and to revitalize the town. Since its founding in 1912, Chandler had become two cities: one affluent, the other the old, impoverished, downtown area.

Seeking a cause for the city center's decay, city officials fixed on illegal immigration and focused on alleged criminal activity by illegal immigrants. The city police and the Border Patrol collaborated on a plan linked to Operation Restoration, and on the first day of the operation, two dozen police officers and five Border Patrol agents moved through the downtown area, chasing suspected illegal immigrants from work sites and filling up buses with those they captured. In all, police eventually removed 432 illegal immigrants, all but 3 from Mexico.

However, the illegal immigrants in Chandler coexist with a large, well-established Mexican American community in which Latinos make up about 15% of the population. As police questioned those leaving markets favored by Latinos, they encountered U.S. citizens, from whom they also demanded identification and immigration papers. The police operations targeted legal residents and U.S. citizens who "looked Mexican."

Four months later, the Arizona attorney general revealed the results of his inquiry into this raid. These included that Chandler police had stopped residents, questioned them, and entered their homes without warrants, relying only on skin color, Mexican appearance, or use of the Spanish language to identify the residents as suspected illegal immigrants. Moreover, the city officials had not requested formal permission from the U.S. attorney general to act against illegal immigrants, as is required by federal law.

The city manager officially reprimanded the police chief for the raid, and a group of Latinos launched a $35 million lawsuit against the city. Latinos commented that it would take 10 or 15 years for people to feel comfortable again in the town.

Source: From "An Ugly Stain on a City's Bright and Shining Plan," by H. Tobar, December 28, 1998, *Los Angeles Times*, p. A1.

Legal Ethics

As professionals, lawyers are subject to detailed rules and codes that govern their actions in relation to their clients and to the justice system in general. An instance of this is the American Bar Association Model Rules of Professional Conduct (1983). Lawyers' duty to the court is specified in such texts, and there are rules governing the conduct of prosecutions and the tactics and strategies defense lawyers may or may not employ in representing their clients. Ethical norms are therefore highly developed within the legal profession, and accountability for violations is ensured through professional associations and the courts, both of which have the power to discipline and even disbar lawyers for unethical conduct. In cases where an ethical rule is unclear, a lawyer can seek advice from within the profession, and this facilitates the task of keeping within the permissible boundaries regulating a lawyer's conduct and practice. Among the general public, however, there is only very limited awareness of professional ethical rules; significant misunderstandings exist about the operation of the common-law adversarial system of justice, a system that gives lawyers a good deal of control over the court process. For example, the public routinely faults defense lawyers for "defending persons they know to be guilty," based on a lack of understanding of the link between the protection of an accused person's rights and the role of the defense lawyer in ensuring that those protections are enforced. Lawyers are required to adhere to the principles of partisanship and neutrality. They must put the interests of the client above the public good and, in representing a client, must disregard questions of personal morality so that the client's interests always take precedence over those of the lawyer.

The primary duty of a prosecutor is not merely to secure a conviction but to ensure that justice is done. Prosecutorial work brings into play a special set of ethical issues that result from the wide discretion that prosecutors (like police) enjoy in the operation of certain functions, such as deciding what crime to indict a person with and those relating to the practice of plea-bargaining. As well, the right of the prosecutor to determine, within a limited framework of rules, what evidence is to be put before the court and what evidence is to be made available to the defense can give rise to serious ethical conflicts. In the United States, many prosecutors are elected officials, and this gives rise to a further set of ethical issues, including community pressures about how the prosecutorial function is exercised in the context of promises made and expectations raised during the election process. Whether the primary concern is for the victim, the community, re-election, or discovering "the truth," prosecutors must make choices and decide their constituency, either generally or in a particular case. The likelihood that judges and prosecutors may become corrupt or act unethically probably increases according to the extent to which they enjoy wide discretionary powers. However, because judges generally perform their functions transparently and in public, the risks of impropriety are reduced. The same cannot be said about prosecutors, who conduct much of their business behind closed doors and who do not open to public scrutiny such processes as plea-bargaining. Sometimes, judges are so blatantly corrupt that they actually manipulate the judicial system to enrich themselves, as can be seen in the following case study.

Case Study: "Pennsylvania Rocked by 'Jailing Kids For Cash' Scandal"

Luzerne County, Pennsylvania, has been shocked by a scandal involving two elected judges, Mark Ciavarella and Michael Conahan, who received more than $2.6 million in kickbacks for jailing juveniles. The two judges have been disbarred and have also resigned from their elected positions. They will serve 87 months' imprisonment under plea bargains for fraud and tax charges. The corruption began in 2002, when Conahan shut down the state juvenile facility and used funds from the county budget to fund a private facility. The federal government began an investigation in 2006.

The two judges engaged in the practice of sending children to private juvenile detention centers owned by Mid-Atlantic Youth Services Corporation under a contract with the court; in return for this, the two judges were paid kickbacks. The private detention center operator is still in business, and the owner denies any involvement or knowledge of the scheme practiced by the two judges. Records indicate that two people paid the judges, one of whom was the former owner of Mid-Atlantic, who claims he was pressured to pay by the judges.

Of the hundreds of children appearing before the judges, many had no lawyers, and about half of those who appeared before Ciavarella were sent to a placement, as compared to only 8.4% across the state. Records showed that numerous minors charged with nonviolent crimes were given harsher sentences than recommended by probation reports.

Pennsylvania has the second-highest number of privatized juvenile detention facilities after Florida and accounts for about 11% of all such private facilities in the United States. Critics say that these private facilities are able to hide illegal and improper activities because they are not subjected to the same inspection and audit requirements as state facilities.

Source: From "Pennsylvania Rocked by 'Jailing Kids for Cash' Scandal," by Stephanie Chen, February 24, 2009, CNN.com Edition.

Punishment

What is the ethical rationale for punishment, and how do we justify its imposition? The sociological approach to understanding why we punish focuses on how the currents and modes of thinking in society affect the climates of tolerance and intolerance. Social theories about punishment treat it as a social phenomenon and explore relations between punishment and society. Philosophical theories apply utilitarian and retributive theories, asking questions about the goals of punishment and its overall purpose. According to these theories, punishment is justified according to theories of deterrence, retribution, just deserts, rehabilitation, incapacitation, and restorative justice. Many believe that punishment deters the crimes of both repeat offenders and potential offenders. Deterrence theory was first proposed by utilitarian philosophers, who contended that it is the fear of the consequences of criminal actions that deters crime. However, numerous research studies have failed to show conclusively that deterrence works, partly because the commission of much crime does not appear to be based upon rational decisions that weigh the potential consequences

(Beyleveld, 1979, cited in Hudson, 1996, p. 23; Blumstein, Cohen, & Nagin, 1978, p. 66; Ten, 1987, p. 9).

The theory of retribution contends that punishment can be justified because it is deserved and that persons ought to be held accountable for acts that harm society. Retributionists argue that the punishment imposed should always be proportionate to the wrongdoing, a standpoint known as *just deserts*. Further, retribution is considered justified in terms of criminals owing and paying a debt to society, that society ought to censure those who break its norms and rules, and that punishment has an expressive function (in that society is expressing its condemnation of an offender) that ought to be communicated to an offender. Retribution or just deserts theory began to gain ground over alternative versions of the purpose and justification of punishment in the 1980s. It has emerged as the premier rationale for punishment and, consistent with its emphasis on proportionality, has led to the development of sentencing guidelines and sentencing commissions charged with determining the extent of punishment that ought to be imposed for particular crimes. Just deserts theory focuses only on the harm involved in the crime and on the culpability of the offender. Critics argue that it lacks any principled basis for determining commensurate sentences for crimes and completely ignores social and other factors that ought to be taken into account in arriving at an appropriate sentence (Hudson, 1996, p. 46; Tonry, 1994, p. 153). Critics of retribution argue that it is nothing more than vengeance, but Nozick (1981, p. 366) points out that, unlike retribution, revenge possesses no limits and may be inflicted on an innocent person, perhaps a relative, and not necessarily on the offender.

The concept of rehabilitation is that punishment ought to be concerned with healing the offender so that he or she may return to society after punishment with little or no chance of becoming a repeat offender. Crime is regarded as a social disease to be treated and cured. To determine the appropriate punishment, the offender's social and economic background must be fully taken into consideration. Previously, indeterminate sentences were imposed that made the release of the offender contingent on the successful completion of rehabilitation programs. The decision to release was exercised by boards, based on their assessment of an individual's progress through rehabilitation, and was not determined exclusively by the court. In the 1970s, opinion turned against rehabilitation as the proper rationale and basis for determining punishment when meta-studies of rehabilitation programs purported to show that "nothing works" (Martinson, 1974). The discredited rationale of rehabilitation has been replaced by the now-dominant theories of just deserts and incapacitation.

Incapacitation theorists argue that the public ought to be protected from the chance of future offenses committed by those who are already convicted criminals and that placing offenders in custody for long periods of time is justified in the pursuit of this end. Opponents of incapacitation contend that offenders are therefore being punished on the basis of predictions of their likely future conduct and that this is arbitrary, unfair, and entirely speculative (Morris 1974, p. 241). They question the ethics of punishing people for crimes they have yet to commit.

Restorative justice proponents emphasize community involvement in determining an appropriate punishment and maintain that a process through which a victim confronts the offender with the harm suffered will help restore that offender to the community with an enhanced capacity to support social cohesion and not reoffend. Restorative justice calls for a return to community punishment practices that disappeared with the emergence of the state as the exclusive authority for administering punishment and providing solutions to crime. This form of justice has generally been employed to deal with minor offenses but has been accepted in some jurisdictions as the most appropriate means of punishing juvenile delinquency.

Correctional Ethics

Over the last two decades, criminal justice policies focusing on crime control—including so-called zero-tolerance practices and incapacitating offenders for very long periods of time under laws such as "three strikes and you're out"—have caused an explosion in the size of the prison population (Harrison & Beck, 2003). Commentators now regularly describe U.S policy as favoring "mass imprisonment" (Christie, 2000). Within justice systems, police and corrections officers have always been empowered to exercise a degree of physical control over citizens; now, contemporary crime-control strategies bring even greater numbers of citizens into direct contact with law enforcement and corrections staff. Heightened tensions between the public and criminal justice officials, arising from policies of mass imprisonment, make it essential that ethical standards of treatment and conduct be observed in prisons and jails.

Like law enforcement, corrections work possesses an institutional culture that has developed over time in conjunction with changes in prison operations, staffing, and disciplinary regimes. An understanding of that culture is vital to an appreciation of the ethical challenges faced by corrections staff. The organization and management of corrections developed from early individualistic methods of controlling people in custody into full-fledged bureaucratic and managerialist regimes of control, with detailed rules and procedures that covered both prison staff and those incarcerated as well as the permitted interactions between them. Historically, prisoners had few rights and were treated harshly and with high levels of brutality, yet in the contemporary period, prisoners regularly test the scope and content of their rights in the courts. How do ethics relate to corrections when prisoners are in custody, sometimes under maximum security conditions and sometimes within lightly guarded facilities? Commentators argue that a person is sent to prison "as" punishment and not "for" punishment; therefore, such practices such as highly controlled visitation, strip searches, and punishment of prisoners through removal of so-called privileges, should be prohibited because they amount to the imposition of additional and unauthorized sanctions (Kleinig, 2001, p. 7). Adopting an ethical standard would therefore mean respecting the dignity, humanity, and rights of prisoners as well as refraining from imposing any further forms of punishment.

The nature of the relationship between guards and prisoners and between guards and their coworkers also raises questions about normative conduct. Obviously, there is a significant power dynamic between inmates and guards, and the guards, in the absence of rules that incorporate ethical standards and norms, potentially have the power to seriously abuse prisoners (Kleinig, 2001, p. 10). Guards are required to demonstrate the ability to manage prisoners but must also accept that they are dependent on good relations with prisoners to protect their personal safety. Guards possess a personal authority derived from character and personality, as well as a legal authority the source of which is the prison rules and regulations. Therefore, an ethical framework that regulates these interactions is required. One extreme school of thought argues, however, that the nature of incarceration makes it virtually impossible to apply ethical standards of conduct and that degradation and brutality are inescapable (Smith, 2001, p. 30).

Research has revealed the prison guard code and the "gray wall of silence," which incorporate key tenets of the business of guarding, including "Always aid an officer in distress," "Don't rat," and "Never make a fellow officer look bad in front of inmates" (Kauffman, 1988, pp. 86–117). The institutional culture of corrections valorizes the dangers and tensions of incarceration and the way these elements combine to engender a sense of suspicion about events in a facility that are out of the ordinary or seem to be violations of prison rules. However, research studies have revealed that guards, despite their apparent absolute dominance, in fact must negotiate the extent of their domination with inmates through a process of contestation (Lombardo, 1989, p. 94). This process can result in the "corruption of authority" and means that rulebooks are often jettisoned in the interests of flexibility and of establishing a modus vivendi. Similar to law enforcement, individual discretion and its exercise are an important part of being a guard and are influenced by the guard culture as well as the relevant rules and the overall prison disciplinary regime. Studies of this culture have revealed that recruits into the corrections industry are socialized to adhere to the elements of the prison guard code that focus on solidarity between coworkers against inmates (Kaufman, 1988, p. 198).

The use of force by corrections staff is a major ethical issue within corrections. In the past, violence was prevalent and expected. Nowadays, despite rules regulating the application of force and accountability (including actions in the courts), some prison systems continue to permit extralegal levels of coercion and force against inmates. The guard culture contends that force is always justified because only the threat of violence or violence itself will ensure control within the facility, and violence deters inmate attacks on guards (Kaufman, 1988, p. 141). Reprisals for attacks by inmates are considered essential and entirely appropriate within the guard culture. Nevertheless, there is also an appreciation within corrections that violence begets more violence and that inmate resistance cannot be repressed by the constant application of force (Kaufman, 1988, p. 71). Nowadays, the use of force is regulated by rules and by the courts, the state, and the federal government. Other forms of conduct that violate ethical norms include institutional and guard attitudes toward rape in prison and the promotion of corruption through smuggling, drug trafficking, and similar activity. The following is a case of male prison rape.

Case Study: Rape in Prison

In 1993, Eddie Dillard was serving time in a California prison. He was a young first-timer, a slight man, and was transferred to share a cell with Wayne Robertson, a huge, muscular man nearly twice the weight of Dillard and who was serving a life sentence for murder. Robertson was known by all as "the Booty Bandit," having earned this nickname through his practice of violently raping prisoners. Before the end of the first day in the cell they shared, the inevitable had occurred: Robertson had beaten Dillard and sodomized him. He continued to do this for the next two days until, finally, Dillard ran out of the cell and refused to return. A correctional officer working on the unit informed the *Los Angeles Times,* "Everyone knew about Robertson. He had raped inmates before and he's raped inmates since." Documentation submitted to a California legislative hearing supported this report, showing Robertson had *committed* more than a dozen rapes inside that and other prisons.

Source: From *No Escape: Male Rape in U.S. Prisons* (pp. 148–149), Human Rights Watch.

Probation and parole were originally linked to plans for the individualized treatment of prisoners, but in their contemporary form they are focused almost exclusively on punishment and the enforcement of court sanctions (Petersilia, 1999, p. 480). Parole officers have always been closer to law enforcement. Now, probation officers adopt a policing posture toward probationers, are armed, and often collaborate with law enforcement officers in raiding premises. Accordingly, both probation and parole officers now exercise substantial degrees of control over probationers and parolees and face ethical concerns like those in corrections and law enforcement.

Ethical Criminal Justice Policymaking

Crime control and how to punish offenders are key elements of justice policymaking. For example, the development of private prisons as a policy option for punishment is an important issue in criminal justice policy and raises significant ethical issues, such as whether the state or government should ever permit outside agencies to punish citizens, whether the profit motive is compatible with the exercise of the right to inflict punishment through incarceration, and how private prisons resolve issues connected with the use of force.

Ethical considerations ought to play a significant role in criminal justice policymaking; however, since the 1970s, policymaking has typically been more concerned with formulating punitive policies than with examining alternative options for punishment and exploring the ethical basis of certain policy approaches. Most policymaking is the outcome of cost–benefit analysis, and that process does not usually incorporate ethical models or arguments. Normally, it is essential in designing policies to advance a justification for a particular approach to a policy issue. Policies may be justified on ideological, empirical, or ethical grounds. Policies grounded in an ethical approach are analyzed under a process that has determined the "rightness or wrongness," or the "good or bad," of a particular approach. There are two central concerns. Firstly, it is necessary that policymakers always act ethically in formulating policies; secondly, there exists an ethical responsibility in making policy about subjects like punishment that have inherently ethical requirements. This latter kind of policymaking can be termed *morality policymaking*. In contemporary policymaking, there is a clear link between morality policymaking and so-called moral panics (Mooney, 2001, p. 116). A moral panic arises when an event is constructed and portrayed as a danger or menace to society and its values. Good examples are the various "wars" declared by different administrations; for example, the War on Poverty, the War on Drugs, and the War on Terrorism. Media, and therefore public, attention to particular forms of criminality has resulted in mandatory minimum sentencing, the War on Drugs, truth-in-sentencing laws, and legislation designed to combat sexual predators and superpredators. The media frequently construct issues like drug abuse as moral panics, and the outcome is often badly conceived laws that are fundamentally unethical. The present mass incarceration of offenders is the result of policy choices based on converging policies and decisions that cannot be said to represent a rational, coherent response to crime. What standards and conditions should be applied to imprisonment? Periodically, the topic of the level of amenities to be supplied to prisoners resurfaces in the media. Politicians who wish to demonstrate a "tough on crime" approach protest that prisoners are given access to weight-lifting equipment, televisions, radios, and "good" food (Banks, 2005, p. 137). The following case reveals one sheriff's view of the standard of amenities to be applied to prisoners in jail.

Case Study: Prison and Amenities

In Maricopa County, Arizona, Sheriff Joe Arpia's policies of housing inmates in tents without air conditioning in the more than 110°F summer weather, clothing inmates in pink underwear and striped uniforms, instituting chain gangs for both men and women, and providing basic and unappealing food such as bologna on dry bread exemplify this attitude that amenities should not be provided to prisoners. Such politicians argue that, if prisoners have standards of incarceration that are superior to the standard of living of the man on the street, then they cannot be said to be suffering punishment. The media fuel this debate by reporting that prisons are "holiday resorts" where prisoners enjoy extravagant amenities and conditions (see Lenz, 2002). In response to this political discourse, the No Frills Prison Act was passed in 1996; it bans televisions, coffeepots, and hot plates in the cells of federal prisoners. It also prohibits computers, electronic instruments, certain movies rated above PG, and unmonitored phone calls (Lenz, 2002).

The assumption underpinning this legislation is that a deterrent effect will be achieved "by making a sentence more punitive, that is, making the inmate suffer more" (Banks, 2005, p. 138). Thus, it is assumed that an inmate will be "less inclined to reoffend knowing the harsh conditions in prison" (p. 138). The problem is that no research exists to support this assumption. Some have argued that there are cost savings to the prison system and to the taxpayers through this approach, but, again, this is not supported, given that the 31 states that allow inmates televisions in their cells do not pay for them (prisoners or their relatives pay for them), and cablevision is paid for out of profits from the prison commissary, vending machines, and long-distance telephone charges (Finn, 1996, pp. 6–7).

Interestingly, prison administrators are often in favor of permitting amenities in the prisons because staff rely heavily on a system of rewards and punishments to maintain control in their institutions (Lenz, 2002, p. 506). They recognize that keeping inmates busy provides important benefits to inmate order and inmate activities. In other words, bored and unhappy prisoners are more likely to cause security problems to which staff, who are in short supply, will have to respond.

Source: From Banks, C. *Criminal Justice Ethics: Theory and Practice, 2nd edition.* Copyright © 2009, Sage Publications.

Policy is usually formulated by elected officials and representatives who react hastily to perceived constituency concerns and to the views of the general public, which are heavily influenced by media representation of an issue as a moral panic. Surveys have revealed that the public has a general tendency toward favoring punitive measures toward offenders. In the U.S., imprisonment is generally regarded as the appropriate form of punishment for most criminality but this is not so in other Western countries where minor crimes are punished much more leniently. As for the ultimate penalty of capital punishment which is a major issue of morality for many citizens, it has found steady support since the 1970s and this is usually reflected in political platforms and in legislative approaches to punishment.

An ethical responsibility includes an obligation to act with integrity. For example, a legislator can be said to act unethically when he or she proposes changes in legislation in the expectation that such action will ensure his or her re-election knowing that it is unlikely to achieve its aims and might even cause fresh injustice. Other acts of policymaking that could be considered unethical include responding to a particular event or series of events by formulating policies that are arbitrary, lack reason or good judgment, and have failed to take account of relevant ethical considerations.

Case Study: "Airlines, Passengers Confront Racial Profiling."

Complaints by Arab Americans against racial profiling by airlines have reportedly increased since 9/11, according to the American-Arab Anti-Discrimination Committee. The committee is aware of passengers with a Muslim or Middle Eastern appearance who have been removed from planes. For example, an Iranian-born U.S. citizen who was a software developer living in Dallas was on his way home from Seattle, and, while reading his paper on an American Airlines plane, was approached by an airline employee holding a passenger manifest. He was told to leave the plane because the pilot did not feel comfortable with him aboard. Reportedly, the pilot did not like how he looked. He was questioned by three airport police about where he lived, his marital status, his religion, and where he worked, and he was treated like a suspect. He was allowed to board the next flight to Dallas, and when the plane landed, apologies were offered by an airline official.

Source: From "Airlines, Passengers Confront Racial Profiling," October 3, 2001, CNN.com/Travel.

The so-called War on Terrorism provokes significant ethical questions and issues. A central issue concerns the normative considerations applicable to this war. Questions include why the United States declared a War on Terrorism after 9/11 and why it created a special prosecution and detention regime for alleged terrorists instead of giving the criminal justice system the responsibility for responding to terrorist acts. After all, terrorist acts normally constitute offenses under the criminal law and can be prosecuted and punished as such. Another issue concerns the extent to which, if at all, torture or so-called enhanced interrogation can be applied to alleged terrorists in custody, even in the cause of averting further acts of terrorism. Third, there is the question of the extent to which rights and freedoms ought to be restricted within the United States in order to fight the War on Terrorism. The argument in this case is that we ought to be prepared to surrender some or even all of those rights and freedoms in the interest of reducing the risk of further terrorist acts. Those rights include privacy and freedom from intrusive surveillance. In addition, pursuing the War on Terrorism is said to require the establishment of specially constituted courts or military commissions to undertake the trials of alleged terrorists, raising the further question of what legal protections and rights those accused should enjoy before such courts or commissions. These are complex issues that impact fundamental values and ethical norms.

The difficulties of ethical policymaking in this field are compounded by questions concerning the fact that there is no single "correct" definition of terrorism and that the nature of the War on Terrorism has been shaped almost entirely by the events of 9/11. It is clear that, though termed a "war" in the same way that previous campaigns have been described as a war on crime or a war on drugs, the War on Terrorism is much more like a conventional war but lacks the attributes of one. Policymakers have constructed the War on Terrorism not as an issue of crime control but as involving issues of national security. In so doing, they have sought to justify exceptional measures, such as illegal international rendition and techniques that some have termed torture (Ackerman, 2004). By defining the campaign against terrorists as a war, the Bush administration justified measures, like the Patriot Act, that have significantly increased surveillance powers over citizens and diminished rights and freedoms. The debate is concerned with whether such measures are ethically appropriate in all the circumstances. Some argue that such measures are immoral simply because they disregard customary and international rules governing the treatment of detainees (by categorizing them as "unlawful combatants"), the rules of war, humanitarian laws of war, and prohibitions against torture and degrading treatment (Emcke, 2005, p. 237).

It has also been argued that depicting a counterterrorist strategy as warfare has the effect of portraying a level of activity inferior to that normally required by actual conventional warfare, as if it were a conventional war between states. Thus, through this process of categorization, the United States has somehow been empowered to conduct '"battles" within the ambit of a never-ending War on Terrorism. For example, in the pursuit of the War on Terrorism, the United States deploys unmanned aircraft, or drones, in the airspace of other states' territories, without their knowledge, in order to conduct assassinations of "known" terrorists. Sometimes, these attacks cause so-called collateral damage to civilians, and some ask whether it is ethically correct to cause injury and death to innocent civilians in this way and whether the effects of this strategy actually mimic the acts of the terrorists themselves (Wilkinson, 2001, p. 23). Therefore, some argue that the War on Terrorism might in fact constitute a greater evil than terrorism itself (Wilkinson, 2001, p. 115). In defending the war and its actions, some have suggested that, so long as citizens can rely on the legislature and the courts for oversight, there is sufficient protection against excesses (Ignatieff, 2004, p. 8). Yet, others point to the lack of executive transparency and the administration's active concealment of surveillance activities that have come to light only through the activities of whistleblowers. In other words, the modern state has the capacity, if it possesses the will, to conduct a wide range of activities in pursuit of a goal that it alone deems critical to public interest and that many would judge illegal and certainly immoral or unethical.

Analyzing Ethical Dilemmas

Ethical theories attempt to provide a means to respond to such critical ethical questions as, How ought I to act in this situation? Thus, for criminal justice professionals, ethical theories provide a foundation and a source of knowledge about how to go about the business of acting ethically in everyday situations. They help provide structure in an otherwise complex environment. A number of ethical theories exist, each offering a varying perspective and approach to ethical dilemmas. It is necessary, therefore, to be aware of the various arguments and perspectives to fully engage with the analysis and resolution of ethical issues. The principal ethical theories are *deontology* and *consequentialism* (also called *utilitarianism*). However, more recently, *virtue ethics* has gained a strong footing in ethical theorizing. Less significant theories include the Greek theories of *hedonism, stoicism,* and *ethical egoism.* Contemporary theorists, such as John Rawls (1973) and Carol Gilligan (1982), have added *social justice* and *feminist ethics* (also called the *ethic of care*) to the theoretical framework.

Principles, Consequences, or Character?

The principal theories of deontology and consequentialism take contrasting positions on the question of how we ought to conduct ourselves in varying situations when faced with the question, How ought I to act? Consequentialists believe that the task of identifying the right way to act in a given situation always depends on the goodness, for everyone affected, of the consequences of acting in a particular way. Therefore, consequentialism always looks at outcomes in determining the proper course of action. In contrast, deontology rejects consequentialism and argues that rules and principles that place limits on our activities and actions ought to guide us in making ethical decisions. Thus, they argue that certain acts are always wrong in themselves, lack moral support, and cannot be employed to justify pursuing any ends, even morally good ones. For example, deontologists absolutely reject the act of lying and argue that lies are wrong because of their nature, even if they result in good consequences. Deontologists emphasize notions of obligation and duty and believe, for example, that it is right to keep promises, regardless of the effects of carrying them out. Often, applying the primary theories will result in similar moral outcomes. For example, a deontologist will argue that stealing goods or breaking promises is always wrong, yet a consequentialist would come to the same conclusion but for different reasons, arguing that it is the consequences of such acts to the public welfare that render them wrong, not their inherent wrongness. Conflicts will arise between these theories, however, when performance of an act normally considered unethical results in an increase in the utility achieved by the result.

Aristotle's virtue ethics has enjoyed resurgence in ethical theorizing, partly because the two principal theories seem to offer little except a choice between a focus on the consequences or a set of absolute rules about how to act. Virtue theories aim to provide us with a picture of the good life and how it can be realized. The good life, in Aristotle's time, was seen as one in which one's full potential as a human person is satisfied. This contrasts with modern ethical theories, which see the good life and morality as separate notions. To the ancient Greek virtue theorists, the chief goal was to achieve a good life and realize our true nature; to them, satisfying this aim was the test of the moral worth of a particular act. From the 16th century on, these concepts were abandoned and modern ethical thinking has discouraged notions of final ends and purposes and the concept of the good life. *Postmodernism* has also impacted ethical thinking; Bauman (1993), for example, argues that few ethical choices can be considered absolutely good or correct, and that such choices are largely based on the application of impulses. He argues that uncertainty and ambivalence, which are the characteristics of postmodernism, apply equally to morality (itself diverse in nature, irrational, and subject to the exercise of power relations), so moral codes are often the outcome of political claims of universalism. Richard Rorty goes further, arguing that philosophy itself is dead in the sense that claims to universal rules and principles are no longer possible or accepted in contemporary societies (Rumana, 2000, p. 4).

A Matter of Principle

Immanuel Kant is regarded as one of the greatest modern philosophers and as the one most responsible for shaping and explaining deontology. In answering the question, What ought I to do? Kant believed that a person should categorically act in a rational manner, in accordance with duty and obligation, and take no account of the consequences (Benn, 1998, p. 172). Kant called this idea the *categorical imperative* and contended that all other considerations were irrelevant. This notion gives rise to the question of how to determine the nature and extent of a duty or obligation. In response, Kant stated that this could be determined by applying the test of whether an individual is willing that a particular act be followed by *all* persons at all times. If so, this gives the act the status of a rule, and it withstands the test of a universal law. Though this seems straightforward, it can pose difficulties. For example, Kant stated that the rule prohibiting lying was a categorical imperative, and therefore it was wrong to lie under any circumstances (Rachels, 1999a, p. 125). In reality, however, a person may lie when faced with moral choices about how to act, such as when it is both wrong to lie and wrong to allow innocent people to be murdered. Thus, two categorical imperatives may conflict with each other. How, then, should this conflict be resolved? One suggestion is to treat moral rules not as absolute categorical rules but as generalizations. Therefore, this would mean, though we should generally always refrain from telling lies, we may abrogate this rule if factors exist that ought to override this imperative.

Kant advanced the important notion that we should always respect others because they are rational human beings with dignity (Hill, 2000, p. 64). Thus, a person should not be treated as a means to an end but as an end in himself or herself. Thus, we ought not to use people to satisfy our own ends; we should always respect others' rights, promote their welfare, and avoid causing them harm. In this way, we will be promoting the worth and dignity of every person—as, for example, in the criminal justice process, in which the right to a fair trial is afforded. This rule would also require that prisoners be treated with dignity, compassion, and humanity.

Considering the Consequences

Consequentialists, or utilitarians, look to the consequences of an act to determine its rightness or wrongness and disregard all other considerations. The question to ask when faced with an ethical question or dilemma is, therefore, Which action will bring about the best possible consequences for everyone affected? This principle is known as the *principle of utility*, and it imposes a duty to act in ways that produce the greatest happiness for everyone affected. Underlying this theory is the thinking of the classical utilitarians, Jeremy Bentham and John Stuart Mill, who regarded happiness as equivalent to pleasure and believed that humans look for pleasure and try to avoid pain, and that this explains how we make choices about how to act (Rachels, 1999b, p. 65). More recent thinking substitutes the idea of *preference satisfaction* for happiness; therefore, we should not aim for pleasure over pain but instead should determine how we can best satisfy human preferences, interests, or desires. Utilitarians can be categorized as either *act utilitarians* or *rule utilitarians*. The former argue that it is possible to measure whether an act causes more pleasure than pain and therefore whether it has more "utility." Given the complications of applying such a rule, act utilitarians follow rules of thumb that rely on past experience. Rule utilitarians, on the other hand, link consequentialism with moral rules and contend that following specific moral rules will result in better consequences. Thus, rule consequentialism aligns to an extent with deontology. An example of rule utilitarianism is that it is generally better to follow the rule that one should speak the truth even when it means that doing so in a specific instance would cause more pain than pleasure, because in the long term telling the truth produces greater benefits overall. Consequentialism is criticized for placing the outcome of an action above the ideals of justice. Also, critics argue that it would require us to give all our resources to others because such an act would promote the general welfare and pleasure of others.

It can be seen that the choice between duty and consequences involves evaluating absolute rules about conduct against calculating which act will provide the most pleasure for the greatest number of people. Consequentialism enjoys a primary role in punishment policymaking in the form of the theory that argues that punishment deters crime. It is claimed that everyone benefits by the imposition of severe penalties for certain crimes to deter others from committing similar crimes.

A Question of Character

Virtue ethics does not ask, What ought I to do? but, What kind of person should I become? According to virtue theorists, the correct course of action can be determined only when that question has been answered. Virtues comprise those personal qualities that we develop through habitual action and that aid us to become persons of excellent character during our lives. Virtues are both natural and acquired qualities, such as intelligence, honesty, generosity, loyalty, integrity, dignity, and self-control. In contrast to deontology's absolute prohibition on lying and consequentialism's acquiescence to lying if the consequences are beneficial, virtue ethics takes the position that lying is dishonest and that dishonesty is a vice, not a virtue. Virtue ethics can be problematic, however. For example, is a suicide bomber acting courageously by dying for a cause he or she believes in? If being generous is a virtue, how generous should one be? Aristotle believed that a good life included happiness in the form of well-being or flourishing and that virtues promote such happiness (Tessitore, 1996, p. 20). Aristotle thought that we should always act in ways that will bring about flourishing, and he advanced the notion of the Golden Mean, which means that when required to make decisions, we should seek the mean, or the average between extremes. An example is to be neither stingy nor lavish but generous—that is, to aim for the Golden Mean. It is easy to see how this idea can be applied to everyday ethical behavior. When applied to questions of conduct, the Golden Mean would be the middle course between forms of radical action.

Aristotle also advocated the notion of practical wisdom, which involves thinking about the circumstances, reasoning correctly, and making the right choices. Those who live with practical wisdom are said to have a kind of insight or perception that guides them in making right decisions (Darwall, 1998, p. 213). Critics argue that virtue ethics must be regarded as contextually and historically tied to an ancient time period, namely Athenian society of the 5th century, which took it for granted that virtues were possessed only by those with great wealth and high social status (MacIntyre, 1984, p. 11). Women and slaves were not considered human, and therefore virtue ethics could not apply to them. Even so, modern philosophers attracted by virtue ethics and its focus on character link it to modern-day social life and the community, emphasizing the need to learn virtues within the family and the community (Blum, 1996, pp. 232–233). As for Aristotle's list of virtues, while some see it as arbitrary, others argue for the universality of virtue whatever the nature of a society or its culture (Hinman, 1998, pp. 334–335). A major criticism of virtue ethics is that it gives us no guidance about how to act in relation to ethical issues. For example, it provides no assistance about such ethical questions as the imposition of capital punishment. However, in favor of virtue ethics, it can be argued that it fulfills an essential role in supplementing other ethical approaches that have provided guidance in deciding how to act (Rachels, 1999a, p. 189). It is also claimed that developing and possessing a virtuous character or a moral self is a prerequisite for resolving ethical dilemmas. Some modern philosophers argue that virtue ethics can stand alone as the ethical basis for ethical action because an action will be correct and moral if performed by a virtuous person acting in character in particular circumstances (Hursthouse, 1999, p. 26). Of course, virtue ethics seems very relevant to the criminal justice system, in which power and authority are susceptible to abuse.

Indifference, Pleasure, or Selfishness?

The ethical theories of stoicism, ethical egoism, and hedonism do not enjoy much support among moral philosophers despite the fact that egoism and hedonism, in their celebration of self-gratification, might be said to resonate with the values of our modern consumer society. Stoicism, like virtue ethics, is historically specific and contends that the path to virtue lies in adopting an attitude of indifference toward external differences, cultivating a life of indifference, and accepting that, while some things are within our power to change and influence, others are not (Prior, 1991, p. 209). Stoics believe in predestiny and the notion that whatever happens has a rational explanation and is always for the best. In some respects, stoicism echoes the claims of virtue ethics about individual character because stoics argue that developing the appropriately stoic frame of mind leads to virtue.

Hedonism comes in the forms of *psychological hedonism* and *ethical hedonism*. The former imagines a life devoted to the pursuit of pleasure and assumes that all action aims to achieve pleasure and avoid pain. Ethical hedonism is a moral version of hedonism and asserts that seeking pleasure is right conduct because pleasure alone is good (Feldman, 1997, p. 109). In this sense, hedonism seems unsatisfactory because it is difficult to accept that seeking pleasure can constitute the sole basis for deciding ethical issues. The theory of ethical egoism contends that right action is action that promotes one's own self-interest, regardless of the interests or concerns of others.

Egoism is separated into two categories, *psychological egoism* and *ethical egoism*. The former holds that all persons are motivated by, and act according to, egoistic concerns. It rejects all altruistic explanations of behavior and argues that acts that may seem unselfish are always performed for egotistical reasons. An ethical egoist argues similarly that morality and reason are satisfied by promoting one's own greatest good and self-interest before anyone else's. The focus on self-interest does not exclude action that might help others, as long as the primary goal is our own interests. Ethical egoism as a theory seems to lack a principled foundation, and some argue that it resembles racism in its focus on the interests of one group alone (Rachels 1999a, p. 94). Others suggest that it precludes any development of sustained relations between persons, because an ethical egoist is so focused on his or her own good that certain acts are precluded, such as assisting those in need, unless such action first serves a self interest (Hinman, 1998, p. 154). In terms of criminal justice, ethical egoism would seem to supply justification for acts that are corrupt or inhumane.

Social Justice

John Rawls's theories seek to fix fundamental principles that would govern a morally good society, and in this sense his search for a set of rules is Kantian. His concern is not with the individual ethical actor so much as with justice, in the sense of fairness, and he regards justice as a founding principle capable of providing guidance concerning how a society ought to conduct itself (Rawls 1973, pp. 50–51). According to Rawls, a moral person is one who possesses a sense of justice and the potential to pursue a conception of the good (1973, p. 121). Achieving this potential requires us to create a just society and to agree on its governing principles. Rawls imagines a group of persons who collectively agree on the nature of this society from a position of ignorance about their class or social position and without taking account of any natural assets or abilities. His argument is that they would choose two principles of justice, one concerned with the equal right to basic liberties and the other with social and economic inequalities (p. 60). The first principle would provide personal liberties, such as the right to vote and to stand for public office, and freedom of speech and assembly. The second principle, part of which is known as the *difference principle,* would comprise the equal distribution of primary goods and services as well as burdens and responsibilities. However, certain inequalities would be considered just if they benefited everyone, especially the least advantaged (p. 75). Thus, there would be no injustice if the least advantaged were better off in an unequal situation than they would be with equality. Consequently, a just society that desires to treat all with equality would give more attention to those victimized by injustice or to those who enjoy a less favorable position because of unfair treatment. This echoes the Kantian principle that persons should always be treated as ends in themselves and not as means to an end.

Rawls sees his principles as purely hypothetical but nevertheless argues that they would be accepted by free and rational persons and would make explicit his notion of "justice as fairness" (1973, p. 11). Rawls describes three stages of moral development in a life: the *morality of authority,* developed by parents; the *morality of association,* which arises through contact with the school and the neighborhood; and finally the *morality of principles*, wherein individuals follow moral positions as a result of earlier moral development and because they seek the approval of the wider society (pp. 476–473). Rawls suggests that, in a society that seeks to achieve social justice, his principles will create harmony and cooperation and reduce injustice. In terms of relevance to the criminal justice system and its institutions, Rawlsian notions of social justice can assist in overcoming not only inequalities in access to justice but also forms of discrimination within the criminal justice system.

The Ethic of Care

Feminist ethical theories focus on the centrality of gender and are critical of other established theoretical approaches for giving too much prominence to the individual, to impartiality, and to universality (Hinman, 1998, pp. 367–369). Feminist theories give importance to relationships, care, and connectiveness. Seminal research by Carol Gilligan and Lawrence Kohlberg has revealed that moral development varies according to gender and that gender shapes the nature of moral inquiry (in Hinman 1998, p. 370). Thus, Gilligan contends that women tend to see moral life in terms of care and responsibility, asking if relationships would be maintained or harm suffered because of an intended action, whereas men see the application of rules in a fair, impartial, and equal manner as the prime consideration (Flanagan & Jackson, 1993, p. 70). Men also show a concern for individual rights and autonomy, but women are more likely to resolve ethical issues by applying solutions that affirm relationships and minimize harm. This does not mean that women should be regarded as inherently emotional beings entirely lacking rational attributes. Both men and women are the products of social conditioning, and gender is socially constructed, and therefore men, too, may follow an ethic of care rather than an individualistic ethical approach (Rachels 1999a, p. 168).

Some question whether the ethic of care possesses enough weight and dimension for an ethical theory and suggest that it is best viewed as complementing virtue ethics (Blum, 1994, p. 208). Also problematic is the scope of the care ethic itself, because, though it is obvious that the ethic of care applies in close family relationships, the question is, To what extent does it (for example) apply to the needy throughout the world? While some regard the familial obligation as absolute and other obligations as secondary, others emphasize the depth of a relationship outside the family circle. Still others argue that our duty can be broad enough to include a communal identity, such as membership of an ethnic group (p. 249). Robin West advocates linking the ethic of care with the ethic of justice so that public institutions would be obliged to exercise compassion or care when dispensing justice (West, 1997, p. 9). She contends that a combined project of care and justice would mean reading and interpreting the law compassionately, for example, taking account of the life circumstances of an accused in a death penalty case. The notion of *peacemaking* has close links with the ethic of care but represents a distinct ethical philosophy variously termed *peacemaking, peacekeeping,* and *peacemaking criminology* (Braswell & Gold, 1998, p. 26). Peacemaking also calls attention to relationships, caring, and mindfulness (thinking about our actions and the needs of others in the long term). In terms of criminal justice policymaking, peacemaking claims nonviolence as a fundamental principle and argues that violence and coercion, in such forms as capital punishment and the excess use of force in policing, should be rejected.

CONCLUSION

This exploration of ethics in criminal justice has highlighted the importance of the theoretical underpinnings of normative and applied ethics to the resolution of ethical issues and dilemmas, and has revealed the nature and scope of the multiple ethical questions that can arise in "doing justice." In law enforcement and corrections in particular, where there is daily direct interaction with suspected offenders and inmates, the level of ethical practice of an agency is greatly influenced by its institutional culture. Codes of ethics and accountability mechanisms, such as civilian oversight and the courts, can resolve individual cases of improper conduct; but systemic racism, corruption, and abusive conduct have proved difficult to eradicate. Sometimes, as in the case of terrorism, questions about how one ought to act are fundamentally about human rights and human dignity. Theoretical approaches to ethical dilemmas and issues apply various mechanisms to evaluate and test the questions that arise, and fresh postmodern perspectives now challenge long-established theories. Shifts in both ethical practice and theory congruent with shifts in the social order ensure that the incorporation of ethical norms and standards will continue to be a testing and challenging field of endeavor in criminal justice.

DISCUSSION QUESTIONS

1. Is there any relationship between the style of policing chosen by a department and the ethical practices it feels are legitimate for its officers to use in carrying out their duties? Which style of policing would support racial profiling, and why?

2. In an ethical correctional system, all prisoners would be treated with humanity and dignity. Explain how prisoner humanity would be respected in the use of force to deal with violence, including prisoner rape, and in the conditions of confinement.

3. One criminal justice policy that many states have supported is prisoner disenfranchisement. Comment on this policy in light of the fact that, for example, if disenfranchisement is permanent, more than 40% of the African American male population will have no say in the policies and laws that have a significant effect on them and on their communities.

4. Is it ever ethically acceptable to torture a person in the War on Terrorism? Support your argument by referring to the criteria of at least one ethical philosophy.

5. Why do modern philosophers regard virtue ethics as an alternative to deontological and consequentialist ethical decision-making approaches? Explain with examples.

REFERENCES

Ackerman, B. (2004). This is not a war. *Yale Law Journal, 113*, 1871–1908.

American Bar Association Model Rules of Professional Conduct. (1983). Chicago, IL: American Bar Association.

Banks, C. (2005). *Punishment in America: A reference handbook.* Santa Barbara, CA: ABC-CLIO.

Bauman, Z. (1993). *Postmodern ethics.* Oxford, UK: Blackwell.

Benn, P. (1998). *Ethics: Fundamentals of philosophy.* Montreal, QC: McGill-Queen's University Press.

Blum, L. (1994). *Moral perception and particularity.* Cambridge, UK: Cambridge University Press.

Blum, L. (1996). Community and virtue. In Roger Crisp (Ed.), *How should one live? Essays on the virtues* (pp. 231–250). Oxford, UK: Clarendon Press.

Blumstein, A., Cohen, J., & Nagin, D. (Eds.). (1978). *Deterrence and incapacitation: Estimating the effects of criminal sanctions on crime rates.* Washington, DC: Panel on Research on Deterrent and Incapacitative Effects.

Braswell, M., & Gold, J. (1998). Peacemaking, justice and ethics. In M. Braswell, B. McCarthy, & B. McCarthy, *Justice, crime and ethics* (3rd ed., pp. 25–39). Cincinnati, OH: Anderson.

Chen, S. (2009, February 24). Pennsylvania rocked by "jailing kids for cash" scandal. CNN.com Edition. Retrieved February 24, 2009, from http://www.cnn.com/2009/CRIME/02/23/pennsylvania.corrupt.judges/index.html

Christie, N. (2000). *Crime control as industry: Towards gulags, Western style?* London: Routledge.

CNN.com/Travel. (2001, October 3). Airlines, passengers confront racial profiling. Retrieved April 3, 2007, from http://archives.cnn.com/2001/TRAVEL/NEWS/10/03/rec.airlines.profiling/index.html.

Crank, J., & Caldero, M. (2000). *Police ethics: The corruption of noble cause.* Cincinnati, OH: Anderson.

Darwall, S. (1998). *Philosophical ethics.* Boulder, CO: Westview Press.

Emcke, C. (2005). War on Terrorism and the crises of the political. In Georg Meggle (Ed.), *Ethics of terrorism and counter-terrorism* (pp. 227–244). Frankfurt, Germany: Ontos.

Feldman, F. (1997). *Utilitarianism, hedonism, and desert: Essays in moral philosophy*. New York: Cambridge University Press.

Finn, P. (1996). No-frills prisons and jails: A movement in flux. *Federal Probation, 60*, 35–44.

Flanagan, O., & Jackson, K. (1993). Justice, care, and gender: The Kohlberg–Gilligan debate revisited. In M. J. Larrabee (Ed.), *An ethic of care: Feminist and interdisciplinary perspectives* (pp. 69–86). New York: Routledge.

Gilligan, C. (1982). *In a different voice: Psychological theory and women's development*. Cambridge, MA: Harvard University Press.

Harrison, P., & and Beck, A. (2003, July). Prisoners in 2002. (Bureau of Justice Statistics Bulletin NCJ 200248). Washington, DC: U.S. Department of Justice.

Hays, T. (2000). Cop gets 15 years in torture case. *Infobeat*. Retrieved January 15, 2001 from http://www.infobeat.com/stories/cgi/story.cgi?id=2567684838-eb5

Hill, T. E. (2000). *Respect, pluralism, and justice: Kantian perspectives*. Oxford: Oxford University Press.

Hinman, L. (1998). *Ethics: A pluralistic approach to moral theory*. Fort Worth, TX: Harcourt Brace.

Hudson, B. (1996). *Understanding justice: An introduction to ideas, perspectives and controversies in modern penal theory*. Buckingham, UK: Open University Press.

Human Rights Watch. (2001). *No escape: Male rape in U.S. prisons*. New York: Author.

Hursthouse, R. (1999). *On virtue ethics*. Oxford: Oxford University Press.

Ignatieff, M. (2004). *The lesser evil: Political ethics in an age of terror: The Gifford Lectures*. Princeton, NJ: Princeton University Press.

Kauffman, K. (1988). *Prison officers and their world*. Cambridge, MA: Harvard University Press.

Kleinig, J. (1996). *The ethics of policing*. New York: Cambridge University Press.

Kleinig, J. (2001). Professionalizing incarceration. In J. Kleinig & M. L. Smith (Eds.), *Discretion, community, and correctional ethics* (pp. 1–15). Lanham, MA: Rowman & Littlefield.

Lenz, N. (2002). "Luxuries" in prison: The relationship between amenity funding and public support. *Crime and Delinquency, 48*(4), 499–525.

Lombardo, L. (1989). *Guards imprisoned: Correctional officers at work* (2nd ed.). Cincinnati, OH: Anderson.

MacIntyre, A. (1984). *After virtue: A study in moral theory*. Notre Dame, IN: University of Notre Dame Press.

Martinson, R. (1974). What works? Questions and answers about prison reform. *The Public Interest, 35*, 22–54.

Mooney, C. (2001). Introduction: The public clash of private values: The politics of morality policy. In C. Mooney (Ed.), *The Public Clash of Private Values: The Politics of Morality Policy* (pp. 3–18). New York: Chatham House.

Morris, N. (1974). *The future of imprisonment*. Chicago: University of Chicago Press.

Nozick, R. (1981). *Philosophical explanations*. Cambridge, MA: Harvard University Press.

Petersilia, J. (1999). Parole and prisoner reentry in the United States. In M. Tonry & J. Petersilia (Eds.), *Prisons* (pp. 479–529). Chicago: University of Chicago Press.

Pope, C., & Feyerherm, W. (1990, June and September). Minority status and juvenile justice processing: An assessment of the research literature (Parts 1 and 2). *Criminal Justice Abstracts*, 327–335, 527–542.

Prior, W. (1991). *Virtue and knowledge: An introduction to ancient Greek ethics.* London: Routledge.

Rachels, J. (1999a). *The elements of moral philosophy* (3rd ed.). Boston: McGraw-Hill.

Rachels, J. (1999b). *The right thing to do: Basic readings in moral philosophy* (2nd ed.). Boston: McGraw-Hill.

Rawls, J. (1973). *A theory of justice.* Oxford, UK: Oxford University Press.

Reiner, R. (1985). The police and race relations. In J. Baxter & L. Koffman (Eds.), *Police: The constitution and the community* (pp. 149–187). London: Professional Books.

Rumana, R. (2000). *On Rorty.* Belmont, CA: Wadsworth.

Russell, K. (1998). *The color of crime: Racial hoaxes, white fear, black protectionism, police harassment, and other macroaggressions.* New York: New York University Press.

Skolnick, J. (1966). *Justice without trial.* New York: Wiley.

Smith, M. L. (2001). The shimmer of reform: Prospects for a correctional ethic. In J. Kleinig & M. L. Smith (Eds.), *Discretion, community, and correctional ethics* (pp. 17–37). Lanham, MA: Rowman & Littlefield.

Ten, C. L. (1987). *Crime, guilt, and punishment: A philosophical introduction.* Oxford, UK: Clarendon Press.

Tessitore, A. (1996). *Reading Aristotle's Ethics: Virtue, rhetoric, and political philosophy.* Albany: State University of New York Press.

Tobar, H. (1998). An ugly stain on a city's bright and shining plan. *Los Angeles Times,* December 28, A1.

Tonry, M. (1994). Proportionality, parsimony, and interchangeability of punishments. In A. Duff & D. Garland (Eds.), *A reader on punishment* (pp. 133–160). Oxford, UK: Oxford University Press.

Walker, S., Spohn, C., & DeLone, M. (2000). *The color of justice: Race, ethnicity, and crime in America.* Belmont, CA: Wadsworth.

West, Robin. (1997). *Caring for justice.* New York: New York University Press.

Wilkinson, P. (2001). *Terrorism versus democracy: The liberal state response.* Portland, OR: Frank Cass.

3

Criminological Theory and Crime Explanation

Dan Okada

Science/Society/Law/Crime/Criminology

In the study of crime, or in the examination of the various constructs that provide the structure from which crime is studied scientifically, it is sometimes forgotten that the process is ultimately an academic exercise. The canons of science dictate value-free investigation and consideration; the political accusation of "flip-flopping" has no relevance to scientific inquiry. The whole point of the exercise is to gather as much information as possible—that is, to gather data—and then to competently assess what has been collected. Not until this analysis has been completed is a decision made one way or another. Scientists must be constitutionally willing to change their minds, because their minds can be made up only on the basis of what they find. This same reminder is provided to criminology students, who are regularly frustrated when they realize that the explanations they have painstakingly committed to memory are "only theories." In the world of academic collegiate criminal justice, where many students hope to pursue law enforcement careers, evidence and analysis lead to successful convictions of those found guilty, or perhaps even to exonerations of those found factually innocent, of the crimes with which they have been charged. Scientific theories are constructed to fail as well as to succeed. A good theory is intended to provoke controversy, to stimulate investigation, to be tested, examined, and perhaps discredited, based exclusively on the data.

Akers (1994) notes that the primary criteria for determining the value of any theory are logic, testability, empirical support, and utility. Although these criteria are appropriate to understanding criminological theory, the hope is that the outcome of this enterprise will be reasonable and effective public policy that minimizes victimization and reduces crime. Criminological theories are created so we can better understand why people behave as they do and so we can therefore respond more effectively to them.

Criminology asks the question, Why? This differs from criminal justice, which asks, What now? Answering the question, Why? offers a range of challenges and opportunities from many perspectives and disciplines. There are many "right" answers. In this regard, criminology students learn that the earliest explanations of criminal behavior were theological. Demonic possession, for instance, was once believed to be the answer (Vold & Bernard, 1983). As technology and the scientific method evolved and influenced scholars, theories likewise evolved. It is important to recognize this evolution to better understand and assess contemporary theories.

A theory is a series of statements that seek to explain or better understand a particular phenomenon. Merton (1968, pp. 50–69) suggests that a more practical application should focus attention on what he calls "theories of the middle range." Because of the nature and complexity of crime, any attempt to construct one broad-based explanation—or what, in this case, Babbie (2009) calls a nomothetic comprehensive, all-inclusive explanation—that addresses all forms of crime would naturally be fraught with frustration. A concentrated, more uniquely directed (idiographic) theory that seeks to explain specific crime typologies would serve end users and students more effectively.

Students learn the myriad explanations, the so-called named theories, that are typically taught as an academic mantra. It is no wonder that many of these explanations are often seen as superfluous or, even worse, irrelevant. If everything is important, then what is truly important? This exercise is confounded by the choice of textbooks from which students are expected to learn[1] and how the information found in them is presented. A cursory review of the texts found in most academic libraries and in the personal libraries of many academics likely reveals that most texts seem to be eerie relatives of each other, containing the same basic intellectual DNA: information with similar skeletal and chemical makeup (the contents), differing only slightly in their cosmetic physiognomy (the cover of the book), and even sharing the same family name: Criminology, Theories of Criminology, or some such.

The student asks, What is the relevance of studying theories? The abstract reasoning needed to outline scientific theories from any academic perspective often holds little attraction for the student who is more interested in the practice of criminal justice. Although examinations that focus on why may not compete favorably against a focus on how, who, and what now, the why is the focus of this examination. It is not the intent of this chapter to offer a lengthy definition of criminology and its parameters. Criminology is the study of crime; this chapter focuses on the causes of crime.

Micro-Level Analyses

Biology

Many criminal justice students gravitate to the social sciences because of their previous inconsistent or modest academic success in what many perceive to be the harder (that is, more rigorous) sciences, such as biology, chemistry, physics, and math, believing that a less arduous journey to a college degree can be found in a "practical" major. Many are then compelled to enroll in a required criminology theory class and, as a starting point, are thrust headfirst into the criminal justice/criminology catechism and exposed to the "father of modern criminology," Cesare Lombroso. Such terms as *atavism* and *born criminal* now enter their vocabularies as they are forced to listen to how the scientific method was first introduced to the study of criminal behavior, along with data collection, hypotheses testing, and ultimately statistical analysis. Eyes roll, shoulders tense, teeth grit, and the fun begins.

Lombroso's education and training led to his role as chief pathologist of the Italian penal system (Sellin, 1938); his foremost contribution to criminology was in asking the question, Why? Why did those convicts to whom he had access commit the crimes for which they were convicted? Given the technology and research methods of this day, Lombroso offered cutting-edge analysis. The answer had to lie in each individual's physiology. Since all these criminals were male and possessed similar physical characteristics that were pronounced and obvious, the traits that each carried from birth had to provide the answer to the question.

While the notion that criminals are born and not made is often found incredible by today's student, the reality remains that certain behaviors and characteristics seem to dispose those who exhibit them to tendencies that may lead to criminal behavior. Although possession of an abundance of body hair or an asymmetrical face, such as Lombroso proposed in his early work (1876), may be disputed as a plausible link to criminal behavior, irritability and impatience that are only occasionally controlled through overt effort are part of an individual constitution that, given the proper catalyst, need, situation, or encouragement, can coalesce in a meaningful way as criminal behavior.

Lombroso never suggested that his findings could be turned into public policy that discriminates against particular social others who possess particular physiological characteristics that he identified. Rather, these "stigmata" simply helped identify those social members who would be "predisposed" to engage in criminal behavior. As an investigatory tool, these characteristics would make detection easier. It can be seen how his broad-based generalizations based on body type, physicality, and even genetics have been turned into such controversial contemporary law-enforcement techniques as racial profiling or even the internment of Japanese Americans during World War II.

Psychology

Psychology has always lent itself easily to analysis involving aberrant or antisocial behavior. Concepts generated by psychological investigators promote cognitive processing, personality disorders, even levels of intelligence as entries in the lexicon of criminological explanation.

The link between psychology and crime is most popularly associated with various personality characteristics possessed by the criminal. Impulsiveness, egotism, incorrigibility, and temperament are often linked to a psychological state that fosters criminality (Agnew, 2005; Lanier & Henry, 1998). Characteristics such as these, according to cognitive psychology, when combined with influences existing in the social environment, render a person more likely to engage in criminality than those not so ably equipped (Walters, 1989). Because of these intrinsic compulsions, when faced with temptation, frustration, anger, or lust, this person can behave criminally. In the absence of the desire to control such urges, short-term hedonism wins out over prosocial behavior. Obviously, the journey to crime is not as simple as this, but cognitive psychologists argue that, without these traits, crime is not as likely to occur.

Yochelson and Samenow (1976) conducted a case study of more than 200 inmates at St. Elizabeth's Hospital for the Criminally Insane in Washington, D.C. Through interviews, self-reflections, and group discussions with patients, Yochelson and Samenow concluded that the factor common to all these criminals was an inherent "criminal personality." Criminals and noncriminals think differently. Through an integration of rational choice, free will, and antisocial decision making, criminals chose to "be" criminals.

Kohlberg (1984) adds to the discussion, suggesting that individual morality could be examined along a behavioral continuum. As we age, we also grow morally. Developmental psychology, behaviorism, and Freudian psychoanalysis all find their way into Kohlberg's model. Moral development is not the same in everyone, nor does it emerge consistently in everyone, but until morality is mastered through the various developmental stages identified by Kohlberg, crime is likely. Kohlberg links overt behavior to the basic philosophy of the existence of crime—that crime is a violation of morality.

In criminal justice settings, psychology offers many links: offender profiles such as those constructed to identify serial killers; the effect of posttraumatic stress disorder (PTSD) on antisocial behavior; and the development of various methodologies seeking to rehabilitate criminals. As a consequence of media portrayals, the various subdisciplines of psychology, such as abnormal, clinical, cognitive, or social psychology, are often the gateway for students who become interested in careers in criminal justice.

Gender

When asked to consider what a "typical" criminal looks like, the first characteristic most respondents would name is maleness. Other characteristics emerge, but maleness is generally the first. Aside from popular culture depictions, a cursory look at the demographics of any criminal justice agency shows that males commit the vast majority of all crimes. The Bureau of Justice Statistics (2009) reports that, in 1998, women made up 22% of all arrests but represented only 6–7% of those sentenced to prison. While the number of female offenders has steadily increased over the past several decades, few would take issue with the notion that males are more criminal than females.

Scholarship that addresses female criminality is often couched in terms of oppression, discrimination, conflict, and economic disadvantage. Using traditional criminological explanations, if it is postulated that men feel strain and anomie in their attempts to secure social capital, then women face greater distress. If men engage in Sykes and Matza's (1957) techniques of neutralization rationalizations when they appeal to higher loyalties such as their gangs or their neighborhoods, women do the same with respect to their families and friends.

Interest in female criminality has grown proportionately, matching the increase in female criminality as well as the changing demographics of the researchers and academics. In the not-too-distant past, women had difficulty finding a place in any area of criminal justice. Along with the increase in number of offenders, women have increased their numbers in virtually every arena of practical and administrative criminal justice. Along with this increase, a criminology has emerged that is devoted to women's crime activity (see Chapter 6 of this book). While the context of feminism has assumed a position of significance in academic examination, a review of crime explanations asks, Do women commit crimes for reasons different from men's? Scholars have answered yes.

Cohen and Felson's (1979) *routine activities* theory, aside from its modest attempt to explain crime causation, highlights crime as the often-random juxtaposition of a motivated offender intersecting with a target of opportunity. No attempt is made to explain why this motivated offender became motivated; yet, under this same construct, the increased number of women engaged in activities outside the home means that more women have the opportunity both to engage in crime and to be victimized by it. Although this does not provide the sole explanation for their behavior, it does provide a perspective for understanding influences on women that might not have been applicable in an earlier historical epoch.

The feminist perspective suggests that women face a number of obstacles that men do not. Although men may profess to understand and even sympathize, they are unlikely to truly understand cultural sexism. To say that criminal justice is a male-dominated enterprise is a gross understatement. There is no area in the crime arena in which men do not prevail. It is disingenuous to suggest that this overt, institutional, and systemic discrimination would not have an eventual response. The suggestion that women might be better equipped to "take it" because of some genetic predisposition to tolerance is discriminatory. The social pressure created by such constant and insidious prejudice may be motivation enough for an aberrant response.

Sexism's complement is paternalism. Chesney-Lind and Shelden (1992) contend that girls are often taken into custody "for their own good." The protective father, in the form of the criminal justice practitioner (even though the officer may be a woman), is taking care of wayward offspring. The underlying suggestion is that women cannot take care of themselves.

Messerschmidt (1993) addresses the gender inequality in criminal justice. He argues that crime is simply one of the resources men have at their disposal to fulfill their destiny, which is male dominance. Males exist in a state of privilege; their wants, needs, desires, motivations, and expressions are accepted as universal. To question their superiority is irrelevant; they simply are. All their activity supports this basic contention. Thus, the more aggressive, the more violent, the more clever, the more insidious the crime, the greater the thrill and reward. Not to act in this fashion is to be thought of as less manly—that is, womanly.

Gender is as critical to behavior as class or race/ethnicity. Societies, for good or ill, differentiate resources, opportunities, and even perspective according to these sociodemographic characteristics. The unfortunate artifacts of discrimination can be seen in correctional settings where women's programs and opportunities for rehabilitation or re-entry are dramatically more limited than male-oriented programs in both number and kind. Programs that do exist tend to focus on such female "trades" as cosmetology or data entry.

Although males dominate the creation, production, and administration of crime, females are no longer lingering in the social background. More and more women are gaining entry into all facets of the crime enterprise. Such scholars as Adler, Belknap, Chesney-Lind, Cook, Daly, Danner, Miller, Morash, and Wonders are as prominent in the criminological literature as Cohen, Cressey, Hirschi, Merton, Sutherland, and other male scholars cited in this chapter. In criminal justice terms, women now constitute the majority of first-year law students, and their numbers are increasing in all practical areas of criminal justice. It is no surprise that their activity in crime creation has also become recognized. Although women are not dominant in this area, at least the recognition that gender matters has taken root in both the study and the practice of crime.

Macro-Level Analyses

Social Learning

Edwin Sutherland attempted to provide a reasonable explanation for the behavior of a particular kind of criminal. Chic Conwell, in Sutherland's *The Professional Thief* (1937), grew up in a comfortable environment but fell into crime after getting involved in drug use and a misguided relationship with a showgirl. This relationship led to contacts with an underworld that enticed him and provided what Katz (1988) might later call "sneaky thrills." Conwell became a thief. This profession required him to acquire techniques, mores, ethics—in short, to learn the techniques and culture of thieving.

Sutherland later interviewed other thieves who were far less scrupulous and more dangerous, who held prestigious positions in American business and industry. These men (no women held such positions back then) were directors and board chairmen of major U.S. corporations during the early to middle 20th century. They practiced collusion, fraud, and larceny against the public and the federal government, passing their trade secrets around like Chic Conwell and his associates did. Because of the stature and position of this previously unrecognized type of offender, Sutherland (1983/1937) coined a new term: the *white collar criminal.*

One element common to both the professional thief and the white collar criminal was their progress from initial naïveté through an apprenticeship and then to interaction with skilled others as they learned to be master criminals. In Sutherland's analysis, the critical factors were the intensity, frequency, and quality of the interaction with more skilled associates, and the knowledge they exchanged. These men engaged in *differential association,* which, according to Sutherland, explained why these criminals did what they did. Sutherland wedded nascent American sociology to a more polished political-economic perspective to develop his understanding of the cause of these kinds of crime. One of the first scholars to write in the field of criminology, he used techniques that contemporary methodologists now recognize as grounded theory and ethnographic data collection.

Sutherland's explanation was a deductive process within which his original seven propositions (1939) eventually grew to nine (1947) and evolved from the explanation of a particular kind of behavior into one of the most popular-criminological theories ever formulated. It has been used to explain behaviors as diverse as juvenile delinquency (Smith & Brame, 1994) and computer crime (Skinner & Fream, 1997).

If nascent criminals can become more accomplished by closely associating themselves with those who know how to be better criminals, then why do we imprison those young criminals whom we capture and prosecute? If differential association makes sense, then incarceration is an illogical response to crime reduction. Herein lies the quandary of social science: After reasonable explanations are constructed and evidence collected, what should be done with the conclusions they produce?

Anomie/Strain

Anomie, according to Durkheim (1893), is a state of social confusion caused by rapidly changing industrial evolution accompanied by societal dislocation. This state is popularly conceptualized as *normlessness.* It is a feeling, an attitude, a psychological state that causes those who experience it to feel confused, frustrated, annoyed, angry, hostile, embarrassed, even resigned or doomed. Angst lingers as they adjust their behavior and thinking to deal with it. This weight can be debilitating or just uncomfortable, but it does exist. Durkheim (1897) contended that some who feel this way may attempt to relieve themselves by committing crimes, and others may kill themselves. While either course may be an overreaction, it must be recognized that some people are not well-equipped to deal with the pushes and pulls of life; for some, extreme measures may seem to be their only viable solution.

The American version of anomie comes from Merton (1938), who proposed that personal stress results from a perceived inability to successfully compete for social capital. Those who have access to cultural capital (money) are more content, whereas those who do not are less so and thus feel anomie. Although the dream of success is universal, the ability to achieve it is not. The causes of this inequality may be structural—education or social status—but the feelings that result from it are shared by everyone.

Merton suggested that those who feel anomie are likely to respond through one of five modalities: *conformity* (dealing with it); *innovation* (creatively circumventing it); *ritualism* (recognizing that success was unlikely but, beyond complaining about it, accepting that they had done all they could); *retreatism* (dropping out, typically through substance abuse, homelessness, etc.); or *rebellion* (creating alternative processes to achieve the rewards impossible through mainstream or traditional means; i.e., becoming involved with gangs, organized crime, etc.). The universality of this theory is that everyone at one time or another faces anomie. We are frustrated by life, our work efforts go unrecognized or are poorly rewarded, and incompetent motorists continually confound us. Although these experiences are all unnerving, Merton contends, at the right moment we adapt to them. This version of anomie has been recontextualized by others and fashioned into theories of *social strain*.

In their study of criminological theories, students are frustrated by the apparent inapplicability of theories to real-world public policy. That is, in learning about the assumptions, propositions, and hypotheses that result from constructing and testing theories, students rightly ask, Now what? Social strain theories, at least, have a direct effect on public policy.

Social strain theories argue that when a person is confronted with the inability to achieve success—when faced with strain that follows the realization that personal talent or training cannot achieve status or desires—crime may result. Obviously, not all such people turn to crime; however, social strain theory suggests that crime is a plausible outcome for those who lack patience or who cannot handle stress well.

The fathers of strain theory are Cohen (1955) and Cloward and Ohlin (1960). Cohen believed that juveniles joined gangs because they sought traditional social status and did not possess the wherewithal to achieve it legitimately. This inability, they believed, was exacerbated because culture dictates upward mobility, which acts as a "middle-class measuring rod." People are naturally competitive. When Cohen's low-income juveniles competed with others of the same class, they saw themselves as more or less equal players in the same game; however, when they compared themselves to those who were middle class or higher, they recognized their inequality. Although their relative status was not a problem when compared with their gang friends, when juxtaposed with those having greater resources, strain ensued. In fact, antagonism may arise, and crime is committed to assuage the strain.

Popular culture also influences some. Television commercials, print ads, product placement in movies, and so forth, show the masses what is "cool," what products are "hot," and, conversely, what is not. Having the "in" thing, which can be attained only if one has enough social capital (money), establishes the standard by which many recognize their deprived status. Their wants cannot be satisfied through prosocial activity. Nefarious, deceitful, criminal means and associations are necessary to achieve success.

In trying to understand juvenile criminality, Cloward and Ohlin believed that equal *opportunity* to acquire social capital would reduce the desire to become delinquent. Juveniles living in urban areas experienced poverty and low-quality education frequently delivered in blighted schools; they faced all the failings associated with the social disorganization found in the inner city (Shaw & McKay, 1942). They were more likely to make life choices that included crime. Thus, if greater opportunities were available to mitigate the influence of society's neglect, their lives would improve, or at least the opportunity to become criminal would be less profound, and crime would be reduced.

Strain and opportunity theories have been credited with influencing President John F. Kennedy's creation of the Department of Health, Education, and Welfare (HEW) and President Lyndon B. Johnson's War on Poverty and the Mobilization for Youth programs (Short, 1975). The theoretical basis of HEW and the War on Poverty was that social problems found in urban areas are the product of unequal distribution of wealth and access. Social programs that provide access to medical and/or psychological treatment, better educational opportunities, and job training and placement could positively affect society. Strain theory holds that, if access to social capital were normalized, prosocial behavior would ensue. Much social science research, as well as the contemporary movement to evidence-based programming, are tangible outcomes of social strain theory.

Conflict

The social upheavals of the 1960s and 1970s caused a reassessment of crime causation explanations in the world of academic criminology. With the increased cultural and social awareness resulting from the civil rights movement, the war in Vietnam, the assassinations of popular political and social icons, the Kent State shootings, and Watergate, these decades were a time of turmoil. Positivist criminology was unprepared, and even thought inappropriate, to explain or understand crime in this era. The state and the ruling moneyed classes, the age-old battle between the haves and the have-nots, and even adolescent immaturity were seen as the genesis of much social unrest and certainly crime. The new generation of scholars questioned authority and focused their inquiries on the inequity, oppression, discrimination, and rage that existed throughout society. Explanations of criminal behavior were found in the creation of law, the war between the classes, and a culture that nurtured exploitation. Controversy exists, but various descriptors were used to identify this perspective: *radical criminology* (Platt, 1974), *new criminology* (Taylor, Walton, & Young, 1973), *Marxist criminology* (Schwendinger & Schwendinger, 1970), *critical criminology* (Quinney, 1973), and *anarchist criminology* (Tifft, 1979). Today, this discussion continues under the term *conflict criminology.*

The conflict perspective is broken down into three areas: conflict between groups (cultures, societies, ethnicities, races, genders, etc.), conflict between classes (the bourgeoisie vs. the proletariats, haves vs. have-nots), and economic conflict caused by inequity in the control of social capital. The struggle is to attain limited social capital—money, services, employment, education—which is unequally distributed. Social justice can be achieved only when all members of society have equal access to all social resources. Until equity is achieved, conflict, and thus crime, will exist.

The controversy surrounding the basic premises of conflict criminology centers on a lingering shortcoming: the difficulty of scientifically testing its propositions. Although equity of status might reduce crimes of exploitation, there is little evidence suggesting that crimes of violence are fewer in societies that profess no class distinctions. In fact, finding existing classless societies is impossible; access to crucial goods and services is class related. Thus, conflict theories become statements of belief rather than scientific assertions. Despite the disagreement that surrounds it, conflict theory must be considered, and thus it fulfills one criterion of a "good" theory: It stimulates thought and efforts to discredit it. Few would maintain that conflict does not contribute to crime. Defining conflict becomes the focus.

Labeling

The foundation for *labeling theory* was created by Tannenbaum's (1938) "dramatization of evil," Merton's (1968) "self-fulfilling prophecy," and Becker's (1963) deviant behavior as an outcome of individual self definition and society's response to it. Lemert (1951) suggests that actors stigmatized with the label *criminal* are destined to live their lives dictated by that label and therefore comport themselves as such. The theory, however, is even more insidious.

According to Merton, many of us live up to, or down to, the expectations others place on us. This is basically the old Chicago School symbolic interactionism. In the framework of labeling theory, the actor has committed a crime, has been adjudicated criminal through a successful degradation ceremony

(Garfinkel, 1965), and thus given a state-endorsed label. The actor internalizes the label believing him- or herself to *be* that label. Whether or not the person is sentenced and processed or eventually reforms is irrelevant. Upon release, that individual now bears the label *ex-convict*; no matters what the person feels she or he is, the state and community now recognize the label and believe that person to be dangerous, suspicious, and contemptible. Employment, housing, and services are denied or grudgingly provided, making reintegration with society at best challenging, at worst impossible. To say that labeling has little to do with this interaction is disingenuous.

Social Control

Although not traditionally thought of as a control theory, Sykes and Matza's (1957) *techniques of neutralization* is an interesting approach to understanding aberrant behavior. It responds to the question, Why do good people do bad things? When faced with the choice to commit a crime or not, individuals "drift," allowing the actor to "neutralize"—that is, rationalize— their decision. Martyrs, people simply in the wrong place at the wrong time, and those who feel they were coerced into crimes they would not normally commit neutralize by "denial of responsibility." Those who believe that their actions would not be noticed or would cause little harm neutralize by "denial of injury." Sometimes, offenders engage in "denial of the victim"—believe that their victims deserved what they got. Offenders who believe their victim "had it coming," for whatever reason, are "condemning the condemners." One of the most often-used techniques rationalizes behavior as supporting or even protecting significant others—the gang, the family, friends, even the state—and thus neutralizes by "appeal to higher loyalties." The actor typically understands what she or he has done, does not deny the action taken, but does not feel culpable.

Most of the explanations discussed in this chapter begin with the question, Why did that actor become a criminal? *Social control theories*, however, answer the question, Why *didn't* the person become a criminal? (Hirschi, 1969). Since the potential to become a criminal is ubiquitous, readily available to anyone, why is not everyone criminal? For social control theorists, the answer is simple: because we are controlled. The method of control becomes the interest of control theory. As in all theory construction, control theories include vestiges of many earlier theories.

Reiss (1951) established the foundation for control theories by arguing from a psychological perspective: When an individual's lack of inner controls is juxtaposed with an absence of effective social controls (like prosocial significant others, effective schools, or family), that person could easily commit crimes. Reckless (1955) followed by adding his own interpretation of control, calling it *containment*. Containment theory stipulates that the self, identified by such diverse psychological constructs as self-concept and superego, is responsible for maintaining a social equilibrium that balances the potential to do crime with the realization that crime is inappropriate. A healthy, prosocial (i.e., contained) self can "insulate" the individual from antisocial influences (Reckless, Dinitz, & Murray, 1956).

One of the most popular control constructs and one of the most widely tested theories followed Reckless. Hirschi (1969) integrated aspects of anomie, social disorganization, differential association, labeling, and containment in proposing *elements of the social bond*. Bond consists of four elements: attachment, commitment, involvement, and belief; when welded together, they form a "bond to the conventional order." Hirschi postulated that the stronger the bond, the greater the chances of prosocial activity. Conversely, the weaker the bond, the more likely crime is to ensue. Conventional behavior is instilled through close interaction with school, work, family, community, and friends. Alienation from or dissonance with these elements—that is, a weaker bond—is more likely to result in crime. Of course, Hirschi never addressed associations with significant others or institutions that are already criminal, like felonious parents or friends, gangs, and other threat groups. The key to Hirschi's bond is the interaction a person has with those who are important to his or her life.

Social disorganization theories are the legacy of the University of Chicago, whose Department of Sociology is hallowed ground for American criminology. Using the city of Chicago as a starting point, faculty examined the urban setting as a social science laboratory. Chicago sociologists collected data from the entities that interested them—people and the places and things they interacted with in the city of Chicago. Today's students often take the resulting dicta as common sense, but for the Chicago alliance, it was all new ground.

That ethnic, cultural, and economic kin shared similar environments generated theories that examined the inner city, the city's concentric zones (Park and Burgess, 1924), prevalent social disorganization (Shaw and McKay, 1942), and existent culture conflict (Sellin, 1938) shared by the groups who lived there. Cities stimulate misbehavior; human interaction happens in cities; and although people are usually cordial, sometimes they act criminally, even violently.

From the family interactions occurring within the confines of any home, to the streets where unsupervised youth might congregate, turning boasts and posturing into conflict or dangerous interaction, the specific geographic location of those interactions—the street/block/corner where people lived and spent time—was related to the types of activities in which those actors engage. Language, words, gestures, and symbols are exchanged and interpreted, or misinterpreted as being provocative. Who one is—one's stature in the community or gang, one's influence or the way that influence was returned—was information to be substantively assessed. In the infancy of criminology, these now-commonplace parameters were first examined. The "hot-spot analysis," "the 'hood," COMSTAT, "broken windows," "turf wars," and "gang" examinations of today, as well as one of the most esteemed scholarly publishing houses in the social sciences, are the contemporary progeny of the Chicago School.

General Theory

Two versions of a broad-based explanation of crime have recently emerged. Gottfredson and Hirschi (1990) expanded on Hirschi's bond concept to create a social control theory they called the *general theory of crime*. At its center is the thesis that the true deterrent of criminality is individual self-control. The failure to control one's impulses leads to crime. The theory sparked controversy by highlighting parenting strategies as the cause of effective or ineffective self-control.

In Agnew's (2006) vision of crime causation, various life influences come together to form a "web of crime," the highlight of his general theory of crime and delinquency. These influences, or domains, are the self, the family, school, peers, and work. Each domain influences the others, prosocially at some times and antisocially at others. Agnew argues that, when an impulsive self who had an ineffective parent has a poor school experience that encouraged interactions with disinterested peers and led to unemployment or underemployment, a web was created that resulted in crime. This web was then influenced, by either low constraints to resist and/or high motivation, to commit crime.

These theories suggest that criminality could be directly affected by more effective parenting strategies and greater accountability by all social enterprises to influence those individuals at society's margins.

CONCLUSION

We are curious about that which tempts, confuses, confounds, and frightens us. Of all human activities, crime is one about which we are the most curious. Criminology is the scholarly attempt to understand crime. While the criminal is a curiosity, becoming his or her potential victim is what more critically concerns us. We understand that the criminal justice mechanism is reactive; it is unlikely to protect any one of us from victimization. Our hope is that criminology, in spite its foibles, has the ability to help us understand and predict who among us, given their constitutions and situations, will commit crimes against us. We seek protection. Alas, that is also our frustration: that, although a plausible explanation increases our awareness of the conditions that could affect crime commission, it largely affects us only intellectually. Ultimately, we want to understand the motivation to commit crime and how to discourage it so that effective public policy can be enacted. Our reality is that there are not too many theories; on the contrary, there are too few.

DISCUSSION QUESTIONS

1. What perspective—sociological, psychological, anthropological, economic, political science, biological, and so forth—is best equipped to explain crime?

2. If reducing crime is the goal, what is the role of science in achieving that goal? What is the role of the state and society?

3. Are there areas of investigation that have not yet been tapped in the attempt to understand the causes of crime? If the role of science is to ask questions and provide answers, what questions have not yet been asked?

4. What is the value of constructing theories of crime causation? Is there an identifiable end product this activity is intended to produce?

5. What are the major considerations and/or variables necessary to constructing a reasonable explanation of the causes of crime? What factors are likely to increase the probability of crime, and what factors are likely to decrease the probability? Do we actually know?

NOTE

1. A cursory review of some of the most insightful and useful works starts with Lanier & Henry (1998); Lilly, Cullen, & Ball (1995); Vold, Bernard, & Snipes (2002); and Williams & McShane (2009).

REFERENCES

Agnew, R. (2005). *Why criminals offend: A general theory of crime and delinquency.* Los Angeles, CA: Roxbury.

Akers, R. L. (1994). *Criminological theories: Introduction and evaluation.* Los Angeles: Roxbury.

Babbie, E. (2008). *The practice of social research* (11th ed). Belmont, CA: Wadsworth/Thomson Learning.

Becker, H. S. (1963). *Outsiders: Studies in the sociology of deviance.* New York: The Free Press.

Bureau of Justice Statistics. (2009). *Criminal offender statistics.* U.S. Department of Justice, Office of Justice Programs. Retrieved September 25, 2009, from http://www.ojp.usdoj.gov/bjs/

Chesney-Lind, M., & Shelden, R. G. (1992). *Girls, delinquency, and juvenile justice.* Belmont, CA: Wadsworth.

Cloward, R. A., & Ohlin, L. E. (1960). *Delinquency and opportunity: A theory of delinquent gangs.* New York: The Free Press.

Cohen, A. K. (1955). *Delinquent boys: The culture of the gang.* New York: The Free Press.

Cohen, L. E., & Felson, M. (1979). Social change and crime rate trends: A routine activity approach. *American Sociological Review, 44*(4), 588–608.

Durkheim, E. (1933/1893). *The division of labor in society.* (George Simpson, trans.). New York: The Free Press.

Durkheim, E. (1951/1897). *Suicide: A study of sociology.* (John A. Spaulding, trans.). New York: The Free Press.

Garfinkel, H. K. (1965). Conditions of successful degradation ceremonies. *American Journal of Sociology, 61*(5), 420–424.

Gottfredson, M. R., & Hirschi, T. (1990) *A general theory of crime.* Stanford, CA: Stanford University Press.

Hirschi, T. (1969). Causes of delinquency. Berkeley: University of California Press.

Katz, J. (1988). *Seductions of crime: Moral and sensual attractions in doing evil.* New York: Basic Books.

Kohlberg, L. (1984). *The psychology of moral development: The nature and validity of moral stages.* San Francisco: Harper & Row.

Lanier, M. M., & Henry, S. (1998). Essential criminology. Boulder, CO: Westview Press.

Lemert, E. M. (1951). *Social pathology.* New York: McGraw-Hill.

Lilly, J. R., Cullen, F. T., & Ball, R. A. (1995). *Criminological theory: Context and consequences* (2nd ed.). Thousand Oaks, CA: Sage.

Lombroso, C. (1876). *L'Uomo delinquente (The Criminal Man).* Milan, Italy: Hoepli.

Merton, R. K. (1968). *Social theory and social structure* (Rev. & enlarged ed.). Glencoe, IL: The Free Press.

Messerschmidt, J. W. (1993). *Masculinities and crime: Critique and reconceptualization of theory.* Lanham, MD: Rowman & Littlefield.

Park, R. E., & Burgess, E. W. (1924). *Introduction to the science of sociology* (2nd ed.). Chicago: University of Chicago Press.

Platt, T. (1974). Prospects for a radical criminology in the United States. *Crime and Social Justice, 1*(Spring-Summer), 2–6.

Quinney, R. (1973). *Critique of legal order: Crime control in a capitalist society.* Boston: Little, Brown.

Reckless, W. C. (1955). *The crime problem.* New York: Appleton-Century-Crofts.

Reckless, W. C., Dinitz, S., & Murray, E. (1956). Self-concept as an insulator against delinquency. *American Sociological Review, 21*(5), 744–756.

Reiss, A. J. (1951). Delinquency as the failure of personal and social controls. *American Sociological Review, 16*(2), 196–207.

Schwendinger, H., & Schwendinger, J. (1970). Defenders of order or guardians of human rights? *Issues in Criminology, 5,* 113–146.

Sellin, T. (1937). The Lombrosian myth in criminology. *American Journal of Sociology, 42*(6):896–897.

Sellin, T. (1938). *Culture conflict and crime.* New York: Social Science Research Council.

Shaw, C. R., & McKay, H. D. (1942). *Juvenile delinquency in urban areas.* Chicago: University of Chicago Press.

Short, J. (1975). The natural history of an applied theory: Differential opportunity and "mobilization for youth." In N. Dermerath, O. Larsen, & K. Schuessler (Eds.), *Social policy and sociology* (pp. 193–210). New York: Academic Press.

Skinner, W. F., & Fream, A. M. (1997). A social learning theory analysis of computer crime among college students. *Journal of Research in Crime and Delinquency 34*(4), 495–518.

Smith, D. A., & Brame, R. (1994). On the initiation and continuation of delinquency. *Criminology 32*(4), 607–629.

Sutherland, E. H. (1937). *The professional thief: By a professional thief.* Chicago: University of Chicago Press.

Sutherland, E. H. (1939). *Principles of criminology.* Chicago: J. B. Lippincott.

Sutherland, E. H. (1983) *White collar crime: The uncut version.* New Haven, CT: Yale University Press. (First published 1937.)

Sutherland, E. H., & Cressey, Donald R. (1947). *Principles of criminology* (4th ed.). New York: J. B. Lippincott.

Sykes, G. M., & Matza, D. (1957). Techniques of neutralization: A theory of delinquency. *American Sociological Review 22*(6), 664–670.

Tannenbaum, F. (1938). *Crime and the community.* Boston: Ginn.

Taylor, I., Walton, P., & Young, J. (1973). *The new criminology: For a social theory of deviance.* London: Routledge and Kegan Paul.

Tifft, L. L. (1979). The coming redefinitions of crime: An anarchist perspective. *Social Problems, 26*(4), 392–402.

Vold, G. B., & Bernard, T. J. (1983). *Theoretical criminology* (2nd ed.). New York: Oxford University Press.

Vold, G. B., Bernard, T. J., & Snipes, J. B. (2002). *Theoretical criminology* (5th ed.). New York: Oxford University Press.

Walters, G. D. (1989). Putting more thought into criminology. *International Journal of Offender Therapy and Comparative Criminology, 33*(3), v-vii.

Williams, F. P., & McShane, M. D. (2009). *Criminological theory* (5th ed.). Upper Saddle River, NJ: Pearson Prentice Hall.

Yochelson, S., & Samenow, S. (1976). *The criminal personality: Vol. 1. A profile for change.* New York: Jason Aronson.

4

Unleashing the Power of Criminal Justice Theory

Peter B. Kraska

This essay addresses three serious concerns about how our field of study, criminology and criminal justice, approaches theory. First, although theorizing about the why of crime is a recognized and institutionalized endeavor, theorizing about criminal justice is unrecognized, underdeveloped, and in serious need of an infrastructure and legitimacy. Second, due to the dominance of the positivist social science model, the power of theory has been severely diminished as an educational tool. Criminal justice theory harbors tremendous transformative powers when used to cultivate critical thinking skills and as a means to raise consciousness. This classic role of academic theorizing, however, has been displaced more often than not by the assumption that the single, ultimate goal of theory is to develop universal causal laws. Third, academe has taken exclusive ownership of theory and, in doing so, has tended to define any theorizing that occurs in the public sphere as mere ideology or pointless rhetoric. The assumption that theorizing is an activity done by academics for other academics seriously diminishes its educative power in public discourse and hence its ability to affect how we collectively make theoretical sense of crime and justice issues.

The goal here, then, is to illuminate the potential power of criminal justice theory for the field of criminal justice studies. This chapter questions the default thinking in our field that studying criminal justice is merely a policy-oriented appendage of criminology proper, and it presents a vision of theory that is at the same time intellectually stimulating and practically transformative.

The Power of Criminal Justice Theory for Our Discipline

As a graduate student, I was required to take numerous "theory" courses. At the same time, I became keenly interested in the intensely punitive turn taken by the American criminal justice system (i.e., the war on crime and the War on Drugs). What I noticed was that all of the "theory" instruction I was receiving focused on the why of *crime*—and paid very little explanatory attention to the why of *criminal justice*. My experiences were typical of our field, and I made an early and unsettling observation: The only recognized theoretical infrastructure and theoretical project we acknowledge in crime and justice studies is crime theory.

Over the years, I've come to recognize this as a serious disciplinary deficiency—one that some of us are attempting to remedy (Bernard & Engel, 2001; Duffee & McGuire, 2007; Kraska, 2004, 2006; Kraska & Brent, forthcoming). Our discipline assumes that theory work is reserved for the why of crime and crime rates. Within our leading scholarly journals, theory development and testing is targeted primarily at explaining crime. Our "theory" textbooks focus almost exclusively on the why of deviance, crime, and delinquency. Even the majority of our introductory criminal justice textbooks, which have the criminal justice system as their explicit object of study, dedicate nearly all their discussion of theory to theories of criminal behavior. Our undergraduate and graduate degree programs assume that the theory component of their curriculum should concentrate almost exclusively on the why of crime. And "teaching theory," as part of these curricula, refers universally to teaching crime theory.

Overall, then, it is taken for granted that the central object of our theorizing in crime and justice studies is crime. Pursuing a recognized and usable theoretical infrastructure about criminal justice—despite the frustration with this state of affairs voiced by some leading scholars in the field over the last three decades—has not been an acknowledged priority and certainly does not constitute a recognized theoretical project (Bernard & Engel, 2001; Duffee & McGuire, 2007; Hagan, 1989; Kraska 2004, 2006; Kraska & Brent, forthcoming; Marenin & Worrall, 1998).

In fact, to make matters worse, studying criminal justice is usually framed as merely a practical endeavor, with little concern for theory development or high-level intellectualism. Theory work is relevant to criminal justice only insofar as theories of crime causation lead to more effective crime control policies and tactics (again, criminal justice behavior is treated as simply the independent variable that affects crime). Embedded in this thinking is the presumption that studying crime control and criminal justice is strictly a "practical," as opposed to a theoretical, endeavor concerned only with what works and the how-to of crime control.

Many criminologists, therefore, see no need for criminal justice theory, since for them crime theory already provides the theoretical foundation for what the criminal justice system should and should not do about crime. Of course, distinguishing between theorizing crime and theorizing criminal justice is not difficult; most crime and justice scholars can appreciate the qualitative difference between explaining crime and explaining crime control. The latter concentrates on making theoretical sense of criminal justice and crime-control phenomena, such as the behavior of the state, the behavior of criminal justice organizations (police, courts, corrections, and juvenile justice organizations), overall trends in the entire criminal justice apparatus, and the private sector's crime-control activities.

Clearly, then, we need different theoretical infrastructures for understanding the nature of crime behavior versus the nature of crime-*control* behavior. And although the two no doubt intersect (see Figure 4.1) in the realm of law creation, the study of criminal justice behavior and crime behavior will require quite different theoretical tools.

The thinking that crime theory constitutes our intellectual core is so reified that many bright and capable academics have difficulty understanding even

Figure 4.1   Venn Diagram of Criminal Justice Theory and Crime Theory

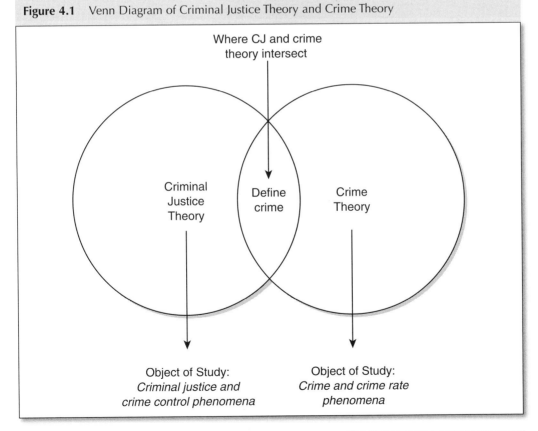

Source: From Kraska, P., *Theorizing Criminal Justice* (2005).

the need for criminal justice theory. One reason is that theorizing criminal justice is inherently a more critical endeavor than theorizing crime. When our object of study shifts from crime to criminal justice, and we are forced to examine, for example, the why of the drug war as opposed to drug use, or the why of the War on Terrorism as opposed to terrorism itself, or the why of police behavior as opposed to the commission of crime, we are essentially problematizing crime control activities and the criminal justice institution as opposed to crime itself. Doing so necessitates the scrutiny of state behavior, of private-sector crime-control activities, and of societal shifts in criminal justice punitiveness.

This is precisely why the "critical" theories found in traditional crime theory textbooks are an odd fit, if not misplaced. In examining the state's oppression of marginalized groups (women, the poor, racial minorities, homosexuals) via the criminal justice system, the truth is that the theories don't belong—because their explanatory gaze is directed less at crime than at the state's creation of and reaction to crime.

Criminal Justice: A Worthy Object of Theorizing

Another difficulty is that, when we theorize criminal justice, our central object of study is even more complex than it is for crime. The terrain of possible foci is vast, ranging from explaining individual practitioner behavior to explaining the growth of the criminal justice system over the last 100 years. Such foci might include theorizing criminal justice practitioner behavior, the system's subcomponents, or its historical development, or perhaps explaining its steep growth in power and size over the last 30 years, a central objective of Garland's (2001) well-known book, *The Culture of Control*. Theorizing could also focus on contemporary trends and issues in crime-control practices, such as privatization, militarization, federalization, the expansion of surveillance, racial profiling, erosion of constitutional safeguards, or trends and issues related to the "wars" on terrorism and drugs. More conventionally, criminal justice theory could seek to explain the behavior of criminal justice policy, agency behavior, and the why of practitioner and organizational decision making.

These varied and important objects of explanation should demonstrate that explanatory frameworks, other than those provided by crime theories, are not only possible but also needed. Traditional criminological theories, despite their obvious interconnection with criminal justice practice, are not designed to function as explanations for criminal justice system or crime-control behavior.

Please note that the claim here is not necessarily a lack of theorizing about the criminal justice system and crime-control activities but rather the lack of a recognized infrastructure; the lack of recognition that a body of theory separate from crime theory even exists; the lack of desire to articulate, let alone teach, criminal justice theory; and due to all of these, lack of access to these theories for students and academics alike.

Developing a Useful Theoretical Infrastructure

To begin the large task of remedying this situation, an avenue is presented for developing an infrastructure (Kraska 2004, 2006; Kraska & Brent, forthcoming). The approach is fairly straightforward: A large volume of existing theoretical scholarship about our reaction to crime is organized around eight explanatory constructs called *theoretical orientations*. These orientations are a type of theoretical lens, framed as metaphors, through which criminologists view and make sense of criminal justice and crime-control phenomena. Formally defined, a theoretical orientation is an interpretive construct that includes a logically coherent set of organizing concepts, causal preferences, value clusters, and assumptions that work to orient our interpretations and understanding of criminal justice phenomena (similar to a paradigm).

The goal is not to develop a single, testable criminal justice theory; on the contrary, the objective is to illuminate the multiple theoretical lenses crime and justice scholars can employ to help us understand the behavior of the criminal justice system and trends in crime control. Figure 4.2 provides a schematic of the eight theoretical orientations.

These metaphors are routinely employed in our field of study. They include criminal justice as (1) rational-legalism, (2) system, (3) crime control versus due process, (4) politics, (5) the social construction of reality, (6) growth complex, (7) oppression, and (8) late modernity. The features of each theoretical orientation are noted beneath it.

Several theoretical orientations in our field are easily identified; the systems are the most obvious. Most academics would agree that the system's framework has dominated our field's thinking and research about criminal justice. The network of governmental agencies responding to our crime problem is universally known as the criminal justice *system*. The system's framework is derived from the biological sciences, Parson's structural functionalism, and organizational studies. It has a strong reformist element, emphasizing the importance of enhancing criminal justice coordination, efficiency, rational decision making, and technology.

Another not-so-common explanatory framework is termed here the *late-modern* theoretical orientation. This theoretical lens situates the criminal justice apparatus (broadly defined) within macro-shifts associated with the current era of social history labeled *late modernity*. Criminal justice and crime-control phenomena are best explained as

Figure 4.2 Criminal Justice Theoretical Orientations

Major Features	Rational/ Legal	System	Packer's C.C. vs. D.P.	Politics	Social Construction	Growth Complex	Oppression	Late Modernity
Intellectual Tradition	neoclassical; legal formalism	structural–functionalism; biological sciences; organizational studies	liberal legal jurisprudence; legal realism; sociolegal studies	political science; public administration	interpretive school; symbolic interaction; social construction	Weber; Frankfurt School; critical public administration	Marx; feminism; critical sociology; race studies	Foucault; govern-mentality literature; postmodernism
Approaches to Knowledge Production	technical legal research; status quo positivism	mainstream positivist social science (critical and status quo focus)	academic legal research; sometime positivist	historical; comparative; positivist social science; theoretical synthesis research	interpretive social science; critical social science; content analysis	critical social science; theoretical synthesis research	critical social science; critical ethnography; feminist approaches	critical social science; theoretical synthesis research; minimal ISS and PSS
Key Concepts Employed	rational–legalistic, rule-bound; taken for granted	functional; equilibrium; efficiency; technology; external forces; open system; closed system	value-cluster; efficiency; crime control values; due process values; needs-based values	ideology; conflict; symbolic politics; policymaking/ implementing; state, community	myth; reality; culture; symbols; legitimacy; moral panic; impression-management institutional theory	bureaucracy building; privatization profit; complex; technical rationality; merging complexes	dangerous classes; gender; patriarchy; racism; class bias; conflict model; structural thinking; dialectics; praxis	actuarial justice; neoliberal politics; exclusive society; safety norm; incoherence in CJ policy

Major Features	Rational/ Legal	System	Packer's C.C. vs. D.P.	Politics	Social Construction	Growth Complex	Oppression	Late Modernity
Reasons for Rapid CJ Expansion in Last 30 Years	legal reaction to increased law-breaking (forced reaction theory)	CJ system reacting to increases in crime (forced reaction theory)	pendulum swing toward crime control values; choosing punitiveness	politicians exploiting problem; politicized drug war; shift in ideology	moral panics; media exploitation; runaway cultural process; crime as scapegoat	dynasty building; growth complex; merging private with public, CJ with military	control of threatening groups; marginalized used as scapegoats; crisis in state legitimacy	crisis in state sovereignty; risk-aversive society; growth complex; moral indifference; social exclusivity paradigm
Assumptions About Agency and Practitioner Motives	well-intended; protecting; serving; rule following; law abiding; professionalism	rational decision makers; efficient; adapting to external forces	role/goal conflict; mixed messages; mimic the value-messages provided from public	responsive to politics; interest-based; ideological pulls; power-players	constructing problems for existing solutions; reacting to moral panics; culturally bound; managing appearances	self-serving; power building; quest for immortality; means over ends; bureaucratic survival; technical over moral thinking	institutional racism, sexism, classism; often unaware of oppressive end result of their own activities	navigating through massive transformations, late-modern forces; good intentions, disturbing results
Issues of Concern	deterrence; defending the virtues and honor of the CJS	abuse of discretion; cutting-edge technology; streamline/ centralize operations	erosion of constitutional rights; governmental intrusiveness	federalization; symbolic politics; ideological intensification	media/ bureaucrat/ political exploitation; mythology	exponential growth; private/public, military/police blur	violence against women; drug war's impact on marginalized; racial profiling	growth of system; changes in social control; rise of surveillance society

Source: From Kraska, P., *Theorizing Criminal Justice* (2005).

adaptations to late-modern social conditions. An impressive body of scholarship has emerged in this area (a few examples include Garland, 2001; O'Malley, 1999; Simon, 2007; and Young, 1999). Five late-modern conditions frame this orientation:

- the rise of actuarial justice and the influence of the risk society,
- the neoliberal shift in macro-politics,
- increasing contradictions and incoherence in crime-control policy,
- the decline of the sovereign state's legitimacy, and
- the ascendance of an exclusion paradigm for managing those perceived to pose a safety threat in an increasingly security-conscious society.

The late-modern orientation is probably the most theoretically vigorous pursuit of criminal justice/crime-control phenomena in the literature today. As shown in Figure 4.2, there are many other possible theoretical lenses through which to view criminal justice behavior. Space limitations obviously inhibit a more detailed examination; further elaboration can be found in Kraska (2004) and Kraska and Brent (forthcoming).

The Power of Theory to Transform Consciousness

As a result of constructing this infrastructure, I've been teaching criminal justice theory, instead of crime theory proper, to students for the last 10 years. And I've come to realize the very real power of theory, and particularly criminal justice theory, to affect students' thinking. Theory work, if approached in the right spirit, harbors tremendous transformative powers through cultivation of critical thinking skills and as a means to raise consciousness.

To fully appreciate its potential, we have to recognize the integral part theory plays not just in such journals as *Criminology* but in our everyday lives. When my 6-year-old daughter Cora was only 3, she asked me, completely out of the blue, "How does a butterfly get the dust on its wings?" After I recovered, and in my feeble attempt to cultivate her theoretical skills, I asked her what she thought. She responded first by positing that "the butterflies are just born that way" (i.e., an inherent part of their biological makeup). I told her that was correct—but then she demonstrated the early signs of a keen theoretical and creative mind. She said, "Daddy, I knew that was the right answer, but I was hoping it was because they pick up different colors of dust from the flowers."

This anecdote demonstrates that the activity of theorizing is essential to everything we think and do, beginning in our earliest years. We craft theory throughout our lives as a way to make sense of our surroundings. The way in which we make theoretical sense of things guides the decisions we make, so that we can navigate those surroundings competently and decently—to solve problems, to think through complex phenomena, to make accurate predictions, to understand others and feel compassion or anger, to make sense of our workplaces and organizational environments. Thousands of times a day, we either assume or assess the why of things, and these assumptions and assessments frame our thinking and actions. Theory is integral not only in everyday life but to all those who work in organizations that deal with criminal or social justice.

Our field's traditional approach to teaching theory diminishes its pedagogical power and practical strength. Overall, the accepted approach involves (1) empirically testing existing crime theories, making minor modifications along the way; and (2) teaching students about these crime theories and examining the evidence that supports and/or refutes them.

Theory is something therefore owned by academics for academics, for the exclusive purpose of developing universal causal laws for the explanation of crime through testing relationships between clearly operationalized independent and dependent variables. Of course, this critique is not meant to diminish the importance of this activity; those of us who do this kind of work are a great asset to our field. What I question is whether this approach *alone* is the most efficacious for teaching and educating our students.

I've learned a lot about teaching theory in the last 10 years that I didn't really recognize for the first 12 years. I now concentrate on teaching criminal justice theory in a way that enhances student's theoretical skills, sensitivities, and lenses, and that cultivates their critical thinking abilities. My views about theory have crystallized teaching graduate students in an in-service leadership program to police administrators, and in another, similar program teaching air force officers who work as military police.

I've taught these nontraditional students theory by exposing them to some of the major theoretical orientations in our field that help us to make sense of criminal justice phenomena. As noted above, I present each of these theoretical orientations as lenses or theoretical filters that provide ideas and organizing concepts that allow students to view their objects of theorizing in a different theoretical light. We talk about how they each harbor a personal theoretical framework that has developed over their lifetime based on what they've learned through direct experience, entertainment, news media, significant others, and the educational system.

They come to realize that their personal theoretical frameworks are always under construction, and the process of learning to interpret their surroundings through differing theoretical filters is a vital part of their educational experience. I concentrate on the eight theoretical lenses noted earlier. The idea is for students to read, think deeply about, and apply, through numerous engagement oriented exercises, these varying theoretical lenses. The objective is to develop critical theoreticians who can

- raise vital questions and problems, formulating them clearly and precisely,
- gather and assess relevant information,
- use abstract ideas to make theoretical sense of things effectively,

- come to well-reasoned, explanatory-based conclusions and solutions, and test them against relevant criteria and standards,
- think open-mindedly, reflectively, and creatively, with an ability to view their objects of theorizing with multiple theoretical lenses,
- communicate effectively with others in figuring out explanations and solutions to complex problems, and
- more competently navigate their way through an increasingly complex social and criminal justice environment.

I've found that these in-service police and military students have a tremendous capacity to develop their personal theoretical frameworks. One explanatory framework I've found particularly enlightening for these in-service students is the metaphor of *growth complex*. The growth complex theoretical orientation illuminates the possibility that organizations (or entire institutional systems) can devolve into entities more motivated by their own bureaucratic interests than by the public good. The underlying assumption is that *any bureaucracy's most basic instinct is to survive and grow*. Growth complex thinking, therefore, casts the criminal justice apparatus in an intensely critical light.

The criminal justice growth complex is an entity comprising numerous interrelated and interdependent parts—an intricate structural matrix of criminal justice and noncriminal justice governmental bureaucracies, politicians, private companies, media agencies, academic institutions, and myriad interests. While not operating in harmony necessarily by design or even by intent, the net effect is nonetheless a complex of loosely and tightly connected organizations and interests that generate a synergy ideal for expansion. In the quest for survival, growth, and influence building, the overall goal of pursuing the public interest through democratic processes and values (participation, accountability, fairness, and a concern for human dignity) is relegated to the back burner. The growth complex orientation views the criminal justice apparatus as an entity that seeks out and constructs new problems for its solution, that actively pursues its own self-serving agenda as opposed to working toward the public good, and that is increasingly influenced by the private-sector objectives of profit and growth. In its simplest terms, garnering power and size becomes not a means to a laudable end but an end in itself. (Please recall that this is only one lens and therefore only illuminates one potential dimension of criminal justice functioning).

I've found that the reason this theoretical orientation resonates with military and police practitioners is that its theoretical premises coincide with their real-world experiences (data and theory are consistent). The growth complex lens influenced one police administrator in dramatic fashion. He was in charge of securing grants for his department and apparently good at his job. He wrote an excellent paper during the semester, applying growth complex thinking to his job. After the class was over, he e-mailed me about a year later and wanted me to know that that he was under a lot of pressure in his department from other administrators to renew a federal grant that the department had secured based on false premises (I'm being purposely vague). He argued against renewal, won the battle, and attributed his action to the new theoretical lenses he adopted. Modifying his personal theoretical framework, of course, affected his values and his value choices. He acted against what he called "mindless bureaucracy-building."

This example demonstrates that it is vital to value the everyday and real-world relevance of theory, and not approach it merely as a body of scientific work found in books and articles. It is indeed an activity, something we do. Theorizing is part of what ought to be happening in a theory class: the application and even crafting of theory—approaching it as an activity, as opposed to simply learning a body of work (Frauley 2005). Remember, we've been crafting theory since the day we were born. We have tested our theories in the real world. Some of us have done a good job; others, a miserable one. The key is to not just have students learn about theory and famous theorists but to apply what they've learned to differing objects of study. Like the way many of us conduct a research methods class—we ask them to conduct research.

The overall point here is that we shouldn't limit the power of theory. It has high potential to foster creativity, empathy, the expansion of our cognitive gaze, a rethinking or at least a clarification of value preferences, and a serious questioning of and introspection about our taken-for-granted reality. Learning theory should be replete with lots of "Aha!" experiences. The purposes of learning theory should include enabling individuals to know themselves and their situation through retrospection and a raising of their consciousness about our complex social world.

The Power of Theory to Affect Public Explanations

My third and final concern is directly related to the second: Academe has taken complete ownership of theory and, as a result, has diminished its significant potential to shape public discourse. I fully realized the gravity of this concern while watching the Hurricane Katrina disaster unfold.

Catastrophic natural disasters, despite all the suffering and pain they inflict, often play out ultimately as stories of human triumph, heroism, and community solidarity. We construct them as testaments to the true decency of humankind. The urgent task at hand, to take care of each others' most basic needs, trumps at least temporarily some of our uglier societal faults, such as class/race/gender divisions and prejudices, self-centeredness, entrenched political conflict, and a lack of social caring.

Hurricane Katrina, which hit the coasts of Alabama, Louisiana, and Mississippi on August 29, 2005, was different. While human triumph and decency were evident, the lasting legacy of Katrina will be that it washed away the veil of denial and neglect and laid bare the ugly societal faults that are usually pushed to the periphery. It seemed to stir up and inflame some of our deepest contemporary fears: poor racial minorities free to loot and victimize others, a sign of things to come as the result of global warming, and a government so inept in homeland security matters that it failed on almost all accounts.

Just as with the terrorist attack of September 11, 2001, we have a strong collective desire to make sense of these types of catastrophic events, both for therapeutic reasons and to prevent or minimize the harm they cause. What exactly does "making sense" mean, though? "Making sense," for some people, means resorting to religious explanations (e.g., "It must be God's will"); for others, it means filtering the event through a rigid ideology in order to reaffirm the truth of that ideology (e.g., "It's the fault of our welfare system; only those dependent on welfare would be unable to get out of New Orleans"). For the social scientist, it means using theory and research to examine rigorously the many unanswered questions.

Each of these endeavors seeks explanation, or a theoretically based narrative—an attempt to construct and find meaning in a highly complex and unsettling event. Traumatic events such as 9/11 and Katrina bring about a state of collective cognitive dissonance in which reality as previously constructed and perceived comes into serious question. Comfortable ideas, expectations, and assumptions are shattered, creating what Garfinkel called a temporary state of "meaninglessness." Theory helps us to put the pieces back together (Kraska & Neuman, 2008, p. 65).

Kishonna Gray and I examined real-world theorizing found in the public sphere after Hurricane Katrina (Gray & Kraska, 2006). Examining this catastrophe provided a valuable opportunity to study how theory operates in the real world. Katrina exposed a host of theoretical questions that are rarely examined, at least outside of academe, and generated an incisive public discourse about power structures, economic inequalities, racial injustice, governmental ineptitude and corruption, and accountability. Contrast this rich, contextualized coverage during Katrina with the public theorizing following 9/11, an insular and uncritical discourse emphasizing themes of xenophobia and evildoers.

Many regarded as unpatriotic any theorizing that fell outside these narrow parameters. The unique example of real-world theorizing found in the post-Katrina public sphere was essential to study, both for theoretical and practical reasons. Unfortunately, the social science community has constructed a disciplinary straitjacket around the notion of theory, limiting theory to testing the relationship between measurable variables by academics and generally for other academics. Academics have unwisely taken exclusive ownership of theory, rendering it an entity separate from everyday thinking. Not only is this an untenable position, for most if not all social science theory emanates from real-world thinking and ideas, it ignores the fact that "public theorizing" is of far greater consequence than what we do in academe. Indeed, the field of crime and justice studies tends to lose sight of what ought to be the premier goal of academic theory: the influencing and shaping of public thinking (i.e., public theory).

One particularly revealing theoretical moment emerged soon after Katrina hit. Kanye West, a music industry star, was standing next to comedian Mike Meyers and said the following on live national television during a post-Katrina fund-raising event:

> I hate the way they portray us in the media. You see a black family, it says, "They're looting." You see a white family, it says, "They're looking for food." It's been five days waiting for federal help because most of the people are black. . . . So anybody out there that wants to do anything to help . . . please.

After Meyers made another comment, Kanye West concluded his analysis by saying, "George Bush doesn't care about black people."

Kanye West's comments instantly became the cultural flashpoint for those who agreed and disagreed with his assertion. It is critical to note that West never said (despite the assertions of many reactionaries and some in the mainstream media), that George Bush *hated* black people. Several news reports even misquoted West by using the word *hate*. This popular culture moment highlighted the prominent role that race-based explanations played in public dialogue about the Katrina disaster. It would be a mistake to discount West's narrative as mere "sounding off" with little theoretical significance.

Of course, had he said *hate*, it would have implied a type of overt prejudice, a type of intentional racism that most would agree has diminished significantly in the last 50 years and is widely condemned as illegitimate in mainstream society. Framing and interpreting West's assertion, therefore, as one of overt bigotry made it easy to de-legitimize.

The phrase *doesn't care about black people*, however, connotes something entirely different. It is the essence of what is called *structural racism*—in which, even though intentional bigotry is not evident, the historical patterns and arrangements of race-based exclusion continue. Long after the bulk of white people have ceased to actively hate and consciously discriminate against racial minorities, there still exists an array of social and economic arrangements, constructed during a time of explicit hatred, that work to the disadvantage of racial minorities.

Where racial prejudice is kept alive by hate, structural racism thrives under conditions of indifference. West emphasized a lack of caring, positing that the abysmal response to the disaster was due to a lack of concern for African Americans. He captured succinctly an important theoretical organizing concept: that the enduring legacy of hate-based racism is a new form of racism, one based in conscious and unconscious indifference, neglect, apathy, and uncaring. It took indifference for our government at many levels to ignore a federally funded task force of scientists who since 2002 have predicted exactly this fate for the population of poor African Americans in New Orleans if a hurricane the magnitude of Katrina were to hit. It took indifference for Chertoff, the director of Homeland Security, to go to a conference the day after the disaster and not attend to a single detail of the relief operation (and for President Bush to remain on vacation). It took indifference to wait five days to provide any type of substantive humanitarian relief to those stuck in new Orleans, while in the meantime the area was being "secured" by military and police forces.

The purpose of this example is to illustrate that our field of study needs to broaden our notion of theory and to recognize that we should not divorce our academic theorizing from public theory. The aftermath of Katrina gave a small glimpse of the potential of theoretical discourse within the public sphere to make a difference—a difference brought about by cracking the veneer of taken-for-granted ideology to reveal other possible explanations and richer theoretical narratives.

CONCLUSION: EMBRACING CRIMINAL JUSTICE THEORY

The transformative powers of theory, both in our private lives and in the public sphere, should be acknowledged and cultivated. We should find ways to encourage our theoretical curiosity and the creation of multiple theoretical lenses. This can assist us in seeing through reified and counterproductive dominant explanations, not just about terrorism but the war on terrorism, not just about drugs but the war on drugs—explanations that will help us discuss the undiscussable, confront the uncomfortable, and reveal the taken-for-granted. Competent, meaningful, accurate, and deep theorizing is an essential precursor for thoughtful, substantive, humane solutions.

In a 1998 article, Marenin & Worrall (p. 465) asserted that "criminal justice is an academic discipline in practice but not yet in theory." Our field has not placed high value on this endeavor for two primary reasons. The first has already been discussed: Crime theory suffices. The second is more difficult to overcome: While exploring the why of crime has prima facie importance, our field has neither articulated nor acknowledged the value provided us by theorizing criminal justice. Some assume, in fact, that studying criminal justice is inherently and necessarily atheoretical because it concentrates on practice. The notion that practice can somehow be severed from theory has been thoroughly debunked in most other major fields of study. Theory and practice are implied in one another; no policy analysis, implementation, strategic plan, or practitioner action is devoid of theory. To deny the integral role theory plays in all these instances is to remain ignorant of its influence.

As noted, theorizing criminal justice is an inherently critical endeavor providing important insights into the "system's" irrationalities, missteps, and disconcerting implications. Theoretically based scrutiny focused on criminal justice and crime control should not be misconstrued as inappropriately critical. It simply approaches criminal justice as a research problem—similar to the way we study crime.

Nor should theorizing criminal justice phenomena be viewed as an endeavor intended exclusively for practical change. Numerous scholars in our field find studying our society's reaction to crime intellectually stimulating in and of itself, much like biologists who study the animal kingdom or astronomers who study the solar system. Studying humans and organizations that attempt to control wrongdoing (and that sometimes engage in wrongdoing in the attempt) yields intriguing insights about the nature of society, our political landscape, and cutting-edge cultural trends. In short, how we react to crime tells us a lot about ourselves and where our society might be headed.

I'm certain criminal justice theory will eventually become a normalized presence in our criminal justice and criminology degree programs, our textbooks, and our doctoral training. The realization is growing that nothing less than our disciplinary integrity is at stake. However, as this process unfolds, it is critical to avoid the shortcomings evident in the development of crime theory. In order for criminal justice theory to reach its full potential, we must (1) develop its infrastructure in a manner that renders it both intellectually stimulating and accessible, (2) teach it in a way that acknowledges our positivist tradition yet allows space for the classic function of transforming consciousness, and (3) apply it to the real world through policy prescriptions based on research findings, yet attempt as well to actively influence public theories about criminal justice issues. Criminal justice theory holds significant potential power; let us hope it is wielded constructively.

DISCUSSION QUESTIONS

1. Is it really possible for criminal justice students to theorize? Or, is it more appropriate that they read and learn about pre-existing theories and the research that tests their veracity?

2. Why is it likely that the field of criminal justice will proceed slowly and with many obstacles in developing the idea of criminal justice theory?

3. What types of "public theorizing" typify such major criminal justice efforts as the War on Terror or the War on Drugs?

4. What is structural racism, and how is it still relevant to the operations of the criminal justice system today?

REFERENCES

Bernard, T., & Engel, R. (2001). Conceptualizing criminal justice theory. *Justice Quarterly, 18*(1), 1–30.

Duffee, D. E., & Maguire, E. R. (2007). *Criminal justice theory: explaining the nature and behavior of criminal justice.* New York: Routledge.

Frauley, J. (2005). Representing theory and theorising in criminal justice studies: Practising theory considered. *Critical Criminology, 13*(3), 245–265.

Garland, D. (2001). *The culture of control: Crime and social order in contemporary society.* Chicago: University of Chicago Press.

Gray, K., & Kraska, P. B. (2006). *Hurricane Katrina meltdown: Examining the relevance of everyday theory.* Paper presented at the meeting of the Academy of Criminal Justice Sciences, Baltimore, MD.

Hagan, J. (1989). Why is there so little criminal justice theory? Neglected macro- and micro-level links between organizations and power. *Journal of Research in Crime and Delinquency, 26*(2), 116–135.

Kraska, P. B. (2004). *Theorizing criminal justice: Eight essential orientations.* Prospect Heights, IL: Waveland Press.

Kraska, P. B. (2006). Criminal justice theory: Toward legitimacy and an infrastructure. *Justice Quarterly, 23,* 2.

Kraska, P. B., & Brent, J. (forthcoming). *Theorizing criminal justice: Eight essential orientations.* (2nd ed.). Prospect Heights, IL: Waveland Press.

Kraska, P. B., & Neuman, L. (2008). *Criminal justice and criminology research methods.* Boston: Pearson.

Marenin, O., & Worrall, J. (1998). Criminal justice: Portrait of a discipline in progress." *Journal of Criminal Justice, 26*(6), 465–480.

O'Malley, P. (1999). Volatile and contradictory punishment. *Theoretical Criminology, 3,* 175–196.

Simon, J. (2007). *Governing through crime.* Boston: Oxford University Press.

Young, J. (1999). *The exclusive society: Social exclusion, crime and difference in late modernity.* London: Sage.

PART II

Offenses and Offenders

5 Juvenile Delinquency

David L. Parry

Available statistics reveal that persons under 18 years of age accounted for approximately 15.4% of all arrests in the United States in 2007, a percentage that has declined steadily since reaching its peak level of 19% in 1996 (Federal Bureau of Investigation, 1996–2007, 2008). As in previous years, most arrested youth fell within the delinquency-prone 15–17 age group, and the vast majority were charged with theft, minor assaults, vandalism, drug offenses, liquor law violations, disorderly conduct, or status offenses such as running away from home or curfew violations. Contrary to the overblown myths and hysterical rhetoric fueling what Howell (2009) has dubbed a "moral panic" over supposedly escalating juvenile violence, Columbine-style school shootings, and a wave of juvenile superpredators, fewer than 1 in 20 juveniles arrested in 2007 were charged with a serious violent crime, and the total number of juvenile arrests—estimated at roughly 2.18 million (Puzzanchera, 2009)—had decreased 20% in the preceding 10 years.

So, who are these delinquents? Where do they come from, and why do they do it? What pathways do they follow into delinquency and—for most—back out as they mature into young adults? What is "delinquency," anyway, and how much of it *really* occurs? These are among the many questions raised in this chapter. The answers are elusive, and the literature exploring them is voluminous. The goal, therefore, is not to present an exhaustive review but rather to selectively examine several key aspects of the delinquency problem, highlighting exemplary statistics and research findings as a vehicle for exploring some of the central issues that must be confronted if we are to better understand and more effectively respond to the delinquency around us and the young people engaged in it.

_____ **What Is Delinquency?**

Let us begin by taking a look at the meaning of the term *juvenile delin-quency*. Traditionally, juvenile courts have exercised jurisdiction in three distinct types of cases. Although statutory language varies, the *delinquency jurisdiction* of these courts generally authorizes intervention in any case involving a minor charged with an act that would be a crime if committed by an adult. It is thus differentiated from their jurisdiction over *status offenders* (youth who engage in activities permissible for an adult but prohibited for children) and *neglected or dependent youth* (those who have no parent or who are the victims of parental neglect or abuse).

This deceptively straightforward definition of juvenile delinquency as a legal category masks significant state-by-state variations that make exceedingly difficult our effort to pin down exactly who and what we are studying when we try to *understand* delinquency. First, who falls within the delinquency jurisdiction of the juvenile court varies tremendously across states. The Illinois statute, commonly heralded as the first anywhere in the world to authorize creation of a separate court for juveniles, for example, limited the delinquency jurisdiction of juvenile courts to "any child under the age of 16 years who violates any law of this State or any city or village ordinance" (An Act to Regulate the Treatment and Control of Dependent, Neglected and Delinquent Children, 1899). Only three states today restrict delinquency jurisdiction so severely. Most cap it at the 18th birthday, while 10 states limit it to youth under 17 (Snyder & Sickmund, 2006), and Connecticut legislation taking effect in 2010 will reduce even further the number of under-16-only states (An Act Implementing the Provisions of the Budget Concerning General Government, 2007).

Further complicating matters, juvenile courts have almost universally retained authority to transfer youth under the age cap to criminal court for prosecution as adults if the judge deems the child unamenable to effective treatment within the juvenile justice system, and many states also automatically (i.e., by statute) exclude certain categories of youth (usually those above a specified age) who are charged with very serious offenses from juvenile court jurisdiction and/or grant prosecutors discretion to file such cases directly in criminal court if they choose to do so (see discussion in Griffin, 2003). At the other extreme, statutes in most states allow for extended juvenile court jurisdiction over adjudicated delinquents placed on probation or committed to a juvenile correctional facility until well beyond the age at which original jurisdiction ends—most commonly until the youth turns 21 or even, in a handful of states, to age 25 (Snyder & Sickmund, 2006). The term—the label—thus applies not only to the *act* but also to the *person* (the teenager or, occasionally, the child) who committed it, and even to the young adult still under juvenile court jurisdiction despite advancing age.

The definition of juvenile delinquency gets even murkier when we consider the offenses that underlie the delinquency label. For example, underage drinking is regarded by many as a status offense because it is prohibited only for those under 21 years of age. In most states, however, it is prosecutable as a misdemeanor for "minors" who are younger than 21 but above the maximum age for juvenile court jurisdiction, rendering it a delinquent act for those under that age. A similar dilemma confronts us regarding possession of marijuana, a misdemeanor under federal law and the laws of most states, and therefore a delinquent offense for juveniles in those jurisdictions. But courts in one state have repeatedly struck down criminal penalties for possession of small amounts within the home (*Ravin v. State*, 1975; *Noy v. State*, 2003), and in several others marijuana possession has been reclassified as a noncriminal infraction subject only to a monetary fine—as recently occurred in Massachusetts (An Act Establishing a Sensible State Marihuana Policy, 2008).

These and other variations in statutory provisions applicable to the delinquency jurisdiction of juvenile courts have significant implications for efforts to understand delinquency as a *social* problem. We saw, for example, that even preteens may sometimes be convicted and punished as adult criminals in the eyes of the law, whereas other young people may technically remain "juvenile delinquents" until their mid-twenties. Does this mean researchers seeking to gauge the extent of delinquency or to understand its causes should rely on after-the-fact decisions by juvenile justice system officials, or on legislatively established age caps for juvenile court jurisdiction, in determining whether to regard particular behaviors as delinquency or as adult crime? Similarly, do variations in state laws mean we should consider teenaged marijuana smokers to be delinquent if they live in California but not if they live in Massachusetts? What about underage drinking—delinquency or not?

How Much Delinquency?

These definitional challenges become especially problematic in any effort to gauge the extent of juvenile delinquency and the characteristics of juvenile offenders, even more so given the monumental obstacles to accurate measurement. Nonetheless, we can gain at least a general sense of the frequency and distribution of juvenile offenses by examining data derived from official arrest records, and we can further flesh out the picture by examining additional information gleaned from unofficial sources based on surveys tapping self-reported delinquency.

Arrest Data

Frequency and rate estimates for arrests of persons under 18 years of age—the closest feasible approximation of youth whose delinquent behavior actually falls within the jurisdiction of juvenile courts in their respective home states—are developed annually at the National Center for Juvenile Justice (NCJJ), based on Uniform Crime Reports (UCR) data compiled by the Federal Bureau of

Investigation and distributed in its *Crime in the United States* series. Prepared under a cooperative agreement with the Office of Juvenile Justice and Delinquency Prevention (OJJDP), the NCJJ estimates for 2007 peg nationwide arrests of "juveniles" at just over 2.18 million that year (Puzzanchera, 2009). Among the eight Part I offenses (formerly the Crime Index), the comparative infrequency of violent offenses is striking. These four offenses (murder, forcible rape, robbery, and aggravated assault) together accounted for less than 5% of all arrests of juveniles in 2007; arrests of juveniles for murder, despite their prominence in news reports and in popular culture, occurred just once in every 1,600 juvenile arrests. Part I property offenses (burglary, larceny-theft, motor vehicle theft, and arson) constituted a much greater share of juvenile arrests—nearly 20%—with the large assortment of generally less serious Part II offenses making up the remainder. Representation of juveniles among *all* arrestees ranged as high as 38% for vandalism and an eye-popping 47% for arson, but for other offenses it was far lower: 25% to 27% for most Part I property offenses, 28% for disorderly conduct, 27% for robbery, 10% for murder, and 13% to 15% for the remaining Part I violent offenses, with their representation among arrestees for other offenses ranging widely, from a high of 23% for weapons violations to less than 5% for drunkenness, fraud, prostitution, and driving under the influence.

Females accounted for 29% of all juvenile arrests in 2007 and for 35% of arrests for property offenses, but their representation dropped to just 17% for violent offenses (Federal Bureau of Investigation, 2008; Puzzanchera, 2009). In contrast with the underrepresentation of females, African American youth, representing about 17% of the under-18 population, were substantially over-represented both among juveniles arrested for property offenses (32%) and even more so among those arrested for violent offenses (51%), with their representation spiking to fully two-thirds (68%) of all juveniles arrested for robbery and 57% of those arrested for murder.

Turning briefly to trends over time, juvenile arrests declined by just over 20% overall between 1998 and 2007 (Federal Bureau of Investigation, 2008; Puzzanchera, 2009). Arrests for specific offenses fell by at least 18 percentage points for every Part I offense except robbery—which went up by 6%, about the same as it did for adults—and by comparably large amounts for most Part II offenses as well. In contrast, the number of adults arrested for violent offenses in 2007 fell just over half as much as for juveniles (8% for adults versus an average of 14% for juveniles). Arrests for property offenses declined just 2% for adults while falling by nearly a third for juveniles. The differences were especially noteworthy for motor vehicle theft, which declined by more than half for juveniles but by only 7% for adults, and for burglary and larceny/theft, both of which declined by over 30% for juveniles while dropping very little (larceny/theft) or even increasing (burglary) among adults.

Comparing trends by gender, arrests for violent offenses declined by roughly the same amount for male and female youth (14% for males versus 13% for females), while the gender gap in arrests for property offenses narrowed considerably, with arrests falling by 39% for males compared with a decline of just 18% among females. Comparing racial trends in terms of changes in rates per 100,000 youth rather than frequency of arrests, Puzzanchera (2009) reports roughly comparable declines in arrests for property offenses of 45% or more across all racial groups since 1993. But he describes a widening gulf between African Americans and other youth in rates of arrest for violent offenses—due in large measure to a 37% increase between 1999 and 2007 in the African American rate of arrest for robbery versus a 17% *decrease* for whites. Overall, the rate of arrest for violent offenses went up 5% among African Americans during that time, while the white rate decreased by 25%.

Self-Report Surveys

Although arrest data offer important insights about delinquency patterns and trends, they are of questionable reliability as barometers of the frequency with which young people actually engage in delinquent behavior (see discussions in Brame et al., 2004; McCord, Widom, & Crowell, 2001; Puzzanchera, 2009; and Snyder & Sickmund, 2006). Alternative measures—especially those based on surveys tapping participants' self-reported involvement in unlawful behaviors—have therefore become an essential adjunct to official records in assessing the extent of delinquency.[1] Self-report data reveal levels of participation in at least minor forms of delinquency that in some studies approach or even exceed 90% (see Moffitt, 1993; Thornberry, Huizinga, & Loeber, 2004), and the cumulative prevalence of self-reported involvement (i.e., the proportion of youth admitting *any* past engagement) in acts characterized as serious violence runs as high as 30% to 40% of males and 16% to 32% of females in some accounts (see discussion in Office of the Surgeon General, 2001). Self-report data also indicate smaller race and gender differences in rates of juvenile offending than do arrest statistics, although the extent of such differences varies tremendously across studies, with some researchers finding no differences at all and others reporting even wider gaps than those found in officially recorded arrests (see discussions in Jensen & Rojek, 2009; Lauritsen, 2005; Zahn et al., 2008).

Adolescent Development, Risk Factors, and Pathways to Delinquency _____

Systematic assessment of the underlying causes of juvenile delinquency falls well outside the scope of this chapter and, in any event, would carry us into territory addressed in Okada's discussion of criminological theory and crime explanations in Chapter 2. But several strands in contemporary delinquency research warrant our attention here insofar as they offer valuable insights about ways in which delinquency is conditioned by the nature of adolescent development, risk factors that increase the likelihood of escalating antisocial behavior, and pathways leading toward increasingly serious delinquency that carry important practical implications for delinquency prevention and juvenile justice policy.

Moffitt's (1993) well-known distinction between adolescence-limited and life-course-persistent offenders provides a useful starting point for discussing the place of delinquency in the life-course trajectories of youth. While large proportions of youth engage in delinquent behavior during adolescence, only a small minority continue their antisocial behavior into adulthood. Even fewer develop into career offenders, cycling in and out of jails and prisons while most of their peers "grow out of it" as they mature and take on law-abiding, adult social roles. In contrast with the *discontinuity* displayed in the transitory delinquency of adolescence-limited offenders, who commit their first offenses as young teenagers and then *desist* as they enter adulthood, Moffitt describes a pattern of striking *continuity* across the entire life span in the antisocial behavior of life-course-persistent offenders. These offenders—estimated at roughly 5% to 6% of the population[2]—are likely to exhibit "difficult" temperaments and aggressive tendencies even in infancy, to have their first police contacts for delinquent behavior before reaching puberty, to become immersed in delinquency as teenagers, and to develop into career offenders in adulthood.

Normal Adolescent Behavior?

Many delinquency researchers share Moffitt's belief that some level of engagement in delinquent or otherwise antisocial behavior is an entirely normal part of adolescent development. Some, like Moffitt, view adolescence-limited offending through a social learning lens, as a self-reinforcing way for adolescents to cope with the uncomfortable paradox of attaining biological maturity years before the autonomy and privileges of adult status are extended to them, a temporary digression that is soon cast off as the transition to young adulthood brings new opportunities and altered contingencies that make desistance increasingly rewarding (Moffitt, 1993).

Others, looking to the lessons of developmental psychology for answers, have sought an explanation in the still-developing decision-making capabilities of adolescents. In one such approach that reflects broadly shared insights, researchers examining the impact of psychosocial immaturity on adolescents' competence to stand trial (an initiative of the MacArthur Foundation Research Network on Adolescent Development and Juvenile Justice) have systematically explored the ways in which teenagers differ from adults in cognitive capacity (reasoning ability) and judgment (common sense). Their findings indicate that, although the cognitive abilities of most youth appear to approximate those of adults by mid-adolescence, their decision making is still deeply impacted by heightened sensitivity to peer influence, comparatively cavalier attitudes toward risk, and a temporal perspective emphasizing short-term benefits over longer-term consequences (Grisso et al., 2003; Scott & Grisso, 1997; Steinberg & Scott, 2003; see also Grisso & Schwartz, 2000). This cluster of psychosocial factors is argued to affect adolescents' judgment in ways that lead them to use information differently, to deploy their reasoning skills differently or less reliably, and to weigh costs and benefits of their actions differently than would an adult in a comparable situation, thus increasing their vulnerability to external pressures supporting delinquent behavior (Scott & Grisso, 1997).

Risk and Protective Factors

The efforts of Moffitt (1993) and others to isolate characteristics that can help predict the direction a young offender's life will take—toward persistent offending in adulthood or toward desistance as he or she matures—have spawned extensive research seeking to identify risk factors that are predictive of later patterns of serious, violent and/or chronic offending, and the pathways leading toward escalating antisocial behavior.

A sense of the wide variety of factors that have been found to place a child at increased risk for later involvement in such behavior can be gathered from the following enumeration of individual, family, school, peer, and community characteristics that researchers participating in the Office of Juvenile Justice and Delinquency Prevention's Study Group on Serious and Violent Juvenile Offenders determined to be at least somewhat predictive of later violence, based on their findings in an exhaustive meta-analysis of 66 rigorous, separately conducted longitudinal studies published between 1959 and 1997:

Individual factors: Pregnancy and delivery complications; low resting heart rate; internalizing disorders; hyperactivity, concentration problems, restlessness, and risk taking; aggressiveness; early initiation of violent behavior; involvement in other forms of antisocial behavior; beliefs and attitudes favorable to deviant or antisocial behavior

Family factors: Parental criminality; child maltreatment; poor family management practices; low levels of parental involvement; poor family bonding and family conflict; parental attitudes favorable to substance use and violence; parent-child separation

School factors: Academic failure; low bonding to school; truancy and dropping out of school; frequent school transitions

Peer-related factors: Delinquent siblings; delinquent peers; gang membership

Community and neighborhood factors: Poverty; community disorganization; availability of drugs and firearms; neighborhood adults involved in crime; exposure to violence and racial prejudice. (Hawkins et al., 2000, p. 2)

Not surprisingly, risk factors have been found to differ substantially in their predictive value, and research has shown that particular factors may be stronger—or weaker—predictors of later behavior when observed in young children as compared to adolescents. In another meta-analysis by members of the Study Group on Serious and Violent Juvenile Offenders, Lipsey and Derzon (1998) found that the predictive value of particular factors differed considerably for young children as compared with adolescents. For children aged 6 to 11, commission of a general juvenile offense (i.e., *any* juvenile offense committed by a child in this age group) was found to be the single strongest predictor of serious or violent behavior at age 15 to 25, followed by substance abuse and, in a second rank of predictive variables, gender (i.e., being male), family socioeconomic status (SES), and antisocial parents. For 12- to 14-year-olds, the strongest predictors were weak social ties and antisocial peers, with commission of general offenses following in the second rank but having noticeably less predictive value than was observed for the younger group. By contrast, antisocial peers had very little impact on later behavior for 6- to 11-year-olds, while substance abuse and family SES carried only minimal predictive value for the older group. Curiously, broken homes and abusive parents were ranked among the weakest predictors for both groups, although later research has emphasized the importance of child maltreatment as a predictor of various forms of violence and other antisocial behavior, especially if it occurs during adolescence (Maas, Herrenkohl, & Sousa, 2008; Thornberry et al., 2004).

Many of the risk factors identified here have found additional support in more recent studies, and other factors not specifically examined in the earlier studies have also been identified (see, for example, Herrenkohl et al., 2000; Thornberry et al., 2004). Researchers have also observed a *cumulative* effect of risk factors, such that exposure to multiple risk factors increases the likelihood of later antisocial behavior (Farrington, 1997; Herrenkohl et al., 2000). Other research has shown that the deleterious effects of exposure to one or more risk factors may be mitigated by the presence of *protective* factors that help insulate the child from negative influences—for example, intolerant attitudes toward deviance, supportive relationships with parents or other adults, or a strong commitment to school (see discussions in Office of the Surgeon General, 2001).

Pathways to Delinquency

Considerable attention has been paid in recent years to the developmental "pathways" followed by adolescents as they progress toward deeper involvement in delinquency. The most ambitious research to date in this regard has taken place within the broader context of three coordinated longitudinal studies undertaken in furtherance of yet another major Office of Juvenile Justice and Delinquency Prevention initiative—the Program of Research on the Causes and Correlates of Delinquency. Based on an initial analysis of the offense trajectories of boys tracked over an extended period in the Pittsburgh Youth Study, project director Rolf Loeber and his associates identified three distinct patterns of escalating delinquency (Kelley, Loeber, Keenan, & DeLamatre, 1997):

> **Authority Conflict** is the first and earliest pathway. The pathway begins with stubborn behavior (stage 1) and can be followed by defiance (stage 2), such as refusal and disobedience. This, in turn, can be followed by authority avoidance (stage 3), such as truancy and running away from home. The authority conflict pathway applies to boys prior to age 12, because after that age some youth are likely to enter the pathway at the highest levels with behaviors such as truancy and staying out late at night.
>
> **Covert** acts and their escalation are addressed in the second pathway. This pathway tends to start with minor covert behaviors (stage 1), such as lying and shoplifting, and can be followed by property damage (stage 2), including vandalism and fire-setting, and later by more serious forms of property crimes (stage 3), such as burglary.
>
> **Overt** or increasingly aggressive acts make up the third pathway. This sequence starts with minor aggression (stage 1), such as annoying others and bullying. This can be followed by physical fighting (stage 2), including gang fighting, and then by violence (stage 3), such as attacking someone, strong-arming, and rape. (pp. 8–9)

The three-pathway model has been replicated in a variety of contexts, including various subsets of the Pittsburgh sample and in both the Rochester Youth Development Study and the Denver Youth Survey. Summarizing their findings in a later report, the project directors of the three causes and correlates studies reiterate the conclusion that youth tend to follow an orderly sequence as they move from less serious to more serious delinquency, even in those instances where they progress on multiple pathways, engaging in a wider variety of delinquent behaviors as they get older (Thornberry et al., 2004). Referencing related aspects of the studies, they emphasize the predictive importance of early onset (i.e., childhood aggression beginning before age 13), child maltreatment, and gang membership as precursors of escalating involvement in delinquent behavior. But they also caution that accurate differentiation between those whose behavior persists and escalates over time and those who desist following a period of experimentation remains distressingly elusive.

Different for Girls?

Seeking to remedy the general dearth of attention paid to delinquent girls even as the gender gap in arrest rates narrows (see Chapter 6 of this book; Puzzanchera, 2009; Zahn et al., 2008), researchers have begun compiling an empirical record addressing the developmental pathways girls follow and the risk and protective factors that influence their delinquent involvement. While some have concluded that girls tend to follow the same developmental pathways as boys and that the risk factors for male and female delinquency are similar, others have found girls to follow distinctive routes and to respond differently to certain risk factors (see discussion in Howell, 2009).

With remarkable consistency, research on female delinquency points to a cluster of life circumstances shared by large proportions of delinquent girls. For example, in one study of girls in the California juvenile justice system, 92% of offenders reported a history of physical, emotional, and/or sexual abuse, 95% lacked a stable home environment, 9% had experienced some form of school failure, and 75% had a history of drug or alcohol abuse (Acoca & Dedel, 1998; see also Acoca, 1999). In another, focus groups with system-involved girls in ten California counties revealed a set of risk factors for delinquency, including family issues (family conflict, parental absence, parental criminality or drug abuse, poor communication); sexual, physical, and emotional abuse; running away from home; substance abuse; gang involvement and fighting; school difficulties and negative attitudes toward school; and early and inappropriate sexual behavior (Bloom, Owen, Rosenbaum, & Deschenes, 2003). The themes of sexual victimization, family disruption, educational failure, substance abuse, and running away also permeate Chesney-Lind's examinations of the lives of female delinquents and the ways in which gender stratification and its consequences condition not only their delinquency but also their "invisibility" once drawn into the juvenile justice system (see especially Chesney-Lind, Morash, & Stevens, 2008; Chesney-Lind & Shelden, 2004). These themes appear as well in Howell's (2009) discussion of girls' delinquent careers. Linking together findings from numerous studies of female delinquents, OJJDP's former deputy administrator and long-time director of research and program development builds the case for a sequence of six "stepping-stones" for girls following a pathway toward serious, chronic, and/or violent delinquency. Describing a process grounded in the notion that the "gendered" nature of risk factors girls experience in common with boys may exacerbate the impact on girls, Howell traces a pathway leading from physical and/or sexual child abuse to mental health problems, drug abuse, running away from home, youth gang activity, and, finally, juvenile justice system involvement.

CONCLUSION

We have learned, for example, that delinquency is "normal" in adolescence but that most of us desist from illegal activity as we enter adulthood. In fact, age consistently ranks among the strongest correlates of criminal behavior (Farrington, 1986; Federal Bureau of Investigation, 2008; Hirschi & Gottfredson, 1983), and the pervasiveness of delinquent involvement during adolescence followed by desistance in early adulthood is now well documented (see Moffitt, 1993; Thornberry et al., 2004). Even among serious juvenile offenders, a life-course trajectory leading toward desistance in adulthood appears to be the norm rather than the exception (MacArthur Foundation Research Network on Adolescent Development and Juvenile Justice, n.d.; Mulvey et al., 2004; Sampson & Laub, 2003).

These patterns offer at least a modicum of support for the arguments of labeling theorists that juvenile court intervention is unnecessary or even counterproductive for most youthful law violators (Lemert, 1967; Schur, 1973). Does this mean we should follow their advice and avoid intervention altogether, or intervene only if it is absolutely essential in order to protect public safety? Or does it direct us to heed the findings of research on risk factors and pathways to escalating delinquency, doing our best to identify potential life-course-persistent offenders as early as possible so we can steer them in a different direction while leaving the adolescence-limited offenders alone as much as possible?

As the researchers involved in the causes and correlates studies discovered, early intervention is crucial to the success of efforts to divert youth from pathways leading to increasingly serious and persistent delinquency; so a "this too will pass" approach risks waiting until the opportunity to intervene effectively is long past (Kelley et al., 1997, p. 17; see also Thornberry et al., 2004). But categorizing young offenders based on the presence of known risk factors is not a panacea, either. Aside from questions about the fairness of treating youth differently based on personal characteristics rather than the nature of the offense, even the most sophisticated research still lacks the ability to accurately distinguish "persisters" from "experimenters" (Kelley et al., 1997). Statistical association between a particular characteristic and later antisocial behavior cannot be taken as an indication that a youth exposed to that risk factor, or even to a constellation of factors, will necessarily become a serious or chronic offender later in life. It also bears emphasis that the findings of individual studies, or even of a combination of studies, cannot be taken as definitive with respect to factors that predict later delinquent behavior. Aside from variations in the overall quality of study design and execution that impact results, the focus of research varies considerably from one study to the next. Some studies investigate predictors of *violent* behavior, while others expand the focus to encompass predictors of *serious* delinquency, whether violent or otherwise, or even to *any* delinquent involvement. Yet others investigate predictors of *chronic* antisocial behavior continuing into adulthood, or narrow the focus to risk factors for engagement in particular *types* of delinquent activity or other antisocial behavior (e.g., gang membership, sex offenses, intimate partner violence). Likewise, the independent variables that are tested differ across studies, and study samples differ in ways that greatly affect results (e.g., risk factors may be very different for males and females or for youth of different racial groups, so findings based on a study of one group cannot be generalized to others). Even the measures of delinquency (arrest data, self-reports, etc.) differ tremendously from one study to the next in ways that impact results.

These observations offer just a hint of the many ways in which delinquency research can be used to stimulate consideration of policy innovations carrying the potential to divert youth from deeper involvement in delinquent behavior. But they should also serve as a caution against thoughtlessly translating research into policy without recognizing the probabilistic nature of the findings and the potentially conflicting implications for preventing or responding to delinquency arising from different lines of research.

DISCUSSION QUESTIONS

1. If delinquent behavior is really a normal part of adolescent development that most youth engage in to some degree, what should be done about those who are caught, and what characteristics of the offense and the offender do you think should be taken into consideration in deciding how to respond in a particular case?

2. In light of what we know about adolescent development, the pervasiveness of adolescence-limited delinquency, and the distribution of crime across age groups (i.e., the correlation between age and crime), what maximum age for juvenile court jurisdiction would you consider most appropriate?

3. Given the importance of early onset as a risk factor for later involvement in serious, violent, and chronic offending, should young children who are caught committing delinquent acts be treated differently from adolescents who commit comparable offenses?

4. Based on what we know about risk factors and pathways to delinquency, what elements would you recommend including in a prevention program in order to maximize its effectiveness in steering young people away from delinquency? What differences would you recommend in prevention programs targeting the following groups?

   a. adolescents and preteens
   b. males and females
   c. youth at high risk to become life-course-persistent offenders and those likely to remain adolescence-limited offenders

5. How might research on adolescent development, risk factors, and pathways to delinquency be used to facilitate correctional intervention with youth who have been caught committing delinquent acts?

NOTES

1. Although the many shortcomings of early self-report studies have not been entirely alleviated, increasing sophistication of the sampling frames, measures of delinquency, and question formats employed in contemporary survey instruments has greatly enhanced their utility as indicators of delinquent behavior (Brame et al., 2004; Hindelang, Hirschi, & Weiss, 1981; Huizinga & Elliott, 1986; Thornberry & Krohn, 2000).

2. This figure is commonly traced to Wolfgang, Figlio, and Sellin's (1972) seminal finding that about 6% of boys born in Philadelphia in 1945 were responsible for over half of all offenses committed by youth in the birth cohort. Moffitt (1993) cites a broad array of subsequent studies that have obtained comparable results with respect to various measures of serious and chronic antisocial behavior among children, adolescents, and adults.

References

Acoca, L. (1999). Investing in girls: A 21st century strategy. *Juvenile Justice, 6*(1), 3–13. Retrieved from http://www.ncjrs.gov/pdffiles1/ojjdp/178254.pdf

Acoca, L., & Dedel, K. (1998). *No place to hide: Understanding and meeting the needs of girls in the California juvenile justice system*. San Francisco: National Council on Crime and Delinquency.

An Act Establishing a Sensible State Marihuana Policy. (2008). Mass. Acts ch 387, Mass. Gen. Laws ch. 94C, § 32L-N.

An Act Implementing the Provisions of the Budget Concerning General Government. (2007). Public Act 07–4, § 73 *et seq.*, Gen. Stat. Conn. ch. 815t, § 46b-120.

An Act to Regulate the Treatment and Control of Dependent, Neglected and Delinquent Children. (1899). Illinois Juvenile Court Act Approved April 21, 1899. Laws of the State of Illinois, enacted by the Forty-First General Assembly at the regular biennial session. 1899 Ill. Laws 131.

Bloom, B., Owen, B., Rosenbaum, J., & Deschenes, E. P. (2003). Focusing on girls and young women: A gendered perspective on female delinquency. *Women & Criminal Justice, 14*(2/3), 117–136.

Brame, R., Fagan, J., Piquero, A. R., Schubert, C. A., & Steinberg, L. (2004). Criminal careers of serious delinquents in two cities. *Youth Violence and Juvenile Justice, 2*(3), 256–272.

Chesney-Lind, M., Morash, M., & Stevens, T. (2008). Girls' troubles, girls' delinquency, and gender responsive programming: A review. *The Australian and New Zealand Journal of Criminology, 41*(1), 162–189.

Chesney-Lind, M., & Shelden, R. G. (2004). *Girls, delinquency and juvenile justice* (3rd ed.). Belmont, CA: Wadsworth.

Farrington, D. P. (1986). Age and crime. In M. Tonry & N. Morris (Eds.), *Crime and justice: An annual review of research* (Vol. 7, pp. 189–250). Chicago: University of Chicago Press.

Farrington, D. P. (1997). Early prevention of violent and nonviolent youthful offending. *European Journal on Criminal Policy and Research, 5*, 51–66.

Federal Bureau of Investigation. (1996–2007). Crime in the United States, 1995–2006. Retrieved from http://www.fbi.gov/ucr/ucr.htm

Federal Bureau of Investigation. (2008). Crime in the United States, 2007. Retrieved from http://www.fbi.gov/ucr/cius2007

Griffin, P. (2003). *Trying and sentencing juveniles as adults: An analysis of state transfer and blended sentencing laws*. Pittsburgh, PA: National Center for Juvenile Justice. Retrieved from http://www.ncjjservehttp.org/NCJJWebsite/pdf/transfer bulletin.pdf

Grisso, T., & Schwartz, R. G. (Eds.). (2000). *Youth on trial: A developmental perspective on juvenile justice*. Chicago: University of Chicago Press.

Grisso, T., Steinberg, L., Woolard, J., Cauffman, E., Scott, E., Graham, S., et al. (2003). Juveniles' competence to stand trial: A comparison of adolescents' and adults' capacities as trial defendants. *Law and Human Behavior, 27*(4), 333–363.

Hawkins, J. D., Herrenkohl, T. I., Farrington, D. P., Brewer, D., Catalano, R. F., Harachi, T. W., & Cothern, L. (2000). *Predictors of Youth Violence.* Washington, DC: Office of Juvenile Justice and Delinquency Prevention. Retrieved from http://www.ncjrs.gov/pdffiles1/ojjdp/179065.pdf

Herrenkohl, T. I., Maguin, E., Hill, K. G., Hawkins, J. D., Abbott, R. D., & Catalano, R. F. (2000). Developmental risk factors for youth violence. *Journal of Adolescent Health, 26*(7), 176–186.

Hindelang, M. J., Hirschi, T., & Weiss, J. G. (1981). *Measuring delinquency.* Beverly Hills, CA: Sage.

Hirschi, T., & Gottfredson, M. R. (1983). Age and the explanation of crime. *American Journal of Sociology, 89*, 552–584.

Howell, J. C. (2009). *Preventing and reducing delinquency: A comprehensive framework* (2nd ed.). Thousand Oaks, CA: Sage.

Huizinga, D., & Elliott, D. S. (1986). Reassessing the reliability and validity of self-reported data. *Journal of Quantitative Criminology, 2*(4), 293–327.

Jensen, G. F., & Rojek, D. G. (2009). *Delinquency and youth crime* (4th ed.). Long Grove, IL: Waveland Press.

Kelley, B. T., Loeber, R., Keenan, K., & DeLamatre, M. (1997). *Developmental pathways in boys' disruptive and delinquent behavior.* Washington, DC: Office of Juvenile Justice and Delinquency Prevention. Retrieved from http://www.ncjrs.gov/pdffiles/165692.pdf

Lauritsen, J. L. (2005). Racial and ethnic differences in juvenile offending. In D. Hawkins and K. Kempf-Leonard (Eds.), *Our children, their children: Confronting race and ethnic differences in American criminal justice* (pp. 83–104). Chicago: University of Chicago Press.

Lemert, E. M. (1967). *The juvenile court: Quest and realities.* In The President's Commission on Law Enforcement and Administration of Justice, Task Force on Juvenile Delinquency. *Task force report: Juvenile delinquency and youth crime—Report on juvenile justice and consultants' papers* (pp. 91–106). Washington, DC: U.S. Government Printing Office.

Lipsey, M. W., & Derzon, J. H. (1998). Predictors of violent or serious delinquency in adolescence and early adulthood: A synthesis of longitudinal research. In R. Loeber & D. P. Farrington (Eds.), *Serious and violent juvenile offenders: Risk factors and successful interventions* (pp. 86–105). Thousand Oaks, CA: Sage.

Maas, C., Herrenkohl, T.I., & Sousa, C. (2008). Review of research on child maltreatment and violence in youth. *Trauma, Violence, & Abuse: A Review Journal, 9*(1), 56–67.

MacArthur Foundation Research Network on Adolescent Development and Juvenile Justice. (n.d.). Creating turning points for serious adolescent offenders: Research on pathways to desistance (Issue Brief 2). Retrieved from http://www.adjj.org/downloads/7230issue_brief_2.pdf

McCord, J., Widom, C. S., & Crowell, N. A. (Eds.). (2001). *Juvenile crime, juvenile justice.* Washington, DC: National Academy Press. Retrieved from http://books.nap.edu/catalog.php?record_id=9747

Moffitt, T. E. (1993). Adolescence-limited and life-course-persistent antisocial behavior: A developmental taxonomy. *Psychological Review, 100*, 674–701.

Mulvey, E. P., Steinberg, L., Hecker, T., Fagan, J., Cauffman, E., Schubert, C., et al. (2004). Theory and research on desistance from antisocial activity among adolescent serious offenders. *Youth Violence and Juvenile Justice, 10*(10), 1–24.

Noy v. State, 83 P.3d 545 (Alaska App. 2003).

Office of the Surgeon General. (2001). *Youth violence: A report of the Surgeon General.* Washington, DC: U.S. Department of Health and Human Services, Office of Public Health and Science, Office of the Surgeon General. Retrieved from http://www.surgeongeneral.gov/library/youthviolence

Puzzanchera, C. (2009). *Juvenile arrests 2007.* Washington, DC: Office of Juvenile Justice and Delinquency Prevention. Retrieved from http://www.ncjrs.gov/pdffiles1/ojjdp/225344.pdf

Ravin v. State, 537 P.2d 494 (Alaska 1975).

Sampson, R. J., & Laub, J. H. (2003). Life-course desisters? Trajectories of crime among delinquent boys followed to age 70. *Criminology, 41*(3), 555–592.

Scott, E. S., & Grisso, T. (1997). The evolution of adolescence: A developmental perspective on juvenile justice reform. *Journal of Criminal Law and Criminology, 88*(1), 137–189.

Schur, E. M. (1973). *Radical nonintervention: Rethinking the delinquency problem.* Englewood Cliffs, NJ: Prentice Hall.

Snyder, H. N., & Sickmund, M. (2006). *Juvenile offenders and victims: 2006 national report.* Washington, DC: Office of Juvenile Justice and Delinquency Prevention. Retrieved from http://ojjdp.ncjrs.gov/ojstatbb/nr2006/downloads/NR2006.pdf

Steinberg, L., & Scott, E. (2003). Less guilty by reason of adolescence: Developmental immaturity, diminished responsibility, and the juvenile death penalty. *American Psychologist, 58*(12), 1009–1018.

Thornberry, T. P., Huizinga, D., & Loeber, R. (2004). The causes and correlates studies: Findings and policy implications. *Juvenile Justice Journal, 9*(1), 3–19. Retrieved from http://www.ncjrs.gov/pdffiles1/ojjdp/203555.pdf

Thornberry, T. P., & Krohn, M. D. (2000). The self-report method for measuring delinquency and crime. In D. Duffee (Ed.), *Criminal justice 2000: Vol. 4. Measurement and analysis of crime and justice* (pp. 33–84). Washington, DC: National Institute of Justice. Retrieved from http://www.ncjrs.gov/criminal_justice2000/vol_4/04b.pdf

Wolfgang, M. E., Figlio, R. M., & Sellin, T. (1972). *Delinquency in a birth cohort.* Chicago, IL: University of Chicago Press.

Zahn, M. A., Brumbaugh, S., Steffensmeier, D., Feld, B. C., Morash, M., Chesney-Lind, M., et al. (2008). *Violence by teenage girls: Trends and context.* Washington, DC: Office of Juvenile Justice and Delinquency Prevention. Retrieved from http://www.ncjrs.gov/pdffiles1/ojjdp/218905.pdf

6

Gender Matters

Trends in Girls' Criminality

Meda Chesney-Lind

Crime Wave?

In 2006, girls accounted for nearly a third (29.1%) of juvenile arrests (Federal Bureau of Investigation, 2007). From the 1960s to the 1980s, girls accounted for between 17% and 22% of juvenile arrests, one fifth of the total (Chesney-Lind & Shelden, 2004, pp. 9–11). This is a remarkable increase in their "share" of official delinquency and one that requires exploration.

The forces that create criminal behavior may be different for adolescents, and we now suspect that this has been particularly the case for the last two decades. If one were to use arrests as a gauge of delinquency trends, female activity has been trending differently from that of their male counterparts. The much-discussed "crime drop" in juvenile delinquency in the 1990s was more correctly a "boy" crime drop, fueled by a decline in gun- and drug-related violence among boys and young men (Blumstein & Wallman, 2000).

Looking specifically at arrest data, it appears that boys' arrests peaked in 1993 and then began dropping, but during the same decade, girls' arrests continued to climb. According to FBI reports (FBI, 2003, p. 239), between 1993 and 2002 girls' arrests increased 6.4%, whereas boys' arrests decreased by 16.4%. Between 1997 and 2006, the data do not show a stark increase in female offenses; nonetheless, their arrests decreased by a far smaller percentage than boys', 17.6% compared to 26.4% (FBI, 2007, Table 33). This said, in the most recent year for which we have data, girls' arrests seem finally to have leveled off (decreasing by 1.7% between 2005 and 2006), whereas arrests of boys began to move up, particularly serious violent crime.

Juvenile delinquency has long been assumed to be a male problem, and girls were either ignored or excluded from consideration, particularly by researchers who worked during the formative years of criminological theory building. Hirschi (1969) excluded self-report data on females from analysis in his classic *Causes of Delinquency*. Others regarded delinquency as quintessentially male; the delinquent was the "rogue male," according to Cohen's (1955) classic book on gangs.

Seminal criminological theories assumed delinquency to be male and therefore focused on male offenders in research settings that accessed boys and young men involved in these typically male offenses (see Chesney-Lind & Shelden, 2004). As a result, programs were aimed at male delinquency prevention and intervention (see Lipsey, 1992; Girls Incorporated, 1996). Yet, at virtually all levels within the juvenile justice system, there are more girls than ever. The academic, policy, and programmatic neglect of girls' issues, coupled with recent arrest trends, suggests that it is clearly time to consider female delinquency in its own right, not as an afterthought to boys' delinquency.

Delinquency: Gender Matters

The picture of female delinquency that emerges from the available data reflects the existence of substantial gender differences in both self-reported and official delinquency. For starters, girls are less "serious" delinquents than boys. If one examines gender differences in court populations around the country, for example, girls' delinquency differs from boys' in that it is less chronic and less serious. Based on an in-depth study of one large, urban court system, Snyder & Sickmund (1999, p. 80) found that 73% of females (compared to 54% of males) who enter the juvenile justice system never return on a new referral. They also noted that, of the youth who came to court for delinquency offenses, only 3% of females had committed a violent offense by the age of 18, compared to 10% of boys; likewise, only 5.5% of girls, compared to 18.8% of boys, had more than four referrals to court (p. 81).

The significant role played by minor offenses in girls' delinquency also emerged in the Annie E. Casey Foundation study of youth in detention in several cities. Researchers found that many more girls than boys were detained for "minor" offenses, such as public disorder, probation violations, status offenses, and traffic offenses. Finally, it was also learned that "rather than histories of violence, detained girls had more status offenses and misdemeanors in their histories" (American Bar Association/National Bar Association [ABA/NBA], 2001, pp. 18–19). This research documented that race as well as gender matters in girls' detentions; African American girls make up half of those in secure detention, according to this study, and Latinas, 13% (ABA/NBA, 2001, pp. 20–21).

The American Correctional Association's (ACA, 1990) earlier study of girls held in state training schools found that substantial numbers of girls were incarcerated for probation or parole violation (15%), followed by aggravated assault (9.5%), larceny theft (9%), and runaway (6.5%). Roughly half the girls were white (50.5%), nearly a third were black or partly black (31.7%), 6.2% were Hispanic, and 7.7% were Native American (p. 47).

Most were between 16 and 17 years of age, and 18.6% were mothers at the time of their incarceration.

That same study found disconcertingly high rates of sexual abuse among incarcerated girls; over 60% had been the victim of some form of physical abuse, and 54% reported being the victim of sexual abuse. This finding may or may not explain why over 80% of the girls in training schools report that they have run away from home at least once, and a staggering 50% have run away from home six or more times.

The ACA study also found that 60% of this population needed substance abuse treatment at intake and that over half were multiply addicted. They also reported that many of these girls took drugs (34.4%) or drank alcohol (11.4%) as a form of self-medication to make themselves feel better. In addition, a majority stated that they used alcohol (50%) and marijuana (64%) regularly. Of the girls who were substance dependent, most started using between the ages of 12 and 15 (pp. 59–60). Although models that delineate the relationship between delinquency and substance abuse have largely involved adolescent males, evidence for females also indicates that substance abuse is highly correlated with disruptive behavior (Girls Incorporated, 1996).

These portraits of officially delinquent girls, particularly the ACA study, point out two important themes in girls' delinquency, particularly the form that brings girls into the juvenile justice system. First, while most girls' delinquency involves offenses that are not as legally serious as those committed by boys, this does not mean that they do not have serious problems, particularly those who stay in the system. Just because girls are arrested and referred to juvenile courts for legally less serious offenses, these "trivial" offenses often mask significant and ongoing problems, like sexual abuse, for which gender-responsive programming might well be appropriate.

Girls' Crime, Girls' Offenses

An overview of girls' arrest patterns reflects and amplifies the themes found in the portraits of official delinquents (see Table 6.1) and seems a logical starting point in discussing key themes in female delinquency. In 2006, girls were most frequently arrested for larceny theft, a property offense which, as we shall see, for girls means shoplifting (Campbell & Harrington, 2000; Chesney-Lind & Shelden, 2004).

Girls were also arrested in large numbers for running away from home, an offense for which only juveniles can be taken into custody. Finally, large numbers of girls, particularly in recent years, were arrested for the seemingly nontraditional offenses of simple assault and disorderly conduct. Boys' arrests are more diffuse, meaning that the top offenses account for slightly over half of all boys' arrests (58.9%), whereas for girls over two thirds (68.4%) of their arrests are accounted for by these five offense categories. The data also indicate that girls' arrests for simple assault have replaced runaway arrests as a key theme in girls' official delinquency.

Table 6.1   Rank Order of Arrests for Juveniles, 1997 and 2006 (Figures based on percent distribution within each gender cohort)

Male		Female	
1997	*2006*	*1997*	*2006*
(1) All Others (17.3)[1]	All Others (18.4)	Larceny-Theft (22.9)	Larceny-Theft (18.3)
(2) Larceny-Theft (16.3)	Larceny-Theft (10.9)	Runaways (16.2)	All Other (16.1)
(3) Drug Abuse (8.6)	Other Assaults (10.5)	All Other (15.3)	Other Assaults (12.9)
(4) Other Assaults (8.1)	Drug Abuse (10.4)	Other Assaults (8.9)	Disorderly Conduct (10.7)
(5) Curfew (6.6)	Disorderly Conduct (8.7)	Disorderly Conduct (6.6)	Runaway (10.4)

	Male		Female	
	1997	*2006*	*1997*	*2006*
Arrests for Serious Violent Offenses	4.9	5.2	2.5	2.7
Arrests for All Violent Offenses[2]	12.9	15.7	11.1	15.6
Arrests for Status Offenses[3]	10.9	9.5	23.9	17.1

Source: Federal Bureau of Investigation, *Uniform Crime Reports,* 2006. Table 33. Retrieved on February 14, 2008, from http://www.fbi.gov/ucr/ucr.htm

Notes: [1] "All Others" refers to a variety of offenses, usually against state and local ordinances. Among the most common are public nuisance, trespassing, failure to appear on warrants, contempt of court, and, for juveniles especially, violation of various court orders (e.g., probation, parole) and certain status offenses. This category does not include traffic offenses. Status offenses other than runaway and curfew also account for a large proportion of girls' arrests for other offenses (Chesney-Lind & Shelden, 2004).

[2] Also includes arrests for other assaults, a Part II crime.

[3] Arrests for curfew and runaway.

Girls' Violence: When She Was Bad

Female aggression and violence have been much in the news in recent decades. Whether it was the female revolutionary of the 1970s, the girl gangbanger of the 1980s, the violent girl of the 1990s, or the mean girls who ushered in the new millennia, the last few decades have seen a cavalcade of girls' acting out in ways that seem far worse than merely unfeminine (see Chesney-Lind & Irwin, 2008). Quite often, the media frame is one that juxtaposes girls' aggression or violence with stereotypical images of a girlhood devoid of behavior of this sort. The *Newsweek* issue on youth violence, as an example, included an insert on girls' violence complete with a picture of an African American girl wearing a bandanna over her face, peering at the camera over the barrel of a gun, with the headline "Girls Will Be Girls" (Leslie, Biddle, Rosenberg, & Wayne, 1993, p. 44). In many ways, this gender juxtaposition makes sense in a country that grew up reading Longfellow's (1992, p. 513) poem about his daughter: "When she was good, she was very, very good, but when she was bad she was horrid."

Of course, the reality is much more complex. First, it turns out that self-report data routinely show that girls act out violently and have been since the earliest self-report data were published (Elliot & Voss, 1974). Second, there appears to be very little evidence that these patterns have changed in the last decade, despite the media frenzy on the topic. The Centers for Disease Control and Prevention (CDC) in Atlanta has monitored youthful behavior in a national sample of school-age youth in a number of domains (including violence) at regular intervals since 1991 in a biennial survey entitled the Youth Risk Behavior Survey. As an example, a review of the data collected over the 1990s and into this century reveals that, although 34.4% of girls surveyed in 1991 said that they had been in a physical fight in the previous year, by 2001 that figure had dropped to 23.9%, a 30.5% decrease in girls' fighting; boys' violence also decreased during the same period but less dramatically—from 50.2% to 43.1%, a 14.1% drop (CDC, 1992–2002).

While girls had long reported that they were acting out violently, their arrests, particularly in the 1960s and 1970s, did not necessarily reflect that reality. Instead, girls' arrests tended to emphasize petty and status offenses; by the 1990s, that had changed dramatically, as more girls were arrested, particularly for such seemingly "masculine" offenses as simple assault. Between 1997 and 2006, despite an overall decrease in girls' arrests, girls' arrests for simple assault continued to climb, increasing by 18.7%, while boys' arrests for the same offense declined by 4.3%.

Research increasingly suggests that these shifts in girls' arrests are not products of a change in behavior, with girls getting "more" violent. Not only do other measures of girls' criminality fail to show an increase in girls' violence, there is ample evidence that girls are being more heavily policed, particularly at home and in school (see Chesney-Lind & Irwin, 2008). Specifically, girls are being arrested for assault because of arguments with their parents, often their mothers (see Buzawa & Hotaling, 2006), or for "other assault" for fighting in school because of new zero-tolerance policies enacted after the Columbine shootings (see New York ACLU, 2007). In decades past, this violence would have been ignored or labeled a status offense, like being "incorrigible" or a "person in need of supervision." Now, an arrest is made.

Girls are also staying in the system after being arrested for these new "violent" offenses. Between 1985 and 2002, the number of girls' delinquency cases referred to juvenile courts increased by 92%, compared to a 29% increase for males (Snyder & Sickmund, 2006). Arrests of girls for crimes of violence clearly played a role in this pattern: "For females, the largest 1985–2002 increase was in person offense cases (20%)." Finally, like the pattern seen in girls' arrests, girls have proportionately more person offense referrals than boys: 26% compared to 23% (Snyder & Sickmund, 2006, p. 160).

Girls' arrests for crimes of violence have also ushered in a dramatic increase in the incarceration of girls. Between 1991 and 2003, girls' detentions rose by 98%, compared to a 29% expansion by boys (Snyder & Sickmund, 2006, p. 210). Girls detained for "violent" offenses were far more likely to be held on "other person" offenses, like simple assault. Well over half (57.3%) of the girls but less than a third of the boys (32.4 %) were held for these minor forms of violence (Sickmund, Sladky, & Kang, 2004). Likewise, girls' commitments to facilities increased by an alarming 88% between 1991 and 2003, while boys' commitments increased by only 23% (Snyder & Sickmund, 2006, p. 210).

Media sensationalization aside, girls' behavior, including violence, needs to be placed within a larger discussion of girls' place in a society that expects and normalizes aggression and violence from boys while encouraging girls and women to be nice, pretty, and feminine. It is important to chart the contexts that produce violence in girls (see Morash & Chesney-Lind, 2008).

Some hints of these issues can be found in the backgrounds of girls who act out violently. In her analysis of self-reported violence in girls in Canada, Artz (1998) noted that girls who reported problems with violence reported significantly greater rates of victimization and abuse than their nonviolent counterparts, and girls who were violent reported greater fear of sexual assault, especially from their boyfriends. Specifically, 20% of violent girls stated they were physically abused at home, compared to 10% of violent males and 6.3% of nonviolent girls. Patterns for sexual abuse were even starker; roughly 1 out of 4 violent girls had been sexually abused compared to 1 in 10 nonviolent girls (Artz, 1998). Follow-up interviews with a small group of violent girls found that they had learned at home that "might makes right" and had engaged in "horizontal violence" directed at other powerless girls. Certainly, these findings provide little ammunition for those who would contend that the "new" violent girl is a product of any form of "emancipation." Histories of physical and sexual abuse, then, may be a theme in girls' physical aggression, just as it is in their runaway behavior.

Aggressive and violent girls are, ironically, often quite committed to the "ideology of familial patriarchy . . . [which] supports the abuse of women who violate the ideals of male power and control over women" (DeKeseredy, 2000, p. 46). This ideology is acted out by those males and females who insist that women be obedient, respectful, loyal, dependent, sexually accessible, and sexually faithful to males. Artz (1998) builds upon that point by suggesting that violent girls, more often than not, buy into these beliefs and "police" other girls' behaviors, thus preserving the status quo, including their own continued oppression.

Such themes are particularly pronounced among girls who have the most serious problems with delinquency. Artz, Blais, and Nicholson (2000, p. 31) found that the majority of their girl respondents were also male focused, expressed hostility to other girls, and wanted very much to have boyfriends—always making sure that they had at least one, both in and out of jail. One girl strongly identified with the boys and saw herself as "one of the guys," also admitting that she had "always wanted to be a boy." Only one girl spoke little about boys—at 18 years of age, she was the oldest girl in the center. All the girls used derogatory terms to describe other girls, and when they spoke about girls, their words reflected views of females as "other." Many saw other girls as threats, particularly if they were pretty or "didn't know their place." A "pretty" girl, or a girl that the boys paid attention to, was a primary target for girl-to-girl victimization because she had the potential to unseat those who occupied the top rung on the "pretty power hierarchy" (Artz, Blais, & Nicholson, 2000, p. 124). An "ugly" or "dirty" girl (a girl designated a slut) was also a primary target for girl-to-girl victimization because she "deserved" to be beaten for her unappealing looks and for her "unacceptable" behavior.

Such a perspective is puzzling, but the sad reality is that marginalized girls who have been the victims of male power often see that sort of agency as the only source of power available to them. Most of these girls regarded their victims as "responsible" for the violence that they committed, since they were acting as "sluts," "total bitches," or "assholes" (p. 189). Clearly, where these girls live, "you've gotta watch your back" (p. 189) because "the world is a piece of shit" (p. 189). Those girls who have problems with violence suggest that both girls' and women's victimization, as well as girls' violence toward other girls, are really twin products of a system of sexual inequality that valorizes male violence as agency and has girls growing up "seeing themselves through the eyes of males" (Artz, 1998, p. 204).

_____ Running Away: Girls Coping With Trauma and Abuse

Running away from home and prostitution remain the only two arrest categories in which more girls than boys are arrested. Many more girls are arrested for running away than for prostitution, despite the public fascination with the latter. In 2006, 38,461 girls were arrested for running away, whereas less than 1,000 were arrested for prostitution. In 2006, girls constituted over half (56.4%) of those arrested for this one status offense. This means that, despite the intention of the Juvenile Justice and Delinquency Prevention Act of 1974, which, among other things, encouraged jurisdictions to divert and deinstitutionalize youth charged with status offenses, arrests for these offenses remained substantial. Having said this, it should be noted that the arrest rates for runaways have been decreasing significantly for both girls and boys; from 1997 through 2006, these arrests decreased by 47.1% for girls during the same period that arrests of girls for simple assault increased by 18.7% (FBI, 2007, Table 33).

For many years, statistics showing large numbers of girls arrested and referred to court for status offenses were taken as representative of the different types of male and female delinquency. Yet, studies of actual delinquency show that girls and boys run away from home about equally. As an example, Canter

(1982) found in the National Youth Survey that there was no evidence of greater female involvement, compared to males, in any category of delinquent behavior. Indeed, males were significantly more likely than females to commit status offenses. A study of inner-city adolescents who had been referred to a diversion program found that, while youth showed considerable, and expected, gender differences in official arrests, with males being referred for law violations and girls being referred for status offenses and "personal problems," self-report data from the same group "found that girls did not actually commit more status offenses than boys" (Rhodes & Fischer, 1993, p. 4). National self-report data collected from youth ages 12 to 16 also showed no gender difference in runaway behavior; roughly 10% of both boys and girls reported that they had "ever" run away from home (Snyder & Sickmund, 1999, p. 54).

Thorne (1994), in her ethnography of gender in grade school, found that girls used "cosmetics, discussions of boyfriends, dressing sexually, and other forms of exaggerated 'teen' femininity to challenge adult, and class- and race-based authority in schools." She also found that "the double standard persists, and girls who are overtly sexual run the risk of being labeled sluts" (p.156).

Contemporary ethnographies of school life echo the validity of these parental perceptions. Orenstein's (1994) observations also point to the durability of the sexual double standard; at the schools, she observed that sex "ruins girls" but "enhance[s] boys" (p. 57). Parents, too, according to Thorne (1994), have valid reasons to enforce the time-honored sexual double standard. Concern about sexual harassment and rape, to say nothing of HIV/AIDS, if their daughters are heterosexually active, has caused "parents in gestures that mix protection with punishment, (to) often tighten control of girls when they become adolescents, and sexuality becomes a terrain of struggle between the generations" (Thorne, 1994, p.156; see also Lamb, 2003). Finally, Thorne notes that, sadly and ironically, as girls use sexuality as a proxy for independence, they reinforce their status as sexual objects seeking male approval—ultimately ratifying their status as the subordinate sex. Whatever the reason, parental attempts to adhere to and enforce the sexual double standard will continue to be a source of conflict between parents and their daughters.

Another reason for different responses to running away from home speaks to differences in boys' and girls' reasons for running away. Girls are, for example, much more likely than boys to be the victims of child sexual abuse. According to the *Third National Incidence Study*, girls are sexually abused 3 times more often than boys (Sedlak & Broadhurst, 1996). Sexual abuse typically starts early; both boys and girls are most vulnerable to abuse between the ages of 7 and 13 (Finkelhor, 1994). Not surprisingly, the evidence also suggests a link between this problem and girl delinquency—particularly running away from home, since girls are more likely to be the victims of intrafamilial abuse (Finkelhor, 1994). Moreover, this abuse lasts longer and has more serious consequences than stranger abuse (Finkelhor, 1994).

Widom (1995) found that victims of child sexual abuse are 27.7 times more likely than nonvictims to be arrested for prostitution as adults; it is speculated that some victims become prostitutes (if female) or abusers (if male) because they have a difficult time relating to others except on sexual terms. Not all studies find a link between sexual abuse, running away, and prostitution, however. In a comparison of prostitute and nonprostitute youth, Nadon, Koverola, and Schludeermann (1998) found that prostitute youth were not significantly more likely than an appropriate comparison group to report sexual abuse. However, adolescent prostitutes ran away from home significantly more often than adolescent nonprostitutes. Nadon and colleagues state that "it was determined prostitution may be a particular survival strategy for girls in very difficult circumstances" (p. 206).

Another study that tracked the gendered consequences of running away for girls and boys (Tyler, Hoyt, Whitbeck, & Cauce, 2004) found that, for females, running away from home for the first time was associated with engaging in deviant subsistence strategies, survival sex, and victimization by a "friend or acquaintance." For boys, survival sex was associated with stranger victimization; for homosexual boys, though, victimization came at the hands of an acquaintance or friend (Tyler et al., 2004, p. 503).

Most girl runaways have fled homes where abuse, including sexual abuse, was a prominent theme. Yet, ironically and tragically, their lives on the streets are almost always even more abusive because, like all other aspects of life, the streets are gendered. Once on the streets, girls quickly discover both the dangers involved in street life and the narrow range of survival options available to them. They also discover that they are in possession of a form of sexual capital that they can access, whereas boys tend to engage in a wider variety of survival strategies.

The tragedy here is that a girl who runs from physical and sexual abuse is forced to confront terrible choices: She does not want to return to an intolerable home, yet she cannot legally go to school, get employment, or find housing without risking return. In short, her legal options are criminalized by a system that has traditionally encouraged her to return home and obey her parents. Even systems that want to explore other sorts of placement possibilities face numerous challenges, not the least of which is a shortage of programs for girls (Freitas & Chesney-Lind, 2001). Faced with abysmal choices, some girls turn to survival sex, which they may not even recognize as sexual exploitation (Beyette, 1988), or some other form of sex work, like prostitution. For some, but not necessarily all, girl runaways, survival sex and possibly prostitution become a way to survive in the absence of few other earning skills (Campagna & Poffenberger, 1988; Miller, 1986).

_____ Wild in the Streets: Girls, Drugs, and Alcohol

A review of trends in girls' arrests for substance abuse also reveals a gendered pattern. Specifically, girls' arrests tend to increase for most offenses during the last decade, whereas boys' arrests decreased. As an example, the

FBI (FBI, 2007, Table 33), reports that girls' arrests for disorderly conduct increased by 19.0%, while boys' arrests decreased by 22.1%. Likewise, girls' arrests for driving under the influence showed a 39.3% increase, as compared to a 6.4% decrease seen in boys' arrests.

Reviews of self-reported drug use, like the Youth Risk Behavior Surveillance System, indicate that male and female use of alcohol has actually declined in the most recent decade for which data are available (1993–2003), while marijuana and cocaine use have actually increased slightly among respondents. Moreover, there is an apparent gender convergence. In 1993, 50.1% of boys reported "current alcohol use," whereas 45.9% of girls did; in 2003, only 43.8% of boys and 45.8% of girls reported use. With marijuana, 20.6% of boys reported use in 1993, compared to 25.1% in 2003; for girls, 14.6% reported use in 1993, compared to 19.3% in 2003 (CDC, 1994; 2004).

In the area of drug use, at the point of arrest, in 1997, 29% of arrested girls tested positive for one or more illegal drugs, compared to 57% of boys, largely due to marijuana use (Belenko, Sprott, & Petersen, 2004, p. 6). In subsequent interviews with arrested youth, 33% of arrested and detained girls and 34% of boys reported some alcohol use, and 61% of girls, compared to 75% of boys, were drug involved (Belenko, Sprott, & Petersen, 2004. p. 6).

In delinquent girls, depression is a major problem, whether we are discussing runaway youth, aggressive youth, or youth with substance abuse issues. In fact, girls in general are more likely to report problems of depression and anxiety than boys, and these trends are magnified among girls in the juvenile justice system (Belenko, Sprott, & Petersen, 2004, p. 21).

Kataoka and colleagues (2001) found that female juvenile offenders were three times more likely than girls who were not in the system to show clinical symptoms of anxiety and depression. As mentioned earlier, many of the girls in the justice system have extensive histories of abuse, which can explain their choices to self-medicate in response to that traumatic history. The links between posttraumatic stress disorder and drug use are certainly more pronounced in girls than in boys. Deykin and Buka (1997) found that almost half (40%) of reported substance-abusing girls showed current prevalence of PTSD, compared to slightly more than one tenth of boys (12.3%).

Shoplifting: You Shoplift as You Shop

Property crimes, particularly larceny theft, accounted for 1 out of 5 girls' arrests in 2006; in contrast, this offense accounted for only 1 in 10 boys' arrests. There is evidence that this offense is gendered, with the bulk of girls' larceny thefts involving shoplifting, while boys are more involved in buying stolen goods, and thefts from cars or bicycle theft (Campbell & Harrington, 2000; Chesney-Lind & Shelden, 2004). Girls' "share" of this offense has also increased over time, from 34.1% to 40.8% (FBI, 2007).

Such a gender shift is also apparent in the self-report data. Data collected from high school seniors suggest that, while roughly a quarter (25.9%) of girls said they had taken something from a store without paying for it at least once in the past year, that was about the same as a decade earlier (25.2%); for boys, the comparable figures were 30% in 2002 and 36% in 1994. Thus, although male shoplifting has been dropping, these data suggest that female involvement has stayed about the same (Bureau of Justice Statistics, 2003, Table 3.47). These data show that larceny theft committed by boys has declined over time, possibly as a result of increased surveillance in malls (Hayward, 2004, p.189), though it is not clear why this would have affected boys' but not girls' levels of shoplifting.

Increasingly, discussions of women's crime and changes in the volume of female offending have focused on the role played by economic marginalization and patterns of women's employment in property crimes (see English, 1993; Heimer, 2000). Specifically, females have experience as employees in retail settings and, as a consequence, often know the routines that characterize security in these establishments, even if they do not work there (English, 1993). As retail employees, they are also likely to augment often-meager salaries by stealing or shoplifting where they work (Franklin, 1979). Men, if they steal from the workplace, tend to be employed in higher-level positions; if they steal, they are less likely to be caught (because they are less heavily supervised), they steal larger amounts, and they are often not prosecuted (Franklin, 1979).

According to self-report studies, however, males are more likely to shoplift. An English study found that males outnumbered females by a 2:1 ratio. Recall, though, that recent U.S. data show that, although the gender gap has closed, that is because boys report doing less shoplifting. Another study found males to be more likely than females to shoplift, but the male–female ratio for youths "cautioned by the police" or actually sentenced was only 1.7:1 (Morris, 1987, p. 31). Morris (1987) suggests that females are more often detected by store personnel because the latter expect women to shoplift more than men and therefore watch women more.

Explanations of male and female shoplifting have generally been simplistic and gender biased. A common explanation for female shoplifting, according to Morris (1987, p. 65), is that it is "a result of subconscious motivations (kleptomania), depression (for example, resulting from the menopause) or poverty (for example, mothers on welfare who steal food)." A common explanation of male shoplifting is that it results from "peer-group pressure and the search for excitement."

One consideration that rarely appears in work on shoplifting is that young people, especially girls, may be inordinately sensitive to the consumer culture: They steal things they feel they need or indeed may actually need but cannot afford. For example, Campbell (1981) notes that women—young and old—are the targets of enormously expensive advertising campaigns for a vast array of personal products. They also constitute a large proportion of those who shop, spend more time doing so as a pastime, and consequently are exposed to greater temptation (Campbell, 1981, pp. 122–123). Temptation is probably most pronounced for girls, whose popularity is tied very closely to physical appearance and participation in fashions and fads (see Adler & Adler, 1998).

Participation in the teen consumer subculture is costly, and if a young woman cannot afford participation, she is likely to steal her way in. It is no surprise, then, that girls are more likely than boys to shoplift cosmetics and clothes (Campbell, 1981, pp. 122–123). Moreover, because girls spend more time shopping, they undergo more scrutiny by store detectives, who report they are suspicious of young people in groups, particularly if they are not dressed well (May, 1978). In short, girl subculture, where popularity is based on an appearance that includes "expensive clothing" and other "material possessions" (Adler & Adler, 1998, p. 47), may be particularly hard on girls from poor families. They are bombarded daily with the message that they are acceptable only if they look a particular way, and yet they do not have the money necessary to purchase that look.

In general, shoplifting by girls must be placed within the context of girls' lives in a youth- and consumer-oriented culture. Here, the drawbacks of not having money are evident, and for girls there are few avenues to success. Shoplifting, then, is a social cost attributable to goods attainable only with money that many of them do not have.

CONCLUSION

Girls are an increasingly large proportion of those being arrested. The arrest data show large numbers of girls arrested for assault, yet there are reasons to suspect that the increases seen in the arrest data are reflective not of actual behavior but rather of changes in the policing of girls. That said, girls' aggression and violence are best understood from within the context of their situations in their families, in their schools, and on the streets. Research on girls engaging in physical violence suggests that violent girls are often themselves the victims as well as the victimizers. Unfortunately, the victims of this aggression are often similarly situated girls, not those who are victimizing her.

Initially, arrests for running away were actually proxies for suspected sexual activity in girls, and there is still some evidence that the gender difference in girls' and boys' arrests for these offenses are products not of their behavior but rather of their parents', who report their daughters' running away but not their sons'. Girls on the run are often forced by current laws to live like escaped convicts. Unable to attend school, get a job, or even live apart from their abusive families, girls are forced into criminal behavior simply to survive. Sometimes, that behavior further criminalizes them and involves them in other risky behaviors, like survival sex, prostitution, and/or drug use.

Shoplifting accounts for many juvenile female arrests, and studies indicate that girls may well shoplift for reasons that are very much a product of a youth culture that, particularly for girls, stresses the importance of appearance.

What forces will shape the female delinquency of the new millennia? Those who study and work with these offenders must consider not only class but also gender and race when crafting their theories. Those who hope to effectively prevent and intervene in this behavior would do well to consider the gendered way in which youth experience adolescence. In short, delinquency theory, which has long focused (uncritically) on boys' delinquency with a particular emphasis on the role of class, would do well to consider gender both in crafting an approach to the problem and in developing responses that will help rather than further stigmatize and victimize.

The need to focus on the unique forces that bring girls into the justice system is very clear, as girl incarcerations are soaring at a time when no such dramatic increase is seen in the incarceration of boys. These trends, driven largely by the arrest and referral of girls for simple assault, threatens to undo more than 30 years of efforts to remove youth from institutional settings. It also means that the mass incarceration that has so heavily impacted adult women, particularly women of color, might well be visited upon their younger sisters unless a vigorous campaign of education and advocacy is not launched.

DISCUSSION QUESTIONS

1. Do females engage in crime for reasons different from their male counterparts and therefore require justice system treatment that is also different? Does this also cause them to engage in different sorts of crime activities?

2. Are girls subject to situations and conflict in their homes from which their brothers are excluded?

3. Must the justice system amend its previous practices to account for the influx of gender differences that were not present in previous decades? What should the justice system do?

4. What is the role of social patriarchy in the handling of female offenders versus male offenders? Are girls subjected to judicial treatment that is different from that faced by their brothers or other male offenders? Is there a remedy for this discrepancy?

REFERENCES

Adler, P., & Adler, P. (1998). *Peer power: Preadolescent culture and identity*. New Brunswick, NJ: Rutgers University Press.

American Bar Association and the National Bar Association. (2001). *Justice by gender: The lack of appropriate prevention, diversion and treatment alternatives for girls in the justice system*. Chicago: American Bar Association.

American Correctional Association. (1990). *The female offender: What does the future hold?* Washington, DC: Author.

Artz, S. (1998). *Sex, power and the violent school girl.* Toronto, ONT: Trifolium Books.

Artz, S., Blais, M., & Nicholson, D. (2000). *Developing girls' custody units.* Unpublished report.

Belenko, S., Sprott, J. B., & Petersen, C. (2004). Drug and alcohol involvement among minority and female juvenile offenders: Treatment and policy issues. *Criminal Justice Policy Review, 15*(1), 3–36.

Beyette, B. (1988, August 21). "Hollywood's teen-age prostitutes turn tricks for shelter, food." *Las Vegas Review-Journal.*

Blumstein, A., & Wallman, J. (2000). *The crime drop in America.* Cambridge: Cambridge University Press.

Bureau of Justice Statistics. (2003). *Sourcebook on criminal justice statistics.* Washington D.C.: Author. Retrieved on February 14, 2008, from http://www.albany.edu/sourcebook/pdf/t347.pdf

Buzawa, E. S., & Hotaling, G. T. (2006). The impact of relationship status, gender, and minor status in the police response to domestic assaults police response to domestic assaults. *Victims and Offenders, 1,* 323–360.

Campagna, D. S., & Poffenberger, D. L. (1988). *The sexual trafficking in children.* Dover, MA: Auburn House.

Campbell, A. (1981). *Girl delinquents.* New York: St. Martin's Press.

Campbell, S., & Harrington, V. (2000). *Youth crime: Findings from the 1998/1999 youth lifestyles survey.* Home Office Research Findings 126. London: Home Office.

Canter, R. J. (1982). Sex differences in self-report delinquency. *Criminology, 20,* 373–393.

Centers for Disease Control and Prevention. (1992–2004). *Youth risk behavior surveillance—United States, 1991–2004.* CDC Surveillance Summaries. U.S. Department of Health and Human Services. Atlanta: Author.

Chesney-Lind, M., & Irwin, K. (2008). *Beyond bad girls: Gender, violence, and hype.* New York: Routledge.

Chesney-Lind, M., & Shelden, R. (2004). *Girls, delinquency, and juvenile justice* (2nd ed.). Belmont, CA: Thompson/Wadsworth.

Cohen, A. K. (1955). *Delinquent boys: The culture of the gang.* New York: The Free Press.

DeKeseredy, W. (2000). *Women, crime, and the Canadian criminal justice system.* Cincinnati, OH: Anderson.

Deyken, E. Y., & Buka, S. L. (1997). Prevalence and risk factors for posttraumatic stress disorder among chemically dependent adolescents. *American Journal of Psychiatry, 154,* 752–757.

Elliot, D., & Voss, H. (1974). *Delinquency and dropout.* Lexington, MA: D. C. Heath.

English, K. (1993). Self-reported crimes rates of women prisoners. *Journal of Quantitative Criminology, 9,* 357–382.

Federal Bureau of Investigation (FBI). (2007). *Crime in the United States, 2006.* Washington, DC: U.S. Government Printing Office.

Finkelhor, D. (1994). Current information on the scope and nature of child sexual abuse. *The future of children, 4*(2), 31–53.

Franklin, A. (1979). Criminality in the workplace: A comparison of male and female offenders. In F. Adler & R. Simon (Eds.), *The criminality of deviant women.* Boston: Houghton Mifflin.

Freitas, K., & Chesney-Lind, M. (2001, August/September). Difference doesn't mean difficult: Workers talk about working with girls. *Women, Girls, & Criminal Justice,* 65–78.

Girls Incorporated. (1996). *Prevention and parity: Girls in juvenile justice.* Indianapolis, IN: Girls Incorporated National Resource Center.

Hayward, K. J. (2004). *City limits: Crime, consumer culture, and the urban experience.* London: Glasshouse Press.

Heimer, K. (2000). Changes in the gender gap in crime and women's economic marginalization. In G. Lafree (Ed.), *Criminal justice 2000: Vol. 1. The nature of crime: Continuity and change* (pp. 427–483). Washington, DC: National Institute of Justice.

Hirschi, T. (1969). *Causes of delinquency.* Berkeley: University of California Press.

Horowitz, R., & Pottieger, A. E. (1991). Gender bias in juvenile justice handling of seriously crime-involved youths. *Journal of Research in Crime and Delinquency, 28,* 75–100.

Johnson, N. G. (2003). On treating adolescent girls: Focus on strengths and resiliency in psychotherapy. *Journal of Clinical Psychology, 59,* 1193–1203.

Kataoka, S., Zima, B., Dupre, D., Moreno, K., Yang, X. & McCracken, J. (2001). Mental health problems and service use among female juvenile offenders. *Journal of the American Academy of Child and Adolescent Psychiatry, 40,* 549–555.

Lamb, S. (2003). Not with my daughter: Parents still have trouble acknowledging teenage sexuality. *Psychotherapy Networker, 27* (May/June).

Leslie, C., Biddle, N., Rosenberg, D. & Wayne, J. (1993, August 2). Girls will be girls. *Newsweek,* p. 44.

Lipsey, M. (1992). Juvenile delinquency treatment: A meta-analytic inquiry in the variability of effects. In T. A. Cook et al. (Eds.), *Meta-analysis for explanation: A casebook* (pp. 83–127). New York: Russell Sage.

Longfellow, H. W. (1992). "There was a little girl." In J. Bartlett & J. Kaplan (Eds.), *Familiar Quotations* (16th ed., p. 513). Boston: Little, Brown.

May, D. (1978). Juvenile shoplifters and the organization of store security: A case study in the social construction of delinquency. *International Journal of Criminology and Penology, 6,* 137–160.

Miller, E. M. (1986). *Street woman.* Philadelphia: Temple University Press.

Morash, M., & Chesney-Lind, M. (2008). Girls' violence in context. In M. Zahn (Ed.), *The Delinquent Girl* (pp. 182–206). Philadelphia: Temple University Press.

Morris, A. (1987). *Women, crime, and criminal justice.* New York: Blackwell.

Nadon, S., Koverola, C. & Schludeermann, E. (1998). Antecedents to prostitution: Childhood victimization. *Journal of Interpersonal Violence, 13,* 206–221.

New York Civil Liberties Union. (2007) *Criminalizing the classroom: The over-policing of New York City schools.* New York: Author.

Rhodes, J. E., & Fischer, K. (1993). Spanning the gender gap: Gender differences in delinquency among inner-city adolescents. *Adolescence, 28*(112), 879–889.

Sedlak, A., & Broadhurst, D. (1996). *Executive summary of the Third National Incidence Study of Child Abuse and Neglect.* Washington, DC: National Center on Child Abuse and Neglect, U.S. Department of Health and Human Services.

Sickmund, M., Sladky, T. J., & Kang, W. (2004). Census of juveniles in residential placement databook. Washington, DC: U.S. Department of Justice. Retrieved on February 14, 2008, from http://www.ojjdp.ncjrs.org/ojstabb/cjrp/

Snyder, H. N. (2001). *Law enforcement and juvenile crime*. National Report Series Bulletin. Washington, DC: U.S. Department of Justice, Office of Justice Programs, Office of Juvenile Justice and Delinquency Prevention.

Snyder, H. N., & Sickmund, M. (1999). *Juvenile offenders and victims: 1999 national report*. Washington, DC: Office of Juvenile Justice and Delinquency Prevention: National Center for Juvenile Justice.

Snyder, H. N., & Sickmund, M. (2006). *Juvenile offenders and victims: 2006 national report* (NCJ 178257). Washington, DC: U.S. Department of Justice, Office of Justice Programs, Office of Juvenile Justice and Delinquency Prevention.

Thorne, B. (1994). *Gender play: Girls and boys in school*. New Brunswick, NJ: Rutgers University Press.

Tyler, K., Hoyt, D., Whitbeck, L., & Cauce, A. (2004). The impact of childhood sexual abuse on later sexual victimization among runaway youth. *Journal of Research on Adolescence, 11*, 151–176.

Widom, C. S. (1995). *Victims of childhood sexual abuse: Later criminal consequences*. Washington, DC: National Institute of Justice, U.S. Department of Justice.

7

Race and Crime

Helen Taylor Greene

The concepts of race and crime have been inextricably linked in the study of criminology and criminal justice for more than a century. Today, most colleges and universities offering undergraduate and graduate degrees in criminology- and criminal-justice-related programs have either a required course or an elective course on race and crime. Usually, such courses explore the economic, historical, political, and sociological contexts of race and crime. Some courses include analyses of ethnicity, class, gender, and comparative perspectives. Most examine contemporary issues, including disproportionate minority confinement, bias/hate crimes, immigration and crime, racial profiling, and sentencing disparities. This chapter presents an overview of race and crime that includes discussions of definitional issues, crime and victimization statistics, theoretical explanations of race and crime, contemporary research on selected topics, and future issues.

Definitional Issues

The definition of race is complex. Historically, race was conceptualized biologically and based primarily on physical characteristics. Beliefs about the superiority of whites and the inferiority of others, especially people of color, prevailed. Over time, according to the American Anthropological Association (1997), the concept of race acquired a cultural and ideological context in the United States and elsewhere in the world that

> . . . magnified the differences among Europeans, Africans, and Indians, established a rigid hierarchy of socially exclusive categories, underscored and bolstered unequal rank and status differences, and provided the rationalization that the inequality was natural or God-given. (p. 1)

Biological differences between individuals, especially color and hue, provide the foundation for what many refer to as the social construction of race (Aguirre & Turner, 2007). Are individuals who look different on the outside different on the inside? If not, why are race and ethnicity (used here interchangeably with the term *minorities*) at the center of so many controversies nationally and internationally?

Today, the U.S. Bureau of the Census recognizes five racial/ethnic categories: American Indian and Alaska Native, Black (including African American and Negro), Native Hawaiian and other Pacific Islanders, White, and Latino or Hispanic; and there is now a category for "some other race" with numerous combinations to choose from. In spite of more categories, race does not capture heterogeneity—that is, differences within racial groups. All members of a racial group are not the same; there are cultural, subcultural, and class differences not only between but also within racial/ethnic groups. In 2000, the U.S. Bureau of the Census also noted that racial categories were sociopolitical constructs and not scientific or anthropological in nature (Gabbidon & Greene, 2009).

The complexities of race in America were an important topic during the election of President Barack Hussein Obama. Obama's mother was white, his father was African, and he was raised for many years by his white grandparents in Hawaii. Does that make him white? African? African American? In March 2008 in a speech on race, President Obama stated, "I have brothers, sisters, nieces, nephews, uncles and cousins, of every race and every hue, scattered across three continents . . ." (*New York Times,* 2008, para. 8). His race, and that of many other Americans, is not easily categorized as either black or white. At an earlier time in our country, President Obama would have been classified as black and, depending on the time period, referred to as mixed, mulatto, colored, Negro, and African American because of his skin color. In the past, Americans with any Negro blood, especially if they did not look white, were considered black.

Unlike race, crime is easier to define. In the early 20th century, Paul Tappan provided a definition of crime as an intentional act in violation of criminal, statutory, and case law that is committed without a defense or excuse, that is penalized as a felony or misdemeanor by the state (Tappan, 2001). Over time, behaviors labeled as crimes change, although some—including murder, rape, burglary, and theft—always have been considered crimes. In both past and present, many factors—including values, industrialization, immigration, and technological developments—have led to the criminalization and the decriminalization of many behaviors. For example, when legislative efforts to outlaw the sale and use of alcohol failed (the National Prohibition Act, also known as the Volstead Act), these activities were decriminalized. Decades later, as the use of automobiles increased, so did driving under the influence of alcohol or drugs. Due to increased attention, especially from Mothers Against Drunk Drivers (MADD), penalties for vehicular homicides by drunk drivers have increased. Today, the prevalence of computers has led to increases in cybercrimes, and many crimes that already existed, such as child pornography, bullying, fraud, and identity theft have moved to the Internet.

Even though whites commit numerous crimes, the study of race and crime has been concerned primarily with crimes committed by blacks and other minorities. In the past, acts considered criminal for blacks were not necessarily viewed as such when committed by whites. For example, prior to the Civil War, slave owners were rarely punished for beating, branding, raping, and killing their slaves. According to Kennedy (1997), the law protected whites in order to maintain their supremacy. Both before and after the Civil War, the law was used to maintain social control and "keep the Negro in his place" (Work, 1937, p. 111) as well as to control immigrant whites and other minorities.

Some of the focus on minorities in the study of criminology and criminal justice devolves from their disproportionate involvement in crime, especially violent personal crimes. According to Young (1996),

> The concept of disproportionality has become the mainstay of discussions on race and crime. . . . (W)hen authors review trends and patterns of crime and introduce the "variable" race the comparisons are between Blacks, whites and others and the emphasis is on the disproportionate involvement of nonwhites, in particular Blacks. (p. 74)

Even though whites commit violent crimes, especially bias or hate crimes, these crimes do not receive as much attention as violent crimes committed by minorities, especially blacks (Walker, Spohn, & DeLone, 2007). Corporate and other white-collar crimes committed by whites don't receive much attention, either. This fixation on "black crime" contributes to the racialization of crime (Covington, 1995)—a belief that the majority of blacks (and perhaps other minorities) commit crimes.

Overreliance on official statistics, such as those in the Federal Bureau of Investigation's *Uniform Crime Reports*, contributes to misperceptions about race and crime in the United States. For example, most students are often surprised to learn that (1) most Americans, regardless of race, are not arrested; and (2) even though blacks are vastly overrepresented in arrest statistics, most persons arrested are white. Crime and victimization statistics in the study of race and crime are discussed next.

Crime and Victimization Statistics

The two major sources of statistics on crime and victimization are the Uniform Crime Reports (UCR), which are collected and compiled by the Federal Bureau of Investigation (FBI), and the National Crime and Victimization Survey (NCVS), which are compiled for the Bureau of Justice Statistics by the U.S. Bureau of the Census. Both the UCR and NCVS collect and report information on race, although they do so differently. The Bureau of Justice

Statistics (BJS; http://www.ojp.usdoj.gov/bjs/) provides statistics about many aspects of crime and criminal justice that include race; it also provides users with the capability to analyze some crime and justice data online (http:// bjsdata.ojp.usdoj.gov/dataonline/index.cfm). Other governmental and non-governmental sources of information on crime and victimization also permit analyses by race; two are the Death Penalty Information Center (www .deathpenaltyinfo.org/) and the Sentencing Project (www.sentencingproject .org/). What do the two major sources (the UCR and the NCVS) tell us about race, crime, and victimization?

FBI Uniform Crime Reports

In the "Crimes Reported" section of the 2007 FBI UCR, the estimated size of the United States population was 301,621,157. An estimated 1,408,337 violent crimes were reported in 2007, about 466.9 violent crimes per 100,000 inhabitants. An estimated 9,843,481 property crime offenses were reported in 2007, a rate of about 3,263.5 offenses per 100,000 inhabitants. Larceny-theft offenses accounted for over two thirds (66.7%) of all property crimes in 2007. Both reported violent crimes and property crimes declined compared to 2006 UCR data.

In the "Persons Arrested" section of the UCR, information is provided by race in four categories: (1) White, (2) Black, (3) American Indian or Alaskan Native, and (4) Asian or Pacific Islander. In this section, the population is estimated to be 225,477,173. There were 10,656,710 reported arrests, including 7,426,278 whites, 3,003,060 blacks, 142,969 American Indian or Alaskan Natives, and 84,403 Asian or Pacific Islanders. For the traditional Part I offenses (murder/nonnegligent manslaughter, aggravated assault, robbery, forcible rape, burglary, larceny-theft, motor vehicle theft, and arson), most individuals were arrested for larceny-theft, regardless of race, followed by arrests for aggravated assault and burglary. When examining the percent distribution by race, blacks are overrepresented in reported arrests for all Part I crimes, and whites are overrepresented for arson (see Table 7.1). Though not shown in Table 7.1, whites are also overrepresented in several Part II offenses, including vandalism, sex offenses, and driving under the influence (FBI, 2008).

How do the UCR arrest data contribute to understanding race and crime? The answer to this question is unclear and requires taking into consideration the following weaknesses of the UCR data:

- Arrests of Hispanics/Latinos usually are included in the White category.
- Many (crimes and) arrests are not reported (this is often referred to as the "dark figure" of crime), and others are not recorded by the police.
- The UCR utilize estimates of the total population, crimes reported, and persons arrested that might be inaccurate.
- Police biases can result in different racial and class arrest decisions.

Table 7.1 Persons Arrested by Race for Part 1 Crimes, 2007

Total	Total arrests				Percent distribution				
	White	Black	American Indian or Alaskan Native	Asian or Pacific Islander	Total	White	Black	American Indian or Alaskan Native	Asian or Pacific Islander
TOTAL	10,656,710	7,426,278	3,003,060	142,969	100.0	69.7	28.2	1.3	0.8
Murder and nonnegligent manslaughter	10,067	4,789	5,078	101	100.0	47.6	50.4	1.0	1.0
Forcible rape	17,058	10,984	5,708	153	100.0	64.4	33.5	1.2	0.9
Robbery	96,584	40,573	54,774	635	100.0	42.0	56.7	0.6	0.7
Aggravated assault	326,277	208,762	109,985	3,156	100.0	64.0	33.7	1.3	1.0
Burglary	228,346	156,442	68,052	2,191	100.0	68.5	29.8	1.0	0.7
Larceny-theft	894,215	610,607	261,730	11,885	100.0	68.3	29.3	1.3	1.1
Motor vehicle theft	88,843	55,229	31,765	1,041	100.0	62.2	35.8	1.2	0.9
Arson	11,400	8,510	2,666	119	100.0	74.6	23.4	1.0	0.9

Source: From *Crime in the United States 2007*, U.S. Department of Justice, September 2008, Table 43.

The National Crime Victimization Survey

The National Crime Victimization Survey (NCVS) was designed and implemented as an alternative source of information on the extent of crime and victimization. It is conducted annually and includes a sample of 76,000 households and about 135,000 people over the age of 12. The survey has been redesigned several times, most recently in 2006, to improve data collection. Participants are asked about their experiences as victims of personal and household crimes. The Bureau of Justice Statistics publishes an annual bulletin titled *Criminal Victimization*. In the 2007 bulletin, the reported victimization rate for violent crimes was 20.7 per 1,000 persons and 146.5 per 1,000 households for property crimes (Rand, 2008). The overall rate of violent crime and personal theft for blacks was 24.3; for whites, 19.9; and for Hispanics, 18.6. Victimization rates for specific offenses vary by race. For example, blacks have a 4.9, Hispanics a 3.9, and whites a 1.9 rate of robbery victimizations per 1,000. For aggravated assault, Blacks have a 4.4, Hispanics a 3.0, and Whites a 3.2 rate per 1,000. In 2007, victimization rates for persons of two or more races are included in the NCVS. The victimization rate for this group is higher than that for whites, blacks, Hispanics, and others (See Table 7.2).

Table 7.2 Rates of Violent Crime and Personal Theft, by Gender, Race, Hispanic Origin, and Age, 2007

Demographic characteristic of victim	Population	Victimizations per 1,000 persons age 12 or older						Personal theft[a]
		Violent crimes						
						Assault		
		All	*Rape/ Sexual assault*	*Robbery*	*Total*	*Aggravated*	*Simple*	
Gender								
Male	122,122,700	22.5	0.1^	3.4	19.1	4.5	14.5	0.9
Female	128,222,170	18.9	1.8	1.4	15.6	2.4	13.2	0.7
Race								
White	203,470,370	19.9	1.0	1.9	17.0	3.2	13.9	0.6
Black	30,385,450	24.3	0.5^	4.9	18.8	4.4	14.4	1.9
Other race[b]	13,340,930	11.4	1.2^	1.8^	8.3	2.7	5.7	1.1^
Two or more races	3,148,100	73.8	5.5^	10.8	57.5	13.3	44.2	0.6^

Demographic characteristic of victim	Population	Victimizations per 1,000 persons age 12 or older							
		Violent crimes							Personal theft[a]
						Assault			
		All	Rape/ Sexual assault	Robbery	Total	Aggravated	Simple		
Hispanic origin									
Hispanic	34,423,520	18.6	0.3^	3.9	14.5	3.0	11.4		1.0^
Non-Hispanic	215,499,050	21.0	1.1	2.2	17.8	3.5	14.3		0.7
Age									
12-15	16,755,440	43.4	1.0^	4.2	38.2	2.8	35.5		0.6
16-19	16,981,750	50.1	2.4	6.4	41.4	7.2	34.2		1.6^
20-24	20,752,030	35.2	2.9	3.5	28.7	7.5	21.2		1.1^
25-34	40,349,730	24.7	1.2	3.4	20.1	4.8	15.3		1.1
35-49	65,636,410	17.7	10	1.4	15.3	3.2	12.1		0.6
50-64	53,677,450	11.6	0.3^	1.7	9.5	2.3	7.2		0.3^
65 or older	36,192,050	2.5	0.1^	0.6^	1.8	0.3^	1.5		0.8^

Source: Table 4, "Criminal Victimization, 2007," by Michael R. Rand, 2008, *Bureau of Justice Statistics Bulletin*, p. 4.

Note: The Nations Crime Victimization Survey includes as violent crime rape, sexual assault, robbery, aggravated assault, and simple assault. Because the NCVS interviews persons about their victimizations, murder and manslaughter cannot be included.

^Based upon 10 or fewer sample cases.

[a]Includes pocket picking, completed purse snatching, and attempted purse snatching.

[b]Other race includes American Indians, Alaska Natives, Asians, Native Hawaiians, and other Pacific islanders.

Like the UCR, the NCVS also has limitations:

- It includes only people over the age of 12.
- Victimization data are based on respondents' recall of incidents involving the respondent or someone in their household.
- Minorities are probably underrepresented because they are underrepresented in population statistics and may be reluctant to participate in the survey.

In spite of the limitations of both sources, both seem to indicate that crime and victimization are important to any discussion of race and crime, for both sources show patterns of arrests for crime, victimization, and race that require explanation. Some of these explanations found in the race and crime theoretical research are presented next.

Theoretical Perspectives on Race and Crime

Why do African Americans and some other minorities continue to be over-represented in crime and victimization statistics? Why do we continue to focus on the overrepresentation of some minorities in crime and victimization data and ignore the law-abiding behavior of most others? Why do we downplay the role of criminal justice system professionals, especially police and prosecutors and their discretionary decisions concerning arrest, charging, and negotiating pleas? The first question has perplexed criminologists and other scholars for decades. Both criminological and criminal justice theories offer explanations. In the criminological research, explanations include biological, sociological, and psychological explanations that focus on the individual, the environment, or both. The second question relates to the idea, presented earlier, that race is a social construct. Although criminal justice theoretical research is more limited, it focuses on the fairness of the criminal justice system, an issue raised by the third question. According to Duffee and Allan (2007), "Theories of criminal justice raise questions about why the government is doing what it is doing" (p. 18). Justice—including just processes, outcomes, and the just use of state power—is central to criminal justice theory (Castellano & Gould, 2007).

Few contemporary criminology and criminal justice theories examine how religion has influenced explanations of race and crime in the United States, even though religion was an important source of beliefs about evil and sin. Gabbidon and Greene (2007) point to the story of Noah's son Ham in the Bible as a possible source of the (Hamatic) myth that black people were "evil" and criminal (p. 6). The role of religion in the United States and the acceptance of this myth during the colonial and antebellum eras is important to understanding prevailing beliefs about the criminality and inferiority not only of blacks but also of Native Americans, Asian Americans, and Latino Americans. It is still unclear how much influence religion has on American criminology. Some criminology and criminal justice texts include discussions of the contributions of religion to penal philosophy and the corrections movement, but few discuss the interconnectedness of religion, race ideology, and the administration of justice.

Classical and positivist criminological theories have predominated in the study of criminology for hundreds of years. Classical and neoclassical theories focus on several key concepts, including utilitarianism, hedonism, free will, and rational choice. These theories did not address race and crime specifically. Positivists believe that criminal behavior is determined by biological, psychological, and/or sociological factors. Even though sociological theories predominate today, Cesare Lombroso's research on physical characteristics was influential in the United States, where beliefs about the inferiority of blacks and Native Americans already existed. Though less popular, biological research continues in the United States (Moffitt, 1993; Rowe, 2007; Rushton, 1995; Walsh & Beaver, 2008; Wilson & Herrnstein, 1985).

W. E. B. Du Bois, Monroe N. Work, Clifford R. Shaw, and Henry D. McKay were among the earliest scholars to refute the biological approach and the fixation on the individual. Instead, they focused on the role of environment and social disorganization in crime (Du Bois, 1899/1973, 1904; Work, 1900, 1913; Shaw & McKay, 1942). Du Bois (1899/1973) and Work (1900) noted the impact of slavery, discrimination, and segregation on black criminality and pointed to social, economic, and political conditions that contributed to blacks' involvement in crime. Du Bois conducted a study of Negroes in Philadelphia for the University of Pennsylvania, published in 1899 and titled *The Philadelphia Negro: A Social Study*. One of his conclusions was that "[c]rime is a phenomenon of organized social life, and is the open rebellion of an individual against his social environment" (Du Bois, 1899/1973, p. 235). Monroe N. Work, who studied at the University of Chicago and later worked at Tuskegee Institute, emphasized how historically the law was used against Negroes rather than to protect them. As a result, many Negroes not only feared the law, but also evaded and had little respect for it (Greene & Gabbidon, 2000).

Although the research of Du Bois and Work was not widely known, other scholars in the early 20th century also pointed to the deleterious effect of social conditions on criminality. Shaw and McKay, researchers affiliated with the Chicago School of Sociology, examined delinquency areas in Chicago and concluded that "within similar areas, each group, whether foreign-born or native, recent immigrant or older immigrant, black or white, had a delinquency rate that was proportional to the rate of the overall area" (Vold & Bernard, 1986, p. 170).

Unlike other immigrants who found themselves in "delinquency areas" and eventually were able to move out of them, many blacks seem to be trapped there, creating the *Truly Disadvantaged*, a term coined by William Julius Wilson (1987). These areas experience concentrated indicators of social disorganization that include poverty, crime, school dropouts, drug use and sales, inadequate housing, high incarceration rates, teen pregnancies, and unemployment. Over time, several factors, including housing inequality and socially isolated residents, foster cultural adaptations that undermine both social organization and the control of crime (Sampson & Wilson, 1995).

One criticism of social disorganization theory is that all minorities in socially disorganized communities are not involved in criminal behavior (Gabbidon, 2007). Several researchers have examined social capital and/or collective efficacy to explain variations in levels of crime. The term *social capital* refers to social ties, levels of trust, and the ability of individuals to work together for the good of the community. Communities with low levels of positive social capital and cohesion are more apt to succumb to negative social networks that value criminal behavior (Poteyeva, 2009).

Many other sociological explanations of criminality and delinquency, such as subcultural theories, the colonial model, conflict theory, critical race theory, the general theory of crime, social control, strain theory, and social inequality, are useful to the understanding of race and crime. Theoretical research on Latinos, Native Americans, and Asian Americans is still limited, and more is needed. Is social disorganization theory applicable to these groups? Does another theory provide a better explanation for crimes (and arrests) committed by individuals in these groups? What about white Americans? What is the best theory to explain corporate crimes, serial killings, human trafficking, and selling drugs? The next section examines research on contemporary race and crime issues.

Contemporary Race and Crime Issues

What are the most important contemporary issues in the study of race and crime? Issues related to aspects of race and policing (racial profiling, police use of force), race and corrections/sentencing (the War on Drugs, disparities, mass incarceration, prisoner reentry), and race and juvenile justice (disproportionate minority confinement, gangs, violent juvenile offenders) are often identified. Discretion—that is, decisional latitude—permits justice practitioners to be guided not only by the official policies of their agencies but by their own values, and perhaps biases, as well. As a result, another explanation for the disproportionate representation of blacks and other minorities in the criminal justice system is discriminatory practices. Even though discrimination and injustices that existed in the past are less prevalent today, vestiges of both remain (Walker, Spohn, & DeLone, 2007). In the next section, research is presented on three issues of race, crime, and justice: racial profiling, prisoner reentry, and disproportionate minority contact.

Racial Profiling

According to the Institute on Race and Justice at Northeastern University, *racial profiling* has been defined in many ways. It usually refers to targeting individuals by using race/ethnicity as indicators of criminality (del Carmen, 2009). Racial profiling can occur whether or not those targeted are actually engaged in any crimes. Today, racial and ethnic profiling is believed to occur in several situations, including traffic stops (Harris, 2002; Withrow, 2006), ethnic profiling related to perceived terrorist threats (Abu-Lughod, 2009), and consumer racial profiling (Jordan, Gabbidon, & Higgins 2009). According to del Carmen (2009) various forms of racial profiling existed in the United States during the Jim Crow and immigration eras in the 19th and 20th centuries. More recently, drug courier profiles have been used by federal, state, and local law enforcement officials to identify suspected drug dealers. After several lawsuits, the existence of racial profiling was finally acknowledged by criminal justice practitioners. As a result, many states mandated data collection, with varying methodological approaches (Higgins, Gabbidon, & Jordan, 2008).

Profiling by private security officers in retail settings (consumer racial profiling) has received attention as well. Higgins, Gabbidon and Jordan (2008) analyzed data from the 2004 Minority Rights & Relations/Black-White Social Audit (Gallup) poll and found that blacks were more likely than whites to believe that racial profiling is widespread.

Prisoner Reentry

Jeremy Travis, a former director of the National Institute of Justice and president of John Jay College of Criminal Justice in New York City, was instrumental in drawing attention to the issue of prisoner reentry when he published his 2005 book, *But They All Come Back: Facing the Challenges of Prisoner Reentry*. According to Travis, the growth of the prison population (mass incarceration) during the past two decades has resulted in large numbers of ex-offenders returning to families, to communities, and often to crime. The most recent reentry data indicate that almost 750,000 prisoners were released in 2006. The overrepresentation of racial and ethnic groups in prison means that their communities are more burdened by returning ex-offenders. Unfortunately, institutional and community corrections agents had not prepared for "mass reentry," and suddenly thousands of ex-offenders were returning with neither resources to assist them nor employment opportunities. During the past five years, efforts have been made in some jurisdictions to smooth the transition back into society that involve corrections officials (in facilities and in the community), law enforcement, faith organizations, families, and communities. The challenges of reentry include not only the lack of resources and limited employment but also family issues, transportation, health, and housing issues (Greene, Polzer & Lavin-Loucks, 2006). The current sentencing policies, including mandatory sentencing and the three strikes law, guarantee that prisoner reentry will continue for decades to be a problem that requires innovative solutions.

Disproportionate Minority Contact and Confinement

The term *disproportionate minority contact and confinement*, or DMC, refers to the overrepresentation of minorities at various stages in adult and juvenile justice systems, especially confinement. The U.S. Congress has legislated core requirements in revisions to the Juvenile Justice Delinquency Prevention Act DMC since 1988. States are required to identify and address the problem in order to receive federal funding through formula grants (Gabbidon & Greene, 2009). The Office of Juvenile Justice and Delinquency Prevention (OJJDP) is responsible for monitoring DMC progress and providing technical assistance to the states. Unfortunately, progress in this area has been limited; DMC continues to exist at many stages and in several states.

Future Issues in the Study of Race and Crime

The next decade will present traditional crime and justice problems as well as new ones. If the historical relationship between economics and crime holds true, we can expect more crime in the coming years, especially if unemployment continues to increase. Unlike the past, more attention will be paid to white-collar crime and fraud as a result of the massive business failures in the banking, security, and housing industries in recent years. The race and crime conundrum may become less important as crime and victimization data reflect increases in other types of crime. As long as social and economic disparities exist, street crime will occur. The next decade presents an opportunity to reinvest in crime and delinquency prevention, youth development, and other strategies that have taken a back seat to homeland security and terrorism in recent years. Reducing involvement of minorities in crime must be a priority, as well as halting what the Children's Defense Fund (2009) and others refer to as the "cradle-to-prison pipeline." Justice agencies must also develop cultural competencies of employees in an effort to overcome hidden biases.

Another future issue is the changing demographic trends in the United States. Today, Latinos are a majority in many cities and counties in the United States. Researchers should resolve the dilemma of counting this group so that we have a better understanding of ethnic trends in criminal justice. Relatedly, the victimization trends for mixed races require more research, since this category has not appeared in the past, and rates of victimization are high in this group. Two other important issues in the future study of race and crime are DNA analysis and human trafficking. The role of DNA in solving crimes, uncovering wrongful convictions, and maintaining DNA databanks is of great import. Lastly, human trafficking requires greater emphasis on how this global problem relates to race, ethnicity, crime, and justice.

Discussion Questions

1. Why is the historical context of the problem of race and crime in the United States important?

2. What do crime and victimization statistics tell us about race and crime?

3. What is the best explanation of the overrepresentation of some minorities as crime perpetrators and victims?

4. What are the implications of the past decade's shift in population characteristics for the study of race and crime?

5. What do you think is the most important emerging research or policy issue related to the study of race and crime? Explain your answer.

REFERENCES

Abu-Lughod, R. (2009). Arab Americans. In Greene, H. T., & Gabbidon, S. L. (Eds.), *Encyclopedia of Race and Crime* (pp. 27–30). Thousand Oaks, CA: Sage.

Aguirre, A., Jr., & Turner, J. H. (2007). *American ethnicity.* New York: McGraw-Hill.

American Anthropological Association. (1997). *AAA's Statement on Race.* Retrieved on February 7, 2009, from http://www.understandingrace.org/about/statement.html

Castellano, T. C., & Gould, J. B. (2007). Neglect of justice in criminal justice theory: Causes, consequences, and alternatives. In D. E. Duffee & Edward R. Maguire (Eds.), *Criminal justice theory: Explaining the nature and behavior of criminal justice* (pp. 71–92). New York: Routledge Taylor & Francis Group.

Children's Defense Fund. (2009). *Cradle to prison pipeline.* Retrieved from http://www.childrensdefense.org/helping-americas-children/cradle-to-prison-pipeline-campaign/

Covington, J. (1995). Racial classification in criminology: The reproduction of racialized crime. *Sociological Forum, 10,* 547–568.

del Carmen, A. (2009). Profiling, racial: Historical and contemporary perspectives. In H. T. Greene & S. L. Gabbidon (Eds.), *Encyclopedia of race and crime* (pp. 666–668). Thousand Oaks, CA: Sage.

Du Bois, W. E. B. (1899/1973). *The Philadelphia negro.* Millwood, NY: Kraus-Thomson.

DuBois, W. E. B. (Ed.). (1904). *Some notes on Negro crime, particularly in Georgia.* Atlanta, GA: Atlanta University Press.

Duffee, D. E., & Allan, E. (2007). Criminal justice, criminology, and criminal justice theory. In D. E. Duffee & E. R. Maguire (Eds.), *Criminal justice theory: Explaining the nature and behavior of criminal justice* (pp. 1–26). New York: Routledge Taylor & Francis Group.

Federal Bureau of Investigation (2008). *Crime in the United States, 2007.* Retrieved on February 7, 2009, from http://www. fbi.gov

Gabbidon, S. L. (2007). *Criminological perspectives on race and crime.* New York: Routledge.

Gabbidon, S. L., & Greene, H. T. (2009). *Race and crime* (2nd ed.) Thousand Oaks, CA: Sage.

Greene, H. T., & Gabbidon, S. L. (2000). *African American criminological thought.* Albany: State University of New York Press.

Greene, H. T., & Gabbidon, S. L. (2009). *Encyclopedia of race and crime.* Thousand Oaks, CA: Sage.

Greene, H. T., Polzer, K., & Lavin-Loucks, D. (2006). Prisoner reentry and transition in Dallas, Texas. *Williams Review, 1*(1), 37–62.

Harris, D. (2002). *Profiles in injustice.* New York: The New Press.

Higgins, G. E., Gabbidon, S. L., & Jordan, K. (2008). Examining the generality of citizens' views on racial profiling in diverse situational contexts. *Criminal Justice & Behavior, 35,* 1527–1541.

Jordan, K., Gabbidon, S. L., & Higgins, G. E. (2009). Exploring the perceived extent of and citizens' support for consumer racial profiling: Results from a national poll. *Journal of Criminal Justice, 37*(4), 353–359.

Kennedy, R. (1997). *Race, crime, and the law.* New York: Vintage Books/Random House.

Moffitt, T. E. (1993). Adolescence-limited and life-course-persistent antisocial behavior: A developmental taxonomy. *Psychological Review, 100,* 674–701.

The New York Times (March 18, 2008). Barack Obama's speech on race. Transcript. Retrieved on June 29, 2009, from http://nytimes.com/2008/03/18/us/politics/18text-obama.html

Poteyeva, M. (2009). Social capital. In H. T. Greene & and S. L. Gabbidon (Eds.), *Encyclopedia of race and crime* (pp. 756–757). Thousand Oaks, CA: Sage.

Rand, M. R. (2008). Criminal victimization, 2007. *Bureau of Justice Statistics Bulletin* (NCJ 224390). Retrieved on February 7, 2009, from http://www.ncjrs.gov/app/Topics/MorePublications.aspx

Rowe, D. C. (2007). *Race and crime.* New York: Oxford University Press.

Rushton, J. P. (1995). Race and crime: International data for 1989–1990. *Psychological Reports, 76,* 307–312.

Rushton, J. P., & Whitney, G. (2002). Cross-national variation in violent crime rates: Race, r-K theory, and income. *Population and Environment, 23,* 501–511.

Sabol, W. J., & Couture, H. (2008). *Prison inmates at midyear 2007.* (NCJ221944). Washington, DC: Bureau of Justice Statistics. Retrieved from http://www.ojp.usdoj.gov/bjs/pub/pdf/pim07.pdf

Sampson, R. J., & Wilson, W. J. (1995). Toward a theory of race, crime, and urban inequality. In J. Hagan & R. D. Peterson (Eds.), *Crime and inequality* (pp. 37–54). Stanford, CA: Stanford University Press.

Shaw, C. & McKay, H. (1942). *Juvenile delinquency and urban areas: A study of rates of delinquents in relation to different characteristics of local communities in American cities.* Chicago: University of Chicago Press.

Tappan, P. (2001). Who is a criminal? In S. Henry & M. Lanier (Eds.), *What is crime: Controversies over the nature of crime and what to do about it.* Lanham, MD: Rowman & Littlefield.

Travis, J. (2005). *But they all come back: Facing the challenges of prisoner reentry.* Washington, DC: The Urban Institute Press.

U.S. Department of Justice. (2008). *Crime in the United States 2007.* Retrieved from http://www.fbi.gov/ucr/cius2007/data/table_43.html

Vold, G. B., & Bernard, T. J. (1986). *Theoretical criminology* (3rd ed.). New York: Oxford University Press.

Walker, S., Spohn, C., & DeLone, M. (2007). *The color of justice* (4th ed.). Belmont, CA: Wadsworth.

Walsh, A., & Beaver, K. (Eds.). (2008). *Contemporary biosocial criminology.* New York: Routledge.

Wilson, J. Q., & Herrnstein, R. (1985). *Crime and human nature: Intelligence and crime construction.* Cambridge, MA: Harvard University Press.

Wilson, W. J. (1987). *The truly disadvantaged.* Chicago: University of Chicago Press.

Withrow, B. L. (2006). *Racial profiling: From rhetoric to reason.* Upper Saddle River, NJ: Prentice Hall.

Work, M. N. (1900). Crime among Negroes in Chicago. *American Journal of Sociology, 6,* 204–223.

Work, M. N. (1913). Negro criminality in the South. *Annals of the American Academy of Political and Social Sciences, 49,* 74–80.

Work, M. N. (1937). Problems of adjustment of the race and class in the South. *Social Forces, 16,* 108–117.

Young, V. D. (1996). The Politics of disproportionality. In A. T. Sulton (Ed.), *African-American perspectives on crime causation, criminal justice administration, and crime prevention* (pp. 69–82). Boston, MA: Butterworth-Heinemann.

8

Culture, Media, and Crime

Dimitri A. Bogazianos

Introduction

This chapter argues for a more complex way of understanding the relationship between culture, media, and crime. Such an argument suggests that simple or "simplistic" explanations—even if understandable at the everyday level—are not only incomplete but also potentially dangerous when enshrined in criminal justice policy. No matter what our original intentions, the criminal justice policies we create from our explanations of this relationship will affect thousands, if not millions, of lives in countless unforeseeable ways. We should therefore approach such issues, however briefly, with the attention, complexity, and seriousness they deserve, even if for only a semester, a quarter, or a lecture. The intersection of culture, media, and crime is important to understand because the stakes are high.

While such statements may seem obvious to both academic and popular critics, the "commonsense" understandings of this intersection that continue to influence real policy rarely reflect the social complexities they purport to address. This chapter, therefore, argues that all such intersections in the "real" world—whether concerning gangsta rap, jailhouse tattoos, violent video games, or Internet pornography—deserve, at the very least, to have analytical gridworks composed of multiple theoretical perspectives and complimentary methodologies applied to them. What follows, hence, is a necessarily brief but thoroughly accessible presentation of the key elements that any basic analytical gridwork intended to examine the intersection of culture, media, and crime should include. Accordingly, my notes and references are few and provided primarily to give interested readers a baseline from which they might explore further; they are not meant to constitute an exhaustive literature review. The immediate goal of this presentation is to bring it all together—to bring the various elements of and approaches to criminal justice into a comprehensive whole that might then be used to analyze *any* intersection of culture, media, and crime, whether in the past, present, or future. Of course, understanding this intersection first depends on how we understand the three key terms that make up this chapter's title: *culture, media,* and *crime.*

Key Terms

"Culture," as historian and cultural critic Raymond Williams famously wrote, "is one of the two or three most complicated words in the English language" (Williams, 1985, p. 87). In large part, this complexity exists because of the multiple, overlapping layers of meaning we associate with it. At the very least, the word suggests both process and product—the norms governing the ways in which people become fully social beings as well as the artistic, symbolic, and expressive output that people raised in their cultural environments create. In effect, culture refers to *ways of life* as well as to the creations that represent those lifeways—cultivation and creation. Similarly, then, as its prefix suggests, the term *subculture*—which is often used in explanations of crime and punishment—is clearly related and generally refers to cultural processes and products that exist either within larger, mainstream cultural formations or, as many have argued, outside the mainstream in marginal or marginalized ways. Hence, we can refer to "subcultures of crime" as well as to "subcultures of music," for example.[1]

Likewise, if we take culture to be both process and product, then *media*—the second word in our title—is clearly related to culture, as the products of culture quite often are "fixed" in tangible forms and circulated through physical, sonic, and visual mechanisms. At its most basic, *media* refers to *mediums*—the stuff through which something else is communicated, such as books, films, and compact discs. Clearly, therefore, culture and media are inherently linked, which suggests that media cannot exist without the cultural contexts that help create them and that, in turn, cultures cannot be fully understood without the mediated creations that represent them.[2]

Perhaps most important is the word *crime*—something we all "know" yet do not always agree upon. Defining just what crime is has concerned writers, critics, and, indeed, the general public for a very long time (and probably always will). Some hold to a more legalistic understanding: Crime is whatever the criminal law says it is. In this version, law makes crime, since prohibited acts, logically, cannot be prohibited without the laws that prohibit them. Other versions understand crime more generally, arguing that legal proscriptions are often little more than the codification of widely held sentiments about morality, law, and order and that, essentially, the criminal law most often reflects—and that if not, it should reflect—informal community standards and normative codes of behavior. Obviously, crime refers at least, but not only, to behaviors that enough people in positions of relative law-making power find so undesirable that such acts should be punished.

There is, therefore, far more to the intersection of culture, media, and crime than simple cause and effect. Take Japanese animation styles, for example. Some, though by no means all, display images of extreme violence and explicit sexuality, yet Japan has one of the lowest violent crime rates in the world. Clearly, there is no easy one-to-one correlation between the individuals who create such images, the cultural contexts that give them meaning, the socio-political structures within which both exist, and the behavior—criminal or not—of the people who consume the final products.

Think about what it takes for a popular song to go from creation to consumption. On one end of the creative continuum, we can imagine a "true" artist who slaves away in relative isolation, disregarding money or status and instead creating "purely" for art's sake. On the other end, we can imagine something like the boy bands that were so popular in the late 1990s, which—like *American Idol* in the 2000s—auditioned thousands of young people for only a few spots. In either case, however, the creation of a song takes a lot of time and at least some talent. Once created, the song must be recorded, which—even in the cheapest, most bare-bones home studios—requires access to equipment and the knowledge of how to use it all. Then, if one is lucky enough to get an audience and attract the attention of record labels, distributors, or music publishers, contracts of all sorts will come next, necessitating either a very high level of skill in interpreting legal documents or the money to pay lawyers who have those skills if one does not. Perhaps most important, bringing a song to an audience in such a complex business environment requires patience, for such complexity can put serious strains on even the closest relationships. For any song, then, to get to an audience, it must first go through a maze of social and legal arrangements. These complex processes often lie at the core of the intersection of culture, media, and crime and have been analyzed from multiple perspectives throughout the years.

Key Approaches

For convenience's sake, we can organize approaches to the role of media in social, and hence criminal, life into four broad categories: top-down, bottom-up, from-the-middle, and across-the-whole. As in any similar effort, of course, this organization is a rule of thumb, and the categories are frames of reference rather than definitively distinct boxes with no overlap. In reality, elements of all four can be found in individual theories; the differences, therefore, are primarily due to individual emphasis, not logical exclusivity.

Let's think of tattoos, for example. The practice of tattooing has existed in all parts of the world since prehistory. However, in modern European American societies, until quite recently tattoos have been worn primarily by people in criminal subcultures or the military. In the 2000s, though, tattoos are worn by everyone from urban hipsters to suburban teenagers and soccer moms, most of whom (happily) will see the inside of a jail cell only on television. In essence, then, getting a tattoo in the 2000s actually *means* something different from what it did only 20 years ago. Times change, of course, and the significance of social practices change with them. "Common sense," however, changes as well. It was once "common sense," for example, to use cocaine in a wide variety of legitimate medical practices. The point here is that these kinds of changes in social meaning must be explained, not explained away by dismissive references to "commonsense" explanations that "everyone," somehow, already knows. Rather, the question is this: Why at *this* time, in *these* places, under *these* conditions, have tattoos become mainstream? One "commonsense" answer might be that "people just want to look cool." But people have always wanted to look cool, and styles of cool change with the times. In mid-1980s America, for example, it was considered cool—and therefore "common sense"—for men in rock bands to tease their long hear with large quantities of hairspray and perform for adoring female fans wearing women's makeup and spandex pants. So, again, "common sense" is never an explanation, only an avoidance of a basic question: Why here and now?

A top-down approach to analyzing this intersection, then, might argue that the spread of tattooing beyond its "original" meanings and associations has been due primarily to the entertainment industry's constant search for new markets and new ways to make money. In effect, the approach suggests that tattoos have been commodified—turned into things that can be bought and sold rather than having to be learned the old-fashioned way, through in-depth participation in a real subculture. The emphasis in this approach focuses on the needs of the current economic system to keep making money by finding and exploiting new areas of social life previously left alone by the marketplace. In a top-down approach, then, a tattoo is simply another commodity that ultimately works in the service of the current economic order; therefore, the meanings of tattoos for the people who create them and wear them do not, in the end, determine why tattooing has spread and become mainstream.[3]

A bottom-up approach, on the other hand, might actually agree with many of the points just made but argue that, regardless of the entertainment industry's commodification of tattooing, the practice first started in organic subcultures that used tattoos primarily to differentiate themselves from the mainstream, thereby representing a rejection of, say, conventional middle-class values as well as pride in being part of an alternative cultural form. A bottom-up approach, then, might focus on tattooing's original, uncommodified existence, which was later co-opted by the entertainment industry for profit. Clearly, both top-down and bottom-up approaches are critical of current economic conditions; in the latter, however, the actual participants in the original alternative subcultures are often, though not always, understood to be active agents in creating, re-creating, revising, and critiquing the ways in which their practices get incorporated into the mainstream. Bottom-up approaches, therefore, often critique—sometimes only implicitly—the top-down approach's potential to see individual participants as mere pawns in a much larger game. Of course, as a rejoinder, top-down approaches often critique the bottom-up approach's potential to overemphasize the role of individual participants, and neglect the degree to which cultural formations, no matter how "alternative" they may seem, still work in the service of maintaining current economic exploitation.[4]

A from-the-middle approach might agree with many of the points made in both approaches discussed above but argue, instead, that the *interactions* between middle-level participants, such as tattoo artists and clients, have the most influence in determining the meanings tattooing takes on as it spreads beyond its earlier associations. A from-the-middle approach, consequently, emphasizes that the creation of meaning is always a social process in which creators and consumers share in the creation of meaning, and that the distinctions between the two are often blurred. From-the-middle approaches, then, tend to focus on the day-to-day working environments that form in specific cultural industries and suggest—sometimes only implicitly—that neither top-down nor bottom-up approaches pay enough attention to the relationships between, for example, producers and performers, editors and authors, or directors and actors.[5]

An across-the-whole approach, however, might take a different tack entirely and instead focus primarily on in-depth analysis of the tattoos themselves. Often derived from linguistic models of analysis, which suggest that words have meaning only because they are different from other words, across-the-whole approaches argue that meaning does not rely on individuals, cultures, or interactions but is created through the systematic differences between things. We understand the word *cat*, for example, primarily because it is different from other words, like *dog*, not because of some inherent correlation between the word *cat* and the flesh-and-blood thing the word represents. Across-the-whole approaches, then, might chart the subtle but systematic changes in actual tattoos throughout a specific historical period in order to show how individual choices made about tattoos—both creating and wearing them—are governed by the whole archive of tattoos in a period, which often heavily influences, if not wholly determines, the universe of possible choices, making it incredibly difficult for any one tattoo artist or client to create something completely "outside the box." Each single tattoo, then, can only ever be a variation in a larger pattern of possibility set by the whole range of already-created tattoos. Differences in the lettering, color, or themes of specific tattoos make sense, then, only because they are explicitly referencing the letters, colors, and themes from which they depart. In this view, there is no such thing as a pure, freely chosen action. Clearly, criticisms of this approach often revolve around its explicit departure from the intentions of flesh-and-blood human beings. However, the approach does allow for analyses that are simultaneously deep and far reaching.[6]

It is worth repeating that these four approaches are not mutually exclusive perspectives and, indeed, can be integrated with each other in various ways. In any case, complex explanations of the relationship between culture, media, and crime must take account of one fundamental reality: Individual actions are always situated in cultural contexts that are themselves grounded in specific times and places, which are in turn thoroughly influenced by the dominant economic, political, and linguistic structures. Indeed, one might argue for a combination of all four—that artists and clients shape the immediate meanings of tattoos, but that these interactions are grounded in the meanings created within specific subcultures, and that, by consciously searching for the next exploitable commodity, the entertainment industries have come to profit from the subcultural credibility that tattoos often give to entertainers and athletes. And, finally, when such meanings become diffused throughout social life to significant degrees, the commodities themselves become structures in their own right, like archives of meaning that influence individual choices even when the individuals themselves are unaware of being influenced. Fundamentally, then, a complex explanation of the relationship between culture, media, and crime must be able to address at least three different levels of social reality, even if one level becomes emphasized over the others—individual, cultural, and structural.

Key Levels of Analysis

By *individual*, we can mean, at least, self-conscious, self-aware, human beings who behave in ways that show both instinct and intention, unconscious desire and purposeful action, nature and nurture. To state the obvious, people have reasons for doing the things they do. Often, though, there is a tendency to explain the intersection of culture, media, and crime only in terms of what specific individuals intended. Indeed, intentionality is at the core of our criminal law; without guilty minds, bad acts can be only accidents. There is a problem with overly individualistic explanations, however: If multiple people create similar work, for example, yet believe they are doing so for different reasons, their intentions alone cannot explain their creations. That is, people can intend all kinds of different things but still create very similar work. In effect, something other than the personal is influencing their creativity. Enter culture.

As I've stated, culture means both process and product, cultivation and creation. But overly culturalist explanations of this intersection also run into their own problems. This is the "birds of a feather" explanation: People behave the way they do because they have been acculturated to do so by their social contexts. The problem here is that simply being a part of a cultural environment that seems to accentuate or justify criminal behavior does not by itself explain why only some people raised in such cultures actually become criminals while many others do not.

Finally, by *structural* we can mean those social forces that are bigger than individuals, which move out of any one individual's control but affect us just the same. Economic booms and depressions, for example or, as many have argued, linguistic rules—"discourses"—that, many believe, condition the very possibility of saying what we mean or being the free, rational people we think we are. Clearly, the potential critiques of purely structural accounts of this intersection revolve around the neglect of the human individual—that, at bottom, no matter how influential they may be, structural forces can always be subverted, challenged, and changed by individuals who resist such pressures.

People, then, do not do things simply because their cultures tell them to or because their structures force them to; individuals always make choices. Inescapably, however, individuals create and consume media within specific cultural formations that exist within structural conditions that both enable and constrain individual action.

Key Methodologies

Methodologically, these levels have been addressed through a variety of approaches. Just as in all social analysis, quantitative methods—those that create statistical summaries and predictions—allow for the "big picture" to be sketched out. In addition to statistical breadth, qualitative methods, including interviews, observations, and media analyses, allow for more in-depth portraits. In media studies generally, both quantitative and qualitative approaches have been focused on understanding two key social processes: production and reception. Generally, *production* refers to those processes through which media products become products—how they are produced. *Reception*, therefore, focuses on how those products then get consumed—how they are received and used by their audiences. Hence, some studies might focus on observing and interviewing how musicians understand the music they create, what they hope their audience might take from their sounds. Other studies, instead, might focus on the fans of the same music, how they actually interpret the sounds those musicians create. Often, then, different perspectives on the same product, music, reveal radically different perceptions of its meaning, worth, and significance. Alternatively, and aligned with the across-the-whole approach discussed earlier, other studies might focus on the music itself and examine how, for example, rap lyrics constantly reference, quote, and sample—"cut and mix," "chop and screw"—a wide range of previous musical styles, thereby suggesting that the meaning of any one rap song depends on what earlier material it references and the ways in which it does so.[7]

CONCLUSION

While I have tried to suggest throughout this chapter that common sense is never simple, there is still a lot of sense to common sense. After all, few parents, for example, need social scientists to tell them if and when their children should be exposed to violent or sexual imagery. This "commonsense" approach to the intersection of culture, media, and crime—which serves us well at the everyday level—seems at least a bit incomplete, however, when used to create laws that punish real people. Prohibition—the nearly 15-year experiment in making the production and distribution of alcohol illegal in the United States—is a classic case in point, as it reflects a clearly well-intentioned effort to "clean up" our cities. It also allowed for the growth of large-scale criminal networks to supply the banned substances, and it drastically curtailed peoples' personal freedom to choose how they spent their time and money.

When seemingly commonsense explanations—e.g., "bad" substances cause "bad" behavior, which then leads to social chaos—are simplistically applied to complex social issues, often we all pay the price. Hopefully, then, this chapter can convince its readers that such intersections deserve a multi-dimensional approach and that only through richer understandings of complex social issues can the larger goal of forming fair, just, and humane criminal justice policy be achieved. This is a lofty goal but a crucial one. It assumes that the stakes are high and that what we do about pressing social issues is first influenced by the ways we think about them. Focusing on structural situatedness, for example, should not by itself absolve individuals of responsibility for their actions. But neither should individual explanations dismiss out of hand the cultural and structural contexts in which all individual action is inextricably embedded. In effect, the goal is to explain without explaining away—to think complexly about complex social issues and to have explanations and policies that reflect that complexity. Lives are at stake.

DISCUSSION QUESTIONS

1. Can you think of any current criminal justice policies that are based on simplistic cause-and-effect assumptions?

2. How might you integrate the various approaches and levels discussed in the chapter in a coherent, unified way in order to analyze a specific current event, case, or policy?

3. Can you think of any unintended consequences of current criminal justice policies that affect more than their intended targets?

4. What practical issues are involved with trying to incorporate more complex understandings of culture, crime, and media into criminal justice policy? How might such barriers be overcome?

NOTES

1. The concept of subculture has played a crucial role in criminological theorizing from the earliest days of sociological criminology in the United States and England to the present. See, for example, Becker (1997); A. Cohen (1955); S. Cohen (2002);

Polsky (1967). See also its uses in the more recent work of cultural criminologists, e.g., Ferrell, Hayward, & Young (2008); Ferrell & Sanders (1995). The classic treatment of subculture in media studies is Hebdige (2002).

2. Studies of media are far too numerous to mention, but two of the most famous and important are Febvre & Martin (1997) and McLuhan (1964).

3. Top-down approaches are often derived from or associated with the critical theory of the Frankfurt School. Its influence has been far too extensive to adequately summarize, but two key texts are Horkheimer & Adorno (1995) and Marcuse (2002).

4. Bottom-up approaches are often associated with cultural studies, whose influence also has been too extensive to adequately summarize. Key texts, among many, are Benjamin (1969); Gilroy (1993); Hoggart (1957); and Williams (1977).

5. From-the-middle approaches are often associated with symbolic interactionism, social constructionism, and the sociology of culture. Key texts dealing with crime are Bailey & Hale (1998); Best (1999); Ferrell & Websdale (1999); and Potter & Kappeler (1998).

6. Across-the-whole approaches are often associated with structuralism and poststructuralism, whose influence on all academic disciplines is, again, far too extensive to adequately summarize; without question, however, the key text for criminology is Foucault (1995).

7. An example of a production study is Grindstaff (2002). An example of a reception study is Ang (1985).

REFERENCES

Ang, I. (1985). *Watching Dallas: Soap opera and the melodramatic imagination.* London: Methuen.

Bailey, F. Y., & and Hale, D. C. (Eds.). (1998). *Popular culture, crime, and justice.* Belmont, CA: Wadsworth.

Becker, H. S. (1997). *Outsiders: Studies in the sociology of deviance.* New York: The Free Press.

Benjamin, W. (1969). *Illuminations.* New York: Schocken Books.

Best, J. (1999). *Random violence: How we talk about new crime and new victims.* Berkeley: University of California Press.

Cohen, A. (1955). *Delinquent boys.* New York: The Free Press.

Cohen, S. (2002). *Folk devils and moral panics.* New York: Routledge.

Febvre, L., & Martin, H. (1997). *The coming of the book: The impact of printing 1450–1800.* London: Verso.

Ferrell, J., Hayward, K., & Young, J. (2008). *Cultural criminology: An invitation.* London: Sage.

Ferrell, J., & Sanders, C. R. (Eds.). (1995). *Cultural criminology.* Boston: Northeastern University Press.

Ferrell, J., & Websdale, N. (Eds.). (1999). *Making trouble: Cultural constructions of crime, deviance, and control.* New York: Aldine de Gruyter.

Foucault, M. (1995). *Discipline and punish: The birth of the prison* (Alan Sheridan, Trans.). London: Vintage.

Gilroy, P. (1993). *The black Atlantic: Modernity and double consciousness.* Cambridge, MA: Harvard University Press.

Grindstaff, L. (2002). *The money shot: Trash, class, and the making of TV talk shows*. Chicago: The University of Chicago Press.

Hebdige, D. (2002). *Subculture: The meaning of style*. London: Routledge.

Hoggart, R. (1957). *The uses of literacy: Aspects of working-class life with special reference to publications and entertainment*. London: Chatto and Windus.

Horkheimer, M., & Adorno, T. W. (1995). *The dialectic of enlightenment*. New York: Continuum.

Marcuse, H. (2002). *One-dimensional man: Studies in the ideology of advanced industrial society*. London: Routledge.

McLuhan, M. (1964). *Understanding media: The extensions of man*. New York: Signet.

Polsky, N. (1967). *Hustlers, beats, and others*. Harmondsworth, UK: Penguin.

Potter, G. W., & Kappeler, V. E. (1998). *Constructing crime: Perspectives on making news and social problems*.

Williams, R. (1977). *Marxism and literature*. Oxford: Oxford University Press.

Williams, R. (1985). *Keywords: A vocabulary of culture and society*. New York: Oxford University Press.

9

Crime and Economics

Consumer Culture, Criminology, and the Politics of Exclusion

Stephen L. Muzzatti

What does the American Dream mean today? For Niko Bellic, fresh off the boat from Europe, it is the hope he can escape his past. For his cousin, Roman, it is the vision that together they can find fortune in Liberty City, gateway to the land of opportunity. As they slip into debt and are dragged into a criminal underworld by a series of shysters, thieves, and sociopaths, they discover that the reality is very different from the dream in a city that worships money and status and is heaven for those who have them and a living nightmare for those who don't.[1]

Introduction: A Spectre Is Haunting Criminology . . .

The connection between crime and economics is complex and multifaceted. Perhaps because of this density, thorough coverage of the topic of crime and economics has proven to be so elusive to mainstream or administrative criminology, particularly in the United States, despite some ostensibly elaborate and occasionally very high-profile attempts to address it. In some respects, the topic is anathema to criminology. While such an assertion may read as sacrilegious to orthodox criminologists, it is not anywhere near as wildly unsubstantiated as some of orthodoxy's high priests might retort. As any devoted reader of the indecipherable articles that fill such journals as *Criminology* and *Justice Quarterly* (to say nothing of moribund textbooks and stale government reports) can undoubtedly attest, a plethora of criminological studies purport to address the matter of crime and economics. However, many (dare I suggest most) of these studies, if they address economics at all, do so in a disjointed, limited, and myopic way. In various degrees, these studies attempt to account for the impact of economics on crime rates, ethnoracial or subcultural variations in offending, policing practices, criminogenic age cohorts, victimisation risks, incarceration, recidivism, and a host of other issues. They do so in a sophisticated and nuanced fashion, symbolically representing crime's factors with *lambda* and *chi*, employing elaborate multiple-regression models and the latest statistical alchemy (see Ferrell, Hayward, & Young, 2008; Muzzatti, 2006, 2009). They ultimately tell us very little about crime and economics. Whilst I do not mean to cast any aspersions upon the researchers involved or question the countless hours of work and effort they devote to these projects, most fall victim to a fatal ontological flaw: They fail to address capitalism.

It seems that *capitalism* is a bad word in criminology. It is not something to be discussed in polite company (such as at the American Society of Criminology's annual meetings) lest you be labelled a leftist ideologue or, worse, a reductionist; and it is certainly not something to be committed to print (except occasionally, in esoteric, European-based criminology journals). Academic criminology's gatekeepers have long been aware of the potential consequences associated with allowing an unbridled thrashing of the "C-word" and work diligently to prevent it from sullying the good name of the discipline.[2] Aside from a few serpentine flashes, any emancipatory potential to be found in criminology is met with the Marcusian repressive tolerance of programme committees, blind-reviewers, institutional ethics boards, tenure and promotion committees, and outside funding sources, such as the National Institute of Justice (NIJ). It is far easier and more respectable to facilitate work on "nuts, sluts, and preverts" and "the exotic, the erotic, and the neurotic" under the aegis of "value-free" voodoo criminology and the numbers game than to risk the ire of editors, publishers, and granting agencies, to say nothing of the grief that one will undoubtedly suffer at the hands orthodox criminology's high priests and most of the lesser clergy who totter along in ideological lockstep (see Liazos, 1972; Muzzatti, 2003; Young, 1999 and 2007.)

I am fortunate that editors Mary Maguire and Dan Okada were not only open to but enthusiastic about including in this collection an ontological and epistemological challenge to the crime and economics canon. For that I am grateful. Of course, readers should note that any shortcomings or foibles are mine alone. Readers should also be aware that, in addition to the term *capitalism*, they will encounter throughout this chapter a number of other profanities well outside criminology's polite lexicon (ex. *political economy, late modernity,* etc.) as I attempt to historically and genealogically reconstruct a criminology of capitalism.

Reading the Profane: Theorising Crime and Capitalism

While it is true that many contemporary American criminologists fail to address the role of capitalism in matters of crime (whether causation, creation, reification, or commodification), some late 19th- and early 20th-century European scholars paid it considerable attention. In the following section, I briefly address the work of two often-overlooked criminological theorists, Germany's Karl Marx and Holland's Willem Bonger, as a means of contextualising extant issues of crime and capitalism in 21st-century America.

Karl Marx (1818–1883)

Considering his vast corpus of work, it is perhaps not surprising that many criminologists overlook Karl Marx's writing on crime. With the exception of his article "Debates on the Law on the Thefts of Wood" in 1842[3] and a few pieces for the *New York Daily Tribune*[4] in the 1850s, Marx rarely addressed the topic of crime specifically. However, he wrote extensively about capitalism as an economic and political system and the way this system essentially produced two classes of people: *capitalists* and *proletarians*. Because capitalists owned the means of production, they also were able to exert almost total control over social institutions (including but not limited to what we today understand as the criminal justice system) and were able to entrench their beliefs and values as *the* beliefs and values of society. In contrast, the proletarians owned and controlled nothing and hence were obliged to exchange their ability to work for a wage at the discretion of the capitalists. For Marx, the social production of concrete material relations—relations by which people secured their material existence—permeated all aspects of life. Because of this, the capitalist ruling class was able to translate its economic power into political and ideological power. Through his endeavour to illustrate that the material basis for systemic inequality produced conflict (which can manifest itself as crime), Marx provided the requisite conceptual tools for answering questions about crime.

At the risk of oversimplifying, Marx theorised that the criminal and criminal law are inextricably bound to the larger economic order. In *The German Ideology* (1846), Marx and his coauthor, Friedrich Engels, describe crime as the struggle of the isolated individual against the prevailing conditions. In other words, it was the economy, specifically industrial capitalism, that determined crime's incarnations. The creation and enforcement of law were at the discretion of the capitalist class. Though this posit was ignored by most American criminologists, these correlates of crime and inequality are certainly no less true today than when Marx and Engels first described them.

Willem Adriaan Bonger (1876–1940)

Between the time of Marx's death and the first decade of the 20th century, a criminology of the capitalist economic system was emerging in several European nations, notably France, Germany, and Italy.[5] The late 1880s, in particular, saw a proliferation of these works by Italian criminologists, such as Bruno Battaglia, Napoleone Colajanni, and Filippo Turati. However, to the considerable detriment of Anglo-American criminology, few of these stellar contributions were ever translated into English.[6] A notable and instructive exception was the translation of Dutch criminologist Willem Bonger's book, *Criminalite et Conditions Economiques* (1905).

As a young man, Bonger studied law at the University of Amsterdam. It was here that he became well acquainted with the work of Marx and was inspired to study the political economy of crime by G. A. van Hamel, a renowned penologist who was his criminal-law professor. While Bonger made several major contributions to criminology in the areas of racism and criminal justice, suicide, penal philosophy, militarism, and war, it was the English translation of *Criminality and Economic Conditions* (1916) that proved to be his most enduring and the one most relevant to this chapter.

According to Bonger, capitalism is criminogenic. Put simply, capitalism's brutality creates conditions under which crime is not only produced but flourishes. For Bonger, crime and capitalism are connected in three fundamental ways. Bonger employed the historical materialism of Marx and Engels in illustrating the first of these connections: the development of criminal law in unison with the aggrandisement of property rights. Hence, for Bonger the history of theft is the history of private property. Much of criminal law was created to protect the property of the haves from the have-nots. Connected to this was Bonger's second major posit: that crime is engendered by the miserable conditions forced upon the working class in the emergence of industrial capitalism. Finally, and most prescient for the consideration of crime under late modernity, Bonger theorises that the economic logic of capitalism promotes endless greed and fosters crime.

Both Marx and Bonger addressed the myriad ways capitalism produces crime, including the miserable conditions under which the majority of the population languished, the biased creation and application of law, and the destructive values of avarice and individualism that permeated industrial society. However, with the notable exception of what came to be known as the conflict criminology[7] of William Chambliss, Elliot Currie, Julia and Herman Schwendinger, Steven Spitzer, Tony Platt, and Richard Quinney in the 1970s and 1980s, few American criminologists took up these themes with vigour.[8]

Banality and Viciousness in Late Modernity _____

Whilst the conditions of 21st-century America are very different from the early and high industrialism of Marx and Bonger's Europe, capitalism rages on, leaving a broad swath of destruction and human suffering, including but not limited to what is narrowly defined as crime. Contrary to the vociferous pronouncements of capitalist running dogs, market-order cheerleaders, and neoliberal apologists, globalisation and the concomitant postindustrialisation have not made the American landscape a better, safer, or more humane environment. Massive transnational corporations the size and scope of which the authors of the Sherman Antitrust Act could nary imagine continue to steal and murder with impunity, street crime is ever more racialised, minor transgressions increasingly come to be addressed through the criminal justice system's formal and punitive mechanisms, and living-wage jobs are nearly impossible to find and even more difficult to keep.

Under such conditions, it is little wonder that people are adrift and cling desperately to anything that promises more stability than late modernism's liquidity (see Bauman, 2000). Unfortunately, there is relatively little available on which people, particularly young people, can moor themselves. As Hall, Winlow, and Ancrum (2008) illustrate with great aplomb, because the global capitalist project is increasingly reliant upon *finance* capital rather than *productive* capital, material reality has readily been displaced by a fictitious realm of fleeting visceral pleasure and ephemeral amelioration. Hence, unlike pre-deindustrialised generations, in which social worth was determined through the relationship to the means of production and other stratified forms of social meaning, under late modernity our selves and our subjectivities are increasingly determined through our consumption practices (Ewen, 1977, 1988; Hayward & Yar 2006; Muzzatti, 2008, 2009). In his seminal work on crime and consumer culture, Hayward (2004) illustrates that the products and services we acquire and access through our consumer exercises are the primary indices of identity. While there is nothing inherently new about capitalism's unapologetic promotion of consumerism as a gateway to social integration, the process has accelerated rapidly over the past decade, reaching gargantuan proportions. Today, the creation and expression of identities via the celebration of consumer goods have all but supplanted other, more traditional forms of identity expression. This, in combination with the aforementioned withdrawal of meaningful, living-wage employment opportunities, seriously undermines the life world, moral codes, and habitus of ordinary people (Bordieu, 1984; Hall et al., 2008).

_____ Youth and the Vicissitudes of Late Modernity

Commenting on his experiences living and working in 1830s Manchester, Engels (1845) wrote of the English working class's children,

> And children growing up in this savage way, amidst the demoralising influences, are expected to turn out good-goody and moral in the end! Verily the requirements are naive, which the self satisfied bourgeois makes upon the working man! (p.168)

Again, although he was writing about a place very different from 21st-century America, Engels's insight should not be lost on those of us who strive to better understand the contemporary workings of consumer capitalism and its impact on the everyday/night lived experiences of young people. Although it is not my intention to demonise America's youth (that is the purview of the corporately owned news media), it behooves us to realise that the 18- to 25-year-old demographic is responsible for a not insignificant portion of traditional street crime, particularly violent street crime. So, too, and perhaps equally as telling, young people disproportionately find themselves the subjects of the orthodox criminological lens. Historically, orthodox criminology's treatment of youth delinquency and crime has been no better, and in some respects worse, than its "efforts" to address capitalism. However well intentioned, the canon—from "inverted values" and "generating milieus of gang delinquency" through "subcultures of violence" and "elements of bonding"—has provided little insight into youth involvement in criminality and has reified class bias both within academic criminological discourse and, more disturbingly, among criminal justice policymakers and practitioners[9].

The criminalisation of youth and class is itself part of the ideological work of capitalism. By suggesting that a particular working-class or underclass age cohort holds a monopoly on crime, orthodox criminology transmits a political economy of values that serves the interests of global capital while positioning the marginalised subject group for optimal regulation and control. It does so in part by atomising or individualising social problems and furtively sheathing late capitalism's destructive values beneath a veneer of spectacle and the *carnivalesque* (see Presdee, 2000).

Consuming Crime and Culture

Scything through capitalism's veneer, it is evident that lives of late-modern subjects have been so thoroughly colonised by consumerism that the goals–means discrepancy (i.e., "strain") Merton described over 70 years ago seems almost benign in comparison. Indeed, living in a world where work, if it exists at all, is increasingly deskilled, wages are pitifully low, and growing segments of the former middle classes slip into a vortex of unsecured debt, it is little wonder that consumption itself is now *the* strategy employed to demarcate, compartmentalise, and control the general public (see, relatedly, Bauman, 2000, 2007; Wilson, 1987). This transformation has served only to intensify capitalism's inequality. According to Bauman, late-modern consumer society is now polarised between indemnified, privileged, and dutiful consumers on the one hand, and on the other, the increasingly swollen ranks of the marginalised and criminalised classes, who, as a result of either inability or unwillingness, have failed to acquiesce to the hegemonic dictates of consumerism. The first of these groups, the "Seduced," exhibit the requisite desire and fixation required by unmediated consumer societies. More important, though, they are in a position to satisfy their desire through continual cycles of unre-flexive hyperconsumption. Standing in stark contrast to the "Seduced" are the "Repressed," a group that embodies what one might describe as the *collateral damage* of consumerism. This throng of uncommoditised or failed consumers represent an ever-growing, marginalised mass who, through neg-ligence or wilfulness, fail to adequately acquit themselves of their consumer "duties." The Repressed's insufficient and/or disreputable consumption pat-terns do not satisfactorily integrate them into the acceptable echelons of con-sumer society (Muzzatti, 2004, 2009). Though highly stylised, the opening soliloquy by "Mark Renton," the heroin-addicted antihero from the film *Trainspotting*, sardonically captures the nihilism that is both the predictable and not unreasonable consequence of such a vicious bifurcation:

> Choose Life. Choose a job. Choose a career. Choose a family. Choose a fucking big television, choose washing machines, cars, compact disc players and electrical tin openers. Choose good health, low cholesterol, and dental insurance. Choose fixed interest mortgage repayments. Choose a starter home. Choose your friends. Choose leisurewear and matching luggage. Choose a three-piece suite on hire purchase in a range of fucking fabrics. Choose DIY and wondering who the fuck you are on a Sunday morning. Choose sitting on that couch watching mind-numbing, spirit-crushing game shows, stuffing fucking junk food into your mouth. Choose rotting away at the end of it all, pishing your last in a miserable home, nothing more than an embarrassment to the selfish, fucked up brats you spawned to replace yourself. Choose your future. Choose life.[10]

Late Modernity, Crime, and Pseudo-Pacification

What is of importance in terms of this chapter (and something overlooked by Bauman) is the way in which late modernity's ideological work not only serves to incessantly remind us of this bifurcation but also acts to control and manipulate us by illustrating the consequences of lax or ineffectual consumption work (Muzzatti, 2008, 2009). As Hall and his colleagues poignantly illustrate, late capitalism systematically organises conditions of social insecurity while simultaneously lauding aggressive competition and individual hubris (Hall et al, 2008). Unlike the "norms" of the Mertonian framework, late modernity's norms are created in the fantasy world of venture capitalism, hyperwealth, and unlimited personal and natural resources. Such arrangements are potentially criminogenic, as they detach people from reality, breed frustration, and undermine any true sense of community and solidarity by fostering irresponsible and wholly instru-mental attitudes toward other people (ibid). A rank, dog-eat-dog individ-ualism and fortress mentality are vital components of late modernity's depoliticalisation process, which lulls the populace into a state of false insecurity. Alternately described as *anelpis* (Hall & Winlow, 2004, p. 277, quoting Taylor) and *vertigo* (Young, 2007, p. 12), this malaise of late modernity is characterised by total cynicism, no opinions (except as they relate to the incontrovertibly mundane), no hope, a sense of entitlement, unrealistic expectations, giddiness, unsteadiness, uncertainty, and insecurity. Perhaps most significantly, it is evidenced by misplaced fear; not a legitimate fear of government, corporations, or other authority, but a misplaced and unrealistic fear of other people.

Capitalism produces numerous contradictions. In late modernity, we live in isolation from our neighbours and cut ourselves off from all but a small number of intimates, yet we pay high monthly fees to have cable companies and satellite providers pump mediated images of the outside world into our homes. We distrust strangers and move briskly to maintain our physical distance from those we do not recognise on the street, but we loudly discuss our most intimate personal details on mobile phones in shopping malls and post the prosaic intricacies of our lives on social networking sites for anyone to see. We are suspicious of those who migrate to our shores, because they may "take our jobs," or not work, and "live off our tax dollars." We fear terrorism but fail to scrutinise the foreign policy of our own government lest we be labeled un-American. Perhaps capitalism's greatest obfuscation is found in the fact that we continually feed our cravings for inexpensive consumer goods but fail to consider the real costs—economic, social, and environmental, at home and abroad—of doing so.[11]

Selling Crime, Marketing Transgression, and Commodifying Violence _____

Even in their most surreal nightmares, it is unlikely that either Marx or Bonger could have envisaged the leviathan proportions and seemingly infinite tentacles of 21st-century capitalism. However, given their respective historical contexts, both offered some discerning commentary on the saleability of crime. In the first volume of *Theories of Surplus Value* (1863), Marx's insights into the marketability of crime are perhaps even more poignant under today's conditions of late modernity than when it was first written. According to him (as quoted in Greenberg, 1981)

> [t]he criminal produces not only crime but also criminal law, and even the inevitable text-book in which the professor presents his lectures as a commodity for sale in the market . . . but also art, literature, novels and the tragic drama, as *OEdipus* and *Richard III* . . . (pp. 52–53)

In a similar vein and in stark contrast to most contemporary criminology textbooks, Bonger begins *Criminality and Economic Conditions* (1916) not with the conventional hyperbolic pieties about the current state of crime and justice but instead with several pages devoted to Thomas More's fictional account of the traveller Raphael Hythloday.[12] Although these examples focus on suffering under petty mercantilism and other precapitalist economic formations, they do address the narcissistic individualism that capitalism has exacerbated under late modernity.

While several early British conflict criminologists examined the way the news media used crime to sell (see Cohen, 1972; Cohen & Young, 1973; Hall, Critcher, Jefferson, Clarke, & Roberts, 1978), only in the last decade or so have criminologists seriously investigated the connection between crime and the entertainment media. A new wave of cultural criminologists has applied the contributions of such Frankfurt School theorists as Max Horkheimer and Theodor Adorno (1946) to an understanding of the role played by the culture industries in transmitting corporate consumerism's destructive values. Ferrell and Sanders were among the first of this new wave to examine on how mass or common culture is recast as crime. They theorise that the criminalisation of everyday life is a cultural enterprise of the powerful and must be investigated as such (Ferrell & Sanders, 1995, p. 7). Similarly, Presdee's (2000) analysis of carnival desire and the sensuality of wickedness demonstrates how our everyday/night responses to late modernity come to be defined as criminal. Analogising mediated crime to the board game Monopoly, Presdee examines the way in which crime, like monopoly capitalism, is dehistoricised, whitewashed, and transmogrified into mass-marketed pleasure. Citing a range of examples, from Internet bondage sites and arson to stolen-car racing and weapon bazaars, Presdee explores the contradictions and irrationality of a commodity-oriented society from which criminalised culture emanates.

More recently, cultural criminologists have been attentive to the processes and products associated with what they have variously described as the "marketing of transgression" (Hayward 2004) and the "commodification of violence" (Ferrell, Hayward, & Young, 2008). This visual representation of crime and transgression, they argue, is not only central to the production of news but now a vital component of the entertainment media—gripping the collective imagination of television viewers, moviegoers, Internet browsers, video gamers, and other audiences. To a certain extent, of course, there is nothing intrinsically new about the use of this type of imagery in the service of consumerism; certainly crime and violence have been used to sell movie tickets, TV programs, video games, and music for decades. However, what is new, as Ferrell, Hayward, and Young illustrate, is the force and range of these "illicit" messages (2008, p. 140) and the effect this has had on the tectonic landscape of the late-modern entertainment media. In particular, there appears to be a far greater willingness among *mainstream corporations* to utilise allusions to crime and transgression to give their products edgy appeal whilst still serving the conservative interests of consumer capitalism and its control functions. Considering late capitalism's oligopolistic media ownership patterns, it is perhaps not surprising that the same racialised and class-biased images of the new "dangerous classes" (i.e., chavs and hoodies in Canada and the United Kingdom; ghetto-fabulous bangers in the United States) that are meant to frighten the public on the news are also now employed to entertain us and sell us a host of products and services.

CONCLUSION: NOTHING TO LOSE BUT OUR CHAINS

This chapter's epigram from the enormously popular video/PC game *Grand Theft Auto IV* poignantly illustrates the harsh and unforgiving landscape of late modernity. Whilst the narrative framing of the Bellic cousins is fictional, the brutality of capitalism that undergirds the storybound Liberty City is all too real in 21st-century America. Inexplicably, orthodox criminology continually fails to address this crimogenesis.

Irrespective of whether we conceptualise such a paucity of attention as obstinacy or as benign neglect, the end result differs little; the material conditions that influence our lives—and, indeed, the single most influential factor not only in the production, distribution, and consumption of crime but a driving force that has transformed human existence more in the last 200 years than anything in the previous millennia—remain unstudied by our discipline.

If there is a silver lining to this cloud, it is that late-modern capitalism's multiple appendages, coupled with orthodox criminology's inability/unwillingness to address it, leaves many openings available to those inclined to challenge the hegemony of these twin sacred cows. Certainly, from environmental racism and the prison industrial complex through the disappearance of work and crimes of globalisation, the fissures are legion.

The intention of this chapter, as astute readers likely surmised several pages back, was to provide neither a comprehensive assessment nor, for that matter, a general overview of the literature on crime and economics. In fact, some readers may be uncomfortable with this chapter's leap from Marx and Bonger to a 21st-century criminology of capitalism. I am among them.[13] However, my intention here was to produce not a definitive piece but rather a heuristic tool through which readers can intellectually and politically confront the intersecting convenient fictions of late capitalism and orthodox criminology. As such, perhaps much of this chapter was superfluous; perhaps all that was required was the epigram.

DISCUSSION QUESTIONS

1. Other than the specific disciplinary constraints intimated by the author, why has American criminology failed to adequately address capitalism?

2. The author cites *Grand Theft Auto IV* as a crime–capitalism narrative. Draw on your own experiences with popular culture texts to provide another example.

3. Make a list of several street crimes and white-collar, corporate, or state crimes, and illustrate their connections to capitalism.

4. The author enumerates several examples of how capitalism fosters contradictory forms of human behaviour. Provide examples of other such contradictions.

NOTES

1. *Grand Theft Auto IV*, www.gta4.net
2. See, for example, William Chambliss (1989).
3. The article was the third of three that Marx was commissioned to write on the Proceedings of the Sixth Rhine Province Assembly for *The Rheinische Zeitung*. The paper published only the first and the third.
4. "Capital Punishment" (February 18, 1853) and "Population Crime and Pauperism" (September 16, 1859).
5. See Bonger (1916, pp. 673–700).
6. Sadly, instead of translations of these, English-language criminology was introduced to the racist, misogynistic, and bigoted work of Lombroso and other biodeterminist European criminologists. The seeding of this "pathological" theory to the American criminological canon was certainly fuelled by, and served as an accelerant for, the eugenics movement and facilitated the growth of a home-grown pathological school (ex. Henry Goddard, Ernest Hooton, Eleanor and Sheldon Glueck).
7. In the intervening years, the paradigm alternately came to be known as radical or Marxist criminology. Today, it is generally referred to as critical criminology and encompasses a variety of traditions, including left realist, peacemaking, social justice, anarchist, convict, state, feminist and cultural criminologies.
8. A parallel but perhaps slightly more effervescent trajectory also emerged in the United Kingdom at this time, including the work of Stanley Cohen, Stuart Hall, Carol Smart, Ian Taylor, Paul Walton, and Jock Young.
9. See Selke, Corsaros, & Selke (2002).
10. *Trainspotting* (1996), a screenplay by John Hodge based on Irvine Welsh's novel.
11. Many of the same structural conditions that facilitate the crimes by the capitalist state abroad also contribute to the social harms it inflicts on people in America (see Tifft & Sullivan, 1980).
12. Published as a novel in 1516, St. Thomas More's *Utopia* described a land of economic equality.
13. Among my most egregious offences herein is relegating the rich, vibrant work of many of America's founding conflict criminologists to passing references and footnotes. It was a conscious decision made in keeping with space limitations. I hope that readers can take more from the chapter than a redundant and woefully incomplete history lesson.

REFERENCES

Bauman, Z. (2000). *Liquid modernity*. Cambridge, UK: Polity Press.

Bauman, Z. (2007). Collateral casualties of consumerism. *Journal of Consumer Culture, 7*(1), 25–56.

Bonger, W. A. (1905). *Criminalite et Conditions Economiques*. Amsterdam: G. P. Tierie.

Bonger, W. A. (1916). *Criminality and economic conditions* (F. H. Norcross, Trans.). Boston: Little, Brown.

Bourdieu, P. (1984). *Distinction: A social critique of the judgement of taste*. Cambridge, MA: Harvard University Press.

Chambliss, W. (1989). On trashing Marxist criminology. *Criminology, 27*(2), 231–238.

Cohen, S. (1972). *Folk devils and moral panics: The creation of the Mods and Rockers*. Oxford, UK: Blackwell.

Cohen, S., & Young, J. (Eds.). (1973). *The manufacture of news*. Beverly Hills, CA: Sage.

Currie, E. (1997). Market, crime and community: Toward a mid-range theory of post-industrial violence. *Theoretical Criminology, 1*(2), 147–172.

Engels, F. (1845/1973) *The condition of the working-class in England*. Moscow, USSR: Progress Publishers.

Ewen, S. (1977). *Captains of consciousness: Advertising and the social roots of consumer culture*. Toronto, ON: McGraw-Hill.

Ewen, S. (1988). *All consuming images: The politics of style in contemporary culture*. New York: Basic Books.

Ferrell, J., Hayward, K., & Young, J. (2008). *Cultural criminology. An invitation*. London: Sage.

Ferrell, J., & Sanders, C. (Eds.).(1995). *Cultural criminology*. Boston: Northeastern University Press.

Greenberg, D. (Ed.). (1981). *Crime and capitalism*. Palo Alto, CA: Mayfield.

Hall, S. Critcher, C., Jefferson, T., Clarke, J., & Roberts, B. (1978). *Policing the crisis: Mugging, the state and law and order*. London: Macmillan.

Hall, S., & Winlow, S. (2004). "Barbarians at the Gate": Crime and violence in the breakdown of the pseudo-pacification process. In J. Ferrell, K. Hayward, W. Morrison, & M. Presdee (Eds.), *Cultural criminology unleashed* (pp. 275–286). London: Glass House Press.

Hall, S., Winlow, S., & Ancrum, C. (2008). *Criminal identities and consumer culture: Crime, exclusion and the new culture of narcissism*. Devon, UK: Willan.

Hayward, K. (2004). *City limits: Crime, consumer culture and the urban experience*. London: Glass House Press.

Hayward, K., & Presdee, M. (2009). *Framing crime: Cultural criminology and the image*. London: Routledge.

Hayward, K., & Yar, M. (2006). The "chav" phenomenon: Consumption, media and the construction of a new underclass. *Crime, Media, Culture, 2*(1), 9–28.

Horkheimer, M., & Adorno, T. (1946/1972) *The dialectic of enlightenment*. New York: Herder and Herder.

Lasch, C. (1979). *The Culture of narcissism: American life in an age of diminishing expectations*. New York: W. W. Norton.

Liazos, A. (1972). The poverty of the sociology of deviance: Nuts, sluts and preverts. *Social Problems, 20*, 103–120.

Marx, K. (1863/1969). *Theories of surplus value*. London: Lawrence and Wishart.

Marx, K., & Engels, F. (1846/1976) *The German ideology*. Moscow, USSR: Progress Publishers.

Merton, R. (1938). Social structure and anomie. *American Sociological Review, 3*(5), pp. 672–682.

More, T. (1516/1965) *Utopia* (P. Turner, Trans.). Harmondsworth, UK: Penguin Books.

Muzzatti, S. (2003). Anarchy against the curriculum. In M. Schwartz & M. Maume (Eds.), *Teaching the sociology of deviance* (5th ed., pp. 9–14). Washington, DC: American Sociological Association.

Muzzatti, S. (2004). Criminalising marginality and resistance: Marilyn Manson, Columbine and cultural criminology. In J. Ferrell, K. Hayward, W. Morrison, & M. Presdee (Eds.), *Cultural criminology unleashed* (pp. 143–153). London: Glass House Press.

Muzzatti, S. (2005). Bits of falling sky and global pandemics: Moral panic and severe acute respiratory syndrome (SARS). *Illness, Crisis and Loss, 13*(2), 117–128.

Muzzatti, S. (2006). Cultural criminology: A decade and counting of criminological chaos. In W. DeKeseredy & B. Perry (Eds.), *Advancing critical criminology: Theory and application* (pp. 63–81). Lanham, MD: Lexington Books.

Muzzatti, S. (2008). They sing the body ecstatic: Television commercials and captured music. In M. Pomerance & J. Sakeris (Eds.), *Popping culture* (5th ed, pp. 191–201). Toronto, ON: Pearson.

Muzzatti, S. (Forthcoming). Drive it like you stole it: Imagery and automobile advertisements. In K. Hayward & M. Presdee (Eds.), *Framing crime: Cultural criminology and the image,* London: Routledge.

Presdee, M. (2000). *Cultural criminology and the carnival of crime*. London: Routledge.

Selke, W., Corsaros, N., & Selke, H. (2002). A working class critique of criminological theory. *Critical Criminology, 11*(2), pp. 93–112.

Taylor, I. (1983). *Crime, capitalism, and community*. Toronto, ON: Butterworths.

Taylor, I. (1999). *Crime in context: A critical criminology of market societies*. Boulder, CO: Westview Press.

Tifft, L., & Sullivan, D. (1980). *The struggle to be human: Crime, criminology and anarchism*. Orkney, UK: Cienfuegos Press.

Wilson, W. J. (1987). *The truly disadvantaged: The inner city, the underclass, and public policy*. Chicago: University of Chicago Press.

Young, J. (1999). *The exclusive society*. London: Sage.

Young, J. (2007). *The vertigo of late modernity*. London: Sage.

10

Sex Crimes

Mary Maguire

John and Sage were only 14 years old when they met. Like many adolescents, they responded to hormones and their need for attention by engaging in a sexual relationship. Their relationship was short lived, and unfortunately for John, methamphetamine was his method of choice for soothing loneliness and depression. After several encounters with law enforcement through his teens and twenties, John eventually entered a rehabilitation center and became clean and sober by his 29th birthday. He was working his 12-step program and enjoying his work in construction when he received an unexpected call from Sage, his childhood girlfriend of 15 years past. Their sexual relationship had resulted in a daughter, of whom John was unaware. Sage reported that their daughter, Carissa, now age 14 herself, was out of control and too much for Sage to handle. Under duress, John agreed to help by allowing Carissa to live with him. The transition was difficult; although Carissa was John's biological daughter, they were strangers to each other. Carissa used drugs and regularly skipped school. The stress of responsibility for a child whom he could not control was more than John could manage with new sobriety, and he soon relapsed into methamphetamine use. With both John and Carissa using drugs and often home together, their relationship did not resemble a typical parent–child union. Carissa felt like she was falling in love with John and began to make sexual advances toward him. Eventually, the two entered into a full sexual relationship, which continued for over a year. Today, Carissa is in foster care, and John is serving time in prison for his sex crime.

Unlike John, Mark does not have a history of drug use. His family owns a successful business in the community, and Mark worked for his father. Uncomfortable with confrontation, Mark was a passive adolescent who grew into a passive man. In his everyday life, Mark was overly conciliatory and found maintaining relationships with women difficult. As a result, he began to use prostitutes to meet his sexual needs. The anonymity of the prostitutes allowed Mark to show emotions in a way that he could not with friends and family. As a result, his encounters with prostitutes became dangerous. After securely locking the women he chose in his spare warehouse, he would rape, humiliate, assault, and terrorize his victims. Wanting to believe that his victims enjoyed the act, Mark sent them to the bathroom to wash their faces and "clean up" if they cried too much. Fearing for their lives or safety, as chain saws were always within reach, Mark's victims complied. Mark served time in prison for his sex crimes and is now in the community on parole.

Stories like John's and Mark's are only a part of what we regularly ingest through multiple media venues regarding sexuality and sex crimes. As consumers, we are inundated with sexual images. Whether it is the prepubescent children, like Carissa, in the Calvin Klein advertisements, the cleavage displayed on the covers of magazines sold in grocery stores, or the senior adult couples in the TV commercials for any number of pharmaceuticals, we are fed a steady diet of sexual images. We are equally intrigued by the steady narrative of sexual missteps of the power elite. Presidents, senators, congressmen, governors, and mayors alike are guilty; we listen to a seemingly never-ending stream of stories, from dalliances to misdemeanor sex crimes. Our interest in sexual deviance, however, has not informed our understanding of it. One might wonder if it is our ingestion of media spin regarding sexual deviance or our general lack of understanding of sex crimes that has allowed sweeping sex-crime legislation to proliferate in the past 10 years. Ironically, more stringent sex-offender management policies, such as residency restrictions, public notification laws, chemical castration, and GPS monitoring (Levenson, 2007), are being implemented as the rates of sex crimes decline. Data from the Federal Bureau of Investigation's (FBI) report *Crime in the United States, 1986–2005*, show that sexual offenses against adolescents dropped by 79%, and the number of cleared cases against children of all ages declined by 39%.

It is unclear to what extent stringent postprison management techniques keep communities safe by helping offenders reintegrate as a responsible, contributing members of society. Considerable work has been done on identifying types of offenders, on understanding motivations and drives of offenders, and on the effects of the justice system response to offenders. This chapter discusses each of these areas and then asks readers to consider the implications of our present-day understanding of sex offenders.

Sex Crimes Defined

Statutory definitions of sexual assault vary from state to state. A *sexual assault* is a statutory offense that occurs when one person, either by force or by threat, causes another person to engage in any form of sexual act. Sexual assault often occurs when one person touches another in a sexual way; however, touching does not have to occur for an act to be considered a sexual offense. Simply to offend or annoy another person sexually is considered a sexual offense. For example, exhibitionism—an act wherein a person exposes him- or herself in a sexual way to another person, who is unwilling—is a sex crime with no physical contact.

Did You Know?

1. Convicted rape and sexual assault offenders serving time in state prisons report that two thirds of their victims were under the age of 18, and 58%—or nearly 4 in 10 imprisoned violent sex offenders—said their victims were age 12 or younger.
2. In 90% of the rapes of children under 12 years old, the child knew the offender, according to police-recorded incident data.
3. Among victims 18 to 29 years old, two thirds had a prior relationship with the rapist.
4. Four datasets (the FBI's *Uniform Crime Reports* arrests, state felony court convictions, prison admissions, and the National Crime Victimization Survey) indicate that most sex offenders are older than other violent offenders, generally in their early thirties, and more likely to be white than other violent offenders.

Source: Data from *Sexual Offenses and Offenders*, by L. Greenfeld (1997), Bureau of Justice Statistics.

There is no single profile for perpetrators. Sexual assault takes many forms and definitions, which may vary from state to state. Several researchers have created typologies of sexual offenders and sex crimes (Groth, 1979; Hale, 1997; Knight & Prentky, 1990). Sex offenders are largely categorized as rapists, child molesters, female offenders, juvenile offenders, and cyber offenders. This chapter focuses primarily on rapists, child molesters, and cyber offenders. Reliable information about offense rates of female offenders is hard to obtain, as sexual victimization is significantly underreported. National statistics indicate that fewer than 10% of those arrested for sex crimes are women (FBI, 2006). As such, this chapter uses the pronoun *he* to refer to offenders, but the reader should be aware that, although their numbers are small, some sex offenders are women.

Rape

The U.S. Department of Justice defines *rape* as "unlawful sexual inter-course with a female, by force or without legal or factual consent" (FBI, 2002, p. 29). Although researchers' categorizations of rape have provided useful explanatory power, standard definitions follow the statutes and are outlined by the *Uniform Crime Reports*. They are (1) forcible rape, (2) statu-tory rape, and (3) rape by fraud. *Forcible rape* is the carnal knowledge of a female by force and against her will. This includes assaults as well as attempts to commit rape by force or threat of force. *Statutory rape* is the carnal knowl-edge of a girl under statutory age (usually between 16 and 18 years of age, depending on the state of residence) with or without her consent. This per-tains exclusively to sexual intercourse and not to other types of sexual con-tact. *Rape by fraud* is engagement in a sexual act or relationship with a consenting adult female under fraudulent conditions or false pretenses.

While an understanding of statutory definitions is imperative, an under-standing of the nuances of offenders is vital for assessing future risks of indi-viduals. The Massachusetts Treatment Center (MTC) has a unique ability to increase our understanding of sex crimes, for it houses exclusively those who are civilly committed subsequent to being identified as sexually dangerous, as well as state inmates who are sex offenders. After extensive work with these offenders, researchers at the MTC have developed an empirically based model of rape typologies that has been tested both inside the MTC (Knight & Prentky, 1987) and by outside researchers (Barbaree, Seto, Serin, Amos, et al., 1994; Harris, Rice, & Quinsey, 1994). The model, called the Massachusetts Treatment Center Rapist Typology Version 3 (MTC:R3), places rapists in four categories according to motivation (opportunistic, pervasively angry, sexual, and vindictive). The model further separates these four groups into nine sub-types. The subtypes are differentiated by six temperamental or cognitive dimen-sions (aggression, impulsivity, social competence, sexual fantasies, sadism, and naïve cognitions or beliefs). These categories provide rough profiles and insight into offender motivation.

The *vindictive rapist* is an individual who directs his anger toward an undeserving target. His offenses are motivated not by sexual feelings but by anger; therefore, he is violent and aggressive in his attack. In the absence of any sexual feelings, this offender rapes to harm, humiliate, or degrade women. He usually rapes strangers; however, his victims might possess par-ticular traits that either trigger or appeal to the offender (for example, Asian women, blonde women, or victims with a particular body type). Additionally, simply due to his own affect, he is more likely to behave violently toward women in his everyday life.

Similarly, the *pervasively angry rapist* is marked by anger that pervades each area of his life and is not gender specific. These individuals often have a long history of childhood and adult antisocial behavior and exercise random violence in their lives. Their attacks are often unplanned and without premeditation. Their offenses are characterized by extreme violence, and they cause significant injury to their victims.

Unlike the vindictive rapist and the pervasively angry rapist, the *nonsadistic sexually motivated rapist* is motivated not by anger but by feelings of inadequacy. His ability to overpower and gain control of a victim helps him compensate for various feelings of impotence. The sexually motivated rapist is often shy and lacks social skills. Through rape, he can "prove" not only sexual adequacy but his own self-importance. His assaults are committed in response to sexual arousal produced by stimuli in the environment. The sexually motivated rapist, sometimes referred to as the "gentleman rapist," is likely to fantasize that the victim will enjoy the sex and return to him for more, even if she resisted the first time. We see these offender characteristics in the case study of Mark at the beginning of the chapter. Mark allowed his unexpressed anger and feelings of powerlessness to motivate him. His assaults had characteristics of the pervasively angry rapist and later escalated to resemble sadistic behavior.

The *sadistic sexually motivated rapist* combines sexual arousal with pain and violence in order to commit the act. This offender often believes that women enjoy being controlled and dominated by men. He is more likely to beat, violate, and possibly kill his victims. He is more likely to be involved in domestic disputes and has difficulty being loyal in committed relationships.

Last, the *opportunistic rapist* engages in spontaneous rape when the opportunity presents itself. Marked by impulsivity, he views the victim strictly as a sexual object. Although he does not necessarily employ overt aggression, he has no concern for his victim's fear or pain. Motivated only by his own desire, he will use no more force than necessary to gain control of the victim. With this type of offender, the rape is usually secondary to another crime, such as burglary or robbery.

Pedophilia

The clearest distinction between the rapist and the pedophile is the targeted victim. Unlike the rapist, who chooses adult women or men as victims, the pedophile is attracted to or assaults children. The term *pedophilia* encompasses acts of child molestation and sexual abuse. The American Psychiatric Association (2000) defines *pedophilia* as having recurrent and intense sexual urges toward children or experiencing sexual fantasies about children that cause distress or interpersonal problems.

The MTC has also grouped pedophiles into four categories according to their behavioral patterns: fixated pedophile, regressed pedophile, exploitative pedophile, and aggressive pedophile (Knight, Carter, & Prentky, 1989):

- The *fixated pedophile* is exclusively attracted to children, or "fixated" on a particular developmental stage. Generally, victims are between the ages of 1 and 13, and the victim is at least 5 years younger than the offender. The fixated pedophile is more likely to be socially awkward, shy, and timid toward adults. He feels more comfortable associating with children and prefers children as both sexual and social objects. Sexual contact does not occur until the child and the pedophile have become well acquainted. The fixated pedophile does not use aggression to manipulate children and generally focuses on caressing and fondling, as opposed to sexual intercourse.

- The *regressed pedophile* may not be primarily interested in children at all. For this offender, the interest in children is usually sparked by rejection or humiliation from a peer. Feelings of inadequacy related to finding a psychosexually equal partner lead this offender to target a child as a sexual partner. The offender regresses to a younger developmental stage himself to feel comfortable sexually with a child victim. He prefers female victims who do not live near him and usually seeks intercourse with his victim.

- The *exploitative pedophile* takes advantage of a child's developmental weaknesses in order to receive sexual pleasure. He is less concerned about the child as an individual and is solely motivated by a desire for sexual dominance. He is more likely to molest stranger victims and will use aggression and physical force. Due to his impulsive nature, this offender is more likely to have a prior criminal record.

- The *sadistic pedophile* uses the infliction of pain and violence on his victims to become sexually aroused. This offender generally has a long history of violence beginning in early adolescence. He may prefer same-sex relationships and is often responsible for child abductions and murders.

Cyber Offenders

The *cyber offender* is an individual who uses the Internet in the commission of a sexual offense. In some cases, Internet offenders exhibit a more addictive personality than the so-called classic offender (Young, 2005). However, just as with classic sex offenders, there is considerable variation in cyber offenders, who range from the online stalker to the child-porn website operator. They are typically well versed in the use of the Internet.

The majority of cyber sex crimes involve adolescent victims, not younger children, and only about 5% of offenders use deception to manipulate their victims. About 80% are honest and direct about their intent to engage in sexual activity. Most of the victims in these cases are at-risk teens who crave romance and affection or sexual information and understanding (Mitchell, Finkelhor, & Wolak, 2003).

Cyber offenders might be individuals with no criminal record or indication of an interest in children (Young, 2005). Some have occupations that provide opportunities to work with children (Robertiello & Terry, 2007), but the Internet provides an anonymous forum for exploration of a range of fantasies. Cyber sex offender typologies are not as well studied, but there have been some significant attempts to increase understanding. The police department in Keene, New Hampshire, completed a 3-year law enforcement project in 2000 that resulted in the arrest of 200 cyber offenders and developed a typology for Internet sex offenders. The Keene project delineated four categories of online offenders: the chatter, the manufacturer, the traveler, and the collector:

- The *chatter* chats online and engages in online grooming and sexual conversation, commonly referred to as *cyber sex*. This contact often escalates from contact online to phone contact and can lead to a face-to-face meeting.
- Unlike the chatter, the *manufacturer* makes child pornography. He takes photos of children in public or in his own home and posts them online. He may collect child erotica instead of pornography.
- The *collector* is often single and socially isolated. He collects and trades sexually explicit photos and child pornography. He looks for specific characteristics in his victims and often has a job with access to children.
- The *traveler* often fits the MTC "fixated" typology and is most often thought of when cyber offenders are discussed. He targets adolescents and engages in extensive "grooming" behavior to build a relationship through online chat. He will travel to his target or pay for the child to travel, which usually culminates in a face-to-face meeting. This offender is often a collector of pornography.

Theoretical Explanations

Understanding the differences between sex offenders helps us to develop more targeted treatment strategies and community safety procedures. These typologies also point to differences in motivation and drive of offenders, and their distinct characteristics also contribute to our theoretical understanding of sexual offending.

Multiple single-factor theories exist to aid our understanding of sexual offending. *Developmental theories* illuminate the difficulties with age-appropriate attachment and with adult intimacy experienced by sex offenders. Caregiver inconsistency at early developmental stages has been found to be a predictor of the degree of sexual violence perpetrated in adulthood (Prentky, Knight, & Lee, 1997). Resultant attachment disorders can include severe anxiety, distrust of others, insecurity and lack of ego strength, dysfunctional anger, and an inability to develop healthy adult relationships. Individuals who lack normal adult social skills are more likely than healthy adults to use children to fulfill psychosexual needs.

The *biosocial theory* also provides an explanation for inappropriate sexual activity. Hormonal levels, in particular an increase in testosterone, are associated with increased sex drive as well as with aggression (Walsh, 2002). Some argue that a biosocial explanation points to a predisposition of some offenders toward unusual sexual preferences.

Due to the nature and variance of sex crimes, *multifactor theories* provide a more robust explanation of the complexity of sexual offending. The *integrated theory* (Marshall & Barbaree, 1990) provides a comprehensive model for understanding sexual offending. This theory asserts that negative early life influences, such as poor or violent parenting, negatively affect one's self-esteem and the ability to manage emotions, to solve problems, and to form meaningful relationships. Consequently, normal adolescent developmental milestones cannot be successfully met, and individuals experience peer rejection and social isolation. This, in turn, exacerbates their existing vulnerabilities at a time when they are experiencing heightened hormonal changes and developing sexual feelings. The inability to successfully learn the skills to manage new sexual feelings and to develop adult relationships leaves socially compromised individuals to resort to unhealthy ways to meet their needs and manage their impulses.

Other theorists (Malamuth, 1996; Malamuth, Heavey, & Linz, 1996) have developed the confluence model, which also provides significant explanatory power regarding sexual offending. This model is based on three primary components: motivators, disinhibitors, and opportunities. Like the integrated theory, the confluence model asserts that individuals who are exposed to childhood physical and sexual abuse will be more vulnerable to developing antisocial coping skills and will be challenged to form healthy adult relationships. The confluence model asserts that individuals who suffer severe and persistent abuse are more likely to develop a delinquent orientation that leads either to the use of sexual power to elevate their peer status or to aggression toward women as a means of domination, control, and humiliation.

Criminal Justice Response to Sex Crimes

In some cases, laws that direct sexual contact between adults are useful in protecting human dignity and community safety. For example, in *Lawrence v. Texas* (2003), the Supreme Court ruled that sodomy among consenting same-sex adults is not a criminal act and sanctions the notion that consenting adults should be free to engage in nonharmful acts together in the privacy of their own homes. The utility of sex crime legislation can also be seen in the states' removal of the marital rape exemption. Amendments to state marital rape laws that make it a crime to rape one's wife are a result of advocacy in the 1970s, and they add to a body of legal safeguards around sexual conduct. Unfortunately, not all legislation that intends to ensure public safety necessarily does so. It is yet to be determined whether the criminal justice response to sex crimes in general provides effective legal safeguards or merely exacerbates issues surrounding sex offenders and compromises community safety.

Sex offender registration and notification laws are examples of laws of unknown utility and questionable constitutionality. Registration laws require sex offenders to register their addresses with local law enforcement. This is essentially a private exchange between the offender and law enforcement that is meant to aid law enforcement in tracking offenders. Notification laws require the offender to be listed in a community notification system that provides multiple forms of identifying information (address, demographics, a photo, and specific sex crimes committed) to the general public. These laws are intended to deter offenders from committing new sex offenses, to increase community awareness of possible danger, and to assist law enforcement in finding sex offenders if needed.

Although California implemented the nation's first sex offender registry in 1947, it was not until the high-profile rapes and murders of Polly Klaas, Megan Kanka, and Jessica Lunsford that heightened public awareness and subsequent national registration laws were enacted. The offenders in these crimes had each served prison time for a sex offense. The Kanka family heightened attention to recidivism and lobbied to have communities notified of sex offenders living nearby; Megan's Law was passed in 1994. In 1996, it was added as an amendment to the Jacob Wetterling Crimes Against Children and Sexually Violent Offender Registration Act. Through a clause in The Jacob Wetterling Act, states that do not implement a community notification program can lose 10% of their funding under the Omnibus Crime Control and Safe Streets Act of 1968.

On the 25th anniversary of the abduction and subsequent murder of Adam Walsh, son of John Walsh (host of the television program *America's Most Wanted*), President George W. Bush signed the Adam Walsh Child Protection and Safety Act of 2006. This law creates three tiers of sex offenders, representing increasing risk of dangerousness and reoffense. Tier 1 offenders must register their addresses annually for 15 years. Tier 2 offenders must register their home addresses every 6 months for 25 years; and Tier 3 offenders must register their addresses every 90 days for life. The Adam Walsh Act provides for a national registry, and failure to register is a felony.

Effects of Sex Offender Management Legislation

In the social science community, it is widely believed that sex offender legislation is not meeting its intended goals. The laws are not based on empirical evidence and were instituted without analysis of the long-term consequences to the offender or the community; they provide little evidence of true community safety (Levenson et al., 2007; Sample, 2006; Tewksbury, 2002). In particular, there have been many challenges to the Adam Walsh Act. The registry portion of the act was ruled unconstitutional by a federal judge in Florida, and the ACLU argues that this change constitutes cruel and unusual punishment by punishing sex offenders for crimes for which they have already paid.

Aside from constitutionality issues, it is not clear how the public safety is ensured. Prescott and Rockoff (2008) found that, although there is a small decrease in crime when a notification system is in place, the benefit is lost with an increased number of offenders on the registry. In other words, convicted sex offenders can become more likely to commit crime because of the associated social costs of being publicly registered. Additionally, the information provided by sex offender notification is not always accurate (Lees & Tewksbury, 2006); but even if one assumes that it is, most scholars do not believe there is a strong link between notification and a reduction in offending (Lovell, 2007; Tewksbury, 2002; Zevitz, 2006).

Similarly, Anderson and Sample (2008) found that, although people are generally aware of the registry, most people do not access the sex offender registration site to get information; the few who did took preventative measures as a result. This finding lends credence to the argument that the notification laws are not serving their ultimate goals of increasing public awareness and subsequent public self-protection.

Others, however, have found that notification laws cause considerable stress to offenders as they attempt to reintegrate into the community (Lees & Tewksbury, 2006; Levenson & Cotter, 2005). Sex offenders report harassment, social isolation, and severe social and occupational loss as a result of public notification. Residents of Long Beach, California, mobilized in 2008 to force out a group of sex offenders who had moved into their community. Similarly, the manager of a hotel in Hayward, California, forced seven sex offenders placed there by the California Department of Corrections and Rehabilitation to leave following angry calls from the community (Graham, 2006).

Another common sex offender management tool is restricted residency of offenders. Residency restrictions are sometimes referred to as "sex offender zoning laws" or "exclusionary zones," and often encompass approximately 2000–2500 feet around places where children regularly gather (such as schools and parks). Many local communities have instituted their own, sometimes stricter, residency restrictions that have forced offenders to move out of the community. In some densely populated urban areas like San Francisco, when boundaries are drawn around all schools and parks, there is virtually no room left where an offender may live.

California's Proposition 83 expanded restrictions to all sex offenders (not just those who offend against children) and passed with over 70% voter approval. Availability of housing for offenders released from California's prisons has plummeted. With a one-size-fits-all policy, a person who has been released from prison for adult rape also cannot live near a place where children regularly gather. A report of the California Sex Offender Management Board (Singer, Maguire, & Loving, 2008) found that, since the passage of Proposition 83, the number of sex offenders registered as transient had increased by 60%. This not only leads to problems with tracking paroled sex offenders, but it reduces the social stability of the offender. Factors such as employment instability and reckless behavior are known risk factors for reoffending (Hanson & Bussiere, 1998) in general. So, it behooves those entrusted with developing policy that ensures community safety to consider the total impact of their decisions. Unfortunately, residency restrictions, although popular, have not proven effective.

CONCLUSION

People are inclined to think that a sex offender is a sex offender—that he commits one type of crime. This is a myth. Sex offenders vary widely in type and motivation; some respond well to treatment, others do not. Due to significant differences in motivation and type of offender and in type and severity of offense, sex offenders pose a challenge for categorization. Public policy cannot always effectively incorporate such nuances in a way that strengthens policy. In the case of sex offender policy, public panic and legislators struggling to find solutions have led to legislation that offers limited success at best and in some cases exacerbates the problem it aims to solve.

Current policies that have led to new problems, such as the contribution of residency restrictions to sex offender homelessness, can be re-evaluated in light of the empirical evidence. Informed legislation is that which is based on evidence of efficiency. With community safety in mind, legislators have an obligation to consider new re-entry schemes for sex offenders. Darwin noted that it is not the strong who survive but those who are most adaptive to change. Change is needed with sex offender community management. With an increasing number of convicted sex offenders being released from prisons, communities need reformed policy that provides appropriate housing, treatment, and supervision for offenders; this is what will change a false sense of security to a viable and meaningful effort toward community safety.

DISCUSSION QUESTIONS

1. Using the information in the chapter, provide a possible theoretical explanation for an offender who is classified as a regressed pedophile.

2. Given the theoretical model you developed in question 1, develop a policy that would assist law enforcement and/or corrections in appropriately managing someone with this type of drive and motivation.

3. Discuss where communities might be in 5 years if nothing changes in the realm of sex offender management.

4. With your understanding of sex offender typologies and unique motivations, how should the criminal justice system have responded differently to the behavior of John and Mark? What would you recommend as an appropriate course of action regarding each of them?

REFERENCES

American Psychiatric Association. (2000). *Diagnostic and statistical manual of mental disorders* (4th ed., Text Revision DSM-IV-TR). Washington, DC: American Psychiatric Association.

Anderson, A., & Sample, L. (2008). Public awareness and action resulting from sex offender community notification laws. *Criminal Justice Policy Review, 19,* 371.

Barbaree, H., Seto, M., Serin, R., Amos, N., & Preston, D. (1994). Comparisons between sexual and nonsexual rapist subtype: Sexual arousals to rape, offense precursors, and offense characteristics. *Criminal Justice and Behavior, 21,* 95–114.

Bureau of Justice Statistics. (1998). *National crime victimization survey.* Washington, DC: Department of Justice.

Bureau of Justice Statistics. (2009). *Criminal offender statistics: Summary findings.* Retrieved on March 1, 2009, from http://www.ojp.usdoj.gov/bjs.

Federal Bureau of Investigation. (2002). *Uniform crime reports–2001.* Washington, DC: U.S. Department of Justice.

Federal Bureau of Investigation. (2005). *Crime in the United States, 1985–2005.* U.S. Department of Justice. Retrieved on February 3, 2009, from http://www.fbi.gov/ucr/05cius/offenses/clearances/index.html

Federal Bureau of Investigation. (2006). *Crime in the United States, 2005: Uniform crime reports.* Washington, DC: U.S. Department of Justice.

Graham, R. (2006, June 3) Sex offender forced out of Island Motel. *Oakland Tribune.* Retrieved on July 14, 2008, from http://www.oaklandtribune.com. In R. Loving, J. Singer, & M. Maguire. (2008). *Homelessness among registered sex offenders in California: The numbers, the risks and the response.* CASOMB Research Report. Sacramento, CA: California Department of Corrections and Rehabilitation.

Greenfeld, L. (1997). *Sexual offenses and offenders.* (NCJ–163392). U.S. Department of Justice, Bureau of Justice Statistics.

Groth, A. (1979). *Men who rape: The psychology of the offender.* New York: Plenum.

Hale, R. (1997). Motives of reward among men who rape. *American Journal of Criminal Justice, 22*(1), 101–119.

Hanson, R. K., & Bussiere, M. T. (1998). Predicting relapse: A meta-analysis of sexual offender recidivism studies. *Journal of Consulting and Clinical Psychology, 66*(2), 348–362.

Harris, G., Rice, M., & Quinsey, V. (1994). Psychopathy as a taxon: Evidence that psychopaths are a discrete class. *Journal of Consulting and Clinical Psychology, 62,* 387–397.

Knight, R., Carter, D., & Prentky, R. (1989). A system for the classification of child molesters: Reliability and application. *Journal of Interpersonal Violence, 4,* 3–23.

Knight, R., & Prentky, R. (1987). The development antecedents and adult adaptations of rapist subtypes. *Criminal Justice and Behavior, 14,* 403–426.

Knight, R., & Prentky, R. (1990). Classifying sexual offenders: The development and corroboration of taxonomic models. In W. Marshall, D. Laws, & H. Barbaree (Eds.), *The handbook of sexual assault: Issues, theories, and treatment of the offender* (pp. 23–52). New York: Plenum.

Lawrence v. Texas, 539 U.S. 558 (2003).

Lees, M., & Tewksbury, R. (2006). Understanding policy and programmatic issues regarding sex offender registries. *Corrections Today, 68*(1), 54–57.

Levenson, J. S. (2007). The new scarlet letter: Sex offender policies in the 21st century. In D. Prescott (Ed.), *Applying knowledge to practice: Challenges in the treatment and supervision of sexual abusers.* Oklahoma City: Wood 'N' Barnes.

Levenson, J. S., Brannon, Y. N., Fortney, T., & Baker, J. (2007). Public perceptions and community protection policies. *Analyses of Social Issues and Public Policy, 7*(1), 137–161.

Levenson, J. S., & Cotter, L. P. (2005). The effect of Megan's Law on sex offender reintegration. *Journal of Contemporary Criminal Justice, 21*(1), 49–66.

Lovell, E. (2007). *Megan's Law: Does it protect children?* London: Policy and Public Affairs, NSPCC.

Malamuth, N. (1996). Sexually explicit media, gender differences, and evolutionary theory. *Journal of Communication, 46*(3), 8–31.

Malamuth, N., Heavey, C., & Linz, D. (1996). The confluence model of sexual aggression: Combining hostile masculinity and impersonal sex. *Journal of Offender Rehabilitation, 23*(3), 13–37.

Marshall, W., & Barbaree, H. (Eds.). (1990). An integrated theory of the etiology of sexual offending. *The handbook of sexual assault: Issues, theories, and treatment of the offender.* New York: Plenum.

Mitchell, K. J., Finkelhor, D., & Wolak, J. (2003). The exposure of youth to unwanted sexual material on the Internet: A national survey of risk, impact, and prevention. *Youth & Society, 34*(3), 330–358.

Prentky, R., Knight, R., & Lee, A. (1997). Child sexual molestation: Research issues. NIJ Research Report. Rockville, MD: National Criminal Justice Reference Service.

Prescott, J., & Rockoff, J. (2008). Do sex offender registration and notification laws affect criminal behavior? NBER Working Paper No. 13803; 3rd Annual Conference on Empirical Legal Studies Papers; U of Michigan Law & Economics, Olin Working Paper No. 08–006. Retrieved on March 1, 2009, from http://ssrn.com/abstract=1100663

Robertiello, G., & Terry, K. J. (2007). Can we profile sex offenders? A review of sex offender typologies. *Aggression and Violent Behavior, 12*(5), 508–518.

Sample, L. L. (2006). An examination of the degree to which sex offenders kill. *Criminal Justice Review, 31*(3), 230–250.

Singer, J., Maguire, M., & Loving, R. (2008). *The Dashboard: Indicators of sex offender management board.* CASOMB Research Report. Sacramento, CA: California Department of Corrections and Rehabilitation.

Tewksbury, R. (2002). Validity and utility of the Kentucky sex offender registry. *Federal Probation, 66*(1), 21–26.

Walsh, A. (2002). *Biosocial criminology: Introduction and integration.* Cincinnati, OH: Anderson.

Young, K. (2005). Profiling online sex offenders, cyber predators, and pedophiles. *Journal of Behavioral Profiling, 5*(1), 1–19.

Zevitz, R. G. (2006). Sex offender community notification: Its role in recidivism and offender reintegration. *Criminal Justice Studies, 19*(2), 193–208.

11

Terrorism and the Criminal Justice System

Questions, Issues, and Current Applicable Law

Sharla J. "Kris" Cook

Introduction

The attacks on September 11, 2001, brought the problem of al Qaeda–based terrorism to the attention of the American public. However, the United States government and its allies have been dealing with a Middle Eastern, al Qaeda–based terrorist threat for many years. Beginning with the Iranian hostage crisis in 1979, the bombings of the American embassy and the U.S. Marine barracks in Lebanon in 1983, continuing attacks against American servicemen in Yemen and Somalia, and the first attack on the World Trade Center in New York City in 1993, America and its citizens have been targets of terrorists at home and abroad. The 1996 attack on Khobar Towers in Saudi Arabia (in which 19 Americans were killed and hundreds of others wounded), the nearly simultaneous 1998 attacks on U.S. embassies in Kenya and Tanzania, and the 2000 suicide bombing of the *USS Cole* in Yemen demonstrated a consistent and determined pattern of attack on American interests and its citizens (McCarthy & Velshi, 2006; Yungher, 2008.).

The response of the United States to this earlier terrorist threat has been widely criticized as disjointed, ineffective, uncoordinated, and unfocused (Poland, 2004; Yungher, 2008; White, 2008), and as having "neither a common response nor the resources or equipment to counter terrorism" (Poland, 2004, p. 234).

The *9/11 Commission Report* (National Commission, 2004) described multiple mistakes in the U.S. counterterrorism efforts. These failures included inadequate gathering and sharing of intelligence by the Department of Defense (DOD), the Central Intelligence Agency (CIA), the Department of Justice (DOJ), and the Federal Bureau of Investigation (FBI). The report also faulted the Immigration and Naturalization Service (INS), the Federal Aviation Administration (FAA), the State Department, and Congress for underestimating or ignoring the terrorist threat and for failing to adequately develop and deploy defensive measures to detect and counter terrorism.

After 9/11, the Bush administration determined it would not make similar mistakes. It asked Congress for the authority to take strong measures to detect and deter the terrorist threat by "break[ing] down barriers to information sharing, enabling law enforcement and intelligence personnel to share information that is needed to help connect the dots and disrupt potential terror . . . activity" (DHS, 2005, para. 2). Congress responded by passing Public Law 107-56, the Uniting and Strengthening America by Providing Appropriate Tools Required to Intercept and Obstruct Terrorism Act (USA PATRIOT Act) of 2001. The Administration also quickly obtained from Congress the joint resolution Authorization for Use of Military Forces (AUMF; Public Law 107-40, 2001), which stated that

> . . . the President is authorized to use all necessary and appropriate force against those nations, organizations, or persons he determines planned, authorized, committed, or aided the terrorist attacks that occurred on September 11, 2001, or harbored such organizations or persons, in order to prevent any future acts of international terrorism against the United States by such nations, organizations or persons. (Sec. 2a)

The sweeping authority found in the AUMF, and in legal opinions based in part on the AUMF and issued by the Justice Department Office of Legal Counsel (Johnsen, 2008), were subsequently used by the president to issue multiple " . . . military order(s) regarding the detention, treatment, and trial of individuals detained in the war on terrorism . . . and . . . (to set) the minimum standards of treatment for detainees" (Meier, 2007, p. 29). Moving beyond those who had attacked the United States on 9/11, the Bush administration declared a comprehensive Global War on Terror (GWOT) that was virtually without limits and seemingly unending. The president stated, "Our enemy is a radical network of terrorists, and every government that supports them. Our war on terror begins with al-Qaeda, but it does not end there. It will not end until every terrorist group of global reach has been found, stopped and defeated" (Bradley & Goldsmith, 2005).

The Bush administration argued that the president's authority as commander-in-chief and the authority in the AUMF gave him a virtually unlimited range of powers to prosecute the GWOT. Johnsen (2008) suggested it was the expanded interpretation of the GWOT that

. . . provided the context for [the Bush administration's] most contro-versial claims of unilateral authority: to override legal prohibitions on the use of torture and cruel, inhuman and degrading treatment; to hold "enemy combatants" indefinitely without access to counsel or any opportunity to challenge their detention; and to engage in domestic electronic surveillance without a court order. (p. 395)

It is beyond the scope of this chapter to detail all the antiterrorism actions taken by the Bush administration. Rather, this chapter focuses on the Bush administration's actions to detect terrorist plans through increased and enhanced surveillance, especially electronic surveillance methods. Additionally, this chapter focuses on the Bush administration's policies on detention, treatment, and interrogation of suspected captured and detained terrorists.

This chapter also examines legal and political challenges to the Bush administration policies on surveillance, and detention, interrogation, and treatment of suspected captured terrorists. However, before we can begin that discussion, it is important to have some understanding of just how complex the topic of terrorism is.

Researchers in multiple academic disciplines, government agencies, and private think tanks have studied the motivation and actions of terrorists. But they have yet to develop a universally accepted definition of terrorism (White, 2008; Yungher, 2008). As Combs (2006) notes, " . . . [T]errorism is a politi-cal as well as legal and a military issue, [thus] its definitions in modern terms has been slow to evolve" (p. 9).

The level of complexity in modern international terrorism is significant and makes a single definition and counterterrorism approach difficult. Whittaker (2002) noted, "The contemporary world presents terrorism in astonishing complexity and diversity" (p. 20). Badey (1998) commented on that diversity, noting that " . . . after more than thirty years of inter-governmental discourse there is still no commonly accepted definition of international terrorism" (p. 2). He suggests that governmental definitions are written to provide maximum individual agency flexibility when dealing with politically sensitive issues.

As one might expect, various federal agencies have tailored their defini-tions of terrorism to provide the maximum flexibility Badey mentions. The State Department (U.S. Department of State, 2004) defines terrorism thusly:

The term terrorism means premeditated, politically motivated violence perpetrated against noncombatant targets by subnational groups or clandestine agents, usually intended to influence an audience.

The term international terrorism means terrorism involving citizens or the territory of more than one country.

The term terrorist group means any group practicing, or that has significant subgroups that practice, international terrorism. (p. xii)

According to a statement of FBI policy on its Jackson Division website (FBI, 2001),

> The FBI defines terrorism as "the unlawful use of force or violence against persons or property to intimidate or coerce a Government, the civilian population, or any segment thereof, in furtherance of political or social objectives." The FBI further describes terrorism as either domestic or international, depending on the origin, base, and objectives of the terrorist organization. (paras. 4–5)

The DOD, the CIA, and the Defense Intelligence Agency all have different definitions of terrorism (White, 2008). There are some common themes: the *threat and/or calculated use of violence* against *innocents, civilians, or noncombatants* and suggestions that the violence is *politically motivated* or *used to intimidate and to create fear for political purposes* (Combs, 2006; Yungher, 2008). Whatever the formal definition, there is no disagreement that terrorism is a threat that must be fought aggressively and effectively.

Fighting Terrorism Effectively in a Constitutional Democracy

How does one best balance the interests of national security with the interests of liberty? Royce C. Lamberth, a former presiding judge of the Foreign Intelligence Surveillance Court (FISC; cited in Kris & Wilson, 2007), stated,

> Like many competing American values, liberty and security converge in law. We strike the balance between them not only in the many particular statutes, orders, and policies of the government, but also in the ongoing process of Legislative, Executive, and Judicial action—and reaction—within the framework prescribed by the Constitution. Our national security is therefore cast, and continually recast, in the crucible of our legal system. (p. xxxiv)

The process Lamberth describes is exactly what has happened since 9/11. The Bush administration, sometimes working with Congress, has implemented a number of statutes, executive orders, and policies designed to protect and enhance American security. Others, who are more concerned about American values and liberty than security, have mounted challenges to those statutes, orders, and policies in both Congress and the courts (Bazen, 2008). This section of the chapter highlights some of the most important issues in that process, including surveillance and detection, as well as detention, interrogation, and treatment of prisoners.

Surveillance and Detection

As noted, immediately after the 9/11 attacks, Congress and the American public appeared to give the executive branch of government broad leeway to prosecute the Global War on Terror (Johnsen, 2008). In one of the most visible measures of that support, Congress passed the USA PATRIOT Act of 2001 (Public Law 107-56, 2001).

In passing the USA PATRIOT Act, Congress clearly sought to promote the interests of national security by liberalizing intelligence gathering/sharing and by expanding the surveillance authority of government agencies. The USA PATRIOT Act consists of more than 1,000 antiterrorism measures. It expanded the government's authority to investigate terror-related threats, search premises, conduct expanded surveillance, detain suspects, and examine suspicious activities in such areas as immigration and banking. Regarding surveillance, Section 215 permits "roving wiretaps," as well as a wide range of surveillance activities, including the capability to obtain business records via warrant. These records include personal library records, e-mail records, medical treatment, websites visited, political events attended, church membership, and mental health records (Public Law 107-56, 2001).

A major change allowed sharing of investigative information between law enforcement agencies (like the FBI) and intelligence agencies (like the CIA). Section 203 of the USA PATRIOT Act (Public Law 107-56, 2001) permits

> Any investigative or law enforcement officer, to disclose . . . wire, oral, or electronic communication, or evidence derived . . . to any other Federal law enforcement, intelligence, protective, immigration, national defense, or national security official . . . foreign intelligence or counterintelligence, . . . or foreign intelligence information . . . to assist the official who is to receive that information in the performance of his official duties. (p. 280)

Critics of the USA PATRIOT Act believe that it has gone too far, both in the sharing of information between intelligence and law enforcement agencies and in expanding the ability to conduct wiretaps and other electronic searches. They claim that Section 218 of the USA PATRIOT Act " . . . substantially expanded authority to conduct wiretaps and searches under the Foreign Intelligence Surveillance Act (FISA) without probable cause of criminal activity" (Cole, 2005, para. 44). In testimony on the USA PATRIOT Act before the 2005 U.S. Senate Committee on the Judiciary, a critic of the expanded powers granted in the act asserted,

> . . . the number of FISA searches has dramatically increased since the Patriot Act was passed. Yet because of the secrecy that surrounds FISA searches, we know virtually nothing about them. The target of a FISA search is never notified that he was searched, unless evidence from the

search is subsequently used in a criminal prosecution. Even then the defendant cannot see the application for the search, and therefore cannot meaningfully test its legality in court. (para. 4)

The questions raised by critics of the Bush administration's surveillance policies rest in several areas. First, there is a concern that the expanded search authority violates the assumed right to privacy found in the 4th Amendment to the U.S. Constitution, which states,

The right of the people to be secure in their persons, houses, papers, and effects, against *unreasonable searches and seizures* [emphasis added], shall not be violated, and no Warrants shall issue, *but upon probable cause* [emphasis added], supported by Oath or affirmation, and particularly describing the place to be searched, and the persons or things to be seized. (Commission on the Bicentennial of the U.S. Constitution, 1991, p. 22)

Second, critics argued that the new laws were unnecessary, since there were already sufficient methods to conduct electronic surveillance for serious crime (that is, for espionage, treason, and violence). The Foreign Intelligence Surveillance Act of 1978 (FISA) provided procedures for acquiring judicial authorization for electronic surveillance and physical search of persons engaged in espionage or international terrorism against the United States on behalf of a foreign power. Requests are adjudicated by a special 11-member court called the Foreign Intelligence Surveillance Court (FISC). FISC oversees FBI foreign intelligence work and hears FBI applications for orders and warrants. Despite complaints of unnecessary and dangerous delays in getting surveillance warrants, since 1978 the FISC has never ruled against the government (American Bar Association, 2003).

However, the FISA process does take time and effort. As Kris (2007) noted, to get a FISA warrant, the government

. . . must establish . . . that the "target" of the surveillance . . . is a "foreign power," such as an international terrorist group, or . . . a member of an international terrorist group. Second, there must also be probable cause that the target is using, or is about to use, the particular "facility," such as a telephone number or e-mail address, at which the surveillance will be directed. Third, the government's application must propose . . . "minimization procedures" . . . designed to balance the government's need to obtain intelligence against the privacy interests of Americans. (pp. 6–7)

The FISA Act of 1978 requires the signatures of two very senior government officials (the director of the FBI and/or the U.S. attorney general are examples) for every targeted suspect and "facility," and the signature of a

FISC judge. In most cases, the surveillance cannot begin until all those officials agree that the legal requirements of the FISA Act of 1978 have been met (Kris, 2008a). The Bush administration thought that the 1978 FISA Act process was cumbersome and slow ("Spies, Lies, and FISA," 2007). Additionally, the administration suggested that the process took terrorism experts (subject matter and language experts, for example) away from their primary duties of collection and analysis in order to meet FISA requirements for justifying the requested surveillance (Kris, 2008b).

A third concern about the Bush administration surveillance programs was raised by an article published in the *New York Times* (Risen & Lichtblau, 2005), which reported that the Bush administration "*secretly* [emphasis added] authorized the National Security Agency (NSA) to eavesdrop on Americans and others inside the United States to search for evidence of terrorist activity *without the court-approved warrants* [emphasis added] ordinarily required for domestic spying . . ." The same article suggested that a classified 2002 presidential order authorized the NSA to monitor "international telephone calls and international e-mail messages of hundreds, perhaps thousands, of people inside the United States without warrants . . ." Prior to the 2002 presidential order, as the *New York Times* (2005) reported, the NSA's "mission [was] to spy on communications abroad . . . ," not to conduct surveillance of communication in and to the United States. The NSA's surveillance program ignored the 1978 FISA Act and its requirements for legal review and approval (Risen & Lichtblau, 2005).

Once the *New York Times* article broke this news, President Bush acknowledged that the National Security Agency (NSA) had been conducting surveillance of communication flowing into and out of the United States (President Bush's Weekly Radio Address, 2005). President Bush justified this program by saying, "To fight the war on terror, I am using authority vested in me by Congress, including the Joint Authorization for Use of Military Force, which passed overwhelmingly in the first week after September the 11th. I'm also using constitutional authority vested in me as Commander-in-Chief" (Radio Address, 2005). Soon afterward, Congress began a series of hearings to examine issues regarding the NSA program and modernizing the FISA program (Bazen, 2008).

This chapter does not discuss the multiple hearings and ongoing attempts to modernize the FISA. Students who want to know more are directed to an excellent article written by David Kris in 2007, *Modernizing the Foreign Intelligence Surveillance Act: A Working Paper of the Series on Counterterrorism and American Statutory Law, a joint project of the Brookings Institution, the Georgetown University Law Center, and the Hoover Institution.*

The most current modernization of the FISA law is the FISA Amendments Act of 2008. This new law expanded surveillance of persons located outside the United States who are not U.S. citizens or legal residents of the United States. No "probable cause" is required, and the government is not required to suggest that the target is a terrorist or a spy. The program does not allow the government to target American citizens directly; however, if the foreign target calls or e-mails an American citizen, that communication may be monitored (Harris, 2008, p. 28). In what has been a continuing pattern, on the same day the details of the law became publicly known, the American Civil Liberties Union (ACLU) filed a lawsuit challenging the constitutionality of the new law (ACLU, 2008a).

The USA PATRIOT Act also expanded the use of National Security Letters (NSLs). NSLs are self-issued subpoenas that allow investigators in terrorism and espionage cases to require phone companies, banks, credit reporting agencies, and Internet service providers to turn over records on Americans considered "relevant" to an investigation (ACLU, 2008b). Advocates of NSLs suggest they avoid the time and effort to get a search warrant through court order, thus allowing investigators to rapidly and thoroughly detect and deter possible terrorist activities. Specifically, the FBI (2007) noted,

> In the post-9/11 world, the National Security Letter (NSL) remains an indispensable investigative tool. NSLs contribute significantly to the FBI's ability to carry out its national security responsibilities by directly supporting its counterterrorism, counterintelligence, and intelligence missions. NSLs also allow the FBI to obtain information to eliminate concerns about individuals and close down investigations with a high degree of confidence there is no terrorism or adverse intelligence-gathering threat. (para. 1)

Federal court cases in 2007 and 2008 (the U.S. District Court for the Southern District of New York, September 2007, and the U.S. Court of Appeals for the Second Circuit, December 2008) challenged "provisions of the Patriot Act that prevent national security letter (NSL) recipients from speaking out about the secret records demands" (ACLU, 2008b, para. 1). It had been the practice of the FBI to use NSLs to demand customer records from Internet service providers and then to prohibit them from notifying the targeted individual of the request. In both court challenges, the courts found that the statute's gag provisions violated the First Amendment (ACLU, 2008b).

Although it is probably not surprising that the ACLU criticized the NSL program, *internal governmental* sources have also criticized the use and application of NSLs. A 2007 Justice Department inspector general's report (USDOJ, 2008) reportedly found system-wide failures in the issuance, tracking, and accountability of the NSLs. The report found that the FBI had used NSLs without retaining evidence showing that its data collection was legal and without ensuring that all the data obtained matched its needs or requests. The report also found that, on more than 700 occasions, the FBI had obtained telephone toll billing records or subscriber information from three telephone companies without first issuing NSLs or grand jury subpoenas. Instead, the agency had relied on "exigent letters"—that is, letters signed by personnel not authorized by statute to sign NSLs (USDOJ, 2008). It seems apparent that such mistakes undermine confidence in the government's capability to police itself in its detection and surveillance programs.

In the face of that loss of confidence and continued criticism of the USA PATRIOT Act, the U.S. Department of Homeland Security (DHS) released a statement highlighting many of the national security benefits it provides. DHS argued that those benefits include allowing (CIA) intelligence officers and law enforcement officials (FBI) to *share information* to prevent future attacks. The DHS suggested that the updated laws enabled law enforcement to fight a digital-age battle against terrorists who are ahead of us with new technology (DHS, 2005).

In 2005, Congress began a series of hearings to renew the PATRIOT Act. After months of legislative deadlock, the Senate and the House of Representatives finally agreed to pass legislation renewing most of the act. The new law kept most of the original PATRIOT Act, including "16 expiring provisions of the original PATRIOT Act, including one that allows federal officials to obtain . . . records, including those from libraries and bookstores" (Congress Renews, 2006, para. 16).

It seems clear that there will be continued challenges to the USA PATRIOT Act and to other statutes, executive orders, and policies that have guided the government's surveillance and intelligence gathering activities in the post-9/11 world. Those challenges may come from Congress or from the courts. As Reinhardt (2008) noted, "In times of national emergency, courts are likely to view issues almost entirely from a pragmatic standpoint and to give even greater deference to the judgment of the executive branch than in peacetime"; however, he continued, "deference does not mean abdication" (p. 968).

Proponents of both security and liberty have also focused on other issues in the War on Terror, including detention, interrogation, and treatment of prisoners. Their actions in "the ongoing process of Legislative, Executive, and Judicial action—and reaction—within the framework prescribed by the Constitution" (Lamberth, p. xxxiv; cited in Kris & Wilson, 2007) are detailed in the next section.

_____ Detention and Treatment of Suspected Terrorists

Following the attacks on 9/11, under authority of the AUMF President Bush sent U.S. military forces into Afghanistan to target al Qaeda terrorist training camps and al Qaeda leaders. U.S. military forces soon captured and detained Afghan fighters. Questions arose regarding what to do with those captured fighters. Specifically, where should they be held and for how long, and how should they be treated during interrogations (Meier, 2007)? Initially, the Bush administration's position was that the Geneva Convention did not apply to those captured in Afghanistan (Gonzales, 2002, as cited in Jackson, Jensen, & Matsuishi, 2007).

Generally, the United States follows a series of international treaties and international and domestic laws to determine the rules for detention and treatment of personnel captured in a wartime environment. Those international treaties and laws include The Hague Conventions, the Geneva Conventions, various United Nations Conventions, the War Crimes Act of 1996, and the Uniform Code of Military Justice. The treatment of captured personnel depends, in large part, upon their status (Reisman & Antoniou, 1994).

For example, specific privileges (multiple protections) are given to those who qualify as prisoners of war (POWs). Multiple rules, detailed in the Geneva Conventions, govern who qualifies as a POW. The Geneva Prisoner of War (GPW) Conventions Common Article 3 states that signatories must treat POWs humanely, without adverse distinction based on race, color, or religion (Elsea, 2002). Violence, murder, mutilation, cruel treatment, and torture are prohibited, as are outrages upon personal dignity—"in particular, humiliating and degrading treatment, are prohibited" (Elsea, 2007). Article 17 of the GPW provides that "prisoners of war who refuse to answer may not be threatened, insulted, or exposed to any unpleasant or disadvantageous treatment of any kind" (cited in Elsea, 2002, p. 32). Further, "Torture is not permitted in the case of any detainee, regardless of that person's status" (Elsea, 2007, p. 32).

The United Nations Convention Against Torture also prohibits both torture and "cruel, inhuman, and degrading treatment" (p. CRS-13). Further, it states that "no exceptional circumstances whatsoever . . . may be invoked as justification of torture" (Garcia, 2008, p. CRS-3). The War Crimes Act imposes criminal penalties in the United States for breaches of Geneva Conventions that protect detainees anywhere. The acts prohibited in the War Crimes Act include violations of Common Article 3 of the GPW (Garcia, 2007). The Federal anti-torture statute, 8 U.S.C. Section 2340A (1994), also provides for prosecution of U.S. nationals or anyone within the United Sates who commits or attempts to commit torture while outside the United States (U.S. Code Collection, 2009).

As Meier (2007) noted, following internal debate about the status of captured al Qaeda and Taliban detainees, the Bush administration decided that "none of the provisions of the Geneva Conventions applied to the conflict with al Qaeda in 'Afghanistan or elsewhere throughout the world'" (Bush, 2007, quoted in Meier, 2007, p. 30). Meier also reported that "President Bush found that the provisions of the Geneva Convention would apply to the Taliban" (p. 30). Meier went on to explain that the United States characterized captured al Qaeda fighters as "unlawful enemy combatants . . . with many released; others . . . detained in Afghanistan and Iraq [and] . . . The 'worst of the worst' . . . selected for detention . . ." (p. 30) at the military prison at Guantanamo Bay, Cuba. The Bush administration's conclusion that the detainees were "unlawful combatants" meant that such persons could be detained indefinitely, could be tried by military commissions, and were not entitled to any of the prisoner of war protections found in the GPW (Meier, 2007).

Meier further suggested that the Bush administration chose the Guantanamo Bay prison to hold the detainees "to ensure that they would not be entitled to U.S. judicial review of their status" (p. 31), because the administration asserted that Guantanamo Bay was outside the jurisdiction of U.S. courts.

As noted earlier, the GPW provides that "prisoners of war who refuse to answer may not be threatened, insulted, or exposed to any unpleasant or disadvantageous treatment of any kind" (cited in Elsea, 2007, p. 32); Elsea further states, "Torture is not permitted in the case of any detainee, regardless of that person's status" (ibid.). However, the Bush administration was worried that al Qaeda had more attacks planned against America. They also believed that al Qaeda might attempt such attacks using weapons of mass destruction. Administration officials believed it was critical to capture and question al Qaeda operatives to detect and deter those future attacks. They deemed this information "actionable intelligence." Refusing to grant GPW status to al Qaeda operatives meant, in the administration's view, that "aggressive interrogation methods" would not violate the principles of the GPW, other international treaties, or U.S. law (Karl, 2008; Miller, 2008; Taylor, 2003).

Advocates of granting the executive branch sweeping powers to prosecute the GWOT have argued that the scope of constitutional rights must be conservatively interpreted and have suggested that personal liberties must be limited in a time of national emergency (Posner, 2006). Taylor (2003) argued,

> When dangers increase, liberties shrink. That has been our history, especially in wartime. And today we face dangers without precedent: a mass movement of militant Islamic terrorists who crave martyrdom, hide in shadows, are fanatically bent on slaughtering as many of us as possible and—if they can—using nuclear truck bombs to obliterate New York or Washington or both, without leaving a clue as to the source of the attack. (para. 1)

The "Torture Memo"

On the other hand, critics of the Bush administration's policies on detention and treatment of suspected terrorists believe the administration went too far in implementing executive legal interpretations that were not supported by congressional action or judicial review (Johnsen, 2008).

One example cited by Johnsen (2008) is the infamous "torture memo" issued by the Office of Legal Counsel in the Justice Department. That secret 2002 memo "concluded the President, as Commander-in-Chief, possessed the Constitutional authority to authorize government officials to engage in torture, not withstanding a federal statute that criminalized such action" (p. 403). The memo offered an opinion that U.S. law "prohibits only the worst forms of cruel, inhuman or degrading treatment," (Gellman & Becker, 2007, para. 15) and further narrowed the definition of torture, stating that it "must be equivalent in intensity to the pain accompanying serious physical injury, such as organ failure, impairment of bodily function, or even death" (Priest & Smith, 2004, para. 8).

Priest and Smith (2004) noted that the Pentagon had issued similar guidance for military personnel conducting interrogations of suspected terrorists. According to their article in the *Washington Post*, despite a 1994 U.S. law that "bars torture by U.S. military personnel anywhere in the world" (para. 25), a Pentagon working group report concluded that, consistent with President Bush's authority as commander-in-chief, "the 1994 law barring torture 'does not apply to the conduct of U.S. personnel' at Guantanamo Bay. . . . It also said the anti-torture law did apply to U.S. military interrogations that occurred outside U.S. maritime and territorial jurisdiction, such as in Iraq or Afghanistan" (paras. 26–27). But the group also suggested that "both Congress and the Justice Department would have difficulty enforcing the law if U.S. military personnel could be shown to be acting as a result of Presidential orders" (paras. 26–27).

In October 2002, Secretary of Defense Rumsfeld approved new rules for military interrogations at Guantanamo Bay. Those new techniques included yelling at or deceiving detainees, the use of stress positions for up to four hours, the use of the isolation facility for up to 30 days, conducting interrogations lasting 20 hours and longer, removal of comfort items (including religious items), removal of clothing and forced grooming, and use of detainee's individual phobias (such as fear of dogs) to induce stress (Jehl, 2004; Wright & Reese, 2008).

Secretary Rumsfeld also approved scenarios designed to convince a detainee that death or severely painful consequences might be imminent for him or his family. He also approved exposure to cold weather or water (with appropriate medical monitoring), the use of wet towels and dripping water to induce misperception of suffocation (waterboarding), and the use of mild, noninjurious physical contact, such as grabbing, poking in the chest with a finger, and light pushing. In January 2003, Secretary Rumsfeld rescinded his earlier rules for enhanced interrogation (Jehl, 2004; Wright & Reese, 2008).

When the "torture memo" became public knowledge, the Justice Department repudiated its contents, saying, "Torture is abhorrent both to American law and values and to international norms" (quoted in Shane, Johnston, & Risen, 2007, para. 39). But in 2005, the Justice Department issued a new secret opinion which " . . . provided explicit authorization to barrage terror suspects with a combination of painful physical and psychological tactics, including head-slapping, simulated drowning and frigid temperatures" (Shane, Johnston, & Risen, 2007, para. 3).

The Detainee Treatment Act (DTA)

In 2004, photos taken by American soldiers working at the Abu Ghraib prison in Iraq—a prison run by the U.S. military—clearly depicted degrading and humiliating treatment and assaults of detainees by U.S. soldiers. When those photos were made public, the outrage was immediate. Senator John McCain, a former U.S. prisoner of war, sponsored the Detainee Treatment Act (DTA) to ban inhumane treatment of U.S.-held detainees wherever they might be held. In 2005, the DTA became law (Suleman, 2005).

The DTA established standards for interrogation and banned cruel, inhuman, or degrading treatment of detainees in the custody of any U.S. agency. At the administration's request, and in reaction to a case decided by the U.S. Supreme Court (*Rasul v. Bush*; see following section), it also denied detainees access to federal courts to file habeas corpus petitions. The administration argued that detainees in the GWOT should not have the legal protections of habeas corpus or other due process protections enjoyed by American citizens (Suleman, 2005). A writ of habeas corpus is essentially a court order requiring that a prisoner be brought before the court to determine whether there is lawful authority to hold that person. If not, the person should be released (Doyle, 2006).

Court Challenges

There have been numerous court challenges to the detention and military commission tribunal policies of the Bush administration. Several of the most important cases decided in the U.S. Supreme Court are briefly summarized here.

In 2004, the U.S. Supreme Court held in *Hamdi v. Rumsfeld* that it was the role of Congress, not the president, to authorize the detention of combatants. The Court also held that the Constitution guaranteed Hamdi (a U.S. citizen) due process rights in a military tribunal. The Bush administration had argued that Hamdi was an enemy combatant and could be detained indefinitely, without trial or other judicial hearings, until the War on Terror ended (Perkins, 2005).

Also in 2004, the U.S. Supreme Court ruled in *Rasul v. Bush* that U.S. courts have jurisdiction to hear appeals from Guantanamo Bay detainees challenging their status as enemy combatants. The Court overturned a lower court's ruling that no U.S. court has jurisdiction to hear petitions for habeas corpus on behalf of the detainees because they are aliens detained abroad (Roosevelt, 2005). As noted earlier, in reaction to the *Rasul v. Bush* ruling and at the Bush administration's urging, Congress passed the DTA with a provision that denied detainees access to federal courts to file habeas corpus petitions (Suleman, 2005).

In 2006, in *Hamdan v. Rumsfeld*, the U.S. Supreme Court found that President Bush did not have the power, independent of congressional action, to unilaterally establish military tribunals to try detainees. Additionally, they found that the Geneva Convention protections for POWs applied to all detainees at Guantanamo and other "foreign" prisons (Spiro, 2006). In response, the Department of Defense (DOD) issued policies ordering the U.S.

military to comply with Common Article 3 of the GPW in all aspects of its treatment of detainees. DOD Directive 2310.01E "provided a baseline standard of treatment for all detainees . . . and . . . was widely perceived as a repudiation of the harsh interrogation tactics and treatment standards approved subsequent to the attacks of September 11" (White, 2006, cited in Meier, 2007, p. 34).

In response to *Hamdan v. Rumsfeld*, the Bush administration sought congressional approval for its proposed military commission tribunal system to try suspected terrorists. In 2006, Congress approved the Military Commissions Act (MCA). The MCA authorized military commissions to prosecute detainees for war crimes. The MCA also stripped U.S. courts of jurisdiction to hear or consider habeas corpus appeals from anyone held as an enemy combatant. The MCA also prohibited detainees from invoking the GPW as a source of rights in U.S. Courts (Estreicher & O'Scannlain, 2006).

In 2008, the U.S. Supreme Court heard another challenge to the restrictions on habeas corpus in the case of *Boumediene et al. v. Bush*. The Court looked at four questions:

1. Should the Military Commissions Act of 2006 be interpreted to strip federal courts of jurisdiction over habeas petitions filed by foreign citizens detained at the U.S. Naval Base at Guantanamo Bay, Cuba?

2. If so, is the Military Commissions Act of 2006 a violation of the Suspension Clause of the Constitution?

3. Are the detainees at Guantanamo Bay entitled to the protection of the Fifth Amendment right not to be deprived of liberty without due process of law and of the Geneva Conventions?

4. Can the detainees challenge the adequacy of judicial review provisions of the MCA before they have sought to invoke that review? (*Boumediene et al. v. Bush*, 2007)

In a 5-to-4 majority opinion, the Court held

. . . that because the procedures laid out in the Detainee Treatment Act are not adequate substitutes for the habeas writ, the MCA operates as an *unconstitutional suspension* [emphasis added] of that writ. The detainees were not barred from seeking habeas . . . merely because they had been designated as enemy combatants or held at Guantanamo Bay. (2007)

The Latest Developments

President Obama has replaced President Bush. It appears that Obama's approach to fighting the terrorist threat may vary significantly from that of the previous administration. Within days of taking office, President Obama signed executive orders "ordering the closure of the U.S. detention camp at Guantanamo Bay, Cuba, and banning the use of controversial CIA interrogation techniques. But he left open the question of how his administration will deal with any detainees it concludes are too dangerous to be released" (Warrick & Young, 2009, para. 1).

President Obama also ordered the suspension of all judicial proceedings at Guantanamo Bay under the Bush administration's military commissions system. As Warrick and DeYoung reported, "The executive orders left maneuvering room on some Bush policies," and "military commissions established by the previous administration . . . might be preserved in some form for those detainees determined to be 'unreleasable' and 'untriable'" (para. 3). In what probably seemed an ironic twist to former Bush officials, a military judge at Guantanamo rejected Obama's request to suspend a hearing for a *USS Cole* bombing suspect (Judge, 2009). Thus, in that process that Lamberth described so eloquently, "We strike the balance between [liberty and security] . . . in the ongoing process of Legislative, Executive, and Judicial action—and reaction—within the framework prescribed by the Constitution" (p. xxxiv, cited in Kris & Wilson, 2007). Whatever its challenges, seeking that balance is how democracy works.

DISCUSSION QUESTIONS

1. Do you believe the USA PATRIOT Act encroaches on such constitutionally guaranteed freedoms as protection against illegal search and seizure?

2. What is the proper balance between violation of detainees' rights and aggressive interrogation in the interests of national security?

3. What is the proper balance between national security and the national values of fairness, justice, due process, and rule of law? The Fourteenth Amendment ensures American citizens due process if they are suspects in a criminal case.

4. Should Fourteenth Amendment rights be extended to terrorist suspects who may not be American citizens?

5. Can we detain, interrogate, and hold enough terrorists to win the War on Terror?

6. Do our methods stand up to the scrutiny of a skeptical world (especially the Muslim world), which may doubt our commitment to fairness, justice, due process, and the rule of law?

7. Can we afford not to take the measure we have taken to protect our security?

8. Suppose you had just been elected president of the United States; what would you do about the War on Terror, and what would you do to balance the competing concepts of security and liberty?

REFERENCES

Abrams, N. (2007). The U.S. crosses the Rubicon: The Military Commissions Act 2006. *Journal of International Criminal Justice, 5*(1), 2–9.

American Bar Association. (2003). *Section of individual rights and responsibilities report to the House of Delegates: Recommendation.* Retrieved on December 22, 2008, from http://www.abanet.org/leadership/recommendations03/118.pdf

American Civil Liberties Union (ACLU). (2008a). *The Foreign Intelligence Surveillance Act.* Retrieved on December 22, 2008, from http://www.aclu.org/safefree/spying/fisa.html

American Civil Liberties Union (ACLU). (2008b). *Court rules PATRIOT Act's "national security letter" gag provisions unconstitutional: ACLU hails victory in challenge to government's power to silence NSL recipients.* Retrieved on January 12, 2009, from http://www.aclu.org/safefree/nsaspying/38113prs20081215.html

Associated Press. (2009, January 29). Judge refuses to delay Gitmo detainee's trial. *MSNBC World News.* Retrieved on February 1, 2009, from http://www.msnbc.msn.com/id/28914869/

Badey, T. J. (2002). Defining international terrorism: A pragmatic approach. In T. J. Badey (Ed.), *Annual Editions: Violence and Terrorism* (pp. 32–35). Guilford, CT: McGraw-Hill/Dushkin.

Bazen, E. B. (2008). *The Foreign Intelligence Surveillance Act: An overview of selected issues.* Washington, DC: Congressional Research Service.

Boumediene et al. v. Bush, 553 U.S. _____ (2008), 128 S. Ct. 2229. Retrieved on January 22, 2009, from http://www.oyez.org/cases/2000–2009/2007/2007_06_1195/

Bradley, C. A., & Goldsmith, J. L. (2005). Congressional authorization and the war on terrorism. *Duke Law News & Events.* Retrieved on January 22, 2009, from http://www.law.duke.edu/magazine/2005spring/features/bradley.html?linker=2

Bush, G. W. (2002, February 7). *Humane treatment of al Qaeda and Taliban detainees.* (Memorandum). Retrieved from http://www.slatecom/features/whatistorturememos.html

Cole, D. (2005). *Testimony of Professor David Cole before the United States Senate Committee on the Judiciary on the USA PATRIOT Act.* Friends Committee on National Legislation [website]. Retrieved on January 5, 2009, from http://www.fcnl.org/issues/item.php?item_id=1376&issue_id=68

Combs, C. C. (2006). *Terrorism in the Twenty-First Century* (4th ed.). Upper Saddle River, NJ: Pearson, Prentice Hall.

Commission on the Bicentennial of the U.S. Constitution. (1991). The Constitution of the United States. Washington, DC: U.S. Government Printing Office.

Congress renews Patriot Act. (2006, March 7). *CBS News.* Retrieved on January 17, 2009, from http://www.cbsnews.com/stories/2006/03/07/politics/printable1380797.shtml

Department of Homeland Security. (2005). Fact sheet: The USA PATRIOT Act—a proven homeland security tool. Retrieved on October 22, 2008, from http://www.dhs.gov/xnews/releases/press_release_0815.shtm

Doyle, C. (2006). *Federal habeas corpus: A brief legal overview.* CRS report for Congress. Congressional Research Service. Retrieved on January 17, 2009, from http://www.fas.org/sgp/crs/misc/RL33391.pdf

Elsea, J. (2002). *Treatment of "battlefield detainees" in the War on Terrorism.* CRS report for Congress. Congressional Research Service. Retrieved on January 17, 2009, from http://fpc.state.gov/documents/organization/9655.pdf

Elsea, J. (2007). *Treatment of "battlefield detainees" in the War on Terrorism* (Updated). CRS report for Congress. Congressional Research Service. Retrieved on January 17, 2009, from http://www.fas.org/sgp/crs/terror/RL31367.pdf

Estreicher, S., & O'Scannlain, D. (2006). Hamdan's limits and the Military Commissions Act. *Constitutional Commentary, University of Minnesota Law School, 23*, 403–421. Retrieved on January 2, 2009, from http://web.ebscohost .com.proxy.lib.csus.edu/ehost/pdf?vid=4&hid=107&sid=342d4ade-3044-4f1d-b095-d61276458f03%40sessionmgr110s

Federal Bureau of Investigation. (2007, March 9). *Response to DOJ inspector general's report on FBI's use of national security letters.* (Press release.) Retrieved on January 11, 2009, from http://www.fbi.gov/pressrel/pressre107/ns1030907.htm

Federal Bureau of Investigation. (2009). *Counterterrorism.* Retrieved on January 11, 2009, from http://jackson.fbi.gov/cntrterr.htm

Garcia, M. J. (2007). *The War Crimes Act: Current issues.* CRS Report for Congress. Congressional Research Service. Retrieved on January 17, 2009, from http://www .fas.org/sgp/crs/intel/RL33662.pdf

Garcia, M. J. (2008). *U.N. Convention Against Torture (CAT): Overview and application to interrogation techniques.* CRS Report for Congress. Congressional Research Service. Retrieved on January 17, 2009, from http://www.au.af.mil/ au/awc/awcgate/crs/r132438.pdf

Gellman, B., & Becker, J. (2007, June 25). Pushing the envelope on presidential power. *The Washington Post.* Retrieved on October 14, 2009, from http://voices .washingtonpost.com/cheney/chapters/pushing_the_envelope_on_presi/

Harris, S. (1998, July 18). Explaining FISA. *National Journal, 28.*

Jackson, D., Jensen, E. T., & Matsuishi, R. (2007, September). The law of war after the DTA, Hamdan and the MCA. *The Army Lawyer,* 19–27.

Jehl, D. (2004, June 23). Reach of war: Interrogation; files show Rumsfeld rejected some efforts to toughen prison rules. *The New York Times.* Retrieved on January 12, 2009, from http://query.nytimes.com/gst/fullpage.html?res=9B04E7DF1139F 930A15755C0A9629C8B63&sec=&spon=&pagewanted=print

Johnsen, D. E. (2008). What's a president to do? Interpreting the Constitution in the wake of Bush administration abuses. *Boston University Law Review, 88,* 395–419.

Karl, J. (2008, December 15). Exclusive: Cheney holds hard-line stance: In an exclusive interview with ABC News, Vice President Dick Cheney opens up about his hard-line tactics. *ABC News.* Retrieved on January 3, 2009, from http://abcnews .go.com/print?id=6464919

Kris, D. (2007). *Modernizing the Foreign Intelligence Surveillance Act: A working paper of the series on counterterrorism and American statutory law, a joint project of the Brookings Institution, the Georgetown University Law Center, and the Hoover Institution.* Retrieved on January 2, 2009, from http://www.brookings .edu/~/media/Files/rc/papers/2007/1115_nationalsecurity_kris/1115_national security_kris.pdf

Kris, D. (2008a, June 21). *A guide to the new FISA bill: Part I.* Balkinization [blog]. Retrieved on January 2, 2009, from http://balkin.blogspot.com/2008/06/guide-to-new-fisa-bill-part-i.html

Kris, D. (2008b, June 22). *A guide to the new FISA bill: Part II.* Balkinization [blog]. Retrieved on January 2, 2009, from http://balkin.blogspot.com/2008/06/guide-to-new-fisa-bill-part-ii.html

Kris, D., & Wilson, J. D. (2007). *National security investigations and prosecutions.* Eagan, MN: Thomson/West.

McCarthy, A., & Velshi, A. (2006). *We need a national security court*. Foundation for Defense of Democracies [website]. Retrieved on January 2, 2009, from http://www.defenddemocracy.org/index.php?option=com_content&task=view&id=11780050&Itemid=102

Meier, M. W. (2007). A treaty we can live with: The overlooked strategic value of Protocol II. *The Army Lawyer*, 28–41.

Miller, G. (2008). Cheney was key in clearing CIA interrogation tactics. *Los Angeles Times*. Retrieved on December 3, 2008 from http://www.latimes.com/news/nationworld/nation/la-na-cheney16–2008dec16,0,5456856.story

National Commission on Terrorist Attacks upon the United States. (2004). *The 9/11 Commission report: Final report of the national commission on terrorist attacks upon the United States* (Authorized ed.). New York: W.W. Norton.

Perkins, J. (2005). Habeas corpus in the war against terrorism: *Hamdi v. Rumsfeld* and citizen enemy combatants. *BYU Journal of Public Law, 19*(2), 437–471. Retrieved on January 4, 2009, from http://www.law2.byu.edu/jpl/Vol%2019.2/6Perkins.pdf

Poland, J. (2004) *Understanding terrorism: Groups, strategies, and responses* (2nd ed.). Upper Saddle River, NJ: Pearson Education.

Posner, R. (2006). *Not a suicide pact: The Constitution in a time of national emergency*. New York: Oxford University Press.

President Bush's Weekly Radio Address. (2005, December 17). *The Washington Post*. Retrieved on December 29, 2008, from http://www.washingtonpost.com/wp-dyn/content/article/2005/12/17/AR2005121700498_pf.html

Priest, D., & Smith, J. R. (2004, June 8). Memo offered justification for use of torture. *The Washington Post*. Retrieved on January 12, 2009, from http://www.washingtonpost.com/wp-dyn/articles/A23373–2004Jun7.html

Public Law 107-40 [S. J. Res. 23]. (2001, September 18). Authorization for Use of Military Force. Retrieved on December 22, 2008, from http://news.findlaw.com/wp/docs/terrorism/sjres23.es.html

Public Law 107-56 [H. R. 3162]. (2001). Uniting and Strengthening America by Providing Appropriate Tools Required to Intercept and Obstruct Terrorism (USA PATRIOT ACT) Act of 2001. Retrieved on December 22, 2008, from http://frwebgate.access.gpo.gov/cgi-bin/getdoc.cgi?dbname=107_cong_public_laws&docid=f:pub1056.107.pdf

Reinhardt, S. (2008). Weakening the Bill of Rights: A victory for terrorism. *Michigan Law Review, 106*, 963–974.

Reisman, M., & Antoniou, C. T. (Eds.). (1994). *The laws of war: A comprehensive collection of primary documents on international laws governing armed conflict*. New York: Vintage Books.

Risen, J., & Lichtblau, E. (2005, December 16). Bush lets U.S. spy on callers without courts. *The New York Times*. Retrieved from http://www.nytimes.com/2005/12/16/politics/16program.html?_r=2&pagewanted=print

Roosevelt, K., III. (2005). Application of the Constitution to Guantanamo Bay: Guantanamo and the conflict of laws: Rasul and beyond. *University of Pennsylvania Law Review, 153*, 2017–2071. Retrieved on December 14, 2008, from http://scholar.google.com/scholar?hl=en&lr=&q=info:I4dLourPqn4J:scholar.google.com/&output=viewport&pg=1

Shane, S., Johnston, D., & Risen, J. (2007, October 4). Secret U.S. endorsement of severe interrogations. *The New York Times*. Retrieved on January 11, 2009, from http://www.nytimes.com/2007/10/04/washington/04interrogate.html?_r=1&ei=5070&en=0a8e2695f9fdc6a9&ex=1192161600&emc=eta1&pagewanted=print

Spies, lies and FISA. (2007, October 14). *The New York Times.* (Editorial). Retrieved on December 14, 2008, from http://www.nytimes.com/2007/10/14/opinion/14sun1.html

Spiro, P. J. (2006). Hamdan v. Rumsfeld. 126 S. Ct. 2749. *The American Journal of International Law, 100*(4), 888–895. Retrieved on January 17, 2009, from http://www.jstor.org/pss/4126323

Suleman, A. M. (2005). Detainee Treatment Act of 2005. *Harvard Human Rights Journal, 19,* 257–265. Retrieved on January 17, 2009, from http://www.law.harvard.edu/students/orgs/hrj/iss19/suleman.shtml

Taylor, S., Jr. (2003, October). *Rights, liberties, and security: Recalibrating the balance after September 11.* The Bookings Institution. Retrieved on October 8, 2009, from http://www.brookings.edu/articles/2003/winter_terrorism_taylor.aspx

U.S. Code Collection, Title 18, part 1, chapter 118, § 2441. (2009). *War crimes.* Cornell University Law School, Legal Information Institute. Retrieved on January 17, 2009, from http://www4.1aw.cornell.edu/uscode/18/2441.html

U.S. Department of Justice (USDOJ). (2008). *A review of the FBI's use of national security letters: Assessment of corrective actions and examination of NSL usage in 2006.* Office of the Inspector General. Retrieved on October 8, 2009, from http://www.usdoj.gov/oig/special/s0803b/final.pdf

U.S. Department of State. (2004, April). *Patterns of global terrorism, 2003.* Retrieved on January 11, 2009, from http://www.state.gov/documents/organization/31912.pdf

Warrick, J., & DeYoung, K. (2009, January 23). Obama reverses Bush policies on detention and interrogation. *The Washington Post.* Retrieved on October 14, 2009, from http://www.washingtonpost.com/wp-dyn/content/article/2009/01/22/AR2009012201527_pf.html

White, J. (2006). New rules of interrogation forbid use of harsh tactics. *Washington Post, September 7, A1,* as cited in Meier, M. W. (2007). A treaty we can live with: The overlooked strategic value of Protocol II. *The Army Lawyer,* September 2007, 28–41.

White, J. R. (2008). *Terrorism and homeland security* (6th ed.). Belmont, CA: Wadsworth Cengage Learning.

Whittaker, D. J. (2002). *Terrorism: Understanding the global threat.* London: Pearson Education.

Wright, D. P., & Reese, T. R. (2008). *ON POINT II: Transition to the new campaign: The United States Army in Operation IRAQI FREEDOM May 2003–January 2005.* Fort Leavenworth, KS: Combat Studies Institute Press. U.S. Army Combined Arms Center. Available from http://www.globalsecurity.org/military/library/report/2008/onpoint/chap05–07.htm

Yungher, N. I. (2008). *Terrorism: The bottom line.* Upper Saddle River, NJ: Pearson Prentice Hall.

12 Developments in Cyber Criminology

Johnny Nhan and Michael Bachmann

The Emergence of Cyber Criminology

In the past fifteen years, cybercrime has garnered considerable attention from the general public, business communities, government, and academia. Growing concerns over increased victimization,[1] increased damages,[2] and protection of critical infrastructures related to national security[3] have sparked several disciplines in the social sciences and the computer sciences to address cybercrime phenomena. Despite the heightened societal awareness of the problem, an assessment of the current state of cyber-criminological research must conclude that it remains exploratory. The discipline still lacks a clear identity, standardized methodologies, and a consistent theoretical framework. Nevertheless, several central topics have emerged within this young discipline. This chapter explores four of the central developmental directions: (1) definitional issues in cybercrime, (2) meanings and demarcations of Internet space, (3) policing and social control in cyberspace, and (4) theoretical explanations. Due to the difficulty of understanding exactly what constitutes a cybercrime—a problem that is reflected in the first category—these classifications are not mutually exclusive. The chapter is meant not as a comprehensive categorization and explanation of the various different types of cybercrime but as an assessment of the challenges and problems in some of the main areas of current cyber-criminological research.

The chapter begins by exploring different perspectives on the definition of cybercrime. An assessment of discussions related to issues of space will help explain some of the difficulties involved in defining cybercrime. Subsequently, policing and controlling the cyber environment are examined; hacking is used as an example to highlight the conflicts between policing and informal *cyber rights*. The debate surrounding the applicability of traditional criminological theories to cybercrime phenomena are also addressed. The focus in this section is on whether existing criminological theories can be transposed into the cyber environment, or whether formulating adequate explanations of cybercrime demands new or hybrid models. Finally, we discuss the challenges of researching cybercrime in the developing field of cyber criminology. Please keep in mind that this chapter is by no means a comprehensive study of cybercrime and cybercrime types but merely a snapshot of some of the major areas in the current research in criminology.

The Next Terrorist Attack on Cyberspace?

Cybercrime has gotten the attention of the U.S. government in a big way in recent years. Telling signs include the appointment of a cyber czar by President Obama, who in his first speech to Congress, mentioned cybercrime as one of the three greatest dangers facing the United States today. Recently, the U.S. Air Force has added cyber warfare to its role with the new slogan, "Air, Space, and Cyberspace." In part, reasons for this increased attention are increased cyber espionage activities by foreign nations and the recognition that the Internet is a vital component of our critical infrastructures. Cyber terrorism is believed to be a powerful tool that threatens to produce catastrophic disasters ranging from financial system collapse to disruption of electrical grids. Moreover, the Department of Homeland Security considers cyberspace a virtual "safe haven" enabling would-be terrorists to spread propaganda, to recruit and train prospective members, and to fund and plan terrorist operations (Department of Homeland Security, 2007). Major hacker attacks have even permeated popular media; recent plots often involve defusing bomb-like cyber attacks and capturing or even killing hacker villains. It can be argued that we have been waging war on cyberspace.

The U.S. Defense Department is establishing the U.S. Cyber Command to protect government computers. According to Deputy Secretary of Defense William Lynn, cyber attacks cost billions of dollars annually and require the resources of 90,000 Defense Department employees to defend the nearly 7 million computers and devices connected to 15,000 computer networks (Pessin, 2009). No directly attributable deaths have occurred, despite an increase in highly sophisticated cyber attacks originating from China and Russia in recent years.

Defining and Classifying Cybercrimes

The development of a generally accepted definition of cybercrime is obscured by substantive problems similar to white-collar crime, whose definition has been debated for over half a century. Sociologist Edwin Sutherland's address to the 1939 annual meeting of the American Sociological Association, "White-Collar Criminality," sparked controversy by using a class-based orientation of crime "in the upper or white-collar class, composed of respectable or at least respected business and professional men . . ." (Sutherland, 1940, p. 1). Many contemporary scholars of white-collar crime have expanded Sutherland's original orientation to include individuals of nonelite status (Edelhertz, 1970) and more activities. Gil Geis (1991) considers the ramifications of broadening Sutherland's definition, questioning whether a television scam should be regarded as a white-collar crime or merely a petty consumer crime. The blurred distinction between white-collar and conventional crime makes a common definition difficult to establish. Likewise, the emerging field of cybercrime does not have a widely agreed-upon criminological definition and consequently suffers from similar problems.

The broad scope of different types of cybercrime lends itself to substantive definitional debate. The term *cybercrime* denotes a wide range of phenomena, encompassing such disparate activities as attacks on national critical infrastructures and online auction fraud. The vast scale of multifaceted phenomena comprised by the term *cybercrime* renders formulation of a precise general definition extremely difficult (Bachmann, 2008). However, three defining categories have emerged as essential elements of a broad conception of cybercrime: (1) its commission within electronic networks, (2) the role of technology, and (3) the various legal statutes that can be applied.

First, cybercrime is commonly understood as signifying a range of illegal acts that share commission through electronic information and communication networks. For example, Thomas and Loader (2000) define cybercrime as "computer-mediated activities which are either illegal or considered illicit by certain parties and which can be conducted through global electronic networks" (p. 3). This definition distinguishes cybercrime from other crime types by limiting the term to crimes that occur in the "virtual space" of worldwide information networks, particularly the Internet (Castells, 2002).

Second, cybercrimes can also be categorized by the function of technology in their commission. Furnell (2002, p. 22) differentiates between "computer-assisted crimes," in which "the computer is used in a supporting capacity, but the underlying crime or offense either predates the emergence of computers or could be committed without them"—such as fraud, theft, and pornography—and "computer-focused crimes…in which the category of crime has emerged as a direct result of computer technology and there is no direct parallel in other sectors." These crimes include such activities as hacking, website defacing, and virus/worm attacks. A similar distinction is proposed by Gordon and Ford (2006), who isolate three main dimensions of the term *cybercrime*: (1) involvement of computer and hardware devices—that is, the part played by technology; (2) the technology–human-element continuum, which ranges from primarily technological cybercrimes to those that have pronounced human elements; and (3) the "crimeware"—the malicious software that is used for the commission of the crime. Unfortunately, both Furnell's classification and Gordon and Ford's, although useful in analyzing interdependency processes in social and technological developments, are of limited criminological value (Yar, 2005).

Third, cybercrime can be defined legally. Wall (2001, pp. 3–7) suggests translating four existing criminal law classifications into their cybercrime equivalents: (1) "(cyber)-trespass," the unauthorized crossing of the boundaries of computer systems and/or the causation of damage to those systems or their owners; (2) "(cyber)-deceptions/theft," the stealing of money or property through, for example, identity thefts, credit card frauds, phishing e-mails or pharming websites, or violations of intellectual property through online piracy; (3) "(cyber)-pornography/obscenity," the display of obscene or pedophile pornography or racist or otherwise offensive statements; and (4) "(cyber)-violence," inflicting psychological harm or threatening physical harm through, for example, hate speech, harassment, or the dissemination of information assisting in dangerous activities like bomb building.

Compared to Wall's definition, Brenner (2001) offers a more fundamental classification of cybercrime into four legal categories: (1) prohibited conduct (*actus reus*), (2) culpable mental state (*mens rea*), (3) attendant circumstances, and (4) forbidden result or harm. Using a legal orientation, Brenner considers all cybercrime materially indistinguishable from street crime, thereby raising the question (which is also the title of her article), Is there such a thing as "virtual crime" (ibid.)? For example, when comparing theft or embezzlement by a cyber criminal to physical theft, "(the) perpetrators may use different methods to accomplish their thefts, but their conduct, their mental states, the pertinent circumstances and the ultimate result are conceptually indistinguishable" (Brenner, 2001, p. 1).

Beyond the various proponents and opponents who argue for or against certain aspects as essential to an overarching academic definition of cybercrime, a third faction of scholars is forming. These scholars see the definitional debate over cybercrime—and white-collar crime as well—as a mere distraction from meaningful, solution-oriented research. Peter Grabosky (2001, p. 243) questions whether the concept of cybercrime warrants a separate definition or has instead to be considered merely "old wines in new bottles." Ralph D. Clifford (2006) offers a more sensible solution. He questions the practicality of attempting to subsume the vast scale of multifaceted phenomena encompassed by the term *cybercrime* under one legal definition. Instead, Clifford suggests focusing our attention on the rational implications of the various cybercrime-related statutes for investigators, prosecutors, and defense attorneys. Despite Clifford's suggestion to end the debate for an overarching definition, this discussion will likely continue as the line between cyber and crime becomes further obscured by a greater infusion of computers into society.

The Internet Space and Jurisdiction

Some criminologists and social scientists are seeking to understand the Internet structurally. These researchers are primarily concerned with the inherently "borderless" nature of the cyber environment and the resulting difficulties regarding the defining, demarcating, understanding, and ultimately controlling crime on the Internet. The disembodied nature of cyberspace challenges the politically and legally defined borders that govern our physical world. This is not to suggest that cyberspace is entirely disconnected and independent from physical spaces. However, Internet borders are defined by other means. Wilson and Corey (2000) conceptualize electronic space by three distinctions: (1) the physical infrastructure, such as servers, switches, routers, and cables; (2) virtual disparities, or the power relations derived from the digital divide between those who have greater access to the Internet and those who do not; and (3) the demarcation of interaction of places, such as online communities that have informal regulations for interactions and restrictions for membership.

Many legal scholars have attempted to define Internet borders in terms of jurisdiction. Susan Brenner and Joseph Schwerha IV (2004) have examined jurisdictional difficulties in policing international cybercrime. They concluded that persisting legal discrepancies between sovereign countries often hinder investigations; they also found that formal processes governing transnational evidence gathering are "cumbersome" (ibid., p. 112). Kumar (2006) examines the decentralized nature of cyberspace as problematic for determining which court has jurisdiction over civil e-commerce cases. Joel Reidenberg (2005, p. 1953) suggests considering certain types of cybercrime—such as hate, drugs, sex, gambling, and stolen music use—as "denial of service" attacks on the legal system because they pose "technologically based arguments to deny the applicability of rules of law interdicting their behavior."

As is the case with white-collar crime, jurisdictional difficulties and the complexity of cybercrime have also affected prosecutorial strategies. Smith, Grabosky, and Urbas (2004) have found that, like white-collar crime, cybercrime is treated no differently from conventional crime under the court system. However, cross-border jurisdictional legal difficulties and case complexity often affect the practicality of deciding which cases to prosecute. Nhan (2009) found that the strategies ensuing from these difficulties often result in heavy use of plea bargaining and minimal threshold requirements, which often create "free zones" in which lawbreakers are not subject to policing and regulation.

Criminologists and legal scholars are still grappling with the difficulties of fitting geographically defined rules, based on legal and politically defined borders, to the abstract nature of cyberspace. Political and legal institutions have been historically grounded in geographically defined notions of territory. The emergence and growing societal relevance of the Internet poses an unprecedented disruption to this long-established order of power and control. Similarly, institutions of formal social control, namely law enforcement, also experience great difficulties in policing this new, "antispatial" environment.

Policing and Social Control on the Internet

A growing number of criminologists and legal scholars have investigated the fit between law enforcement and cyberspace. Huey (2002) has examined the conceptual difficulties of fitting geographically based law enforcement (which historically has been tied to geographically limited, territorial arrangements in controlling assigned public spaces) to the complex and "abstract" environment of the Internet. She argues that the Internet is not fundamentally different from the physical world; rather, law enforcement's perception of cyberspace is shaped by cultural habits that "bar them from seeing their role as operating outside of geographic space" (ibid., p. 250). This perception of the Internet by police is further skewed by the general lack of understanding of computers and telecommunications technology and the tendency to interpret them as "magic boxes that mysteriously obey commands upon direction" (ibid., p. 244).

A number of criminologists and legal scholars have questioned whether the digital environment demands new policing strategies based on public–private collaborations. Brenner (2004) expounds on the inadequacy of the established policing model to control the vast scale of border-spanning cybercrime. Wall (2007) suggests a similar collaborative model, arguing that the public policing role must adapt to the Internet environment by establishing partnerships with nonstate institutions to create security networks. These concepts are derived from Ericson and Haggerty's (1997) proposed shift in the police paradigm from strict crime control to managing dangers and risks in an information society. The new policing paradigm is derived from Castells's (2000) network theory, which holds that security is produced from interconnected "nodes" (institutional actors) that require the diffusion of policing power to nonstate and hybrid entities (Burris, Drahos, & Shearing, 2005; Dupont, 2006; Wood & Shearing, 2007).

It remains to be determined whether it is even possible to implement entirely new models of policing, given the required larger structural changes to the policing and legal paradigms. The current model of policing cybercrime is still confronted with the restraints of the established criminal justice and legal systems. The primary functions of law enforcement agencies are still to detain suspects and prepare paperwork for court, regardless of the type of crime. In the case of cybercrime, this translates into computer forensics work and issues related to admissibility of digital evidence in court (Moore, 2007).

Current models of forensics employed by law enforcement are challenged by the cyber environment and by increasingly savvy criminals. The volatility and intangibility of evidence associated with these types of offenses holds significant difficulties for law enforcement, owing to the lack of such traditional forensic artifacts as fingerprints, DNA, and eyewitness accounts (Bachmann, 2008; Shinder & Tittel, 2002). Moreover, cyber criminals often employ anonymizing strategies and services, such as encryption algorithms, "spoofing" tools, and public wireless networks and access points to further complicate forensic cyber investigations.[4] The many technical obstacles and time constraints involved in the pursuit of cyber cases serve as additional disincentives for prosecutors and investigators. To face these challenges, law enforcement has increasingly turned to partnership models of policing.

Law enforcement has embraced collaborative efforts to a limited degree, primarily through interagency task forces that partner with the private sector. Nhan and Huey's (2008) study of high-tech crimes task forces in California have found this public–private model effective. Nevertheless, significant cultural and structural frictions still hinder more robust collaborations. Moreover, certain types of cybercrimes that fit well with the current policing model of apprehending offenders (such as illegal piracy) are favored by state and local agencies over more transnational/decentralized and technical cybercrimes (such as hacking). Addressing this issue, Gros (2003) has questioned the notion of sovereignty and emphasized a greater role of collaborative international institutions, such as Interpol and the United Nations, in policing global cybercrime.

Another complication in policing cybercrime is the dichotomy between security and privacy. The question of whether the Internet represents a separate domain that operates by different rules is debated between law enforcement circles, whose members desire greater flexibility in monitoring cyberspace, and citizens' rights groups, which fight for the protection of online privacy. Reitinger (2000) discusses the role of the state and the friction of using encryption technologies to manage anonymity (identity privacy) and confidentiality (content privacy). In addition, electronic evidence has raised Fourth Amendment concerns related to jurisdiction, ownership, culpability, and privacy rights during investigations (Obinyan, Ikegwuonu, & Vanderpuye, 2008). To understand why the Internet seems to be governed by a disembodied normative culture, we look back at the historical developments of the Internet and the hacking culture to see why it is so difficult to police and why people commit cybercrimes.

A Cyber Sting Operation of Online Fraud

The most lucrative form of modern computer crime, and also the most dangerous one for private computer users, is the trade and sale of stolen credit card information, or "carding." According to FBI estimates, the average MasterCard sells for $1; Visa cards sell for $6 each; a hacked PayPal account that includes all verified details can be bought for $100, or $60 for a verified account without all details. Several sites exist in the computer underground that globally trade credit card information, electronic banking logins, credit card magstripe swipes, "dumps," specialized hardware used for skimming attacks, and so forth.

DarkMarket.ws was one of the central trading websites for the global carding scene. At its peak, the site had more than 2,500 registered members. When the site closed on September 16, 2008, the site administrator, known as Master Splynter, posted the site's final closure announcement, explaining that

> [DarkMarket.ws] is attracting too much attention from a lot of the world services (agents of FBI, SS, and Interpol). I guess it was only time before this would happen. It is very unfortunate that we have come to this situation, because…we have established DM as the premier English speaking forum for conducting business. Such is life. When you are on top, people try to bring you down. (Poulsen, 2008, para. 10)
>
> What none of the site's members knew was that Master Splynter was actually FBI Senior Agent J. Keith Mularski from the Cyber Initiative and Resources Unit, part of the National Cyber Forensics Training Alliance (NCFTA). For the past three years, Mularski had infiltrated the carding underground deeper than any other agent before him. The sting operation he ran led to the arrest of 56 major players in the carding scene worldwide and prevented $70 million in economic losses. It was the single most successful operation in the FBI's battle against the global carding underground.

_____ Cyber Rights and Cybercrime: The Case of Hacking

The Internet was originally conceived with a set of principles in mind. It developed from the ARPAnet,[5] a primarily research-oriented network designed to create a global infrastructure based on open and decentralized information sharing. Leonard Kleinrock (2004, pp. 199–200), computer scientist and one of the original architects of the Internet, explains that much of the perception of the Internet as a distinct, disembodied space with separate rules manifests from a set of initial norms. Among those norms are the notions that it serves everyone, that it is an "open" environment, that it is a means to share ideas and works, and that it is empowering, noncentralized, and owned by no one. These mentalities have manifested in various justifications for cybercrime.

Computer hacking is one form of cybercrime that has straddled the dichotomy between the open principles of the Internet and malicious behavior. The hacker subculture materialized in the genesis of computers in the 1960s and 1970s. Rather than simply using existing computer technology, original hacker enthusiasts were united in their passion for technological innovations and by their playful and individualistic quest to satisfy their intellectual curiosity (Hafner & Markoff, 1991; Jordan, 2008). All early contributors who pioneered the "computer revolution" (Naughton, 2000, p. 313) and all those who paved the way for today's superhighways of the Internet were considered prototypical hackers in this original understanding of the term (Levy, 1984).

The early hacking community was characterized by a fundamental distrust of governmental and military monopolies, power, and authority. Early hackers were characterized by their defiance of corporate domination of culture and by their rejection of traditional and conservative values and lifestyles (Yar,

2005). Instead, they advocated the idealistic notions of unrestricted distribution of information, knowledge, and intellectual thought (Lasica, 2005; Thomas, 2002) and the use of computer technology for the higher goals of intellectual discovery, the creation of art and beauty, and improvement of the overall quality of life (Levy, 1984). Furthermore, they challenged the status quo of closed models of software development produced by companies like Microsoft by creating a Free Software/Open Source (FOSS) countermovement dedicated to developing open and free software alternatives (Jordan, 2008).

However, this positive connotation of the word changed during the 1980s, as more malicious hackers drew the attention of the press. The increasingly mission-critical nature of computer networks for many industries and the expanding popularity of electronic financial transactions began to attract people who sought not to understand the systems but to abuse, disrupt, sabotage, and exploit them. Today, the hacker scene is divided into "penetration testers," who, following the spirit of the original hacker scene, hack legally and under contract to improve the security of systems and networks, and "black-hat hackers," who attempt to illegally break into and exploit computers. Holt and Kilger (2008) further distinguished between computer experts who learn how to hack in institutional settings such as universities, whom they term "makecraft hackers," and hackers "in the wild," whom they call "techcraft hackers" (ibid., p. 76). Holt and Kilger showed that techcraft hackers, while exhibiting no differences in their knowledge of ethical conduct, have significantly fewer concerns about breaching the law and compensate for the lack of institutional support with a greater number of hacker peers (c.f. Holt, 2007). Consequently, Holt and Kilger (2008) concluded that social learning mechanisms contribute to the greater rejection of ethical norms among techcraft hackers.

The primary focus of criminological research on hackers concerns their attitudes, ethics, social backgrounds, and behaviors (Bachmann, 2008; Holt, 2007; Holt & Kilger, 2008; Jordan, 2008; Jordan & Taylor, 1998; Thomas, 2002). Bachmann (2008) showed that the common hacker stereotype of the clever, lonesome, deviant male adolescent whose computer proficiency compensates for social shortcomings barely begins to tell the whole story of who hackers are. The most important inadequacy of this stereotype is the notion that hackers are socially inept and invariably young (Bachmann, 2008; Holt, 2007; Holt & Kilger, 2008). More importantly, Bachmann (2008) also revealed that hackers undergo a maturation process over the course of their hacking careers and that the more experienced and seasoned black-hat hackers tend to be the most dangerous. They are more likely to attack higher-profile targets, and many engage in illegal hacking activities with the stronger criminal intent to profit financially. The studies of hackers and the hacking subculture, while gathering important insights into the social dimensions of technical crimes, face several practical methodological challenges, as do the rest of the cyber-criminological studies. These challenges are addressed in the following section.

The Man Who Saved the Internet?

In 2005, Dan Kaminsky, a 26-year-old computer consultant, serendipitously discovered a computer flaw that had the ability to affect the Internet. This may seem like a common occurrence, given the number of software bugs frequently discovered in the endless lines of computer software code that govern Internet traffic. However, Kaminsky discovered a fundamental design flaw that affected the *entire* Internet. This vulnerability, if exploited, could potentially allow hackers to control the traffic of every web page and redirect the data to a hacker-specified address. Internet traffic ranging from e-mail to banking and commerce could be affected. This would potentially cost billions of dollars and simply destroy the Internet.

Kaminsky discovered a serious flaw in the Domain Name System (DNS) that functions as a directory linking Internet Protocol (IP) address numbers to recognizable domain names, such as yahoo.com. Domain name servers work behind the scenes as a backbone of the World Wide Web to facilitate the billions of Internet transactions executed daily.

Fortunately for the general public, Kaminsky first disclosed the serious flaw to security experts. A secret meeting was quickly arranged with stunned representatives from major computer security and networking companies at the Microsoft campus in Redmond, Washington. A group of engineers from such companies as Cisco and Red Hat worked feverishly to patch vital servers before Kaminksy's scheduled presentation of the vulnerability at the DEFCON hacking conference at Las Vegas, Nevada. When Kaminsky finally presented his findings, the major vulnerabilities had been patched, and disaster was averted. (See Davis, 2008; Zetter, 2008.)

Source: From "Secret Geek A-Team Hacks Back, Defends Worldwide Web," by J. Davis, November 24, 2008, *Wired Magazine.*

Methodological Challenges in Researching Cybercrime

The developing field of cyber criminology has yet to overcome a series of distinct methodological and theoretical problems. As discussed, the foremost methodological problem stems from the lack of a general definition of cybercrime. This problem is fundamental because of its implications for the second problem, the operationalization and measurement of cybercrime.

To obtain an accurate assessment of the scope and severity of cybercrimes is a difficult undertaking. Official crime data, often used for criminological studies, are rare for cybercrime, and the few existing datasets are plagued by serious underreporting problems. To begin with, the two most important official crime data sources, the Uniform Crime Report (UCR) and the National Incident Based Reporting System (NIBRS), contain hardly any useful information. The UCR records no cybercrime, and the NIBRS contains only one, highly ambiguous computer-crime variable. Additionally, official crime statistics do not measure incident trends and distributions objectively but are socially constructed; particularly for the measurement of cybercrime, this circumstance poses a significant problem. An accumulation of various compounding factors leads to severe underreporting of cybercrime in official statistics. The most common of these factors are perceptions of the offense as private or trivial. Most people do not know exactly what constitutes a cybercrime and are therefore often confused about the appropriateness of reporting a particular incident (Howell, 2007). The intangibility of evidence and the lack of traditional forensic artifacts make online offenses more difficult to detect than terrestrial crimes. Moreover, the global nature of cybercrimes and the high level of offender anonymity in the online environment are two additional aspects that discourage both victims and law enforcement from reporting such crimes, because they decrease the perceived chance of apprehending the offender. As a result, many police stations prioritize reporting of local problems (Wall, 2001) occurring on their "patch" (Lenk, 1997, p. 129). One can only conclude that underreporting continues to be a serious problem in cybercrime victimization surveys and official statistics.

Victimization surveys are often used by criminologists because they can encompass offenses that are typically underreported in official statistics. However, these surveys cannot completely eliminate all difficulties faced by official measurements. First, undetected crime cannot be reported. Second, systematic errors can result from the survey process, such as various interviewer effects and other sources of bias. Survey researchers have long recognized that even the highest possible optimization of survey instruments will never completely eliminate survey errors (cf. Groves et al., 2004). However, many of the aforementioned problems of official statistics also plague cybercrime victimization surveys, thus rendering them particularly prone to bias. To make matters worse, most surveys measure only corporate or organizational victimization and exclude private computer users systematically. Wall (2001) also hints at various existing intersurvey inconsistencies regarding methodologies and classifications that complicate meaningful comparative analyses and aggregations. Yar (2006, p. 14) specifies three reasons for underreporting by corporations: (1) fear of embarrassment, (2) loss of public or customer confidence (as in the case of breaches relating to supposedly secure e-shopping and e-banking facilities), and (3) potential legal liability relating to the violation of data protection responsibilities. In addition to all of these problems of cross-sectional data, longitudinal measures of cybercrime often also must resolve issues resulting from rapidly changing legal classifications. All these problematic factors continue to affect quantitative criminological studies of cybercrime.

Aside from measurement issues, cyber criminologists face certain theoretical problems. Differences in the cyberspace environment with regard to structural and social features call into question the transferability of traditional criminological theories to cybercrimes.

_____ Theoretical Challenges in Cybercrime Research

Many criminologists have applied existing criminological theory to explain cybercrime. Some criminologists have applied Marcus Felson's (2000) routine activities theory to the subject, explaining that crime occurs out of everyday opportunity (Cox, Johnson, & Richards, 2009; Grabosky, 2001). Yar (2005), however, raises some theoretical concerns regarding the applicability of this theory, principally that some of the theory's core elements lose their relevance when they are transposed from "terrestrial" to "virtual" worlds (ibid.). Although cybercrimes certainly do exhibit many of the characteristics of traditional crimes, the qualitatively new environment in which they are committed is likely to invalidate some of the core components of traditional theories. Criminological theories rely in varying degrees on ecological and environmental propositions. Some of them explain crimes as occurring within particular settings that exhibit specific social, cultural, and economic characteristics. For example, routine activities theories focus on the time–space convergence of motivated offenders with suitable targets and the absence of capable guardians, thereby implying certain environmental settings in which offenses can occur (Cohen & Felson, 1979; Felson, 2000). Disorganization theory and others that focus on ecological factors have initiated crime-mapping projects as well as several measurement and prevention programs aimed at the removal of criminogenic factors from the environment (Akers & Sellers, 2004). The problem regarding the applicability of these theories is that the cyberspace environment has no equivalent to easily distinguishable terrestrial locations. For the explanation of cybercrimes, the irrelevance of spatial distances within cyberspace handicaps criminological theories that rely on assumptions specific to terrestrial environments.

A different group of criminological theories examines the reasons some individuals repeatedly involve themselves in criminal activity while others abstain. These theories correlate categories of crime with certain social characteristics of the offender. For example, a significant amount of empirical evidence in the criminological literature substantiates a correlation between economic disadvantage and engagement in property crime or violent crime. This correlation is reversed with regard to computing skills and Internet access; the more disadvantaged segments of the economic and educational distribution possess them least (Yar, 2006). Conversely, Internet offenders typically have greater economic and intellectual resources and exhibit characteristics substantially different from the attributes of the majority of other criminals (Wall, 2001).

Some cyber criminologists suggests that the appearance of cybercrimes and the inability to simply transpose traditional empirical assumptions and explanatory concepts may require considerable theoretical innovation and new analytical tools (Yar, 2006). Ronald Clarke suggests a radical solution: to completely suspend criminological inquiries into the motivations of cyber offenders and instead focus solely on the crime reduction strategies provided by the "crime science" approach (Clarke, 2004). This interdisciplinary approach applies statistics, environmental design, psychology, forensics, policing, economics, and geography to the study of the characteristics of crime incidents and ignores the traits and motivations of criminal actors. Such methods as crime patterning, hot-spot analyses, and crime-mapping studies are substituted for the analytical and statistical tools of traditional criminology. Clarke demands that criminologists focus on concrete and manipulable factors of crime events and accept the remainder as immutable facts. Given the broad spectrum of opinions represented in the debate over whether and to what extent traditional criminological theories can and should be applied to cybercrimes, this debate is likely to continue in the future.

As a result of the debate surrounding the applicability of traditional theories, new and hybrid theoretical models have been developed to better explain certain types of cybercrime. Jaishankar (2007) underscores the deficiency of theory in explaining cybercrime. He proposes space transition theory to explain cybercrime behavior: The anonymous and unsupervised environment releases repressed propensities for crime in general (Jaishankar, 2008). This theory, although currently still untested, seems to be effective in explaining types of child–victimization-based cybercrimes, such as cyber bullying, pedophilia, pornography, stalking, and other online translations of terrestrial crime (Jaishankar & Halder, 2008).

Theoretical models have been applied to cyberspace security. Wall (2007) applies the nodal governance theoretical model, which stresses diffused policing power to nonstate security stakeholders for the policing of cyberspace. Nhan and Huey (2008) use this nodal framework to create *digital defensible spaces*, an online translation of Oscar Newman's (1973) theory on neighborhood-level self-efficacy. However, this model, too, is currently untested. Clearly, more research in the area of cyber criminology is needed to validate new theoretical approaches.

Despite the growth in both cybercrime and cybercrime research, cyber criminology faces challenges as a new paradigm of study in search of a clear definition, generally accepted methods, and theoretical models. A look at some of the shortcomings of the current research reveals good progress but a much greater need for empirical research and methods. Cyber criminology is slow to emerge from a niche area that is often marginalized by mainstream criminology to occupy a position of high importance.

CONCLUSION: TOWARD A CONCEPTUAL MODEL OF CYBER CRIMINOLOGY

The increased social relevance of cybercrime has finally drawn the attention of mainstream criminology, and criminologists are beginning to recognize the scope of the problem. The challenges to the criminal justice system, which arise primarily from the global dimensions and the complexity of cybercrime, warrant specialized research. Disparate criminal laws and geographical boundaries of jurisdictions pose important limitations for law enforcement efforts because they have no direct equivalent in cyberspace (Koops & Brenner, 2006). An increasing number of cyber criminologists are using these circumstances to justify establishing the discipline as a legitimate subsection of criminology, like white-collar crime.

Like white-collar crime, the development of cyber criminology is hindered by several fundamental problems that stem from the lack of a general definition. The blurred distinction between cyber-enabled crime and conventional, terrestrially based crime occurring online has made measuring and establishing standard research methodologies difficult.

Empirical research is vital to understand these phenomena and to guide the development of effective policies and effective strategies to combat cyber criminals. Much of our knowledge of cybercrime stems from very limited exploratory studies with small samples of cases. Qualitative interviews have greatly increased our knowledge of cybercrime phenomena, but the generalizability of their findings to any larger populations remains questionable. More empirical and cross-cultural studies must be pursued to guide the development of adequate theoretical frameworks and effective policies.

A patchwork of research is emerging from workers in the cyber-criminological field who range from criminologists to lawyers. Like the model of policing proposed by nodal governance researchers, collaboration in the research world is necessary. This way, shortcomings in one field can be supplemented by other noncriminological fields, from computer science to informatics to economics and the humanities.

DISCUSSION QUESTIONS

1. With more computers and Internet technology integrated into everyday life, will most crimes eventually become a form of cybercrime? Which ones will, and which ones never will? Why?

2. How would you change our current criminal justice and legal systems to deal with the lack of traditional borders on the Internet?

3. Why is it important to have a single definition of cybercrime? Why is it so difficult to establish one?

4. What type of police force is necessary to effectively police cyberspace? What changes would have to be made, and how would you describe the ideal "cyber officer"?

5. How would you design a study to measure cybercrime? What are some difficulties you might encounter and how would you attempt to contact cyber criminals?

6. What should cyber criminologists do to overcome the problems currently facing the developing discipline?

7. Is cyber terrorism a real threat, or is it unwarranted fear?

NOTES

1. According to the National White-Collar Crime Center (NW3C), the Bureau of Justice Assistance, and the FBI's Internet Complaint Center (IC3) 2007 Internet Crime Report, 206,884 complaints were received in 2007, compared to 124,515 in 2003. See http://www.ic3.gov/media/annualreport/2007_IC3Report.pdf.

2. The Computer Security Institute's CSI 2008 Computer Crime and Security Survey (Richardson, 2008).

3. According to a 2003 White House report, The National Strategy to Secure Cyberspace, cyberspace is considered the "control system" that interconnects critical infrastructures such as agriculture, food, water, commerce, emergency services, energy, and communications. See http://www.dhs.gov/xlibrary/assets/National_Cyberspace_Strategy.pdf.

4. U.S. Department of Justice (2002). Searching and Seizing Computers and Obtaining Electronic Evidence in Criminal Investigations. Computer Crime and Intellectual Property Section. See http://www.usdoj.gov/criminal/cybercrime/searching.html.

5. Acronym for the Advanced Research Projects Agency, the lead funding agency.

REFERENCES

Akers, R. L., & Sellers, C. S. (2004). *Criminological theories: Introduction, evaluation, and application* (4th ed.). Los Angeles: Roxbury.

Bachmann, M. (2008). *What makes them click? Applying the rational choice perspective to the hacking underground.* [Electronic resource]. Orlando: University of Central Florida.

Brenner, S. W. (2001). Is there such a thing as virtual crime? *California Criminal Law Review, 4*(1).

Brenner, S. W. (2004). Toward a criminal law for cyberspace: A new model of law enforcement? *Rutgers Computer and Technology Law Journal, 30*(1).

Brenner, S. W. (2006). Defining cybercrime: A review of state and federal law. In R. D. Clifford (Ed.), *Cybercrime* (2nd ed.), pp. 1395. Durham, NC: Carolina Academic Press.

Brenner, S. W. (2007). Public-private sector cooperation in combating cybercrime: In search of a model. *Journal of Commercial Law and Technology, 2*(2), 58–67.

Brenner, S. W., & Koops, B. J. (2004). Approaches to cybercrime jurisdiction. *Journal of High Technology Law, 4*(1).

Brenner, S. W., & Schwerha, J. J., IV (2004). Cybercrime: A note on international issues. *Information Systems Frontiers, 6*(2), 111–114.

Burris, S., Drahos, P., & Shearing, C. (2005). Nodal governance. *Australian Journal of Legal Philosophy, 30,* 30–58.

Castells, M. (2000). *The rise of the network society* (2nd ed.). Malden, MA: Blackwell.

Castells, M. (2002). *The Internet galaxy: Reflections on the Internet, business, and society.* Oxford: Oxford University Press.

Clarke, R. V. (2004). New challenges for research: Technology, criminology, and crime science. In E. U. Savona (Ed.), *Crime and technology: New frontiers for regulation, law enforcement and research* (pp. 97–104). Dordrecht, Netherlands: Springer.

Clifford, R. D. (2006). Introduction. In R. D. Clifford (Ed.), *Cybercrime: The investigation, prosecution, and defense of a computer-related crime* (2nd ed.). Durham, NC: Carolina Academic Press.

Cohen, L. E., & Felson, M. K. (1979). Social change and crime rate trends: A routine activity approach *American Sociological Review, 44*(4), 588–608.

Cox, R. W., III, Johnson, T. A., & Richards, G. E. (2009). Routine Activity Theory and Internet Crime. In Schmalleger, F. and Pittaro, M. (Eds.), *Crimes of the Internet* (pp. 302–316). Upper Saddle River, NJ: Pearson.

Davis, J. (2008, November 24). Secret geek a-team hacks back, defends Worldwide Web. *Wired Magazine.* Retrieved on June 1, 2009, from http://www.wired.com/techbiz/people/magazine/16–12/ff_kaminsky

Department of Homeland Security (2007). *The National Strategy for Homeland Security.* Retrieved on June 1, 2009, from http://www.dhs.gov/xabout/history/gc_1193938363680.shtm

Dupont, B. (2006). Power struggles in the field of security: Implications for democratic transformation. In J. Wood & B. Dupont (Eds.), *Democracy, society, and the governance of security* (pp. 86–110). New York: Cambridge University Press.

Edelhertz, H. (1970). *The nature, impact, and prosecution of white-collar crime.* Washington, DC: Law Enforcement Administration, U.S. Department of Justice.

Ericson, R. V., & Haggerty, K. D. (1997). *Policing the risk society.* Buffalo, NY: University of Toronto Press.

Felson, M. K. (2000). The routine activity approach as a general social theory. In S. Simpson (Ed.), *Of crime and criminality: The use of theory in everyday life.* Thousand Oaks, CA: Sage.

Furnell, S. (2002). *Cybercrime: Vandalizing the information society.* London: Addison Wesley.

Geis, G. (1991). White-collar crime: What is it? *Current Issues in Criminal Justice, 3*(1), 9–24.

Gordon, S., & Ford, R. (2006). On the definition and classification of cybercrime. *Journal in Computer Virology, 2*(1), 13–20.

Grabosky, P. N. (2001). Virtual criminality: Old wine in new bottles? *Social and Legal Studies, 10*(2), 243–249.

Gros, J. G. (2003). Trouble in paradise: Crime and collapsed states in the age of globalization. *The British Journal of Criminology, 43*(1), 63–80.

Groves, R. M., Fowler, F. J., Couper, M. P., Lepkowski, J. M., Singer, E., & Tourangeau, R. (2004). *Survey methodology.* Hoboken, NJ: Wiley.

Hafner, K., & Markoff, J. (1991). *Cyberpunk: Outlaws and hackers on the computer frontier.* New York: Simon & Schuster.

Holt, T. J. (2007). Subcultural evolution? Examining the influence of on- and off-line experiences on deviant subcultures. *Deviant Behavior* (28), 171–198.

Holt, T. J., & Kilger, M. (2008). Techcrafters and makecrafters: A comparison of two populations of hackers. *WOMBAT Workshop on Information Security Threats Data Collection and Sharing, 2008*, pp. 67–78.

Howell, B. A. (2007). Real-world problems of virtual crime. In J. M. Balkin, J. Grimmelmann, E. Katz, N. Kozlovski, S. Wagman, & T. Zarsky (Eds.), *Cybercrime: Digital cops in a networked environment*. New York: New York University Press.

Huey, L. J. (2002). Policing the abstract: Some observations on policing cyberspace. *Canadian Journal of Criminology, 44*(3), 248–249.

Jaishankar, K. (2007). Cyber criminology: Evolving a novel discipline with a new journal. *International Journal of Cyber Criminology, 1*(1), 1–6.

Jaishankar, K. (2008). Space transition theory of cyber crimes. In F. Schmalleger & M. Pittaro (Eds.), *Crimes of the Internet* (pp. 283–301). Upper Saddle River, NJ: Pearson.

Jaishankar, K., & Halder, D. (2008). Pedophilia, pornography, and stalking: Analyzing child victimization on the Internet. In F. Schmalleger & M. Pittaro (Eds.), *Crimes of the Internet* (pp. 28–65). Upper Saddle River, NJ: Pearson.

Jewkes, Y. (2006). *Comment on the book "Cyber crime and Society" by Majid Yar*. Retrieved on September 09, 2007, from http://www.sagepub.co.uk/booksProd Desc.nav?prodId=Book227351

Jordan, T. (2008). *Hacking: Digital media and technological determinism*. Malden, MA: Polity Press.

Jordan, T., & Taylor, P. (1998). A sociology of hackers. *Sociological Review, 46*(4), 757–780.

Kleinrock, L. (2004). The Internet rules of engagement. *Technology in Society,* (26), 193–207.

Koops, B.-J., & Brenner, S. (2006). Cybercrime jurisdiction—An introduction. In B.-J. Koops & S. Brenner (Eds.), *Cybercrime and jurisdiction* (pp. 1–9). The Hague, Netherlands: TMC Asser Press.

Kumar, J. (2006). Determining jurisdiction in cyberspace. *Social Science Research Network*. Retrieved on November 15, 2008, from: http://ssrn.com/abstract=919261

Lasica, J. D. (2005). *Darknet: Hollywood's war against the digital generation*. Hoboken, NJ: Wiley.

Lenk, K. (1997). The challenge of cyberspatial forms of human interaction to territorial governance and policing. In B. D. Loader (Ed.), *The governance of cyberspace: Politics, technology and global restructuring* (pp. 126–135). London: Routledge.

Levy, S. (1984). *Hackers: Heroes of the computer revolution*. Garden City, NY: Doubleday.

McMillan, R. (2009, January 21). Three years undercover with the identity thieves. Keith Mularski talks about his role as administrator of online fraud site DarkMarket. *Techworld.com*. Retrieved on June 11, 2009, from https://www .techworld.com.au/article/273738/three_years_undercover_identity_thieves?pp=1 &fp=4&fpid=288

Moore, R. (2007). The role of computer forensics in criminal investigations. In Y. Jewkes (Ed.), *Crime online* (pp. 81–108). Portland, OR: Willan.

National White-Collar Crime Center, Bureau of Justice Assistance, & Federal Bureau of Investigation. (2007). *2007 Internet Crime Report*. Internet Complaint Center.

Retrieved on October 12, 2009, from http://www.ic3.gov/media/annualreport/2007_IC3Report.pdf.

Naughten, J. (2000). *A brief history of the future: The origins of the Internet* (2nd ed.). London: Phoenix/Orion Books.

Newman, O. (1973). *Defensible space: Crime prevention through urban design.* New York: Macmillan.

Nhan, J. (2009). Criminal justice firewalls: Prosecutorial decision-making in cyber and high-tech crime cases. In K. Jaishankar (Ed.), *International perspectives on crime and justice.* New Castle, UK: Cambridge Scholars.

Nhan, J., & Huey, L. J. (2008). Policing through nodes, clusters, and bandwidth. In S. Leman-Langlois (Ed.), *Technocrime: Technology, crime and social control* (pp. 66–87). Portland, OR: Willan.

Obinyan, E., Ikegwuonu, P., & Vanderpuye, S. (2008). The Fourth Amendment impact on electronic evidence. In F. Schmalleger & M. Pitarro (Eds.), *Crimes of the Internet.* Upper Saddle River, NJ: Pearson.

Pessin, A. (2009, June 15). U.S. creates military cyber command to defend computer networks. *Voice of America News.* Retrieved on June 15, 2009, from http://www.voanews.com/english/2009–06–15-voa64.cfm

Poulsen, K. (2008, October 13). Cybercrime supersite "DarkMarket" was FBI sting, documents confirm. *Wired Magazine.* Retrieved on June 11, 2009, from http://www.wired.com/threatlevel/2008/10/darkmarket-post/

Poulsen, K. (2008, October 17). 56 arrested in DarkMarket sting, says FBI. *Wired Magazine.* Retrieved on June 11, 2009, from http://www.wired.com/threatlevel/2008/10/56-arrested-in/

Reidenberg, J. (2005). Technology and Internet jurisdiction. *University of Pennsylvania Law Review, 153,* 1951–1974.

Reitinger, P. R. (2000). Encryption, anonymity and markets: Law enforcement and technology in a free market virtual world. In D. Thomas & B. D. Loader (Eds.), *Cybercrime: Law enforcement, security and surveillance in the information age* (pp. 132–152). New York: Routledge.

Richardson, R. (2008). *CSI computer crime and security survey.* Computer Security Institute. Retrieved on November 25, 2008, from http://www.gocsi.com/forms/csi_survey.jhtml;jsessionid=JQEWDNHGFHE4AQSNDLOSKHSCJUNN2JVN

Shinder, D. L., & Tittel, E. (2002). *Scene of the cybercrime: Computer forensics handbook.* Rockland, MA: Syngress.

Smith, R. G., Grabosky, P. N., & Urbas, G. (2004). *Cyber criminals on trial.* New York: Cambridge University Press.

Stohl, M. (2006). Cyber terrorism: A clear and present danger, the sum of all fears, breaking point, or patriot games? *Crime, Law, and Social Change, 46,* 223–238.

Sutherland, E. H. (1940). White-collar criminality. *American Sociological Review, 5*(1), 1–12.

Thomas, D. (2002). *Hacker culture.* Minneapolis, MN: Regents of the University of Minnesota.

Thomas, D., & Loader, B. D. (2000). Introduction—Cybercrime: Law enforcement, security and surveillance in the information age. In D. Thomas & B. Loader (Eds.), *Cybercrime: Law enforcement, security, and surveillance in the information age.* London: Routledge.

U.S. Department of Justice (2002). *Searching and seizing computers and obtaining electronic evidence in criminal investigations.* Computer Crime and Intellectual

Property Section. Retrieved on October 12, 2009, from http://www.usdoj.gov/criminal/cybercrime/searching.html

Wall, D. S. (2001). Cybercrimes and the Internet. In D. S. Wall (Ed.), *Crime and the Internet*. London: Routledge.

Wall, D. S. (2007). Policing cybercrimes: Situating the public police in networks of security within cyberspace. *Police Practice and Research, 8*(2), 183–205.

White House. (2003). *The National Strategy to Secure Cyberspace*. Retrieved on October 12, 2009, from http://www.dhs.gov/xlibrary/assets/National_Cyberspace_Strategy.pdf

Wilson, M. I., & Corey, K. E. (2000). *Information tectonics: Space, place, and technology in an electronic age*. New York: Wiley.

Wood, J., & Shearing, C. (2007). *Imagining security*. Portland, OR: Willan.

Yar, M. (2005). The novelty of "cybercrime": An assessment in light of routine activity theory. *European Journal of Criminology, 2*(4), 407–427.

Yar, M. (2006). *Cybercrime and society*. London: Sage.

Zetter, K. (2008, July 22). Kaminsky on how he discovered DNS flaw and more. *Wired Magazine*. Retrieved on June 1, 2009, from http://www.wired.com/threatlevel/2008/07/kaminsky-on-how/

PART III

Policing and Law Enforcement

13 A History of American Policing

Craig D. Uchida

Americanpolicing traces its roots in law enforcement and preventive policing to its English heritage and to the birth and growth of cities throughout the nation. Historians have documented these developments through comparative histories of the New York and London police (Miller, 1977; Richardson, 1970), through individual histories of specific departments (Lane, 1967; Schneider, 1980), and through specific issues in policing (Fogelson, 1977; Monkkonen, 1981; Walker, 1977, 1998). Overall, these histories illustrate the way police have developed over time. Historical analyses also show the roots of problems in policing, such as corruption, brutality, and inefficiency.

The Roots of Modern Policing

Like much of America's common-law tradition, the origins of modern policing can be linked directly to its English heritage. Ideas concerning community policing, crime prevention, posses, constables, and sheriffs developed from English law enforcement.

In the 17th and 18th centuries, the English colonies followed the English policing system, adopting the sheriff, the constable, and the town watch. The county sheriff, who was appointed by the governor, became the most important law enforcement agent, particularly when the colonies remained small and primarily rural. The sheriff's duties included apprehending criminals, serving subpoenas, appearing in court, and collecting taxes. The sheriff was paid a fixed amount for each task he performed. As sheriffs received higher fees based on the taxes they collected, apprehending criminals was not a primary concern. In fact, law enforcement was a low priority.

In New York, Boston, and Philadelphia, constables and the night watch conducted a wide variety of tasks. The night watch reported fires, maintained street lamps, arrested or detained suspicious persons, raised the hue and cry when they needed assistance in apprehending criminals, and walked the rounds or beats. Constables engaged in similarly broad tasks: taking suspects to court, eliminating health hazards, and bringing witnesses to court.

Law Enforcement in the West

At the same time that the English were colonizing the Eastern seaboard, the Spanish were exerting their influence, culture, and religion in the areas that were to become Texas and California in the 1800s. For example, in 1718 the Royal Presidio of San Antonio de Bexar was established by the viceroy of New Spain, who also founded the Mission San Antonio de Valero (more famously known as the Alamo). The missions were home to Franciscan missionaries and local Native Americans from various tribes. Security and law enforcement in the area were handled by soldiers posted to the presidio, most of whom were Mexican frontiersmen from the northern territories of New Spain. In 1731, the king of Spain granted settlers a charter and permission to organize a town council, which included the first official law officer in San Antonio, the *alguacil* (constable or sheriff), Vicente Alvarez Traviesco, then 26 years of age (Mission Basilica, n.d.).

Farther west, in 1769, a Franciscan friar named Junipero Serra established the first mission in California, Mission Basilica San Diego de Alcala (Mission Basilica, n.d.), which eventually grew into the larger community of San Diego. The first of 21 missions in California, the San Diego mission relied upon soldiers and the tenets of the Catholic religion for security and enforcement of rules and laws. Converting American Indians to Catholicism was one of Father Serra's primary goals, and to do so he relied on the military for support and security. According to the PBS film project *The West,*

> By law, all baptized Indians subjected themselves completely to the authority of the Franciscans; they could be whipped, shackled, or imprisoned for disobedience and were hunted down if they fled the mission grounds. Indian recruits, who were often forced to convert nearly at gunpoint, could be expected to survive mission life for only about 10 years. (West Film Project, 2001, para. 10).

Forming the New Police in England

During the mid- to late 1700s, European cities grew rapidly because of the Industrial Revolution. London, in particular, expanded at an unprecedented rate. From 1750 to 1820, the population nearly doubled (Miller, 1977), and the urban economy became more complex and specialized. With industrial growth came crime, disorder, riots, and public health problems. Food riots, wage protests, poor sewage control, pickpockets, burglars, and vandals created difficulties for city dwellers. The upper and middle classes, concerned about these issues, sought more protection and preventive measures. The constable-watch system of law enforcement could no longer deal successfully with the problems of the day, and alternative solutions were devised.

Suggestions were made to replace the constable-watch system with a stronger, more centralized police force. Prevention and deterrence would guide the police. Magistrates Henry Fielding, John Fielding, and Patrick Colquhoun, as well as philosopher Jeremy Bentham and his followers, advocated this new policing philosophy. A preventive police force would act as a deterrent to criminals and would be in the best interests of society. The idea of uniformed police officers, however, was opposed by many citizens and politicians in England because it resembled a standing army. The proponents of a police force eventually won out, and after much debate, the London Metropolitan Police Act was approved by Parliament in 1829 (Critchley, 1967).

The Police Act established a full-time, uniformed police force with the primary purpose of patrolling the city. Sir Robert Peel is credited with the formation of the police, for he synthesized the ideas of the Fieldings, Colquhoun, and Bentham into law; convinced Parliament of the need for police; and guided the early development of the force.

Through Peel, the role of the London police was formulated. Crime prevention was the primary function, but to enforce the laws and to exert its authority, the police first had to gain legitimacy in the eyes of the public. To earn acceptance, Peel and his associates selected men who were even-tempered and reserved, chose a simple navy blue uniform, insisted that officers be restrained and polite, meted out appropriate discipline, and did not allow officers to carry guns. Overall, the London police emphasized its legitimacy based on *institutional* authority—that their power was grounded in the English Constitution and their behavior determined by rules of law. In essence, the power of the London "bobby" or "Peeler" (so called in deference to Robert Peel) was based on the institution of the government.

American Police Systems

American cities and towns encountered problems like those in England. eastern cities grew quickly, civil disorders swept the nation, and crime was perceived to increase. The population of New York, for example, grew from 33,000 in 1790 to 150,000 in 1830. Foreign immigrants, particularly Irish and Germans, accounted for a significant portion of the increase. Traveling to America in search of employment and better lifestyles, the immigrants competed with native-born Americans for skilled and unskilled positions and were seen as social and economic threats. Other tensions existed in the city as well. Race became a factor, as those who opposed slavery were met with violence in both the North and the South.

Between the 1830s and 1870s, numerous conflicts occurred because of ethnic and racial differences, economic failures, and moral questions, and during elections of public officials. In New York, 1834 was designated the "Year of the Riots" because so many took place (Miller, 1977). At the same time that the riots occurred, citizens perceived that crime was increasing. Homicides, robberies, and thefts were thought to be on the rise. In addition, vagrancy, prostitution, gambling, and other vices were more observable on the streets. Yet, in spite of the apparent immediacy of these problems, replacements for the constable-watch police system did not appear overnight.

The political forces in the large industrial cities like New York, Philadelphia, and Boston hindered the immediate acceptance of a London-style police department. City councils, mayors, state legislatures, and governors debated over a number of questions and could not come to an immediate agreement over the type of police they wanted. In New York City, for example, although the riots occurred in 1834, the movement to form a preventive police department did not take shape until 1841. Four years later, in 1845, the New York Police Department was created, but officers did not begin wearing uniforms until 1853.

Eventually, American police departments borrowed selectively rather than exactly from the London model. The most notable carryover was the adoption of the preventive patrol idea. A police presence would alter the behavior of individuals and would be available to maintain order in an efficient manner. Differences, however, between the London and American police abounded. The London Metropolitan Police Department was a highly centralized agency. An extension of the national government, the police department was purposely removed from the direct political influence of the people. Furthermore, Peel recruited specific individuals—polite, aloof officers who were trained and followed strict guidelines. In addition, the bobbies were encouraged to look upon police work as a career, not just a job.

American police systems followed the style of local and municipal governments, which were highly decentralized. Mayors were largely figureheads; real power lay in the wards and neighborhoods. City councilmen or aldermen ran the government and used political patronage freely. Police departments shared this style of participation and decentralization. The police were an extension of different political factions rather than an extension of city government. Police officers were recruited and selected by political leaders in a particular ward or precinct. As a result of the democratic nature of government, legal intervention by the police was limited, unlike the London police, which relied on formal control. That is, instead of drawing on institutional legitimacy (i.e., parliamentary laws), each American police officer had to establish his own authority among the citizens he patrolled. The personal, informal police officer could win the respect of the citizenry by knowing local standards and expectations. This meant that different police behavior would occur in different neighborhoods. In New York, for example, the officer was free to act as he chose within the context of broad public expectations. He was less limited by institutional and legal restraints than his London counterpart, entrusted with less formal power but given broader personal discretion.

Policing in the 19th Century

From the Civil War to the beginning of the 20th century, American police departments appeared almost overnight in eastern cities (Monkkonen, 1981). Once New York, Philadelphia, Boston, and Cincinnati adopted the English model, the new version of policing spread from larger cities to smaller ones rather quickly.

Unlike eastern cities, however, the development of policing in the West varied, depending in large part on the way in which the city was formed. For example, San Antonio originated as a Spanish mission and presidio in 1718. According to the San Antonio Police Department's website,

> In the earliest years of [the city's development], (1718–1800), the major law enforcement concerns were with problems related to settling residents' disputes over land and livestock, as well as protecting the settlements from Indian attacks. During the first half of the 19th century, according to most published histories on this period, law enforcement concerns were with the protection of the residents of San Antonio from the constant threat of attack by "marauding Indians and Mexican bandits" as well as other intruders. (SAPD, 2004, para. 2)

The city of Houston was established after Texas had won its independence from Mexico in 1836. Although a constable was selected to serve as the first law enforcement official in 1837, it was not until 4 years later that an official police department was formed and a city marshal appointed.

In Wichita, Kansas, and Fort Worth, Texas, the development of law enforcement was tied to the problems associated with cattle towns: all-night saloons, gambling houses, and gunfights. Wichita, located on the Chisholm Trail, was known for its wild nights in the 1870s. Wyatt Earp was appointed to the force as a policeman in 1875, the second stop (Lamar, Missouri, was the first) in a law enforcement career that would lead him to Dodge City, Pima County, and Tombstone, Arizona. To curb the violence that occurred in Wichita, the city appointed a special police force as toll keepers on the Chisholm Trail Bridge, which crossed the Arkansas River into Wichita. This special force also removed firearms from anyone coming into the city and held them for safekeeping until the cowboys departed. To curtail drunken behavior, the state passed a prohibition law in 1880 (City of Wichita, 2009).

In 1873, Fort Worth was incorporated; the city appointed a marshal with a force of four policemen to reduce high crime, gambling, and drunken behavior. Unlike Wichita, the local businesses in Fort Worth abolished the police force after six months for "economic reasons." The cowboys who passed through the area needed supplies and recreation before taking their cattle onto Kansas and were a financial boon to the saloons and gambling houses. Not until 1876, when Jim Courtright became marshal, did violence abate. Courtright, a well-known gunfighter, hired two policemen to assist him and through his reputation reduced the number of killings while maintaining the flow of money and liquor in the city. For Courtright, legitimization came in the form of his ability to outgun his opponents.

Police Work

Officers

The 19th-century patrolman was basically a political operative rather than a London-style professional committed to public service (Walker, 1998). Primarily selected for his political service, the police officer in urban centers owed his allegiance to the ward boss and police captain who chose him. Similarly, in the West, the city marshal was an elected official who chose his officers.

Police officers were paid well but had poor job security. Police salaries compared favorably with other occupations. On average, in 1880 most major cities paid policemen in the neighborhood of $900 a year. Walker (1998) reports that a skilled tradesman in the building industry earned about $770 a year, while those in manufacturing could expect about $450 a year. In Wichita, Wyatt Earp earned $60 per month as policeman, or $720 per year; the marshal made $91.66 per month, or $1100 per year; and the assistant marshal made $75 per month, or $900 per year (City of Wichita, 2009). In San Diego in 1889, the starting salary for a police officer was $80 per month, although he worked 12-hour shifts, 7 days a week (San Diego Police Historical Association, 2009).

Walking the Beat

Police officers walked a patrol route, or beat, in all types of weather for 2 to 6 hours of a 12-hour day. The remaining time was spent at the station house on reserve. During actual patrol duty, police officers were required to maintain order and make arrests, but they often circumvented their responsibilities. Supervision was extremely limited once an officer was beyond the station house. Sergeants and captains had no way of contacting their men while they were on patrol, as communications technology was limited. Telegraph lines linked district stations to headquarters in the 1850s, but call boxes on the beat were not introduced until late in the 19th century, and the radio and motorized communications did not appear until the 1900s. Police officers, then, acted alone and used their own initiative.

Crime Control and Arrests

Monkkonen (1981) found that, from 1860 to 1920, arrests declined in 23 of the largest cities in the United States. Crimes without victims (vice, disturbances, drunkenness, and other public order offenses) fell dramatically. Overall, Monkkonen estimates that arrests declined by more than 33% during the 60-year period. Further analysis showed that the decline occurred because the police role shifted from controlling the "dangerous class" to controlling criminal behavior only. From 1860 to 1890, the police were involved in assisting the poor, in taking in overnight lodgers, and in returning lost children to their parents or orphanages. In the period 1890 to 1920, however, the police changed their role, structure, and behavior because of external demands placed upon them.

Police Corruption and Lawlessness

One of the major themes of 19th-century policing is the large-scale corruption that occurred in numerous departments across the country. The lawlessness of the police—their systematic corruption and nonenforcement of the laws—was one of the paramount issues in municipal politics during the late 1800s.

Because police officers worked alone or in small groups, there were ample opportunities to shake down peddlers and small businesses. Detectives allowed con artists, pickpockets, and thieves to go about their business in return for a share of their proceeds. Captains often established regular payment schedules for houses of prostitution according to the number of girls in the house and the rates charged. The monthly total for police protection ranged from $25 to $75 per house plus $500 to open or reopen after a raid (Richardson, 1970).

Officers who did not go along with the nonenforcement of laws or who did not approve of the graft and corruption of others found themselves transferred to less-than-desirable areas and beats. Promotions were also denied, as they were reserved for the politically astute and wealthy officer (promotions could cost $10,000 to $15,000).

Reforming the Police

A broad reform effort began to emerge toward the end of the 19th century. Stimulated mainly by the Progressives, attempts were made to create a truly professional police force. The Progressives were upper-middle-class, educated Protestants who opposed the political machines, sought improvements in government, and desired a change in American morality. By eliminating machine politics from government, all facets of social services, including the police, would improve.

These reformers found that the police lacked discipline, strong leadership, and qualified personnel. To improve conditions, the Progressives recommended three changes: (1) centralization of departments, (2) upgrading of personnel, and 3) narrowing of the police function (Fogelson, 1977). Centralization of the police meant that more power and authority would be placed in the hands of the chief. Autonomy from politicians was crucial to centralization. Upgrading the rank-and-file meant better training, discipline, and selection. Finally, these reformers urged that police give up all activities unrelated to crime, including running ambulances, handling licenses for businesses, and sheltering the poor.

From 1890 to 1920, the Progressives struggled to implement their reform ideology in cities across the country. Some inroads were made during this period, including the establishment of police commissions, civil service examinations, and legislative reforms. The efforts of the Progressives still did not change urban departments drastically. Chiefs continued to lack power and authority; many officers had little or no education; training was limited; and the police role continued to include a wide variety of tasks.

Walker (1977) gives several reasons for the failure of reform. First, political machines were too difficult to break. Despite the efforts by the Progressives, politicians could still count on individual supporters to undermine their reforms. Second, police officers resented the Progressives' interventions. Reformers were viewed by police officers as individuals who knew little about police work; therefore, officers saw their proposals for change as ill conceived. Finally, the reforms failed because the idea of policing could not be divorced from politics.

Becoming Professionals

After the failure of the Progressives to change policing, a second reform effort emerged. A small cadre of chiefs sought and implemented a variety of innovations that would improve policing generally. From about 1910 to 1960, police chiefs advocated change and pressed for the adoption of the "professional model."

The professional department included a number of characteristics: Officers were experts, police departments were autonomous, and police were efficient, using modern technology and businesslike practices to control crime and enforce the law. These reforms were similar to those of the Progressives, but because they came from within the police organizations themselves, they met with greater success.

The major innovator among the chiefs was August Vollmer. Serving first as the elected marshal of Berkeley in 1905 and then appointed chief in 1909, Vollmer brought new ideas and science to policing. He is credited with a number of "firsts"—the first records system; the first use of the Modus Operandi investigation system; the first to use forensic science to analyze blood, soil and fiber; and the first to establish a motorcycle patrol unit.

Vollmer emphasized improvement of the quality of police personnel, believing that this would lead to professional officers. He initiated the use of intelligence, psychiatric, and neurological tests in the selection of applicants and was the first police chief to actively recruit college students. In addition, he was instrumental in linking the police department with the University of California at Berkeley, where in 1916 officers began to take summer courses. By 1931, a criminology program had been formally created at Berkeley, and in 1950 the School of Criminology was established, with Vollmer and his protégé, O. W. Wilson, as instructors (Berkeley Police Department, n.d.).

O. W. Wilson followed in his mentor's footsteps by advocating efficiency within the police bureaucracy through scientific techniques. From 1928 to 1939, Wilson served as police chief in Wichita, Kansas, where he conducted the first systematic study of one-officer squad cars. He argued that one-officer cars were efficient, effective, and economical. Despite arguments from patrol officers that their safety was at risk, Wilson claimed that the public received better service with single-officer cars.

Technology Development

Technological changes enabled the police to move toward professionalism. The patrol car, the two-way radio, and the telephone altered the way in which the police operated and the manner in which citizens made use of the police. Motorized patrols meant more efficient coverage of the city and quicker response to calls for service. The two-way radio dramatically increased the supervisory capacity of police administrators, as continuous contact between sergeant and police officer could be maintained. Finally, the telephone provided the link between the public and the police.

Overall, the second reform movement met with more success than the Progressives' attempt, though it did not achieve its goal of total professionalization. On the other hand, the quality of police officers greatly improved during this period. Police reformers and others were able to reduce the influence of political parties in departmental affairs. Chiefs secured greater power and authority over their management abilities but continued to receive input from political leaders and remained political appointees. In terms of efficiency, the police moved forward in serving the public more quickly and competently. Technological innovations clearly assisted the police in this area, as did streamlining the organizations themselves.

Turbulent Times: America in the 1960s

Policing in America encountered its most serious crisis in the 1960s. The rise in crime, the civil rights movement, antiwar sentiment, and riots in the cities brought the police into the center of controversy.

During the decade of the 1960s, crime increased at a phenomenal rate; the crime rate per 100,000 persons doubled in 10 years. As crime increased, so, too, did the demands for its reduction. The police, in emphasizing its crime-fighting ability, had created a false expectation on the part of the public. As a result, the public image of the police was tarnished.

The civil rights movement created new demands for the police. The movement, begun in the 1950s, sought equality for black Americans in all facets of life. Sit-ins at segregated lunch counters, boycotts of bus services, attempts at integrating schools, and demonstrations in the streets led to direct confrontations with law enforcement officers. The police became the symbol of a society that denied blacks equal justice under the law.

Eventually, the frustrations of black Americans erupted into violence in cities across the country. Most of the disorders were initiated by a routine incident involving the police, including the New York City riot of 1964 and the Watts riot in Los Angeles in 1965. By 1966, 43 more riots had broken out across the country. Disorders engulfed Newark for 5 days, leaving 23 dead, while the Detroit riot a week later lasted nearly 7 days and resulted in 43 deaths with $40 million in property damages.

On the final day of the Detroit riot, President Lyndon Johnson appointed a special commission to investigate the problem of civil disorder. The National Advisory Commission on Civil Disorders (the Kerner Commission) identified institutional racism as the underlying cause of the rioting. Police actions were also cited as contributing to the disorders. Direct police intervention had sparked the riots in Harlem, Watts, Newark, and Detroit. In Watts and Newark, the riots had been set off by routine traffic stops. In Detroit, a police raid on an after-hours bar touched off the disorders there. The police thus became the focus of national attention.

The Kerner Commission found several problems in police departments. First, police were brutal and abused their power. Second, training and supervision were inadequate. Third, police–community relations were poor. And fourth, the employment of black officers lagged far behind the growth of the black population.

To partially remedy these problems, President Johnson created a crime commission, and Congress authorized federal assistance to criminal justice. The president's crime commission produced a final report that emphasized the need for more research, higher qualifications for criminal justice personnel, and greater coordination of the national crime-control effort. The federal aid program to justice agencies resulted in the Office of Law Enforcement Assistance, a forerunner of the Law Enforcement Assistance Administration (LEAA).

The Legacy of the 1960s

The events of the 1960s forced police, politicians, and policymakers to reassess the state of law enforcement in the United States. Academicians began to study the police in an effort to explain their problems and crises. With federal funding from LEAA and private organizations like the Police Foundation, researchers began to study the police from a number of perspectives. Traditional methods of patrol development, officer selection, and training were questioned. Racial discrimination in employment practices, in arrests, and in the use of deadly force was among the issues closely examined.

In addition, the professional movement itself came into question, for it created two unintended consequences. The first involved the development of the police subculture. The second was the problem of police–community relations. In terms of the subculture, police officers felt alienated from their administrators, the media, and the public and turned inward as a result. Patrol officers resented the police hierarchy because of its emphasis on following orders and regulations. Officers saw the media and the public as foes because of the criticism and disrespect cast their way. As the crime rate increased, newspaper accounts criticized the police for their inability to curtail crime. As the riots persisted, some citizens cried for more order, while others demanded less oppression by the police on the streets. The conflicting message given to officers by these groups led to distrust, alienation, and frustration. Only by standing together did officers feel comfortable in their working environment.

The second unintended consequence of professionalism was the problems it generated for police–community relations. Modern technology (like the patrol car), removed the officer from the street and eliminated routine contact with citizens. The impersonal style of professionalism often exacerbated police–community problems. Tactics such as aggressive patrol in black neighborhoods, designed to suppress crime efficiently, created more racial tensions.

These problems called into question the need for and effectiveness of professionalism. Some police administrators suggested abandoning the movement altogether. Others sought to continue the effort while adjusting for and solving the difficulties. For the most part, the goal of professionalization has remained operative.

Community Policing

As a result of the problems of the 1960s and 1970s, a third wave of reform of police operations and strategies began to emerge: community-oriented policing.

Community policing came to light as an idea and a philosophy in response to the communication gap between police and community and because of research that questioned police tactics and strategies. A new paradigm emerged, incorporating broken windows theory, proactive policing, and problem-oriented policing, and provided the foundation for the community policing reform era.

Police strategists recognized that simply reacting to calls for service limited the ability of law enforcement to control crime and maintain order. Police on patrol could not see enough to control crime effectively—they did not know how to intervene to improve the quality of life in the community. The reactive strategy used during the professional era no longer was effective in dealing with complex problems in the 1980s and 1990s. Instead, Herman Goldstein (1990) and James Q. Wilson and George Kelling (1982) called for police to engage in proactive work and problem-oriented policing. A whole body of work from police researchers, strategists, and reformers laid the groundwork for the community policing movement.

In its ideal sense, community policing promised to fundamentally transform the way police do business. Reformers argued that police should not be so obsessed with routine "people-processing" activities (e.g., making arrests, filling out reports) but should focus instead on "people-changing" activities (Mastrofski & Ritti, 1995). These included building up neighborhoods, designing custom solutions to local problems, forging partnerships with other community agencies, and a variety of other nonroutine police activities.

Since the 1990s, the implementation of community policing has been inconsistent. Federal funding from 1994 to 1999 enabled police departments to hire community policing officers, purchase new technologies for problem solving, and implement different programs (Roth et al., 2000). With the new millennium and the terrorist events of September 11, 2001, however, emphasis on community policing has waned. It remains to be seen how and in what way community policing will reemerge in the coming years.

CONCLUSION

This chapter has taken a brief look at the development of American police systems from its English heritage through the early years of the 21st century. Major emphasis has been placed on the police role, though important events that have shaped the development of the police have also been discussed. Throughout this review, a number of present-day issues are seen to have their roots in different epochs of American history. For example, the idea of community policing can be traced to the colonial period. Preventive patrol, legitimacy, authority, and professionalism are 18th- and 19th-century concepts. Riots, disorders, and corruption are not new to American policing; similar events occurred in the 19th century. Thus, we can give contextual meaning to current police problems, ideas, and situations. By looking at the past, present-day events can be better understood.

DISCUSSION QUESTIONS

1. What are the differences and similarities between the London model and the American model of policing in the 19th century?

2. How does the democratic form of government in American cities influence the way police departments operate and function?

3. Throughout history, reform movements have tried to change policing. How have they succeeded or failed?

4. Describe and discuss the components of professionalism in American policing.

5. The 1960s posed problems for American police. What were those problems, and how were they resolved?

6. What are the historical roots of community policing?

REFERENCES

Berkeley Police Department. [n.d.]. *Our History.* [Website]. Retrieved on October 13, 2009, from http://www.ci.berkeley.ca.us/police/History/history.html

City of Wichita. (2009). *The Beginnings: Excerpts from "Wichita Police Department 1871–2000."* [Website]. Retrieved October 13, 2009, from http://www.wichita .gov/City Offices/Police/History/History

Critchley, T. A. (1967). *A history of police in England and Wales.* Montclair, NJ: Patterson Smith.

Fogelson, R. (1977). *Big-city police.* Cambridge, MA: Harvard University Press.

Goldstein, H. (1990). *Problem-oriented policing.* New York: McGraw-Hill.

Lane, R. (1967). *Policing the city: Boston, 1822–1285.* Cambridge, MA: Harvard University Press.

Miller, W. R. (1977). *Cops and bobbies: Police authority in New York and London, 1830–1870.* Chicago: University of Chicago Press.

Mission Basilica San Diego de Alcala. (n.d.). *Mission History.* [Website]. Retrieved on October 13, 2009, from http://www.missionsandiego.com/mission_history.htm

Monkkonen, E. H. (1981). *Police in urban America, 1860–1920.* Cambridge: Cambridge University Press.

Richardson, J. F. (1970). *The New York police: Colonial times to 1901.* New York: Oxford University Press.

Roth, J. A., Ryan, J. F., Gaffigan, S. F., Koper, C. S., Moore, M. H., Roehl, J. A., et al. (2000). *National evaluation of the COPS program—Title I of the 1994 Crime Act.* Washington, DC: National Institute of Justice.

San Antonio Police Department (SAPD). (1998–2004). *History of SAPD: Part One: The Early Years: 1718–1900.* [Website]. Retrieved October 13, 2009, from http://sanantonio.gov/sapd/history1.htm

San Diego Police Historical Association. (2009). *History.* [Website]. Retrieved on October 13, 2009, from http://www.sandiegopolicemuseum.com/HistorySet.htm

Schneider, J. C. (1980). *Detroit and the problems of order, 1830–1880.* Lincoln: University of Nebraska Press.

Walker, S. (1977). *A critical history of police reform: The emergence of professionalism.* Lexington, MA: D. C. Heath.

Walker, S. (1998). *Popular justice: A history of American criminal justice* (2nd ed.). New York: Oxford University Press.

The West Film Project. (2001). *New Perspectives on the West: Junipero Serra (1713–1784).* PBS. [Website]. Retrieved October 13, 2009, from http://www.pbs.org/weta/ thewest/people/s_z/serra.htm

Wilson, J. Q., & Kelling, G. (1982). Broken windows: The police and neighborhood safety. *Atlantic Monthly, 249,* 29–38.

14

Police Theory

John Crank, Dawn Irlbeck,
and Connie M. Koski

In this chapter, we review four ways of looking at theory: normative–rational, institutional, conflict and critical, and postmodern. Each of these has something to offer the police scholar, and each has its current limitations. Importantly, they provide us a way to begin to organize this field called police scholarship and to think about where we go next.

Normative–Rational Theory

Most people, when they think of the police, think of them reactively. That is, there is crime, and the police do something about crime. Why do we need police theory? It is obvious that the police exist to do something about crime—if not, then one heck of a lot of citizens are being fooled big time. It is not obvious that we need to know much more than that about them, unless we are looking for a job and want to become police officers.

Normative–rational perspectives look at police organizations as independent actors and ask what they can do to achieve their mission. By *normative* is meant that their work finds its meanings in broad societal norms, in this case those norms that formally sanction behavior. *Rational* means that they can make reasonable decisions and act on them based on a rational assessment of their environment.

Two ways of looking at normative perspectives are presented here. The first way is through the assessment of contingency theory, which is the body of theory aimed at explaining the behavior of police organizations in terms of their fit with their environmental settings. The second is an overview of contemporary crime interdiction practices, those that represent the state of the art in police work today.

Contingency Theory

Contingency theory is a rational approach to theory building, but it is different from traditional notions of organizational rationality. The characteristic feature of contingency theory is that organizations adapt to contingencies they face. Their efforts to achieve particular goals will consequently depend on the nature of the community and the organizational circumstances in which they find themselves.

Donaldson (2001, p. 1) defined *contingency theory* as follows: "[O]rganizational effectiveness results from fitting characteristics of the organization, such as its structure, to contingencies that reflect the situation of the organization." *Structural contingency theory*, which refers to theories or efforts to explain or change organizational structure, refers to perspectives that locate structure in terms of the three contingencies of environment, size, and strategy. Change in any of these contingencies tends to produce changes in organizational structure.

Contingency theory is not universalistic, or, in today's banter, it does not lend itself to "best practices." Donaldson noted that contingency refers to adaptive processes: The relationship between any element of structure and its performance is mediated by contingencies that have to be recognized and addressed. "[A] contingency is any variable that moderates the effect of an organizational characteristic on organizational performance" (2001, p. 7). Consequently, when we seek to understand organizational structure or the behavior of those structures, we take into consideration three issues:

1. There is a relationship between the contingency and the structure.

2. If the contingency changes, the structure changes.

3. The fit between the contingency and the organization determines organizational performance. The better the fit, the more effective the organizational performance.

Contingency theory can be traced to Langworthy (1986), who presaged contingency theory by noting that what works for organizations in some communities will not work in others. Much of the work of empirically assessing contingency theory is traced to Mastrofski, whose work is considered later in this chapter in institutional theory, and to Maguire (see, e.g., Maguire, 2003; Mastrofski, Ritti, & Hoffmaster, 1987). Kuhns, Maguire, and Cox (2007), for example, in an application of contingency theory, showed how organizational emphases with regard to a variety of public safety concerns were related to environmental characteristics, particularly regional factors and levels of violent and property crime.

The police–community/political environment research is a good example of structural contingency theory where the contingency is located in the environment. Since the seminal work of Wilson (1968), researchers have been interested in the relationship between characteristics of the community and the policing structure (see Klinger, 2004; Maguire, 2003; Stucky, 2005).

To illustrate what is and what is not contingency theory, we consider Morabito's (2008) paper on the role of the community environment on police innovation. (Please note that Morabito makes no claims that this is contingency theory.) Morabito hypothesized that particular community political structures would facilitate the adoption of community policing practices. She identified three political structures: (1) jurisdictions with city managers, (2) those with partisan elections, and (3) community characteristics such as residential stability, diversity, and income that she used as a proxy for variations in district-based elections. She also included the contingencies of organizational size and formalization of structure. Her findings showed that form of government and district-based elections, as well as organizational formalization, emerged as significant predictors of innovation.

Morabito's work is community theory, which can be considered a category of contingency theory. However, from a contingency theory perspective, there is an unasked question: What is the environment–organization misfit that structural innovations of community policing addresses? That is, what is the policing problem that community policing addresses and that extant forms of policing do not address? In terms of effectiveness, what is the inefficiency that organizational change toward community policing makes effective?

This three-part question—What is it that (1) community policing addresses, that (2) represents a change in the environment, that (3) resulted from a misfit between community policing and the environment?—is not simply a research question. It is an organizational issue that has haunted community policing since its inception and may account for what appears to be the disestablishment of the community policing movement in the current era. One can argue, from a contingency theory perspective, that the rapid rise and institutionalization of data-driven COMPSTAT, with its focus on effectiveness in terms of arrest-driven results, is a result of the misfit in community and policing created by the community policing movement, visibly indicated by public perceptions that crime was inadequately addressed (although see Willis, Mastrofski, & Weisburd, 2007).

Contingency theory does not seem to work well for understanding police organizations. Maguire (2003) noted that, because departments have unclear outputs and will survive from public need despite their performance, changes in environmental contingencies will have minimal affect on them. However, contemporary trends in policing, with their focus on the production of arrest statistics, may increase the importance of such outputs. That is, the relative unimportance of contingency theory may be passing. This is discussed in the following section on police criminology.

Police Criminology

Police criminology refers specifically to police efforts to do something about crime. Most criminal justice research is police criminology. This area also represents the most applied area of police theory today, in that a great deal of research has focused on the effectiveness of police practices in a wide variety of crime and disorder settings.

The signature work on police criminology is the tome *Preventing Crime: What Works, What Doesn't, and What's Promising* (Sherman et al., 1996). This work represented a comprehensive evaluation of the effectiveness of Bureau of Justice grants to assist state and local law enforcement and communities in preventing crime. It is the most thorough overview of police practices yet undertaken. The work focuses on institutional settings, including labor markets, places, families, and schools, and asks whether research carried out in these settings has had any significant effects on crime. Findings are organized according to two factors: (1) Did the interventions show success, and (2) was the methodology adequate for confidence in the conclusions of the research? A discussion of the principal findings are beyond the scope of this chapter, but any reader interested in police criminology is advised to spend some time in this work.

Police criminology today can be separated into two branches. The first assesses existing practices, and the second looks at innovations. The difference between the two branches is subtle and mostly depends on whether any given practice is part of the regular budget.

Existing Practices: Murder

Murder is perhaps the most important crime police deal with—it is the central focus of a great deal of media attention, and it carries the heaviest penal sanction. Yet, the clearance rate for murder has gone sharply down over the past 50 years. In 1965, the average clearance rate for homicide was 91%. By 2002, it had dropped to 64%. Why?

The work of Cronin and his colleagues (Cronin et al., 2007) represents a solid review and analysis of the many facets of police work related to homicide clearance rates. The authors tracked current organizational practices for homicide: the management of homicide units, the identification of eyewitnesses, interrogation practices, the use of crime labs, and ways of dealing with cold cases in the age of DNA. This research did not identify a single causative agent—police work by all accounts has substantially improved over the past 50 years—but provided a range of suggestions in each of these areas. For example, the authors, noting that as many as 75% of eyewitnesses misidentify suspects, provided a series of recommendations with regard to the use of eyewitness testimony and for the management and organization of lineups. This work is an excellent review of many aspects of police work central to contemporary routine police practices.

New Directions: The Return to the Professional Model

Researchers interested in new directions in policing have voluminous materials that they can select. All the practices in the following list represent different ways the police have developed new directions in the past 30 years, and all focus on the mission of crime control.

COMPSTAT: Crime control through managerial oversight and command responsibility

Lever pulling: Crime control through using all available prosecutorial and police tools to threaten (and carry out) apprehension conviction

Problem-oriented crime control: Identifying and gaining control of underlying problems

Broken windows: Crime control through aggressive order-maintenance activity

Zero tolerance: Nondiscretionary enforcement of all laws, sometimes focusing specifically on minor offenses

Crime mapping: Crime control by visual representation of high-crime areas and real-time response

Third-party policing: Crime control through pressure on third parties who in some way facilitate crime

Intelligence-led crime control: Crime control through higher-quality intelligence/ information in real-time policing

Hot-spot policing: Crime control through greater presence/visibility in high-crime areas

Crackdowns: Heavy use of arrest in areas associated with specific crimes or problems

Interestingly, these changes all have been frequently labeled as community policing, yet none of them involve activities in which the police reach out to the community in some pragmatic way, the sine qua non of community policing. To the contrary, all represent a rejection of mission that is not meaningfully tied to crime suppression and prevention. They appear to have piggybacked on community policing's legitimacy and today are emerging as the functional center of a new police professionalism, with the community policing movement in decline. From a historical point of view, we witness in these practices two features: (1) the emergence of police criminology as a strong area of academic research, and (2) the return of the field of policing to its professional roots, a neoprofessionalism movement with a central focus on the law enforcement mission but with a stronger scientific and intelligence-based foundation for its work.

Institutional Theory

Institutional theory of policing is traceable to the writings of Mastrofski, Ritti, and Hoffmaster (1987) and theoretically elaborated by Crank and

Langworthy (1992; see also Crank, 1994). Briefly stated, *institutional theory* is the idea that organizational structure and policy are concerned with satisfying values carried by important constituencies in their environments. It represents a sharp challenge to contingency theories of police organizations. Put simply, organizations in highly institutionalized environments are concerned with constituent values, not technical efficiency. Police organizations, instead of focusing on clear-cut outputs around a core product such as arrests or traffic stops, for example, turn outward to their institutional environments to determine appropriate organizational structures. This has several meanings:

1. Police departments loosely couple their structures to the technical core so that they can satisfy legitimacy concerns without being held accountable for what they actually do.

2. Departments operate under a "logic of good faith," according to which members support each other and believe in the organization as a matter of faith rather than reliance on measurable outputs.

3. Organizational structures mirror turbulence in the external environment by becoming internally complex. Similarly, organizational complexity is a reflection of environmental conflict. For example, hiring processes tend to build in to their policies and practices broad controversies regarding civil service, gender and race equality, and merit.

4. Organizations respond to environmental change by adding layers of complexity. Hence, departments tended to respond to community policing by adding community policing units and specialized activities rather than restructuring or simplifying organizational structures and processes.

Institutional theory itself is in the process of institutionalization in police theory today. Yet, it faces a broad set of issues. Some of those issues are reviewed in the following sections.

Issue 1: Transmission of Institutional Expectations

How are institutional values transmitted to organizations? If an institution is a causal agent, the specification of that cause agent is critical. Giblin (2006), adapting DiMaggio and Powell's (1983) model, identified three means of institutional transmission: mimetic, normative, and coercive pressures. *Mimetic pressures* are those by which organizations borrow convenient items from member organizations in the organizational sector. *Normative pressures* are related to training, accreditation, and education and refer to pressures to conform to broad normative expectations in the institutional environment. *Coercive pressures* refer to compulsory pressures on organizations to conform to their environments. The law is an example of such a coercive pressure.

Crank (2003), adapting Scott's (1992) model of institutional transmission, identified six ways in which environmental elements are received by police organizations. The first, *imposition*, is the same as coercive pressure, noted above. *Authorization*, the second, is similar to normative pressure in that it refers to the way in which broad norms are defined and enforced. However, it refers to more formalistic sources of authority than the general "normative" category. Third, structure and policy may be *induced* in that they are accompanied with rewards for the organization. Crank and Langworthy (1996) described the adoption of community policing as a process of institutional inducement, by which community policing was induced into police organizations through large grants that helped pay for programs and for officer salaries. *Acquisition*, the fourth, is about how organizations deliberately choose elements from their institutional environment. It recognizes that organizations are autonomous actors. The transmission of COMPSTAT across the institutional settings of police organizations can be described as a process of acquisition. *Imprinting*, fifth, occurs when organizations are first formed. For example, one could argue that a militaristic rank structure was imprinted on police organizations in that most of the early departments were post–Civil War and were staffed by Civil War veterans who brought a military posture to the newly minted field of urban policing. Finally, *incorporation* refers to the tendency of multipurpose organizations such as the police to internally map their external environments. Conflicts in that environment will be elaborated in terms of broad policy statements, as in the example of personnel policies mentioned earlier.

Issue 2: Legitimating Processes

How is it that the process of legitimacy occurs in concrete settings? Vitale (2005) argued that the adoption of quality-of-life policing in New York should be understood in terms of institutional processes. Bratton and Giuliani came to power in New York in an environment in which police were seen as ineffectual in crime suppression. The two had a legitimizing mandate: a "quality-of-life" philosophy focusing on zero tolerance, frequent use of stop-and-frisk, broad use of civil enforcement practices, and the creation of other laws and regulations that aimed at controlling disorderly behavior. Through the ongoing commitments and very public support for quality-of-life policing, the mayor and the chief led the NYPD through broad and profound changes. Quality-of-life policing, with its intense law enforcement focus on arrest practices through command responsibility, was institutionalized across the organization. Vitale noted the unique historical circumstances behind the NYPD's transition, including the recognition that many elements of the new policing were already under way when Giuliani was elected. This is an excellent study of legitimacy lost and regained, and of the transformation of a department to ultimately lead the transformation of policing across the United States.

Others have noted the importance of legitimacy for organizational well-being. Crank and Langworthy (1992) argued that the legitimacy of police organizations was carried out as a ceremonial function. The loss of legitimacy was indicated by the firing of the chief and restored only after the selection of a new chief with a new legitimizing mandate. Katz (2001) discussed how a specialized gang unit emerged from constituency pressure and consequently placed greater stock on ceremonial aspects aimed at satisfying environmental "sovereigns" than on substantive efforts to actually do something about gangs.

Issue 3: Empirical Testing Against Contingency Theory

A small number of authors have taken on what might be called the institutional–contingency debate. This debate is whether police practices and organizational changes are better understood in terms of contingency theory or institutional theory. Two works are noted in this regard.

Willis, Mastrofski, and Weisburd provided a qualitative assessment of three police organizations that adopted COMPSTAT practices. All three organizations took technical issues into consideration, but the speed and pattern of acceptance of COMPSTAT elements suggested that COMPSTAT was adopted in response to "institutional pressures to appear progressive and successful" (2001, p. 148). Although it did not use the term, this study provided an excellent example of *loose coupling* in that actual crime-control practices remained fundamentally unchanged despite a broad administrative refocusing on crime control. This paper also emphasized an important point—that organizational structures are not either institutional or technical but invariably carry some of each in their developments and practices. This has important theoretical implications that deserve further consideration. The theoretical study of organizations should not posit institutional and technical perspectives as contradictory or categorical but should consider each as part of the overall contribution to organizational success. It may be that organizational well-being requires both. That is, it must attend to technical requirements in its work on its product core, formalized in the public sector in terms of the mission or charter of the organization, and also ceremonially dress up its product to impress audiences who would like to know why the public should continue to fund it.

Giblin (2006), looking at the expansion of crime analysis units nationally, used measures derived from both perspectives. Unfortunately, his findings provided little support for either perspective; none of his predictors were significant at the .05 level. However, his data trended in the direction of support for institutional predictors, an interpretation he indicated was justifiable based on relatively small sample sizes.

Issue 4: Understanding the Sweep of Police History

Institutional theory reminds us that there was not a "catechism" of police, as Travis (personal communication, 1992) once noted, but that changes in police structure and practices are a consequence of broad changes in the environment of policing. Crank and Langworthy (1992) noted how the emergence of community policing, responsive to the urban conflicts of the 1960s, was initially aimed at building bridges between the African American community and police. Yet, with an increasingly conservative electorate in the 1980s, community policing had shifted to aggressive, public-order-oriented practices based on "broken windows" justifications for harsh treatment of minor crimes, despite its alienating effects on minority communities.

Ritti and Mastrofski (2002), in what is likely the exemplar of empirical analysis of institutional research, described the spread of community policing across the American landscape as a three-phase institutional process. The first phase, "growing dissatisfaction with a problem," reflected the concerns about policing that emerged from the 1960s and early 1970s. The second phase, called "consensus about what to do about the problem," reflected the spread of community policing as an umbrella term and its creative adaptation in many departments outside those associated with its emergence. The third phase, "effective transmission of practices," was a period of intense assessment of community policing practices in a few large departments across the country. The fourth, "institutional transmission of practices," marked the period in which community policing practices were adopted, not because they were critically assessed but because they were "the right thing to do." They represented the new symbolic face of policing for the public, and carried with them the appropriate discourse legitimizing the uncritical adoption of practices. Particularly useful was the way in which the authors operationalized their analysis. Ritti and Mastrofski's work is particularly helpful for researchers looking for ways of measuring institutional-level variables.

Institutional theory has been around in policing for 15 to 20 years, depending on where one locates its first efforts in policing. It has the support of a small but strong body of theorists and researchers. Its success today is due largely to the works of Mastrofski, who, working alone and with others, has provided a body of research aimed at the empirical measurement of institutional theory. The reader is recommended to look at the body of this work (Mastrofski & Ritti, 1996, 2000; Mastrofski, Ritti, & Hoffmaster, 1987; Mastrofski & Uchida, 1996; Ritti & Mastrofski, 2002; Willis, Mastrofski, & Weisburd, 2007) to examine efforts to quantify institutional theory as well as to empirically compare institutional and contingency theory. This body of work has set the standard for the empirical assessment of institutional theory in policing in the current era.

Conflict Theory

The Traditions of Conflict Theory

Conflict theory refers to a multifaceted set of perspectives loosely organized around the idea that strategies of crime control serve the interests of dominant groups (Holmes, 2000). Contemporary conflict theory can be traced to Blalock's (1967) work on the relationship between minority group presence and various social control efforts by the majority group. Turk (1969) extended Blalock's (1967) work by suggesting that culturally and racially dissimilar subordinate groups are perceived as threatening to the social and political order and are therefore disproportionally subject to arrest and punishment by the criminal justice system. Quinney (1970) expanded this notion when he argued that law is the primary means of establishing order in heterogeneous communities in order to compensate for the declining significance of informal control mechanisms therein. Liska, Chamlin, and Reed (1985) drew upon Blalock's (1967) threat hypothesis to further argue that an increase in the percentage of nonwhites increases the threat of crime perceived by authorities, thereby leading to increases in both the size of the crime-control apparatus and the pressure on that apparatus to control crime.

Law enforcement activities, from a conflict perspective, are a reaction to the threat that minority groups pose to the racial majority. As Jacobs (1979, p. 913) explained, "[C]onflict theorists maintain that the control of crime and deviance proceeds in accord with the wishes of those with power who use this control to further their own narrow interests." For instance, conflict theorists have demonstrated strong relationships between the size of minority populations and police resources and expenditures (Jackson & Carroll, 1981), as well as the size of police forces (Jacobs, 1979).

Three primary variations of conflict theory have emerged, all of which affect police research: the racial threat thesis, the inequality thesis, and the racial disturbance thesis. The racial threat thesis, initially put forth by Blalock (1967), suggests that minority group threat increases with the size of the minority population. This relationship may be curvilinear; that is, threat increases until minority groups reach a certain level, beyond which it diminishes. Results have historically tended to demonstrate that relative strength of police forces in the early 1970s was positively impacted by the size of their cities' black populations. The inequality thesis, on the other hand, is a slightly different version of conflict theory that focuses primarily on economic inequalities in a community rather than on the presence of racial minorities as the source of the threat that generates such social control efforts as heightened policing. From this perspective, places where economic resources are substantially unequal are places where the advantaged have the resources and desire to defend them against those who do not. Additionally, since the police constitute the primary governmental institution responsible for "the coercive maintenance of stability and order," enhanced police strength may be expected in areas where greater economic inequality is found (Jacobs, 1979, p. 914). Finally, the racial disturbance thesis asserts that potential threats influenced by minority group mobilizations, such as significant racial uprisings or riots, may directly affect the amount of resources devoted to policing. It is this facet of conflict theory that has been the least empirically supported in the literature (Jackson & Carroll, 1981; Sharp, 2006).

Overview: Research on Conflict Theory and the Police

In this section, we look at papers that have assessed police practices or structures using conflict perspectives. These perspectives were selected because they developed hypotheses from competing theoretical perspectives or because they offered particularly good assessments and tests of conflict theory. One can see in the review of these papers that conflict theory holds a viable and important place in the small group of theories used to explain police organizational structures and behaviors.

Rational Choice and Conflict

Holmes, Smith, Freng, and Munoz (2008) provided an empirical analysis of police department expenditures and size, drawing on conflict and rational choice perspectives to construct contrasting hypotheses. The strengths of this analysis are that it comparatively analyzes two important and competing theoretical traditions, and that it recognizes that the specification of minority group—in this case, Latino—requires a greater degree of specificity than is usually given.

Rational choice theory maintains that resources are distributed in accordance with the *need* for crime control. Conflict theory counters that resources are allocated with the aim of controlling racial and ethnic minorities. In other words, for rational theorists the police are the principle agents of action, whereas for conflict theorists the police serve as the principal agents of domestic coercion (Bittner, 1970), and resource allocations to police departments largely determine the crime-control capacity of states (Liska, 1992). From rational choice, then, the distribution of resources to policing is tied to community crime rates. The central focus of the minority threat perspective, on the other hand, looks at distribution in terms of "percent minority" (most often white/black).

The authors noted that the effects of minority threat "may depend on factors such as region and the degree of racial and ethnic tension" (Holmes et al, 2008, p. 137). Previous research on the Hispanic minority threat has found that percent Hispanic is related positively and strongly to the incidence of civil rights criminal complaints of police brutality in large southwestern cities. Additionally, it has been found that the dominant group, whose anxieties are fueled by media portrayals and political rhetoric, would marshal their superior political power to ensure allocations of public resources to policing. From conflict theory, then, the authors hypothesized that the perceived threat potential of Hispanics in the Southwest should result in greater allocations of fiscal and personnel resources to policing in southwestern cities with relatively large and relatively poor Hispanic populations, particularly those close to the border with Mexico.

The key contribution of this study's analysis, beyond providing support for conflict perspectives, is the identification of within-group class distinctions as potentially more important indicators of minority threat, at least in the Southwest, than percent Hispanic. Allocations of police resources appear to be tied to the presence of poor Hispanics on both sides of the border, pointing to the relevance of the intersection of class and ethnicity to public policy decisions in the region.

Agency Size and Race Conflict

Sharp (2006) presents hypotheses from racial threat, inequality, and racial disturbance theses to assess the growth of police organizations. It is a creative use of conflict theory to assess police organizational size, more typically studied in contingency theories of the police. The author particularly focuses on the historical legacy of police-force growth in the 1960s–1970s era of racial turmoil and the playing out of racial threat dynamics in that era. The latter may have led to a shift in the base levels of department size.

Findings indicate the following:

1. The baseline or legacy effect of the department's relative force size as of 1980 appeared consistently to be the most important predictor of contemporary organizational size.

2. A city's more contemporary experience with racial disturbances is consistently the next most important predictor of contemporary force size (in other words, more significant than the legacy effect).

3. Although the racial threat thesis is unsupported when it is assessed in terms of the prevalence of blacks in the population, there is evidence for this thesis when all minority groups are included in the analysis.

Findings suggest that contemporary racial threat and racial insurgency, more than historical/legacy influences, are the key predictors of enhanced contemporary police strength (i.e., cities that encountered recent race riots, from 1980 to 2000). This alone, the author acknowledges, does not explain the actual processes by which local policymakers react to race riots; a qualitative, case-study approach is needed to possibly uncover what she describes as the "veiled discourse" (Sharp, 2006, p. 303) that may be at play. She also argues that future research needs to focus on minorities more broadly and move away from the white/nonblack-versus-black dichotomies that have historically been analyzed.

The staffing of U.S. police agencies, the author concluded, appears to be an artifact of the "social control phenomenon of subduing a population perceived to be rebellious" (Sharp, 2006, p. 305). This research also showed that crime rates, though most often studied in terms of functionalism, could be incorporated into conflict perspectives. That is, police-force size is an important part of the material frequently shaped and used by public officials in marketing the fear of crime (see Chambliss, 1999).

Drug Arrests and Conflict

This research provides an assessment of both conflict and social disorganization variables in the prediction of drug arrests in 187 U.S. cities. Mosher (2001) argued that "spatial differences in rates of drug arrests are particularly relevant to the central tenets of conflict theory" (p. 88). Narcotics legislation in the United States, he noted, has been used to control minority populations, especially since the intensity of the War on Drugs increased in the 1980s. Mosher also points out that social disorganization and conflict theories posit that numerous measures of inequality will be related to higher drug arrest rates. Social disorganization, however, generally predicts that the effect of a population's ethnic/racial composition is mediated through structural indicators of the relative disadvantage of minority groups when compared to whites. Contrarily, conflict theory (especially the variation focused on minority threat—e.g., Blalock, 1967) predicts that racial/ethnic composition will have an independent positive effect on drug arrest rates that will hold true even when relative economic disadvantage is controlled for. Finally, conflict theory predicts that police strength would exert a strong independent effect on the drug arrest rate across cities.

Mosher found that percent African American is a statistically significant predictor of variation in possession arrest rates across cities, even when race-specific economic deprivation is controlled for. And when he looked at trafficking arrests, Mosher found percent African American was the strongest predictor of arrest rates. Additionally, cities with more police per square mile had higher trafficking arrest rates. In sum, Mosher's findings provide strong support for the predictions developed from conflict theory.

Conflict and Racial Profiling

One of the more controversial issues in the current era is racial profiling, which refers to the perception that police make decisions to act based on the race of an individual. Petrocelli, Piquero, and Smith (2003) carried out a microlevel analysis of police practices using census tract data from a single city to examine how neighborhood context may influence police behavior. This research asked, To what extent are police stop, search, and arrest decisions a function of neighborhood demographic and socioeconomic characteristics in this particular city? Findings indicated that the percentage of population that was African American was significantly related to the percent of stops resulting in a search, and this was especially the case in black neighborhoods. In addition, the number of police stops were significantly higher in neighborhoods with higher rates of Part I crime. Notably, however, in areas where a higher percentage of the population was black, the chance of stops involving at least one arrest/summons is lower. Similarly, in high crime-rate areas, the chance of stops involving at least one arrest/summons is lower.

These findings, the authors suggest, describe a *hurdle effect*. The likelihood of being stopped seems to be more a function of the crime rate in the area

than of the demographic and/or socioeconomic characteristics. After the initial stop, however, searches appear to be more prevalent in neighborhoods
with higher percentages of black residents. They assert that this could be the
result of one or two things: "ecological bias" (officer responses tied to neighborhood characteristics) or that officers are more likely to search African-
American residents based on general perceptions or stereotypes.

Hence, although they support a race effect, the findings overall do not tend
to support a conflict explanation. Such an explanation would hold that officers are more likely to profile poor, minority areas and to make more stops
in such areas. Instead, the crime rate appears to be a more important factor
in the decision to stop.

Conflict and Communicative Action

Schneider's (1999) research study is based in grounded theory and looks at
conflict and communication among residents of Vancouver, British Columbia.
This study represents an effort to look at Habermas's ideas of communicative
action as a recipe for conflicts between the police and community groups.
Schneider argued that police officers, despite their advocacy of community
policing, might be undermining their policing programs through communication problems with residents of socially disadvantaged neighborhoods (SDNs).
Schneider's definition of communication is broad, ranging from interpersonal,
verbal, or nonverbal personal communications to mass communication, such
as the promotion of a crime prevention program by a police department.

He found that police officers in this jurisdiction engaged in unilingual communication, demonstrated a limited range of understanding of different cultures, showed a lack of empathy with special needs groups, and overused
offensive or overtly authoritative technical jargon. These communication practices perpetuated "an asymmetrical power relationship" between the police
and residents of the neighborhoods, ultimately undermining community policing efforts (Schneider, 1999, p. 354). Community policing programs,
Schneider suggested, typically began with the broad assumption that society
was pluralistic and that all communities had similar problems, needs, and
access to political and economic resources. That assumption resulted in a law
enforcement mind-set that approached crime prevention and community
policing programs with a language geared toward "stable, ethnically homogeneous (i.e., white) middle and upper income neighborhoods" (p. 362). In
SDNs, however, this type of approach inevitably failed to address the unique,
specific needs and demands of poorer, less empowered neighborhoods.

The author concluded that COP principles and practices required a
revised theoretical framework oriented toward (1) reducing power relations
between the police and SDNs and (2) avoiding the technical, authoritative
approaches characteristic of community policing. A more effective approach
would be an "affective-emotional model that places community safety in the
broader context of community and social development," rather than the

rational, detached, and objective approach typically followed in contemporary law enforcement (p. 362). The adoption of Habermas's theory of communicative action would facilitate "undistorted communication as a means to reduce asymmetrical power relations between social groups, address[ing] the epistemological weaknesses inherent in liberal community policing theory" (p. 362; see also Forester, 1989, 1993). Shifts in the power differential between SDNs and the police, however, will not be accomplished by improving communication alone. An effective critical approach of community policing must include contributions to the social, economic, and political development of SDNs, as well as sharing of control of crime-prevention decision making and resources with SDNs by law enforcement agents.

Postmodernism

Postmodernism carries several meanings. In this discussion, we are interested in two: postmodernism as a philosophy of rejection of the modern, and postmodernism as a time period, also sometimes called late modernity. Postmodernism can represent the rejection of modernism or the fulfillment of it, depending on whom one reads.

The Philosophy of Postmodernism

Postmodern theory, which gained prominence in the mid-1970s, is sometimes located under the umbrella of critical theory. However, though postmodernism continues to look at social class as one of the major causes of crime, it adds other dimensions of inequality, such as race and gender, which together are coproductive of the conditions of crime. Like critical criminology, postmodernism is less a theory of crime causation than an attempt to develop a more profound policy response to or deeper understanding of the causes of crime. In addition, postmodernism is interested in how structured inequalities (social class, race/ethnicity, and gender) contribute to and are reinforced by a culture that makes these divisions seem real. These social divisions, while faced as real and substantive, are socially constructed and, if subjected to critical analysis, can be deconstructed or dissolved (Lanier & Henry, 1998).

Postmodernism as a philosophy looks at the symbolic, everyday, and formal uses of language that underpin the socially constructed nature of societies' rules, norms, and values. These languages represent discourses and are central to what is defined as criminal and to the way in which society is a source of crime (Lanier & Henry, 1998). Consequently, postmodernism highlights the significance of language and signs in the arena of crime and criminal justice and offers a source of concepts that capture elements of an emerging reality in the new context and set of conditions in which crime occurs, the current postmodern period (Schwartz & Friedrichs, 1994).

Postmodern is often questioned for its failure to provide answers to the questions it raises. Yet, that expectation reveals a misunderstanding of much of postmodernism. One can look at the brooding works of Cesar Vallejo and Jean-Paul Sartre—who are not normally considered postmodernists—and see a great deal of postmodernism in their dark existentialism. Postmodernism is a rejection—once discourse is shattered, it is unclear that anything remains underneath. Take away the meaning of a word, and sometimes all that is left is the jarring sound of mismatched consonants, conveying nothing. Only the most optimistic wing of postmodernism sees qualities of the human condition that somehow prevail with the deconstruction of the taken-for-granted.

Postmodernism as Historical Epoch

As explained by postmodern theorist T. R. Young (1997), premodern understanding of law and justice was based on the idea of "natural" laws given by God. The existing social hierarchy and its corresponding system of rights and privileges were right and proper, natural. Modernism, carried in Enlightenment ideals, replaced the good of God with the good of the individual. The American justice system, for example, was founded upon a statement of natural law in its Declaration of Independence, which moved the basis of lawmaking from the gods and/or nature to human beings acting in democratic concert. The priest was replaced by the research scientist, and modern criminology pays homage to the data gatherer rather than to the scriptural message. Postmodernism represents the dismantling or rejection of modern discourses. The legacy of modernism and its vanities of progress, far from being a democratic peace, is the firebombing of Dresden and the annihilation of the citizens of Hiroshima in thermonuclear fire.

Some writers recognize the interplay between both the philosophy and the historical sweep of postmodernism. In this regard, T. R. Young noted, "Whereas modern science privileges objectivity, rationality, power, control, inequality, and hierarchy, postmodernists deconstruct each theory and each social practice by locating it in its larger socio-historical context in order to reveal that human hand and the group interests which shape the course of self-understanding" (Young, 1995, pp. 578–579).

Police and Postmodernism

Postmodernism literature on the police tends to view them in terms of adaptation to a postmodernist landscape. Whereas in the modern period, policing was dictated by a militaristic, hierarchical, technical–rational, bureaucratic model of authority, in the postmodern (sometimes called the late-modern) era, the role of the police is seen as more fluid and multilateral. Policing becomes much more complex, characterized by (1) the fragmentation of values and moralities; (2) globalization; (3) a rise in consumerism, including private policing; (4) a hollowing out of the nation-state (Reiner, 1992; Sheptycki, 1995); the emergence of a "risk society" (see, for example, Beck, 1986/1992; DeLint, 1999); and (6) adaptive risk-based policing strategies (see Ericson & Haggerty, 1997). One of the key implications for postmodern policing is the shift to a focus on discourse and mode of consumerism, where the community and community policing become coauthored in the same discourse (Reiner, 1992; see Clark, 2005).

Here, we recommend several papers. Waters (2007) discusses how the rhetoric of police reform is consistent with postmodern notions of discourse. Official discourse about police reform and policing developments, he argues, is overwhelmingly couched in terms consistent with postmodern discourse. This article reviews the terminology of that discourse.

Sheptycki (2002) discusses contradictions between the a modernist police setting and a postmodern one. The fragmented terrain of the policing field poses accountability problems not easily answered by the traditional model of constitutional control in a militaristic hierarchy.

Ericson and Haggerty (1997) focus on the communication systems that institutions develop to identify and manage risks, and on how the police become involved in these systems. The police are seen as being in a complex, ambiguous, shifting, and contradictory field of risk management in relation to other institutions. This excellent work provides a sense of the fluid systems in which police find themselves and how they are adapting to those systems.

Manning and Singh (1997) focus on symbolic violence in the rhetoric of community policing. Using a case study of community policing in one western U.S. city, based on interviews with police, observations, and focus groups, they found that COP rhetoric is used as a public discourse. Yet, the daily interdiction practices of patrol officers are relatively unchanged. Moreover, the absence of a crime-control emphasis alters public perceptions of the police while undercutting police morale.

Miller (2007) argues that data collection, the primary response to concerns over racial profiling, is ineffective, largely because it is driven primarily by police concerns about developing and maintaining the perception of responsiveness to public desires. That is, profiling is a symbolic response to public perceptions of crime and hence difficult to eradicate in view of contradictions between public and legal expectations of police behavior. Using LEMAS data, Miller assesses the extent to which "antiracial profiling policies" are implemented.

CONCLUSION

Through this tour of police theory, one can see that police provide an amazingly colorful and richly detailed palette with which to paint a theory. They provide substantive analysis for policy theory, from institutions to individuals, and encompass us in the sweep of history. We have looked at only a few of the many writings on the police; we leave it to the reader to explore from here. There is much to enjoy on that journey, and an unfair share of pain and suffering as well. Of one thing you can be sure: You will be engaged in a study of people as they really are, sometimes without benefit of social custom and often layered in controversy, and in the end you may learn much about yourself.

DISCUSSION QUESTIONS

1. What is police criminology? Is it scientific criminology?

2. What is institutional theory? Why is legitimacy central to understanding institutional theory?

3. Are the police shifting from the community policing model to a different model, neoprofessionalism? Justify your answer from the book and from personal experience.

4. According to this chapter, what is the relationship between race and the police?

5. What is the link between conflict theory and profiling?

6. Identify three implications of postmodernism for the police.

REFERENCES

Beck, U. (1986/1992). *Risk society: Toward a new modernity* (M. Ritter, Trans.). Newbury Park, CA: Sage.

Bittner, E. (1970). *The functions of police in modern society.* Washington, DC: Government Printing Office.

Blalock, H. (1967). *Toward a theory of minority group relations.* New York: Wiley.

Chambliss, W. J. (1999). *Power, politics, and crime.* Boulder, CO: Westview.

Clark, M. (2005). The importance of a new philosophy to the postmodern policing environment. *Policing, 28*(4), 642–653.

Crank, J. (2003). *Understanding police culture* (2nd ed.). Cincinnati, OH: Anderson Press.

Crank, J., & Langworthy, R. (1996). Fragmented centralization and the organization of the police. *Police and Society, 6,* 213–229.

Crank, J. P. (1994). Watchman and community: Myth and institutionalization in policing. *Law and Society Review, 28*(2), 325–351.

Crank, J. P. (2002). *Imagining justice.* Cincinnati, OH: Anderson Press.

Crank, J. P., & Langworthy, R. H. (1992). An institutional perspective of policing. *The Journal of Criminal Law and Criminology, 83,* 338–363.

Cronin, J., Murphy, G., Spahr, L., Toliver, J., & Weger, R. (2007). *Promoting effective homicide investigations.* Washington, DC: Office of COPS, Police Executive Research Forum.

DeLint, W. (1999). A postmodern turn in policing: Policing as pastiche? *International Journal of the Sociology of Law, 27*(2), 127–152.

DiMaggio, P., & Powell, W. W. (1983). The iron cage revisited: Institutionalized iso-morphism and collective rationality in organizational fields. *American Sociological Review, 48*, 147–160.

Donaldson, L. (2001). *The contingency theory of organizations.* Thousand Oaks, CA: Sage.

Ericson, R., & Haggerty, K. (1997). *Policing the risk society.* Oxford: Clarendon Press.

Forester, J. (1989). *Planning in the face of power.* Berkeley: University of California Press.

Forester, J. (1993). *Critical theory, public policy and planning practice: Toward a critical pragmatism.* Albany: State University of New York Press.

Giblin, M. (2006). Structural elaboration and institutional isomorphism: The case of crime analysis units. *Policing, 29*, 643–664.

Holmes, M. (2000). Minority threat and police brutality: Determinants of civil rights complaints in U.S. municipalities. *Criminology, 38*(2), 343–368.

Holmes, M., Smith, B. W., Freng, A. B., & Munoz, E. A. (2008). Minority threat, crime control, and police resource allocation in the southwestern United States. *Crime & Delinquency, 54*(1), 128–152.

Jackson, P., & Carroll, L. (1981). Race and the war on crime: The sociopolitical determinants of municipal police expenditures in 90 non-southern U.S. cities. *American Sociological Review, 46*, 913–925.

Jacobs, D. (1979). Inequality and police strength: Conflict theory and coercive con-trol in metropolitan areas. *American Sociological Review, 44*(6), 913–925.

Katz, C. (2001). The establishment of a police gang movement: An examination of organizational and environmental factors. *Criminology, 39*, 37–74.

Klinger, D. (2004). Environment and organization: Reviving a perspective on the police. *Annals of the American Academy of Political and Social Science, 593*, 119–136.

Kuhns, J., Maguire, E., & Cox, S. (2007). Public safety concerns among law enforce-ment agencies in suburban and rural America. *Police Quarterly, 10*, 429–454.

Langworthy, R. H. (1986). *The structure of police organizations.* New York: Praeger.

Lanier, M. M., & Henry, S. (1998). *Essential criminology.* Boulder, CO: Westview Press.

Liska, A., Chamlin, M., & Reed, M. (1985). Testing the economic production and conflict models of crime control. *Social Forces, 64*, 119–138.

Liska, A. E. (1992). Introduction to the study of social control. In A. E. Liska (Ed.), *Social threat and social control* (pp. 1–32). Albany: State University of New York Press.

Maguire, E. (2003). *Organizational structure in American police agencies.* Albany: State University of New York Press.

Manning, P. K., & Singh, M. P. (1997). Violence and hyperviolence: The rhetoric and practice of community policing. *Sociological Spectrum, 17*(3), 339–361.

Mastrofski, S. D., & Ritti, R. (1996). Police training and the effects of organization on drunk driving enforcement. *Justice Quarterly, 13*, 291–320.

Mastrofski, S. D., & Ritti, R. R. (2000). Making sense of community policing: A the-oretical perspective. *Police Practice and Research, 1*(2), 183–210.

Mastrofski, S. D., Ritti, R. R., & Hoffmaster, D. (1987). Organizational determi-nants of police discretion: The case of drinking-driving. *Journal of Criminal Justice, 15*, 387–402.

Mastrofski, S. D., & Uchida, C. D. (1993). Transforming the police. *Journal of Research in Crime and Delinquency, 30*(3), 330–358.

Miller, K. (2007). Racial profiling and postmodern society: Police responsiveness, image maintenance, and the left flank of police legitimacy. *Journal of Contemporary Criminal Justice, 23*(3), 248–262.

Morabito, M. (2008). The adoption of police innovation: The role of the political environment. *Policing, 31,* 466–484.

Mosher, C. (2001). Predicting drug arrest rates: Conflict and social disorganization perspectives. *Crime & Delinquency, 47*(1), 84–104.

Petrocelli, M., Piquero, A. R., & Smith, M. R. (2003). Conflict theory and racial profiling: An empirical analysis of police traffic stop data. *Journal of Criminal Justice, 31,* 1–11.

Quinney. R. (1970). *The social reality of crime.* Boston: Little, Brown.

Reiner, R. (1992). Policing a postmodern society. *Modern Law Review, 55*(6), 761–781.

Ritti, R., & Mastrofski, S. (2002). *The institutionalization of community policing.* Unpublished manuscript.

Schneider, S. R. (1999). Overcoming barriers to communication between police and socially disadvantaged neighbourhoods: A critical theory of community policing. *Crime, Law & Social Change, 30,* 347–377.

Schwartz, M., & Friedrichs, D. (1994). Postmodern thought and criminological discontent: New metaphors for understanding violence. *Criminology 32,* 221–246.

Scott, R. (1992). Unpacking institutional arguments. In W. Powell & P. DiMaggio (Eds.), *The new institutionalism in organizational analysis* (pp. 164–183). Chicago: University of Chicago Press.

Sharp, E. B. (2006). Policing urban America: A new look at the politics of agency size. *Social Science Quarterly, 87*(2), 291–307.

Sheptycki, J. (1995). Transnational policing and the makings of a postmodern state. *British Journal of Criminology, 35,* 613–631.

Sheptycki, J. (2002). Accountability across the policing field: Toward a general cartography of accountability for postmodern policing. *Policing and Society, 12*(4), 323–338.

Sherman, L., Gottfredson, D., Mackensie, D., Eck, J., Reuter, P., Bushway, S., & the Members of the Graduate Program. (1997). *Preventing crime: what works, what doesn't, and what's promising.* Washington, DC: U.S. Department of Justice.

Snipes, J., & Maguire, E. (2007). Foundations of criminal justice theory. In D. Duffee & E. Maguire (Eds.), *Criminal justice theory: Explaining the nature and behavior of criminal justice* (pp. 27–49). New York: Routledge.

Stucky, T. (2005). Local politics and police strength. *Justice Quarterly, 22,* 139–169.

Turk, A. (1969). *Criminality and the legal order.* Chicago: Rand McNally.

Vitale, A. (2005). Innovation and institutionalization: Factors in the development of "quality of life" policing in New York. *Policing and Society, 15,* 99–124.

Waters, I. 2007. Policing, modernity and postmodernity. *Policing and Society, 17*(3), 257–278.

Willis, J., Mastrofski, S., & Weisburd, D. (2007). Making sense of COMPSTAT: A theory-based analysis of organizational change in three police departments. *Law and Society Review, 41,* 147–178.

Wilson, J. (1968). *Varieties of police behavior.* Cambridge, MA: Harvard University Press.

Young, T. R. (1995). *The Red Feather dictionary of critical social science.* Boulder, CO: The Red Feather Institute.

Young, T. R. (1997). *A constitutive theory of justice: Architecture and content.* No. 004. Distributed as part of the Red Feather Institute Postmodern Criminology Series. Weidman, MI: The Red Feather Institute.

15

Contemporary Policing

Police Work in the 21st Century

Christopher C. Cooper

Introduction

Policing in the United States has undergone myriad changes over the past 100 years. The political, reform, and professionalization movements all gave way to the much-heralded community policing model. The latter came to represent the face of American policing throughout the late 1980s, the 1990s, and the first decade of the new century. Community policing promotes a formula that encourages police and citizens to collaborate to address problems of crime and quality of life (Cordner, 1997; Mayhall, 1994). Included in this amicable venture is a commitment by the police to get out of their patrol cars and walk their beats to promote one-on-one interaction with the citizens they serve.

The current police movement began soon after the tragic events of September 11, 2001, as a response to the subsequent focus on homeland security (Balko, 2006; Rosenbaum, 1998). A typical officer duty now includes checking bags at mass transit stations in an effort to thwart would-be terrorists (cf. Maguire & King, 2004). These additional responsibilities leave little time for bridge-building with members of the community. Along with this new emphasis came the patrol officer's uniform, which now includes militaristic attire, such as bulletproof vests and even gas masks strapped to officers' legs in jurisdictions like New York City. Some officers have supplemented their side arms with high-powered rifles (Balko, 2006; Cooper, 2009).

Driving this phenomenon is a mixture of hysteria and reality. Certainly, to challenge terrorism, advanced weaponry may be needed. But despite the presence of technologically savvy and well-equipped common criminals, there are countless logical reasons why police on patrol in residential neighborhoods should not be armed with M16 automatic rifles.

American policing has incorporated sloppy versions of urban military tactics. In this climate, community policing models cannot survive, because these new threats to policing are inherently antagonistic to citizens and officers alike. Sharing a cup of coffee in hopes of exchanging useful information has become unlikely.

A more obvious dramatic change in American policing has been its demographic shift from an establishment composed almost exclusively of white males to one that now includes females and officers of color.

A Personal Note

On my first police job, I was assigned a foot beat on one of New York's many beachfronts. I was seldom issued a portable radio; rather, I relied on call boxes for communication. Approximately every 1,000 feet along the boardwalk I patrolled was a call box (basically a telephone inside a locked metal box) from which I could call the dispatcher. Later, when I joined the Washington, D.C., Metropolitan Police, I would sign out a clunky two-way radio about the size of brick and weighing almost as much. As might be expected, there was no shortage of citizens' complaints that an officer had used his radio as a "spanking" device.

When we needed to "run a name"—that is, find out whether a suspect was wanted or had had any previous criminal justice system contacts—we would gather as much information as we could from or about the suspect, write it on a notepad, and then call the dispatcher on our walkie-talkies (or the ones we shared with our partners, for radio shortages were the norm). Sometimes she (the dispatcher) would take 3 minutes, other times 20, to find the requested information.

I recall a crowded, urban Columbia Road in the Adams-Morgan section of the District of Columbia. This was before the area underwent the gentrification that made it unrecognizable today as the previously impoverished, working-class neighborhood it was then. In the evening about 6 p.m., the sidewalks could be very crowded. Street-cart vendors peddled fruit, socks, hot dogs, and other disposable goods; the homeless wandered aimlessly, and people entered and exited the bodegas and shops that lined the boulevard. On this night, my partner and I were assigned to a scout car. We stopped a man who was on foot. Based on our estimate of probable cause, we stopped our car and had him place his hands on the hood. I called in his name and waited. It seemed like the dispatcher took forever to find any relevant information from the various databases before acknowledging what we already suspected, that he was wanted. This bad guy knew he was wanted and opted to flee. I chased him between cars, around dilapidated tenement buildings, and through alleys strewn with trash before I caught him.

Contrast this with today's process of checking suspects. Officers can now enter any information they have about a suspect into their handy laptop computers, and—voila!—local and federal databases are available for their assessment. If the suspect has had previous law enforcement or official contact, information from data files across the country are accessible. Waiting time has been reduced to moments.

There's more. Today's officers can be dispatched, receive assignments, ask for runs/jobs, and engage in various types of communication via their in-car computers. I can still hear the incessant static that marked my two-way radio. The crowded airwave, with so many officers jockeying to talk with the dispatcher, necessitated a strategy for sending and receiving information; you had to be fast. To call in a "priority"—e.g., a police emergency, perhaps a 10–13 or 10–30 ("officer has been shot," etc.; each jurisdiction has its own nomenclature)—or even to get permission to take a break and have lunch required luck and a deft touch getting through the crowded radio frequencies. Situations might include an officer yelling into his radio that he was chasing a suspect with a gun, while another officer was yelling into *his* radio that he needed assistance for a street skirmish that was getting out of control. You had to know how to listen attentively to at least two things at once: your radio and any other conversation you might be having, perhaps a conversation with a citizen or your partner. If you were really good, you had a third ear and could listen to a ball game on your unauthorized transistor radio. Good officers could do all this simultaneously as they proficiently filled in the "run sheet," a document on which we wrote down information conveyed by the dispatcher, such as the type of event, the location, or the time of the dispatch.

As communications have improved, so has armament. Today, semiautomatic pistols are the norm. I trained on a six-shot .38 caliber revolver and then eventually acquired a 9mm Glock. On a potentially dangerous occasion, if I needed to be better armed and needed a shotgun, I had to drive back to the station to sign one out. Once, I had tracked down a man who was wanted for shooting a woman in the head in the Fourth District. Before my partner and I went to get him, my partner signed out a shotgun—but there was no ammunition for it. Oh, well. . . . In some jurisdictions, equipment in today's patrol cars includes shotguns mounted between the front driver's and passenger's seats; ammunition is also provided. Based on my patrol experiences in Washington, D.C., and New York, I sometimes wonder what it would be like to work in a department like those depicted in the media these days, where officers wear mirrored sunglasses and seldom have to run up flights of stairs in a darkened project or wade through discarded syringes, feces, and vomit in pursuit of a determined runaway suspect.

Today's officers have been allowed to discard the traditional navy blue police uniform in favor of ones resembling Hollywood ninjas or GI Joes (cf. Kraska & Kappeler, 1997). Having once been a U.S. Marine, I find it comical to see machismo or role-playing by these officers, whose military aspirations seem to be lived out in residential neighborhoods. I ask, What has happened to individual courage and bravado?

Not that long ago, officers had to be physically fit and prepared to chase after a bad guy or wrestle a recalcitrant, violent person to the ground. I believe that police officers should not be allowed to hide behind mirrored sunglasses, body armor, and M16s. Rather, as I did, police officers should have the personal fortitude and integrity to walk through a dangerous housing project armed only with the gift of gab and a sidearm. Sitting in an air-conditioned scout car is a cop-out and a denigration of the social interaction that good police work requires. Sadly, physical strength and character as means to subdue violent suspects have been replaced by Tasers and pepper spray. Where conflict resolution and social interaction skills enabled us to keep things under control on the beat, many of today's officers put on their sunglasses and pepper-spray away.

The technological–military movement currently afoot is a detriment to effective police–community relations and a perversion of the role of the police officer. In this new age of policing, officers in many jurisdictions no longer walk foot patrols; this is a critical error. In urban centers (e.g., northeast coastal cities), people and structures are close together, and egress and ingress for automobiles is limited. When an officer is on foot, crime enforcement is more efficiently and effectively accomplished through intimate community interaction. Criminals are deterred, and good people sense an improved quality of life. It takes courage to walk a foot beat, especially alone on a dangerous city street. Although generations of police officers patrolled this way and officers in some jurisdictions still do, in many other locales the foot beat is a forgotten tactic because individual officers lack the fortitude or the confidence, and their supervisors and chiefs fail to see the foot beat's inherent value.

With one partner in particular, he and I had to walk; in fact, we wanted to walk. We would begin our graveyard/midnight shift in Anacostia (southeast Washington, D.C.) around 10:30 p.m. and walk until 7:00 a.m., rain or shine, snow or calm. We were physically fit and were in close contact with citizens and criminals alike. Today's Taser-oriented officer would not fare well if compelled to perform this type of policing. We had nowhere to hide, so developing a rapport with the community and earning its trust was crucial.

GPS and Video Recording

When the Rodney King beating video was released, I was walking a foot beat in northeast Washington, D.C. At around 2 a.m. the morning after the story broke, I was in a housing project talking with several other officers. People yelled both jokingly and seriously that we were being videotaped. There was not much validity to those claims then, but now it's different. The proliferation of multifunctional cellular telephones has created a society of YouTube video makers along with other online recording aficionados.

With some justification, video and audio recording capabilities are now regularly installed in police vehicles and at police facilities. In recent months, these recording devices have captured both the good and the bad.

Oakland, CA: According to witnesses, Bay Area Rapid Transit (BART) police officer Johannes Mehserle fired into the back of 22-year-old Oscar Grant while Grant lay face down on a train platform at a train station in Oakland, California. Grant and several others had been pulled off a BART train after reports of fighting, as New Year's Eve revelers shuttled home after midnight. The shooting, captured on cell phone cameras and widely viewed on the Internet, inflamed long-running tensions between law enforcement authorities and many African American residents and black community leaders, who have berated BART officials at several public meetings since the incident (KTVU.com, 2009).

Minneapolis, MN: Consider that before anyone knew about the cameras, the Minneapolis police chief, Timothy Dolan, confidently reported at a news conference that Fong Lee was seen carrying a gun (Hanners, 2009).

Peoria, IL: Two police officers in Central Illinois were charged with beating a man, and the incident was captured on videotape by their squad car camera.

Seattle, WA: Deputy Paul Schene, a King County, Washington, sheriff's deputy, wrote a report of an encounter with a 15-year-old child, claiming that she physically attacked him. About a year later, a video of the incident surfaced. It showed a defenseless 15-year-old girl not in any way attacking Deputy Schene but rather being kicked and slammed to the floor of a jail cell by Schene. Schene was arrested and charged with fourth-degree assault. (KING5.com, 2009).

U.S. cities have been rocked by riots, marches, and protests in response to alleged incidents of police brutality. The trigger that incites these public displays of outrage is often a video version of events that shows police officers using excessive force when such force was not needed. The rampant use of videos makes it far more difficult for police and prosecutors to defend inappropriate police responses. In the prevideo era, if an officer used deadly force and then wrote that the alleged suspect had pointed or reached for a gun, investigators would take the word of that officer, and that would be the end of the story. With the emergence of video-equipped devices, an officer's version of events is not as easily accepted at face value.

Let us assume that the shooting death of Oscar Grant in that Oakland train station had occurred before video footage was so common. The shooter, Officer Mehserle, could write up an incident report describing victim Grant as having resisted arrest and stating that Grant had motioned as if he had a gun. There likely would have been demonstrations, and local elected officials would have called for calm. An investigation would have ensued, and then, months later, Mehserle would likely have been cleared of any wrongdoing.

Enter video footage. This incident was captured on cellular phone video by several random passersby. Unlike most police shooting situations, in which the word of the officer would be accepted over the word of any civilian, the video footage spoke for itself: Officer Mehserle was arrested 12 days later and charged with the murder of Oscar Grant.

It is worth exploring whether or not the police benefit from having their every move videotaped. A second issue is whether or not citizens benefit when their encounters with police are taped or recorded.

The GPS (global positioning system) has become part of our culture. This electronic device enables us to see where we are and how to get from point A to point B. We can avoid traffic congestion and find the nearest gas station. Many automobiles have factory-installed GPS devices, and many cellular telephones include GPS capability. It is no surprise that most contemporary police departments monitor officers and vehicles with GPS devices.

In the not-so-distant past, officers could wander away from their assigned areas/sectors, lie, and tell their dispatchers that they were where they were supposed to be. Tracking devices have changed things; dispatchers and police administrators can now determine the origin of a radio transmission and the location of an officer or patrol car. Once again, paradoxes emerge: the pros and cons of close monitoring of police officers.

My own son wants to become a police officer in a "big" U.S. city. He will not be entering his father's police department. It is no longer likely that he will be contacted by his watch commander and asked to locate a missing scout car and the officers in it, who have overslept at some out-of-the way location and missed their regular check-off call. These days, that patrol car has a GPS tracking device. The days of reporting to the dispatcher a "wrong" location are over. With the touch of a button at the communications center, a car and even a specific officer's location are revealed. Busted.

When my son is admonished that he must rewrite an incident report, he will not be in danger of working into nonpaid overtime; with his laptop, he can make changes painlessly and easily and copy all parties who need the information. The world has changed.

The Age of the Taser

A Taser is a hand-held electronic device that delivers a debilitating and usually nonlethal electric shock. Two types of Tasers are commonly carried. The first fires a small projectile attached to wires that attach to a battery that delivers an electric shock. The second is applied directly to the recipient and then triggered by the officer. The controversy is whether or not police officers should be armed with Tasers.

Numerous reports have attributed serious injuries and even death to police use of Tasers. The deceased are young and old alike; their offenses are often minor, even petty. Jaywalking and questioning an officer's authority are among the infractions committed. Research shows that, in most cases, the victims were unarmed. Amnesty International (2008), in its report on the use of Tasers by police in the United States, found that, between 2001 and August 2008, 334 people died after being subjected to a Taser shock (Preidt, 2009).

In March 2009, a 15-year-old boy in Bay City, Michigan, met an untimely death when—although restrained by handcuffs—he dared to challenge a police officer's authority. The issue was whether he had been drinking alcohol. The boy was surrounded by three officers. His 5-foot, 6-inch, 145-pound body was no match for the burly officers, yet he was Tasered anyway (Gilchrist, 2009).

Increasingly, Tasers are being issued to American patrol officers. In England and Wales, where police officers (generally) do not carry guns, only those of chief officer rank or above (equivalent to U.S. police sergeants and lieutenants) in specially trained units are issued Tasers. A directive to UK officers includes the admonition that the Taser "can only be used where officers would be facing violence or threats of violence of such severity that they would need to use force to protect the public, themselves and/or the subject(s)" (Home Office, 2008, para. 7).

The Taser has replaced personal courage, social skills, and physical prowess in today's officers' tool bag. In many jurisdictions, though not all, the Taser has come to embody an officer's lack of temperament, training, and common sense. The Taser has enabled officers to act in a cowardly manner and with a recklessness that is dangerous to citizens and fellow officers alike. Even in Canada, the Taser is causing havoc. A Toronto, Ontario, police officer Tasered his partner when he shot and missed a suspect. The victimized officer reportedly suffered permanent brain injury as a result. Although the Taser was created to give police officers an alternative to taking a life with gunfire, nonetheless many lives have been damaged or lost by Taser use.

In New York City, although a more careful approach has been adopted, mistakes still happen. Recently, a tragic Taser event occurred when a mentally ill man named Inman Morales was Tasered. Morales stood on a building ledge, naked and wielding a fluorescent lightbulb. When a New York City police officer shot him with a Taser, causing 50,000 volts of electricity to enter him, he plunged to the ground head first. The two officers involved were relieved of their duties, and the NYPD admitted that a "grievous" mistake had been made. The officer in charge, Lieutenant Michael Pigott, committed suicide on the day of Morales's funeral. Morales's death led to the NYPD's requirement that all officers who carry Tasers must undergo retraining.

At about the same time the Michigan boy died, prosecutors in Canada decided not to prosecute Royal Canadian Mounted Police (RCMP) officers who Tasered Robert Dziekanski (The Canadian Press, 2009) at the Vancouver, British Columbia, airport. Dziekanski was a tourist from Poland who was wildly throwing furniture in a temper tantrum when officers Tasered him. Partly owing to the demands of an angry Polish government, the RCMP revised its Taser policies.

Although Tasers have been in police arsenals for more than two decades, they have been available heretofore to only a small number of select officers. The burgeoning number of Taser-related deaths coincides with the increasing issuance of this device to ordinary rank-and-file officers. In the United States and Canada, Tasers have progressed from novelty item to weapon of choice. The product of this evolution has been tragic. Tasers should be the next-to-last alternative to firearms, employed by officers who have had substantial training in their use, and used only in life-threatening situations. They are far too powerful to be routinely issued to any police officer who wants one. Alternatively, police agencies should implement rigid departmental policies limiting the use of Tasers to the most extraordinary circumstances.

21st-Century Police Work Requires a Higher Set of Social Skills

The policing profession has been criticized for hiring too many officers who lack adequate skills in social interaction. An individual who lacks the ability to talk to the public should be disqualified from employment as a police officer.

In an industrialized and advanced society, police officers must be highly educated and professionally trained, and must have competent social interaction and problem-solving skills. To effectively tap the public as a resource to fight crime and to address matters for which they may be summoned, police officers must be skilled at interacting and communicating positively. Citizens expect that U.S. federal and local governments and their elected and appointed officials will perform all mandated duties competently, including the enforcement of human and civil rights. This is accomplished by men and women in uniform exhibiting excellent temperament and solid social and conflict-resolution skills. Perhaps because society has become so litigious, or perhaps because, in this information age, the public is more aware of its rights and the obligations of its governmental agents, police must be equally cognizant of their duties and responsibilities. A competent professional officer must have the social skills and values to interact with the public, demonstrate respect and appreciation for the department's polices, and treat the public with dignity and humility.

Crude officers who try to get away with policing by shouting and using physical force must be replaced by officers who demonstrate critical thinking, education, training, and problem-solving skills, along with physical and personal courage. A better-educated, technologically advanced populace requires the same of its police. Calls for service deserve more consideration than a sloppy threat to lock people up. The 21st-century police officer must be understanding, devoted to the profession, and able to communicate positively with citizens.

Included in a 21st-century police officer's tool box should be the ability (skill set) to know how to either arbitrate or mediate a call for service. Regarding arbitration, for example, an officer's decisiveness in resolving an interpersonal dispute must be obvious: "You give him back his key, right now!" Often, arbitration is not necessary; rather, mediation is the best approach. Mediation can be thought of as empowerment, since the officer does not impose a solution but assists the parties in resolving their dispute themselves (Cooper, 1999a, 1999b, 2002).[1]

In mediation, the officer applies a set of positive social interaction skills to the type of call for service in which arrest might still be an alternative; but two parties are in dispute (e.g., landlord–tenant disagreements), and the officer is expected to do more than just yell. The 21st-century officer must be a problem solver. The challenge is for police agencies to hire men and women who possess the mental and intellectual fortitude to employ tact as well as tactics.

A 21st-Century Phenomenon: The Militarization of Police Work

Many American police departments have militarized their operations (Dunlap, 2001; *The Economist*, 1999) either wholly or substantially (e.g., Pittsburgh, PA; Chicago, IL; Prince George's County, MD; and Broward County, FL; see Balko, 2006; Cooper, forthcoming), such that they are no longer recognizable as police agencies but instead have taken on the appearance of local armies. Traditional blue uniforms have been replaced with green or black camouflage. Revolvers gave way to 9mm handguns which, in turn, have been exchanged for M4 and M16 semi- or fully automatic assault rifles. Some are even equipped with grenade- or rocket-launcher capabilities. Ford Crown Victoria and Chevrolet Lumina automobiles have been replaced with used military armored vehicles. For routine police calls, the Pittsburgh, Pennsylvania, police department dispatches an armored vehicle that resembles a tank (Deitch, 2007; see also AP, 2007, May 8; Plushnick-Masti, 2007).

I take the position that the militarization of U.S. police agencies is an affront to the spirit and ethos of the Posse Comitatus Act of 1878, which stipulates that the military cannot be used as "the police" (the exceptions are few and require catastrophic events). The Posse Comitatus Act (U.S. Code at Title 18, Part 1, Chapter 67 § 1385) reads,

> Whoever, except in cases and under circumstances expressly authorized by the Constitution or Act of Congress, willfully uses any part of the Army or the Air Force as a posse Comitatus or otherwise to execute the laws shall be fined under this title or imprisoned not more than two years, or both.

By the Posse Comitatus Act of 1878 (20 Stat. 152, 18 U.S.C. § 1385),

. . . it shall not be lawful to employ any part of the Army of the United States, as a posse comitatus, or otherwise, for the purpose of executing the laws, except in such cases and under such circumstances as such employment of said force may be expressly authorized by the Constitution or by act of Congress. . . ." (Ops. Atty. Gen. 446, 1854).

Recognizing efforts by some to eradicate the Posse Comitatus Act, Justice Marshall and Justice Douglass, in their dissent in *Laird v. Tatum* (408 U.S. 1, 19; 92 S. Ct. 2318, 1972), wrote,

The alarm was sounded in the Constitutional Convention about the dangers of the armed services. Luther Martin of Maryland said, "when a government wishes to deprive its citizens of freedom, and reduce them to slavery, it generally makes use of a standing army." That danger, we have held, exists not only in bold acts of usurpation of power, but also in gradual encroachments.

Some Police departments across America have created their own standing armies (Chaney, 2008; Chaos-in-Motion, 2008; Chapman, 2008). Referencing the foregoing dissent passage, as the statutory exceptions to the Posse Comitatus Act grow, some police commanders created military rule in residential communities (in particular, in underserved communities and neighborhoods of color). I am speaking not just as a lawyer, a social scientist, and a policeman, but also as an Iraq War veteran and a U.S. Marine Corps infantryman who served with the 2nd Reconnaissance Battalion (cf. Trebilcock, 2000).

The militarization of the police circumvents a primary objective of the Posse Comitatus Act, that of enabling citizens to perceive their day-to-day lives as free of governmental military intervention. Although the act speaks to the behavior of the military and imposes harsh punishment on the military commander who dares use the military as police, the act imposes no restrictions on police commanders who turn civilian police departments into military machines.

Does crime control necessitate and justify the shifting of police departments from police service to military? Are there psychological and cultural issues that underlie the shift? It can be argued that some police candidates avoid military service and instead use policing as an outlet for their machismo. If so, then the behavior of such officers can be understood, although not condoned, as they ride atop armored personnel carriers, traversing the minority communities in ninja-style dress and mirrored sunglasses. Since positive community–police relations are demanded in a free society, more research is needed to document the detrimental affects on civilians of and by those reckless displays of machismo by these ill-equipped police officers.

I realize that some criminals use high-powered weapons; I have encountered some who carried them. However, they are not the norm, and thus there is no justification for the militarization of the police to patrol the streets of Harlem or Atlanta or any other city. Police should have access to appropriate weaponry (high-powered rifles, grenades, etc.) only in response to specific hostile threats. Emergency Response Teams (ERTs) serve this purpose. Something is dramatically wrong with officers on routine patrol in residential communities dressed like soldiers and carrying automatic rifles and grenade launchers.[2]

The good news is that many present and former police commanders are among the most vehement critics of the militarization of the police. Rick Fullmer, sheriff of Marquette County, Wisconsin, disbanded his county's Special Weapons Arms and Tactics (SWAT) unit, stating, "Quite frankly, they [officers] get excited about dressing up in black and doing that kind of thing . . . I said, this is ridiculous. All we are going to end up doing is getting people hurt" (Balko, 2006, p. 16).

Militarization of the police hampers police–community relations and causes citizens to feel threatened by the police rather than served by them. Police officers are trained to protect constitutional due-process safeguards; armies are not. Armies are trained to kill.

DISCUSSION QUESTIONS

1. What types of changes in policing have occurred in the United States in recent years?

2. Do you believe that it is important for police and citizens to collaborate to tackle crime and to address issues of quality of life?

3. What do you think the author means by "the Taser-oriented officer"?

4. Why is it necessary for an industrialized and advanced society to have police officers who are highly educated and professionally trained and who possess excellent social skills?

5. What do you think about police agencies' administering police services with high-powered weapons and officers in battle gear?

NOTES

1. Empowerment is important for a variety of reasons. First, people want to have control over things that are important to them. If such control is in dispute, it is no coincidence that they wish to have ownership of any resolution. This can be achieved only by resolving their own problems.

2. Chicago Police superintendent Weis's position appears to be that the availability of high-powered rifles in the United States justifies police, on a daily basis, on routine patrol, dressing like soldiers and arming themselves with grenade launchers and some of the highest-powered rifles in existence. The logic is flawed; gun ownership in the United States is a norm. Hunters, farmers, and collectors have high-powered weapons. Should police present themselves as soldiers in parts of the country where there are rifle collectors, sport-shooting enthusiasts, farmers, and avid hunters?

REFERENCES

Amnesty International. (2008). *"Less than lethal"? The use of stun weapons in U.S. law enforcement*. London: Author. Retrieved from http://www.amnestyusa.org/uploads/LessThanLethal.pdf

Associated Press (AP). (2007, April 27). Two officers plead guilty in Ga. drug raid death of elderly woman. *Police One*. Retrieved from http://www.policeone.com/officershootings/articles/1240691

Associated Press (AP). (2007, May 8). Is police use of armored vehicles going too far? *MSNBC*. Retrieved from http://www.msnbc.msn.com/id/18556831/

Associated Press (AP). (2008, April 15). 'No knock warrants' targeted by challenge. *Herald-Dispatch*. Retrieved from http://www.herald-dispatch.com/news/x1657952375

Associated Press (AP). (2008, August 8). Police clear name of Maryland mayor after drug raid. *Fox News*. Retrieved from http://www.foxnews.com/story/0,2933,399882,00.html

Associated Press (AP). (2008, August 9). Police clear Berwyn Heights mayor. *The Washington Times*. Retrieved from http://washingtontimes.com/news/2008/aug/09/berwyn-heightsmayor-victim-of-drug-traffickers-po/

Associated Press (AP). (2009, March 18). llionois [sic] police officers arrested after videotaped beating. *New York Daily News*. Retrieved from http://www.nydailynews.com/news/national/2009/03/17/2009-03-17_illionois_police_officers_arrested_after-1.html#ixzz0V04rAHJx

Balko, R. (2006). *Overkill: The rise of paramilitary police raids in America*. Washington, DC: The Cato Institute.

The Canadian Press. (2009, October 6). RCMP lied, Polish lawyer tells Taser inquiry. *CBC News*. Retrieved from http://www.cbc.ca/canada/british-columbia/story/2009/10/06/bc-dziekanski-taser-braidwood-inquiry.html

Chaney, K. (2008, August 15). Officers armed with M4s could hit the streets next month. *Chicago Defender*. Retrieved from http://www.chicagodefender.com/article-1585-officers-armed-withm4s-could-hit-the-streets-next-month.html

Chaos-in-Motion. (2008, May 8). Chicago's military [Web log posting]. Retrieved from http://chaosinmotion.blogspot.com/2008/05/chicagosmilitary.html).

Chapman, S. (2008, April 24). Chicago's misfire on gun violence. *Chicago Tribune*. Retrieved from http://www.humanevents.com/article.php?id=26209

Chicago Sun-Times. (2008, April 26). Chicago cops to be armed with assault rifles. *CBS 2 Chicago*. Retrieved from http://cbs2chicago.com/topstories/police.assault.rifles.2.709234.html

Cooper, C. C. (1999a). *Mediation and arbitration by patrol police officers*. Lanham, MD: University Press of America.

Cooper, C. C. (1999b). Mediation training to improve police social interaction skills. *Conflict Resolution Notes, 17*(1), 6–7.

Cooper, C. C. (2002). *Conceptualizing mediation use by police.* Center for Juvenile & Criminal Justice. Available at http://www.cjcj.org

Cooper, C. C. (Forthcoming). Military wannabes, Officer Friendly evolves to Officer Kill & Destroy: Militarization of police threatens Posse Comitatus. *Police Forum, 19*(2).

Cordner, G. W. (1997). Community policing: Elements and effects. In G. P. Alpert & A. Piquero, *Community policing: Contemporary readings* (pp. 45–62). Prospect Heights, IL: Waveland Press.

Deitch, C. (2007, March 22). Military police: Military-style police tactics reflect—and arguably worsen—distrust between black neighborhoods and police. *Pittsburgh City Paper.* Retrieved from http://www.pittsburghcitypaper.ws/gyrobase/Content?oid=oid%3A24549

Dunlap, C. J., Jr. (Col.). (2001). The thick green line: The growing involvement of military forces in domestic law enforcement. In P. B. Kraska (Ed.), *Militarizing the American criminal justice system* (pp. 43–64). Boston: Northeastern University Press.

Gilchrist, T. (2009, March 23). Bay City teen dies after police use Taser. *Bay City Times.* Retrieved from http://www.mlive.com/news/bctimes/index.ssf?/base/news-13/1237821325230720.xml&coll=4

Hanners, D. (2009, March 31). The final moments of Fong Lee. *Twin Cities Pioneer Press.* Retrieved from http://www.twincities.com/ci_12041325

Home Office Police. *Operational policing: Taser* [Website]. Retrieved from http://police.homeoffice.gov.uk/operational-policing/firearms/taser/

KING5.com Staff & Associated Press (AP). (2009, August 15). Justice Dept. looking into alleged deputy assault. *KING5.com.* Retrieved from http://www.king5.com/news/local/60049797.html

Kraska, P. B., & Kappeler, V. E. (1997). Militarizing American police: The rise and normalization of paramilitary units. *Social Problems, 13,* 1–18.

KTVU.com. (2009, January 5). Bart shooting: Transit police ask for patience. Retrieved from http://www.ktvu.com/news/18412851/detail.html#-

Laird v. Tatum, 408 U.S. 1, 19; 92 S. Ct. 2318 (1972).

Maguire, E. R., & King, W. R. (2004, May). Trends in the policing industry. *Annals of the American Academy of Political and Social Sciences, 593,* 15–41.

Mayhall, P. D. (1994). *Police-community relations and the administration of justice.* Englewood Cliffs, NJ: Prentice Hall.

Plushnick-Masti, R. (2007, May 9). American police forces deploying heavy armor. *Chicago Sun-Times.*

Policing: The sultans of SWAT. (1999, October 2). *The Economist.*

Posse Comitatus Act of 1878 (20 Stat. 152, 18 U.S.C. § 1385).

Preidt, R. (2009, March 17). Taser stun guns can cause brain injury. *ABC News.* Retrieved from http://abcnews.go.com/Health/Healthday/story?id=7098339&page=1&page=1

Rosenbaum, D. P. (1998). The changing role of the police: Assessing the current transition to community policing. In R. W. Glensor, M. E. Correia, & K. J. Peak, *Policing communities: Understanding crime and solving problems, an anthology* (pp. 46–63). Los Angeles: Roxbury.

Trebilcock, C. T. (2000, October). *The myth of posse comitatus.* Retrieved from http://www.homelandsecurity.org/journal/articles/Trebilcock.htm

PART IV

Policy and Jurisprudence

16 Police Organization and Administration

Thomas W. Nolan

There are 17,876 law enforcement agencies in the United States, and they employ more than 836,000 police officers of various types: state and local police, sheriff's departments, agents of the federal government, constables and marshals, and special jurisdiction police (such as campus and tribal police). Only 6% of police agencies employ 100 or more officers, and these account for two thirds of sworn personnel nationwide; almost half of all law enforcement agencies employ fewer than 10 officers (U.S. Department of Justice, Office of Justice Programs, 2003, p. 1). Contemporary observers have used the metaphors "juggernaut" (Gordon, 1990; Websdale, 2001) and "monolith" (Maguire, 2008; Morash, 2005) to describe the criminal justice system generally and policing in particular. Any examination of the ways that law enforcement organizations are organized and administered ought be conducted through these insightful and illuminating prisms.

When considering the topics of the administration and organization of police and other law enforcement agencies in the 21st century, an enlightened, progressive inquiry and analysis will necessarily eschew the traditional emphasis on organizational charts and structures, the span of control, unity of command, line and staff functions, the deployment of field forces, and the various organizational theories of Weber, Hammer, Katz, Maslow, Herzberg, McGregor, and others. Of more critical import (and more informed insight) in understanding how police departments are actually organized and administered (formally and informally) will be an examination of the organizational culture (or subculture) of contemporary law enforcement agencies.

Origins of the Structural Model of Police Organizations

Virtually all law enforcement agencies share—from the 561 departments consisting of but a single officer to the New York City Police Department with over 36,000 officers—an organizational model that is quasi-military, hierarchical, and rigidly structured along clearly delineated lines of authority and responsibility. This categorizes the *formal*, prescribed, and public organization of the police. The question arises as to how the organizational structure that we see present in virtually all police organizations came to assume its form, as the inchoate nature of urban policing during its dawn in the mid-19th century saw little, if any, "uniformity" (literally and metaphorically). "Police were involved in social service activities: they ran soup kitchens, provided lodging for indigents, and spurred moral reform movements against cigarettes and alcohol . . . [they] were union busters and political-machine enforcers" (Pollock, 2007, p. 191). Not yet established in the nascent days of policing were military ranks, uniforms, badges of office, or even the issuance and carrying of firearms. It is suggested here that the hierarchical and quasi-military structure of contemporary law enforcement agencies arose out of expediency and necessity when police departments, in their earlier incarnations, were confronted with rioting, looting, and hooliganism on a scale hitherto unprecedented.

The only organizational model available to those mid-19th-century police administrative neophytes was that of the military. Easily recognized and identified, rapidly deployed, operating under a strict chain of command and span of control, trained in teamwork and coordination, the military structure seemed readily adaptable to the unprecedented exigencies confounding emerging police departments in New York, Boston, Philadelphia, and elsewhere. In London, the Metropolitan Police Act of 1829 created a police department founded on a military model that eventually met with a degree of success; this proved to be the form that would be emulated in the United States.

Throughout its history, this model of police organization has been a somewhat uneasy (if not unholy) alliance of philosophical underpinnings and operational strategies and policies. The contemporary emphasis on community policing and problem-oriented policing philosophies, for example, have often proven inimical to and incompatible with the quasi-military model of police organization. The military emphasis on absolute deference and obedience to authority, rote conformity to group norms, the use of force and violence to overcome resistance, and closely monitored and orchestrated teamwork are all squarely at odds with the realities, practices, and expectations of policing in the 21st century, particularly as they relate to community and problem-oriented policing principles. These philosophies and principles privilege and endorse decision making at the lowest levels of the organizational hierarchy— the street-level police officer—in clear contraindication to military practice. Community policing and problem-oriented policing also place responsibility for the identification and resolution of police-related issues squarely in the hands of the individual officer(s) assigned to a particular area or beat. The model of policing in operational practice in the United States today sees the vast majority of actual police activity conducted not only out of the public eye but also absent any scrutiny, inspection, or observation from police supervisors or managers (and this is especially so in the ±3% of U.S. police departments that comprise but a single officer), again clearly contrary to the military model (U.S. Department of Justice, Office of Justice Programs, 2003).

Police Organization and "War"

Police departments have adopted the military's hierarchical organizational rank structure, at least in part. Consider this modified adaptation: Officers of rank in most U.S. police departments are referred to as "corporal," "sergeant," "lieutenant," and "captain." Some of the more highly militarized departments (such as many state police agencies) use the higher military ranks, such as "major" or "colonel," but chief executive officers of police departments in the United States are never referred to as "general," as they are in other countries where the organizational boundaries between the military and the police are somewhat blurred. Executive officers of U.S. police departments typically use the title "chief," and the Western referent to this appellation lies in the Native American conception of the leader of a tribe or clan. Police chiefs often attire themselves in a somewhat conspicuous display of the trappings and symbols of their office. The hat (headdress) adorned with braided gold oak leaves, the gold stars, the gold shield, the embroidered epaulets, the velvet stripes—all serve to set the chief above and apart from his or her subordinates, not unlike their earlier historical counterparts who were tribal leaders (see more on the "tribe" referent in the police subculture section later in this chapter).

The police have also adopted many of the organizational designations employed by the military. Squads, platoons, units, task forces, even battalions and regiments are commonly used in police organizational charts to describe function, lines of authority and accountability, numbers of sworn officers, duties, hours of work, and other identifying and organizationally pertinent information.

A more recent adaptation of military argot in describing police organizational tactics is manifested in the (now) ubiquitous use of the term *Operation*. Consider Operation Community Shield (Immigration and Customs Enforcement targeting violent gangs), Operation Would You Like Fries (sheriffs undercover in fast-food restaurants to spot impaired drivers), Operation Homefront (police working with clergy and troubled youths), Operation CARE (police warning motorists about safety belts), and Operation Falcon (acronym for Federal And Local Cops Organized Nationally to round up 30,000 petty criminals). In fact, the Boston, Massachusetts, police department recently launched an incursion into that city's inner-city neighborhoods dubbed Operation Rolling Thunder (see Smalley, 2006) without any apparent awareness that its military counterpart and predecessor, begun in 1965, consisted of the aerial bombardment and carpet bombing of North Vietnam by the U.S. Air Force (see Wikipedia, 2009).

The metaphor of the modern-era police chief leading warriors into battle against criminals, gangbangers, terrorists, and drug dealers is telling in its irony. For it is here that the military analogy gains the most traction, even as it seriously risks running aground. At the turn of the 21st century, the police in the United States had been organized largely as the first wave of shock troops on the urban battlefield that too many of our cities had become. Klockars (2005) sees three compelling themes in this analogy:

> First . . . the military analogy sought to confer some honor and respect on the occupation of policing. Second, the idea of a war on crime struck a note of emergency [and] . . . a moral urgency and a rhetorical tone that was difficult to resist . . . Third, the military analogy sought to establish a relationship between local politicians and police chiefs that was analogous to the relationship between elected executives at the national level and the general of the U.S. military. (pp. 445–446)

In this role, the police were seen by many as an army of oppression and occupation (particularly in inner-city communities of color), and in large part the police themselves did little to discourage this perception. That no small number of police departments initiated policies arming the police with assault rifles and dressing them in military "battle-dress uniforms" (BDUs) drove a wedge into solid gains that had been made under community policing and problem-oriented policing initiatives dating from the late 1980s (Slack, 2009). Community partnerships and coproduction initiatives that had been the hallmarks of community policing risked being scuttled as police departments reorganized themselves to meet what they perceived to be the law enforcement exigencies of the 21st century. Thus, at the turn of the new century, the so-called "wars"—on drugs (declared in 1984), gangs, terrorists, and the like—saw the police morph into a military monolith or "juggernaut" whose mission may seem somewhat conflicted when community policing's "three core elements [of] citizen involvement, problem solving, and decentralization" (Skogan, as cited in Weisburd & Braga, 2006, p. 28) square off against the more recent mandate to meet violent crime (particularly when it is gang related) with a formidable and well organized display of force—"In the words of one officer: 'We kick ass'" (Kelling & Wilson, 1982, p. 34).

Police Organization: Subculture, Ethos, and Milieu

While the formal organization of contemporary police organizations is characterized by a quasi-military hierarchical structure governed by formalized rules, policies, procedures, and practices, perhaps an articulation and understanding of the *subculture* of policing provides a richer, more elaborate understanding of the police organization and its membership, for this subculture is neither formally recognized nor often understood by the public.

Police and their organizations have been characterized as insular, isolated, hidebound, conservative, masculinist, morally superior, autonomous, authoritarian, cynical, and ethnocentric (among other things). That the police subculture is insular owes much to the expectations that society has of its police. The police are organized in a fashion that clearly delineates them from other members of the communities that they police, through their distinctive uniforms, badges of office, conspicuously marked modes of transport, and their being openly (and somewhat heavily) armed. The police are expected to maintain order, to prevent the occurrence of crime, and to ensure the safety of the public (among other duties); as a result, police develop the self-image of a crime fighter engaged in a "noble cause." Waddington's observations that the police, in the performance of their duties, do not confront "[an] enemy, but fellow citizens and that makes their position acutely marginal . . . It is why the police are so insular: they find social encounters with non-police friends, acquaintances, neighbours and others fraught with difficulty" (1999, p. 298).

The police are isolated, largely owing to the environment in which they work and the significant degree of discretion they exercise. "Police officers often work alone or in pairs . . . there is no direct supervision. Also, a majority of police-citizen encounters occur in private places, with no other observers present . . . for this reason, policing has been described as low-visibility work" (Walker & Katz, 2007, p. 362). Thus, the means by which the police "work product" is organized contributes directly to the physical isolation of officers from their constituent communities and indirectly toward the perpetuation of a tangible sense of isolation (within the context of the police subculture) that the police themselves experience.

The police subculture is hidebound in its resistance to change. Perhaps nowhere in recent evidence is there a more convincing example of this than the arguably abysmal results of community policing initiatives from the early 1990s to the present. Mastrofski (2006) attributes these failures to the organizational subculture of the police and observes that efforts to change what some observers have dubbed a "monolithic" police culture through community policing and other like-minded innovations are likely to "die on the vine" (p. 53) owing to skepticism on the part of rank-and-file officers who are extremely resistant to change. He goes on to suggest that "police socialization processes" influence officer behavior and the police subculture far more than hiring practices that emphasize diversity and cultural change (p. 51). These socialization processes are the mechanisms that serve to perpetuate, validate, and privilege the status quo. That status quo endorses behavioral practices that vehemently resist changes to the organizational subculture that would alter promotional practices, access to desirable assignments, the marginalization of women and minority officers, the tolerance of violence and brutality, and practices that turn a blind eye to minor acts graft, corruption, and deceit (Nolan, 2009).

The police endorse and validate a conservative worldview in the execution of their duties, and this conservatism is a cornerstone of the organizational subculture of policing. In an environment permeated with gray, the police are habituated to see black and white:

> The police tend to view their occupational world as comprised exhaustively of three types of citizens. These ideal types are: (1) "suspicious persons"—those whom the police have reason to believe may have committed a serious offense; (2) "assholes"—those who do not accept the police definition of the situation; and (3) "know nothings"—those who are not either of the first two categories but are not police and therefore, according to the police, cannot know what the police are about. (Van Maanen, 2005, p. 281)

The police thus construct these conceptual categories as cognitive shorthand to deal with the myriad and occasionally overwhelming banalities and crises in which they are constantly submerged. Under community policing initiatives, police organizational practice "privileges the law abider who cares for his home, his lawn, and his children, and the neighborhood merchant" (Harcourt, 2001, p. 127). The police are organized around a conservative ethic that "embraces an unmediated aesthetic of order, cleanliness, and sobriety" (ibid., p. 135) and one in which the "order or rules of civilian conduct . . . are geared toward producing a more harmonious social environment with strong moral bonds" (ibid., p. 140). The police organize their experiential practice into maintaining a conservative social agenda that embraces conformity and adherence to a middle-class ethic of tacitly understood canons of behavior and comportment. They value patriotism, religious practice, distrust of the media, loyalty, respect for tradition and authority, duty to family, and the unquestioned righteousness of the rule of law.

Organization and Subculture: Initiation and Masculinism

Masculinism is a social construct that "justifies and naturalizes male domination. As such, it is the ideology of patriarchy. It sanctions the political and dominant role of men in the public and private spheres" (Brittan, 2001, p. 53). The police subculture is, for the most part, created, maintained, and structurally organized by the men who establish the discourse, enforce the formal and informal rules, and maintain and assign group and member roles: the leaders, the cadre, the plebeians, the novitiates, and the outsiders. Even though women have been mainstreamed into the ranks of the police since the latter decades of the 20th century, the latest available Bureau of Justice Statistics figures show that "of the 451,737 full-time sworn personnel in all local police departments as of June 2003, approximately 11% were women" (U.S. Department of Justice, Office of Justice Programs, 2003, p. 7).

The training that police officers receive at the intake level is indoctrinary and instills in the initiate the language, behaviors, symbols, and rituals that will ensure effective adaptation and assimilation for the novice. Ritualistic forms of voice, gait, posture, demeanor, language, and dress are all prescriptive and representative of a certain form of tribal initiation. Likewise, the ritualistic assembly in the roll call is a highly masculinized throwback to a secret military convocation that dates to the Roman Legions (roll calls are organizational rituals in which officers are inspected and given their assignments). Outsiders are never allowed to watch or participate in a roll call except on extremely rare occasions that are completely staged for the intrusion. The officers hardly see these assemblies as sites for bonding and reinforcing the subculture of policing; that what is said at roll call stays in the guard room (as the assembly point is referred to) seems only natural.

Let us revisit the particular form of masculinism that presents itself in the military representations of rank and vertical hierarchy. As in the military, those higher up in the vertical scale of rank, those bearing or wearing gold stars and bars, are accorded the respect and attention mandated by the efficient operation of this masculinist enterprise. Beyond that, officers of rank are viewed with mistrust, suspicion, and resentment, and a different construction of hierarchy emerges among the plebeians. For example, "street cops" (those who work more hazardous patrol duty) are depicted in the subculture as more masculine than officers who work in clerical positions or guard prisoners. Likewise, police officers who work in what is (perhaps inaccurately) characterized as more dangerous duty in inner-city neighborhoods (i.e., communities of color) are held in higher masculine esteem than officers who work in the relative tranquility of suburban or downtown communities (Nolan, 2009).

A long-held (and equally misguided) subcultural stereotype depicts those who perform the more glamorous functions associated with plainclothes and undercover police work as more masculine than officers who must perform their duties conspicuously and publicly in uniform. Officers assigned to uniform duty are "in the bag"—a pejorative reference to inability to conceal oneself from public view and to wear the fashionable clothes of a "made" detective or the street clothes of an undercover. Those who work in drug investigations are perceived as more "male" than those who work with sexual assault victims (who are largely female). Thus emerges a fraternity of those engaged in what they perceive as duty fraught with danger, a battle against the underworld replete with the bonding, the secrecy, the faux loyalty, and the war metaphors that have historically accompanied those identified with the organizational subculture of policing (Nolan, 2009).

In an earlier writing (2001), I described how certain highly masculinized police organizations routinely (and perhaps unwittingly) objectified, degraded, and sexualized female officers in coercing them into posing as decoy prostitutes during sting operations targeting "johns." So culturally ingrained are many masculinized organizational practices in police departments that they are often hardly recognized as such, even by progressive administrators.

_____ Organizational Subculture and Moral Superiority

The police see their mission as organized around a trope that is imbued with a sense of moral superiority and in which the police have designated themselves the arbiters of the right/wrong or good/bad dichotomies. Through the use of discretion, police often decide in context-specific situations whether or not to invoke the provisions of the criminal law based on their assessment of the level of moral "injury" or offense present in a particular situation. This is particularly true in drug crimes, gambling, prostitution, and other nonviolent and victimless crimes. The police believe themselves to be

> [p]erpetually engaged in a struggle with those who would disobey, disrupt, do harm, agitate, or otherwise upset the order of the regime. And, . . . as policemen, they and they alone are the most capable of sensing right from wrong; determining who is and who is not respectable; and, most critically deciding what is to be done about it (if anything). Such heroic self-perceptions regarding moral superiority have been noted by numerous social scientists concerned with the study of the police. (Van Maanen, 2005, pp. 280–281)

In fact, during the last two decades the vast majority of police organizational strategy and policy has been driven by community policing and problem-oriented policing strategies, the nexus of which has been Kelling and Wilson's "broken windows" theory. Fundamental to this theory that drove so much of police practice was that the police themselves "defined 'order'"; they themselves identified it, and they decided who had violated local moral norms: "Not necessarily violent people, nor, necessarily criminals, but disreputable or obstreperous or unpredictable people: panhandlers, drunks, addicts, rowdy teenagers, prostitutes, loiterers, the mentally disturbed" (Kelling & Wilson, 1982, p. 29). Thus, the police have assumed for themselves the role of identifying morality and immorality and have organized their mission at the local level in an effort to enforce standards of good and bad behavior as they understand it.

Ethnocentrism is "the tendency to reject and malign other ethnic groups and their members while glorifying one's own group and its members" (APA, 2007, p. 345). Several observers have seen police organizations as akin to such groups whose members have a strong identification with a common history, culture, belief system, means of communicating, shared values, worldview, and designation of out-groups. It is suggested here that the ways in which the police are formally and informally organized are reflective of *in-group bias*:

> The tendency to favor one's own group, its characteristics, and its products, particularly in reference to other groups. The favoring of the ingroup tends to be more pronounced than the rejection of the outgroup, but both become more pronounced during periods of intergroup contact. (APA, 2007, p. 481)

Gendreau (2006) and Andrews and Bonta (2006) have described *theoreticism* as "the practice [that] involves accepting or rejecting knowledge on the basis of one's personal values and experiences" and one that "is a critical problem in the criminal justice field" (Gendreau, p. 226). In organizations (such as the police) that are insular and dogmatic, theoreticism can be especially pernicious in guiding organizational practice at the street level and organizational policy and philosophy at the administrative level. Police organizations collectively and the police themselves are very often skeptical of outsiders ("assholes") and of "knowledges" that do not originate within and conform to the police's worldview and experience (and this is particularly true of academic research).

Police Organization: Autonomy and Authoritarianism

That police organizations conduct the vast majority of their day-to-day operations out of the public eye and with little (if any) oversight by or input from the communities they serve has become routinized and normative as American law enforcement enters the second decade of the 21st century. The police are typically neither licensed nor controlled by any government or professional regulatory entity outside of the agency itself—unlike lawyers, doctors, hairdressers, masseuses, acupuncturists, and even tattoo artists. For the large part, police organizations operate almost completely autonomously. For example, an article in *The Boston Globe* (Slack, 2009) recently reported that, in Massachusetts, "some 82 local police departments have obtained more than 1000 weapons over the last 15 years under a federal program that distributes surplus guns from the U.S. military" (para. 2). The weapons ranged from M16 assault rifles to M79 grenade launchers and were acquired by university police departments and some departments with fewer than 10 officers. No input was sought from affected communities, and the proposal to equip 200 police officers in the Boston police department with the assault rifles was shelved after it was leaked to the news media and the public backlash made the proposal politically untenable. One police official, when questioned about equipping officers with the assault rifles, stated, "'That decision belongs with police officials, not the public,'" and "likened community involvement in arms decisions to public involvement in hospitals' decisions on what type and how many heart stents to buy" (paras. 26–27).

In describing the work environment of policing, Skolnick observed that "police work constitutes the most secluded part of an already secluded system of criminal justice and therefore offers the greatest opportunity for arbitrary behavior" (1994, p. 13). Thus, it is the organizational autonomy of the police that sets them distinctly apart from other "individual practitioners of a craft," as Bittner (2005) has described them. In acting autonomously, "most of what a policeman needs to know to do his work he has to learn on his own" (p. 169).

The perspective that it is the police who are the experts and the professionals in all matters pertaining to public safety and the ensuing regulation of human behavior in the maintenance of public order assumes a standpoint that some have characterized as *organizational authoritarianism* and, in police officers, an *authoritarian personality*:

> Authoritarian personality: a personality pattern characterized by (a) preoccupation with power and status, (b) strict adherence to highly simplified conventional values, (c) an attitude of great deference to authority figures while demanding subservience from those regarded as lower in status, and (d) hostility toward minorities and other outgroups and to people who deviate from conventional moral prescriptions. (APA, 2007, p. 89)

Police Administration and the Civil Service

The vast majority of the more than 17,000 police agencies in the United States operate under some type of civil service or tenured intake and promotion system that serves to severely restrict and delimit the discretion of an administrator or appointing authority in hiring and promoting individuals within a particular police agency. In theory, the civil service system was instituted around the turn of the 20th century in an effort to abolish patronage appointments to local police departments. In practice, it has created and sustained a complicated and convoluted system that is often mired in cronyism and bogged down by administrative trivia. For example, preference provisions written into many civil service laws have given entry-level and promotional preference to military veterans, family members of officers deemed to have died "in the line of duty," civilian "cadets," women, foreign-language speakers, emergency medical technicians, and others. Further, applicant tests and other instruments are administered that, to many observers, are in no way reflective of or capable of measuring the necessary skills or identifying the most qualified applicants for entry-level and promotional positions. Police administrators often complain of being hamstrung by outdated legal requirements that hamper their efforts to place the most desirable and qualified applicants in open positions as well as terminate the employment of those proven unsuitable for police service.

Police Administration and Unions

Police unions and the collective bargaining process can prove vexing and frustrating for police administrators (full disclosure: this author was a long-time elected constitutional officer of a large police union). "Nationwide, 41% of local police departments, employing 71% of all officers, authorized collective bargaining for sworn personnel" (U.S. Department of Justice, Office of Justice Programs, 2003, p. 12). Contemporary police unions began forming in the 1960s and 1970s in response to oppressive working conditions that included abysmal compensation, lack of overtime pay, poor equipment, work schedules that permitted few days off, no vacation, mandatory unpaid call-outs, and draconian residency and travel notification requirements.

Many of today's police unions have negotiated generous compensation packages for their members and have proven formidable adversaries in often contentious and confrontational relationships with police administrators. Protracted and fractured contract negotiations between police unions and the City of Boston threatened to shut down the Democratic National Convention in 2004 until the city's police unions won a significant wage increase from the city in an unprecedented contract package that offered no concessions from the unions to the city (Greenhouse, 2004).

CONCLUSION

Students of criminal justice are offered here a glimpse into the realm of the lived experience and worldview of the police from the perspective of one who has lived it for more than 30 years. It is a dominion that is in many ways mired in a perspective on society jaded by constant exposure to a sliver of the polity that is hardly representative of the society in which most of us live. Yet, for the police, it is all too often their only tangible grasp of the netherworld that is, for them, all too real, all too pervasive, all too unrelenting. Progressive police administrators (and enlightened students) understand that therein lie the value and sacrifice of what the police provide to the rest of us and the price that they pay in serving our communities.

DISCUSSION QUESTIONS

1. How does the formal organizational structure of contemporary police agencies contribute (if you believe that it does) to inconsistencies and difficulties in implementing community policing and problem-oriented policing philosophies and strategies?

2. Police organizations have been described as masculinist in nature and form. What are the manifestations of masculinism in contemporary police organizations? How has masculinism affected and informed the ways that police interact with their constituent communities? What are the implications of such masculinism for the future of police organizations?

3. The police are organized in a quasi-military form that employs military metaphors such as "war" and "operation" (among others) in descriptions of its purpose and mission. What are the implications of using military terms to describe strategies, policies, and tactics that the police employ in our communities? Are these descriptions compatible with community policing initiatives?

4. The police are organized around the enforcement not only of the criminal law but also of moral behavior generally. How do the police engage in the identification and enforcement of morality? What are the implications of having the police enforce standards of behavior? Do the police in fact decide what is appropriate moral behavior?

REFERENCES

Alpert, G., Dunh, R. & Stroshine, M. (2006). *Policing: Continuity and change.* Long Grove, IL: Waveland Press.

American Psychological Association. (2007). *The American Psychological Association dictionary of psychology.* Washington, DC: Author.

Andrews, D., & Bonta, J. (2006). *The psychology of criminal conduct* (4th ed.). Cincinnati, OH: Anderson.

Banks, C. (2009). *Criminal justice ethics: Theory and practice* (2nd ed.). Thousand Oaks, CA: Sage.

Bittner, E. (2005). Florence Nightingale in pursuit of Willie Sutton: A theory of the police. In T. Newburn (Ed.), *Policing: Key readings* (pp. 150–172). Devon, UK: Willan.

Bohm, R., & Walker, J. (2006). *Demystifying crime and criminal justice.* Los Angeles: Roxbury.

Braswell, M., McCarthy, B., & McCarthy, B. (2008). *Justice, crime, and ethics* (6th ed.). Cincinnati, OH: Anderson.

Brittan, A. (2001). Masculinities and masculinism. In S. Whitehead & F. Barrett (Eds.), *The masculinities reader.* Cambridge, UK: Polity Press.

Cohen, H., & Feldberg, M. (1991). *Power and restraint: The moral dimension of police work.* Westport, CT: Praeger.

Delattre, E. (1989). *Character and cops: Ethics in policing.* Washington, DC: American Enterprise Institute.

Gendreau, P. (2006). Offender rehabilitation: What we know and what needs to be done. In C. Bartol & A. Bartol (Eds.), *Current perspectives in forensic psychology and criminal justice* (pp. 223–229). Thousand Oaks, CA: Sage.

Gordon, D. (1990). *The justice juggernaut: Fighting street crime and controlling citizens.* Piscataway, NJ: Rutgers University Press.

Greenhouse, S. (2004, July 23). Convention near, Boston police win raise. *The New York Times.* Retrieved on October 15, 2009, from http://www.nytimes.com/2004/07/23/us/convention-near-boston-police-win-raise.html

Harcourt, B. (2001). *Illusion of order: The false promise of broken windows policing.* Cambridge, MA: Harvard University Press.

Kelling, G., & Wilson, J. (1982). The police and neighborhood safety: Broken windows. *Atlantic Monthly, 127,* 29–38.

Kleinig, J. (1996). *The ethics of policing.* Cambridge: Cambridge University Press.

Klockars, C. (2005). The rhetoric of community policing. In T. Newburn (Ed.), *Policing: Key readings* (pp. 442–459). Devon, UK: Willan.

Leighton, P., & Reiman, J. (2001). *Criminal justice ethics.* Upper Saddle River, NJ: Pearson Prentice Hall.

Maguire, M. (2008). Merry Morash: Understanding gender, crime, and justice. *Journal of Critical Criminology, 16,* 225–227.

Mastrofski, S. (2006). Community policing: A skeptical view. In D. Weisburd & A. Braga (Eds.), Policing innovation: Contrasting perspectives (pp. 44-76). Cambridge: Cambridge University Press.

Mastrofski, S., Willis, J., & Kochel, T. (2007). The challenges of implementing community policing in the United States. *Policing: A Journal of Policy and Practice, 1*(2), 223–234.

Morash, M. (2005). *Understanding gender crime, and justice.* Thousand Oaks, CA: Sage.

Nolan, T. (2001). Galateas in blue: Women police as decoy sex workers. *Criminal Justice Ethics, 20*(2), 63–67.

Nolan, T. (2009). Behind the blue wall of silence. *Journal of Men and Masculinities.* doi:10.1177/1097184X09334700

Pogrebin, M. (2004). *About criminals: A view of the offender's world.* Thousand Oaks, CA: Sage.

Pollock, J. (2007). *Ethical dilemmas and decisions in criminal justice* (5th ed.). Belmont, CA: Thomson Wadsworth.

Rossmo, D. (2009). *Criminal investigative failures.* Boca Raton, FL: CRC Press.

Skogan, W. (2006). The promise of community policing. In D. Weisburd & A. Braga (Eds.), *Policing innovation: Contrasting perspectives* (pp. 27–43). Cambridge: Cambridge University Press.

Skolnick, J. (1994). *Justice without trial* (3rd ed.). New York: Macmillan.

Slack, D. (2009, June 3). Police add assault rifles across the state. *The Boston Globe.* Retrieved on October 15, 2009, from http://www.boston.com/news/local/massachusetts/articles/2009/06/03/police_add_assault_rifles_across_the_state/

Slack, D. (2009, June 15). Even small localities got big guns. *The Boston Globe.* Retrieved on October 15, 2009, from http://www.boston.com/news/local/massachusetts/articles/2009/06/15/details_emerge_on_distribution_of_military_weapons_in_mass/?page=1

Smalley, S. (2006, January 31). Service agencies to join police sweeps of neighborhoods. *The Boston Globe.* Retrieved on October 15, 2009, from http://www.boston.com/news/local/massachusetts/articles/2006/01/31/service_agencies_to_join_police_sweeps_of_neighborhoods/

U.S. Department of Justice, Office of Justice Programs (2003). *Law enforcement management and administrative statistics: Local police departments, 2003.* Retrieved on June 8, 2009, from http://www.ojp.usdoj.gov/bjs/pub/pdf/lpd03.pdf

Van Maanen, J. (2005). The asshole. In T. Newburn (Ed.), *Policing: Key readings* (pp. 280–296). Devon, UK: Willan.

Waddington, P. (1999). Police (canteen) subculture: An appreciation. *British Journal of Criminology, 39*(2), pp. 287–309.

Walker, S., & Katz, C. (2007). *The police in America: An introduction* (6th ed.). Boston, MA: McGraw-Hill.

Websdale, N. (2001). *Policing the poor: From slave plantation to public housing.* Boston, MA: Northeastern University Press.

White, M. (2007). *Current issues and controversies in policing.* Boston, MA: Pearson.

Wikipedia (2009). *Operation Rolling Thunder.* Retrieved on October 15, 2009, from http://en.wikipedia.org/wiki/Operation_Rolling_Thunder

Williams, C., & Arrigo, B. (2008). *Ethics, crime, and criminal justice.* Upper Saddle River, NJ: Pearson Prentice Hall.

17

Public Policy

Frank P. Williams III and Janice Ahmad

I n this chapter, we discuss the issue of public policy and its connection to criminal justice and law. Public policy shapes our everyday life, from the way we get to school and work (be it by driving or on public transportation), to the breaks that employees are granted, to the sanitary conditions of the restaurant at which we eat lunch, to the taxes and fees we pay to maintain the schools, roads, police agencies, and correctional facilities. This short list indicates the extensive impact of public policy that is implemented at the federal, state, and local levels. This impact is particularly true for the criminal justice system in the United States.

Most people will argue that there are two versions of public policy: the formal version and the way public policy is actually practiced. We first explain the formal version of public policy and law, after which we examine public policy as a practical matter, giving examples of recent use and misuse of public policy in law and criminal justice. We then discuss three contemporary influences on the creation of public policy and what we consider to be the future of public policy.

Public Policy: The Formal Version

Simply put, public policy is what the government chooses to do or not do (Dye, 2008). These actions or inactions are based on the social contract—what society expects from government. The social contract evolves and changes according to the principles of the public and policymakers. Changes in the social contract occur for such reasons as emerging problems (health epidemics, inflation/recession, natural disasters, acts of terrorism), principles held by new policymakers, or program evaluation results.

What is an "official" definition of public policy? *Public policy* can be defined as purposive governmental courses of action or inaction. Choices are made and implementation takes place, resulting in outcomes that are subsequently evaluated to determine the policy's impact and effectiveness. This formal process of policymaking follows a systems approach and is reviewed and revised to meet the social contract. Under this model, one would expect public policy to be the product of a carefully considered process.

Public policy is generally created when a problem has been identified and brought to the attention of policymakers. If the problem is perceived as fitting the policymakers' agenda, a public policy may be developed to resolve the problem. In criminal justice, policy agendas are generally based on one of the major goals of the criminal justice system: deterrence, incapacitation, punishment, rehabilitation, reintegration, and restoration (Marion & Oliver, 2006). However, before a policy is developed, the policymaking process must be enacted.

When developing public policy, we must keep in mind that it is not developed in a vacuum; rather, a policy can impact several systems and agencies as well as many people. Policy that does not account for this interconnectedness generally has unintended consequences and is ineffective. Recognizing this, Welsh and Harris (2008) separate the policymaking process into three components: defining and examining the problem, developing goals and objectives, and creating the policy.

The first step in developing public policy is to define and examine the problem. What may seem like a widespread problem when first presented may not be, upon examination, as far reaching as presented. Thorough investigation into the problem will reveal its causes, impact, history, stakeholders, previous interventions and outcomes, agency interconnectivity, and the barriers to and support for change. This examination may reveal more than one approach for resolving the problem, as well as the goals and objectives that need to be met by the public policy.

Stakeholders—people who will be positively and negatively affected and the agencies that will be impacted—must be identified and involved in the policy development process. Their involvement is critical to create the most effective policy, gain support for the policy, and have it implemented as intended. The cost, resources needed, and funding sources must also be determined. Finally, the process involves developing an evaluation component.

Evaluation of the public policy helps to determine if the goals and objectives are being met. During the past few years, we have seen an evaluation component being included in public policies. For example, grant solicitations by the U. S. Department of Justice now require that performance measures be included in the grant application and for funding. Evaluations also guide the review and reassessment process to determine whether the policy should be revised, continued, or discontinued.

Criminal justice is directly and indirectly impacted by public policies. Public policies that reduce fear of crime, punish or rehabilitate offenders, and fund 100,000 more police officers are easily identified as criminal justice policy initiatives and are created in consultation with criminal justice agencies.

However, policies that involve other systems (mental health, education, the workplace) may also greatly impact criminal justice. For example, during the late 1960s and early 1970s many residential mental health facilities were closed because it was deemed that the clients would be best served in the community using community resources. However, this public policy resulted in many mentally ill persons becoming involved in a criminal justice system that was not equipped to handle them and subsequently being treated as criminals rather than as mentally ill people. Had the policymaking process been thoroughly undertaken and the criminal justice system included in the process, perhaps more community resources for treating the mentally ill would have been established, thus reducing the number of mentally ill people in jails and prisons. Therefore, thinking outside the proverbial box needs to be part of the policymaking process. Later in this chapter, we examine how the process actually works; however, striving for and implementing the formal policymaking process should be our goal.

Sources of Criminal Justice Policy

Multiple sources create public policy that impacts criminal justice. These include the U.S. Constitution and court rulings, legislatures enacting statutes, administrative agencies issuing regulatory directives, and governmental agencies developing various procedures. In addition, all these sources are duplicated at the federal, state, and local levels, increasing the number of criminal-justice-related policies. Next, we briefly examine some of these sources.

The United States Constitution outlines the rights of the people and the responsibility of government in our society. Ultimately, all public policies must conform to this doctrine. In the more than two centuries since the Constitution was adopted, amendments have been added, and its meaning has been debated and clarified. The U.S. Supreme Court has impacted criminal justice public policy in such cases as *Miranda v. Arizona* (1966; created the now famous "Miranda Warnings"), *In re Gault* (1967; began due process for juveniles), *Furman v. Georgia* (1972; overturned the death penalty), *Gregg v. Georgia* (1976; reinstated the death penalty with required conditions), and *Roper v. Simmons* (2005; ended the death penalty for those under 18 years of age).

Federal and state statutes create criminal justice policy through the establishment of agencies (the California Commission on Peace Officer Standards and Training, Federal Bureau of Prisons, and Departments of Public Safety); making certain behaviors illegal (speeding, taking property belonging to someone else, ingesting certain substances, white-collar crime); or providing funds for crime-related initiatives (crime-victim compensation, new prisons, hiring of more police officers).

Regulatory agencies are created through federal and state statutes and are authorized to develop and enforce directives to meet the agency's goals and objectives. These directives, in turn, can impact criminal justice policy. Examples include the California Board of Corrections, which regulates jail standards; the United States Department of Agriculture, which determines the type of vegetation and animals that can be brought into the country; and the Court Reporters' Board of California, which sets standards for court reporters. Criminal justice agencies are then required to fulfill the policies issued by these regulatory agencies.

Federal and state legislatures pass several bills each year, many of which change the law under which criminal justice agencies operate or enforce. These statutes are based on policymakers' agendas and are public policy in that they reflect what the government has chosen to do or not do—the basic definition of public policy. Laws making another substance illegal, establishing "three strikes" legislation, or requiring police officers to have 4 years of college are all criminal justice policies that involve making choices, having outputs, and impacting various constituencies. One of the most far-reaching of public policies for criminal justice was the federal decision to create the Department of Homeland Security. This legislative policy and its subsequent administrative policies reconstituted federal criminal justice agencies and affected their duties and responsibilities. The effects filtered down to local levels, creating new positions and relationships. It still remains to be seen what the overall effects will be, but some have predicted that law enforcement might eventually become subsumed under the umbrella of security (Williams, McShane & Karson, 2007).

Agency-level policy in the criminal justice arena also reflects the policymakers' agenda and principles. While public policy at this level is generally specific to the agency and its employees, such policies affect those who are served by and interact with the agency. Some agency-level policies have produced their own problems, frequently because the policymaking process was not correctly implemented. These problems are then brought to the attention of other policymakers for remedy. Cases such as *Schmerber v. California* (1966; permitted warrantless search and seizure of blood in DWI cases), *Gilbert v. California* (1967; permitted handwriting samples without violating the Fifth Amendment), *Chimel v. California* (1969; permitted warrantless search incident to arrest), and *Pell v. Procunier* (1974; limited media access to prisoners) are examples of agency policy that has been examined by other policymakers.

Public Policy as It Is in Practice

Our description of public policy- and lawmaking in the formal sense is influenced (as is usually the case when it comes to actual practice in criminal justice matters) by elements inside and outside the system. In this section, we discuss the roles of politics and ideology as they are played out among the various sources attempting to influence policy and law. There are four primary groups of policy-influencing elements: Moral entrepreneurs, or moral crusaders; lobbyists, think tanks, and those otherwise politically and financially connected to powerful people; vested-interest groups; and the media. We focus primarily on moral entrepreneurs here because many of the other groups can be seen as participants in, or variants of, that process.

Partisanship, Politicization, and Ideology

Any public policy is by definition a part of the political process, because public policy can be made only through that process. However, certain parties both inside and outside the political process attempt to exert power and influence so that the direction and content of public policy match their interests. Within the political process itself, partisanship on certain issues results in setting aside the essential democratic process of our political system to ensure that issues near and dear to the hearts of political majorities (or at least those with substantial political power) are enacted into law. In some instances, it is sufficient that certain viewpoints hold sway and thus become the preferred way of viewing issues of a similar type. In such cases, public policy is no longer a product of group consensus but instead a vehicle to force the values of a powerful group onto others. The recent history of partisan dealings and legislation in the U.S. Congress is a testament to the process of influence leading to politicization of issues. When issues can be politicized, values and sometimes influence itself become more important than the content of policies and laws. In short, values embedded in policies are frequently used to direct far-reaching purposes that have little to do with the policies themselves.

These values are sometimes referred to as *ideologies* in social analysis. An ideology is a basic set of background assumptions that control the way a phenomenon should be viewed and judged. It is "the way things are and should be." As a result, ideologies are rarely questioned by those who hold them. Indeed, to question an ideology would move it from the background of ideas to the foreground and therefore likely abort its power to control thought. In one sense, we all have ideologies, but it is when they are thrust into the political arena that they become most dangerous for public policy. The discussion of partisanship in the previous paragraph suggests that there are at least two opposing ideologies at work in the U.S. political world today. Each group of adherents is busy attempting to control how public realities are viewed. Public policy is used as an instrument to further that control. Thus, public policy by itself is not the important ingredient; the *control* of policy becomes a way to implement ideology, or core values.

Sources of Influence and Information

As noted earlier, there are several important policy-influencing elements. Moral entrepreneurs are among the most influential of these where the making of public policy and law are concerned. As described by Howard Becker (1963), moral entrepreneurs who are rule creators seek to influence and define social norms on a particular issue. They can do this for selfish reasons, but most likely their purpose is the result of a sense of moral outrage and evil to be fought, or as Becker puts it, "a moral crusade" (1963, p. 148). In one of the more common criminal justice scenarios, usually as the product of a crime found abominable by some relative of the victim, the relative takes it upon himself or herself to campaign for a new law or approach to the crime (for example, the killing of Candy Lightner's 12-year-old daughter by a drunk driver resulted in her campaign against DWI and the subsequent creation of MADD in 1980). Even if the crime is statistically rare, the pursuit of "righting the wrong" results in artificially inflated numbers and a claim of common occurrence to justify policy change or a new law. Common characteristics among moral entrepreneurs are doggedly pursuing the issue, grandstanding, making out-of-proportion claims, and appealing to sympathy as a "victim." We would add that, somewhere along the process, many of these people also begin to benefit from their cause, either financially or by the fame they gain. Some have become television personalities, and others have created foundations to disperse donated funds (resulting in their own employment by the foundation). In this sense, they become vested participants in the public policy process, over and above their original interest.

These moral entrepreneurs are part of what Stanley Cohen (1972) termed *moral panics*, and known more generally as *constructed social problems*. The process is identical in all aspects to the process of recognizing social problems. Focusing on a real (or sometimes imagined) issue, the moral entrepreneur begins to call it to the attention of the public with exaggerated claims of its frequency. Those with a vested interest (for example, an agency handling such issues and thereby having a financial stake) pick up the public claims and begin to make media announcements designed to support the image of the problem as a relatively common occurrence. The media then circulate this information, again reporting the claims and the frequency of the problem. The claims tend to escalate the exaggeration and stress the moral offensiveness of the problem. At this point, a group of politicians, sensing both publicity and political image to be gained, usually become involved and propose to become "saviors" by creating law and subsequent public policy against this heinous problem. Thus, law and public policy in the criminal justice arena is often a knee-jerk reaction to an exaggerated problem.

A factor in whether this reaction actually produces results is the timing with which others with actual knowledge of the extent of the problem begin to critique the exaggerations. If this happens fairly soon after the initial pronouncements, the creation of law and policy are less likely to occur. If the critique occurs later in the process, laws frequently have already been passed, and the issue takes on a life of its own, regardless of the evidence against it. Once some organization or agency has gained responsibility for eliminating the issue, the financial incentives that go along with it almost ensure that the social problem will continue to exist. In fact, most documented cases have not only resulted in the survival of the "problem" but actually have resulted in its expansion. In other words, organizations use social problems to gain funding and expand; to the extent they can gain control over these problems, they can redefine problems in ways that best suit their own agendas.

Examples of this moral panic process have been documented time and again. In fact, it is hard to find a social problem, or moral panic, that has *not* undergone this process. Interesting criminal justice examples include the late-19th-century criminalization of oleomargarine (yes, the butter substitute—primarily because of the political strength of the dairy industry; Ball & Lilly, 1982), the creation of "juvenile delinquency" (by women engaged in the child-saving movement; Platt, 1969), the discovery of child abuse (by radiologists who increased their stature in the medical field by defining what constitutes "child abuse"; Pfohl, 1977), DWI (through the creation of a national organization dedicated to eradicating it; Jacobs, 1989), serial murder (a term originally invented by the FBI, who defined it as multijurisdictional murders that only they could handle; Jenkins, 1994), missing children (by claims exaggerating the number by including parental abductions and runaways as if they were stranger kidnappings; Best, 1987, 1990), and sex offenses (by false claims that these were widely perpetrated on children by strangers; Sutherland, 1950; Jenkins, 2004). Virtually every "problem" you can imagine was, at one point or another, exemplified by a moral panic with moral entrepreneurs at work (think about playing pool or baseball, watching movies, reading comic books, and listening to rock music—they were all defined as causes of delinquency).

Some of the characteristics associated with the ability of a moral panic to create law and public policy generally have emotional attributes and include such things as child victims, stranger offenders, and the "randomness" of the offense. Of course, the political power and degree of vested interest of both the claims-makers and those potentially arrayed against the claims have to be factored in. "But," you may be asking, "what's wrong with that?"—after all, most of the examples just listed are clear instances of offenses and problems. The problem is twofold. First, public policy should deal with common occurrences, not phenomena that have been exaggerated to make them seem more pervasive than they are. Second, they absorb limited criminal justice system resources and distract attention from more frequent and more serious issues.

Though we have focused on moral entrepreneurs, there are other common types of people and organizations who push to have their agendas made into public policy. Included among them are lobbyists, think tanks, and the power elite, many groups with a single focus and, of course, the media. We leave you to consider the many ways these groups affect public policy through their efforts (usually self-serving ones); it won't be difficult to think of examples. Moreover, any of these groups can also be moral crusaders. The media, in particular, contribute to the agenda of other groups through their reporting on and coverage of emerging policy initiatives. Media are frequently seen as disinterested bystanders in all of this, but because they are businesses, media have an interest in selling themselves. Thus, any topic imbued with the essence of sensationalism and the right combination of images (the combination of a child, sex abuse, and an adult predator are ideal) will be given substantial coverage. Lately, some media sources have even given up the attempt to appear objective and simply push images of crime and victims as other businesses might push any high-profit item. Finally, it should be obvious that many criminal justice policy initiatives find most, if not all, of these influential sources coming together to push common agendas.

The Use and Misuse of Public Policy

If all this sounds like public policy is frequently manipulated to benefit someone, you are correct. The use and misuse of criminal justice public policy is a virtual certainty. You can be sure that someone or some group has a vested interest in virtually every public policy created in the criminal justice arena. This fact, though, does not mean that policy is being misused; it just means that public policy has utility to people and groups.

One way to critically analyze any public policy is to think about its function. Robert K. Merton (1936; 1968, pp. 82–83) distinguished between two types of functions, *manifest* and *latent*. Manifest functions are those that are intended. For example, in the public policy known as "three strikes," the manifest function was to make sure that dangerous felons were removed from the streets and kept in prison for at least 25 years. Latent functions are the unanticipated consequences of social action, or those functions that are unintended. In the "three strikes" example, latent functions might include application of the law to criminals who are not dangerous, the increased numbers of jury trials because of defendants' refusals to plead guilty or plea bargain, and an increased number of inmates and costly new prison construction.

Another issue to look for in the proposed creation of public policy is a financial motive. Such motives do not usually surface in initial proposals and discussions, because legislation rarely includes immediate funding for most social problems. Nonetheless, an agency can gain funding by showing that it has more to do than previously, thus justifying a larger budget at a later date because of the need to add manpower to deal with the new responsibilities for the problem. If an agency (or some other organization) can capture the ability to define the problem, then even more financial rewards accrue. The examples of the California victims' movement given in the next section exemplify this motive.

Finally, there are cases of purposefully misleading the public to achieve other policy goals. These, too, are exemplified in the victims' movement and in the titles given to legislative bills and acts in general. Thus, while these titles are frequently misleading, they serve the purpose of generating policy statements on (usually) related issues.

Examples of California Public Policy Overreach

The victims' movement in California gives us three good examples of the creation of social policy to benefit victims while actually having another purpose. In 1984, the legislature approved the Roberti-Imbrecht-Rains-Goggins Child Sexual Abuse Prevention Act. With the words *children* and *sexual abuse* in the title, supporting the act was a "no-brainer" for politicians, and they literally lined up to be associated with it. However, the fact was that the act did nothing to specifically support the prevention of child sexual abuse, and it was intentionally mislabeled to gain support (Iglehart, 1990). In truth, the act provided funds for police and prosecutors, instituted harsher punishments for child molesters, extended the statute of limitations for filing charges, and allowed judges and prosecutors (both elected officials) to reap political benefits as they claimed to get tough on crime in the new "get tough" atmosphere.

A second example of intentional mislabeling is the California Child Protection act of 1984. Once again, there was nothing directly in the act to protect children, and the intended beneficiaries were prosecutors and legislators, both of whom could stake political claims of being protectors of children (Iglehart, 1990). The primary nonpolitical benefits were that prosecutors (1) no longer need to prove intent and (2) could confiscate property that was the fruit of child pornography profits, along with the equipment used in its production. The latter meant new money in the budgets of prosecutors as the confiscated property was auctioned off.

Finally, the California Crime Victims Justice Reform Initiative of 1990 (Proposition 115) was passed by voters as part of that state's proposition process. As with the other two acts, the title was intentionally misnamed (Iglehart, 1990). Victims gained little direct assistance with the passage of the proposition. On the other hand, judges, prosecutors, and politicians gained tremendously. Because the public at the time was caught up in a "crime wave" mentality and victims were a popular cause, the proposition provided political gains to its supporters and made it easier for judges and prosecutors to increase conviction rates. Even better for politicians faced with campaign spending caps, campaign money was transferred to support the proposition (along with mention of the candidate's largesse) and thus candidates were able to avoid legal spending limitations and still gain media coverage by "campaigning" for a popular issue. In terms of latent functions, the main message disseminated to the public was that more crime was occurring than ever before, and they were almost certain to be victims, thus pushing fear of crime to a new high (McShane & Williams, 1992).

An Example of Federal Public Policy Overreach

Turning to the federal level, a good example of time and resources devoted to a continuing moral panic is exemplified by fears of pornography and child predators on the Internet. When the Internet was still rather young, a study of pornography on the Internet was published in the Georgetown Law Review by a Carnegie-Mellon University scholar. The author, Martin Rimm (1995), allegedly accessed, reviewed, and counted a sample of "obscene and pornographic" materials on the Internet and then constructed estimates that cyberporn represented as much as 83% of all Internet images. This study was given nationwide coverage by *Time* magazine even before it was published in the law journal. As Williams, McShane and Hsieh (2007, pp. 149–151) report, not only did this lead to an uproar over children being exposed to pornography on the Internet, but two prominent U.S. senators, Exon and Glade, sponsored a bill to eliminate this pornography and regulate such materials on the Internet (SB 314, Communications Decency Act). Another senator, Grassley, scheduled a hearing with the study author as the prime witness.

In reality, the Carnegie-Mellon "scholar" turned out to be an undergraduate student who accessed pay-only, adult-oriented "bulletin-boards" (dial-up subscription services not connected to the Internet) and accessed only one of the "news" groups on the Internet at that time. Thus, the "research" never even sampled Internet content. A scandal erupted; Carnegie-Mellon University disowned the "research," and Senator Grassley pulled his star witness at the last moment, but the cyberporn issue was passed into law as an amendment to the Telecommunications Decency Act (which was ultimately struck down by the federal courts). A 1995 study (Williams & McShane), using a random sample of all Internet sex-oriented newsgroups, estimated that sexual materials on the Internet represented no more than 2% of all materials and that specifically pornographic sexual materials were much lower than that 2%. However, the initial claims and media coverage created a moral panic that has yet to die out.

The issue of predators stalking children over the Internet and arranging meetings was also a by-product of the cyberporn publicity. Parents were told time and again that children were vulnerable and to watch them carefully. Williams and McShane (1995) reviewed evidence on these claims in the early days of the moral panic (1994–1995). Examining those two years using articles from three major newspapers, a total of seven articles were found dealing with actual cases or incidents involving children exposed to pornography or potential sex offenders or persons attempting to distribute pornographic stories and images. In regard to predators attempting to meet with children, three of the seven cases involved attempted contact. In sum, the evidence in those early panic days hardly pointed to a common problem, yet public policy was made in response (though most of it was ultimately discarded by the federal courts). The unanticipated consequences primarily restricted public Internet usage for all users, adults and children alike. More recently, a study by a Harvard University research center (Berkman Center for Internet & Society, 2008) and supported by the various state attorneys general found that evidence of sexual predators using MySpace and Facebook was vastly overblown and reminiscent of a moral panic rather than reality. Regardless, legislating restrictions on social networking sites continues to attract attention.

The Policy Implications of Public Policy

The preceding discussion certainly suggests that formal versions of public policy formulation tend to identify the players and the process but not the actual motivations. There are ways by which this might be overcome, however. While it seems redundant to discuss the policy implications of public policy, it is possible to discuss some contemporary influences on the creation of public policy. Two of those we view as being favorable and one as rather negative.

Evidence-Based Policy

Over the past few years, a new catchphrase has come into play when criminal justice decisions (and policies) are made. The phrase is *evidence-based decision making*, and it represents what criminal justice researchers have been arguing for decades. Instead of making decisions and policy based on many of the elements we have just examined (including gut-level and instinctive decisions), the use of both research evidence and hard data from agency information systems provides a more objective, reality-based, and certainly more defensible way to determine what problems exist and what decisions might be made about them. Several criminal justice program funding organizations, especially the Police Research Foundation, the Edna McConnell Clark Foundation, and the National Institute of Justice (NIJ), now require evidence-based program decisions when they are the funding sources.

The Obama administration has recently used the term *evidence-based* as a mantra and insists that it be used to guide policy decisions. As a result of these requirements and the frequency with which the field is now using the phrase, evidence-based policymaking is likely to be the approach of the future. This should result in better public policies and the laws to support them, particularly when compared to past examples of ideologically driven and gut-level policies. An example is a recent report from the National Academy of Sciences (Committee on Identifying the Needs of the Forensic Sciences Community, 2009). A team of scientific experts evaluated current forensic science practice, technology, and interpretation. They found that a substantial amount of the work of police crime labs was based on faulty, discredited, and/or imprecise science and procedures to match evidence to individuals—in particular, non-DNA tests such as fingerprint comparison, tool analysis, and hair analysis. NIJ will now request research to determine what directions to take in developing policy for handling, testing, interpreting, and presenting criminal evidence.

The Politicization of Public Policy

Though evidence-based policy is likely to be the wave of the future, there is little reason to believe that the informal elements and motivations involved in past policymaking will disappear. Over the past two decades, a movement developed that essentially intended to subvert the use of scientific evidence in federal government agencies and congressional hearings. Using argumentative techniques developed by the tobacco industry after 1980, "fringe science" has been allowed to present itself as "sound science" (Mooney, 2006). While the term *sound science* sounds like a reasonable approach suggesting the use of the best available evidence and scientific positions, the opposite is true of anti-science pronouncements that all scientific opinion is equal. Science itself is highly skeptical, critical, and, above all, not democratic; quality and rigor are valued above all else. That very questioning and skepticism have been used to label real science as "uncertain," "fatally flawed," and thus "junk science" (Mooney, 2006). Various vested-interest groups and ideologues in the federal government have pushed "sound science" as a pseudonym allowing fringe positions (those supportive of their positions) an equal voice with best available evidence in an effort to rig hearings and policy. Because real scientists are skeptical and critical, representatives of these interest groups or ideologies play up small disagreements and uncertainties in best available evidence as if there actually were no good evidence. Pseudoscientists asked to provide evidence in support of the vested-interest position have no such qualms and critical stance; thus they and their political supporters announce their fringe "evidence" as correct.

This process played out in criminal justice as political operatives were appointed to positions in various agencies within the Justice Department. Scientific research reports were suddenly required to be approved by a deputy director who knew very little about research. If the research findings did not match desired conclusions, the wording of the report was changed. Researchers who objected to this found their reports went unpublished. Even worse, the grant process was subverted to provide a substantial amount of money to those with business connections (criminal justice and homeland security technologies) and/or the correct political connections. Peer review of grants (the process of researcher experts being assigned to evaluate proposed research) was largely ignored, so that funded "research" was often poorly constructed and incapable of producing a defensible result. If this subversion of scientific research continues, then there is reason to doubt that evidence-based policymaking will actually produce better-informed, more objective policies.

The Contributions of Academic Criminal Justice

Another factor in the future of public policy development is the emerging majority of criminal justice agency personnel who have been educated in university criminal justice departments. This group is now developing into a critical mass in the field and is much more likely to ask for research results and related evidence before making decisions. As a result, better agency policy decisions will be made, and better advice will be available to lawmakers and governmental agencies. Similarly, academic criminal justice is now more likely to be asked to provide information for the development of legislation and public policy. This trend is a favorable one but threatening to vested-interest groups, ideologues, lobbyists, and moral entrepreneurs. Because legislators and policymakers are ultimately public figures, loud public voices will continue to have a substantial say in criminal justice legislation and policy.

CONCLUSION

So what is the likely direction of public policy formulation? The use of evidence and research results in criminal justice decision making and the creation of agency policy has made great strides. Whether that will play out in the larger public policy realm is much more in doubt. Simply put, there is too much at stake among those with moral positions, ideological agendas, and political futures for public policy to be made in a true evidence-based, research-informed atmosphere. While there is reason to hope that future public policy will be made in a more objective fashion, perhaps the best we can do now is to ask for a voice in the process and offer information to those concerned. Time-sensitive and objective information can be provided to members of the media to counter exaggerated claims often made in the early stages of the policy process. Assuming the best public policy is based on objective reality rather than subjective versions of reality, any increase in the consumption of objective information can only serve to improve criminal justice policies.

DISCUSSION QUESTIONS

1. How should public policymaking be accomplished in a democracy? How closely does that description fit with your experience?

2. How do you see public policy being made in your state? Do various checks and balances come into play, or is it a product of rather unfettered influence? Are there any other ways to make public policy that you might find preferable?

3. When federal mental health agencies deinstitutionalized the mentally ill in favor of community treatment, there was a profound effect on local criminal justice agencies. Thinking about such a policy, what would you have anticipated the effects to be?

4. What do you think of the concepts of moral entrepreneurs and moral panics? Is this an overblown academic position, or does it represent reality? What would you say to someone who says that any moral panic still represents a real problem that must be dealt with? Finally, what examples of potential moral panics can you identify that would call for new criminal justice policies?

5. What do you view as the effect of ideology on the making of public policy? Is there anything wrong with the interplay of ideology and policymaking? How would one create any particular focus to guide policymaking if ideologies did not exist?

6. Rather than affect public policy by public outcry, as moral entrepreneurs do, others attempt to directly influence both the making and the direction of public policy. How would you describe the effect of lobbyists and think tanks on policymaking? In a philosophical vein, what do you think about the fairness of their efforts and their subsequent effects on a democratic society?

7. How do you react to the statement that the discipline of criminal justice may ultimately affect the quality of public policy in the crime and justice area? If you agree, how do you see this happening? If you disagree, what are your reasons?

References

Ball, R. A., & Lilly, J. R. (1982). The menace of margarine: The rise and fall of a social problem. *Social Problems, 29,* 488–498.

Becker, H. S. (1963). Moral entrepreneurs. In H. S. Becker, *Outsiders: Studies in the sociology of deviance* (pp. 147–163). New York: The Free Press.

Berkman Center for Internet & Society at Harvard University. (2008, December 31). *Enhancing child safety and online technologies: Final report of the Internet safety technical task force to the multi-state working group on social networking of State Attorneys General of the United States.* Cambridge, MA: Harvard Law School.

Best, J. (1987). Rhetoric in claims-making: Constructing the missing children problem. *Social Problems, 34,* 101–121.

Best, J. (1990). *Threatened children: Rhetoric and concern about child-victims.* Chicago: University of Chicago Press.

Cohen, S. (1972). *Folk devils and moral panics: The creation of the Mods and Rockers.* Oxford: Basil Blackwell.

Committee on Identifying the Needs of the Forensic Sciences Community, National Research Council, National Academy of Sciences. (2009). *Strengthening forensic science in the United States: A path forward.* Washington, DC: National Academies Press.

Dye, T. (2008). *Understanding public policy* (12th ed.). Upper Saddle River, NJ: Prentice Hall.

Iglehart, R. (1990, October). *The impact of Proposition 115: The Crime Victims Initiative.* Keynote speech delivered to the Association of Criminal Justice Researchers (CA), Claremont, CA.

Jacobs, J. B. (1989). *Drunk driving: An American dilemma.* Chicago: University of Chicago Press.

Jenkins, P. (1994). *Using murder: The social construction of serial homicide.* New York: Aldine de Gruyter.

Jenkins, P. (2004). *Moral panic: Changing concepts of the child molester in modern America.* New Haven, CT: Yale University Press.

Marion, N. E., & Oliver, W. M. (2006). *The public policy of crime and criminal justice.* Upper Saddle River, NJ: Pearson Prentice Hall.

McShane, M. D., & Williams, F. P., III. (1992). Radical victimology: A critique of the concept of victim in traditional victimology. *Crime & Delinquency, 38,* 258–271.

Merton, R. K. (1936). The unanticipated consequences of purposive social action. *American Sociological Review, 1,* 894–904.

Merton, R. K. (1968). Manifest and latent functions. In R. K. Merton, *Social Theory and Social Structure* (3rd ed. Rev. and enlarged), pp. 73–91. New York: The Free Press.

Mooney, C. (2006). *The Republican war on science* (Rev. and updated ed.). New York: Basic Books.

Pfohl, S. (1977). The "discovery" of child abuse. *Social Problems, 24,* 310–323.

Platt, A. (1969). *The child savers: The invention of juvenile delinquency.* Chicago: University of Chicago Press.

Rimm, M. (1995). Marketing pornography on the information superhighway: A survey of 917,410 images, description, short stories and animations downloaded 8.5 million times by consumers in over 2000 cities in forty countries, provinces and territories. *Georgetown Law Journal, 83*(5), 1849–1915.

Sutherland, E. H. (1950). The sexual psychopath laws. *Journal of Criminal Law and Criminology, 40,* 543–554.

Welsh, W. N., & Harris, P. W. (2008). *Criminal justice policy and planning* (3rd ed.). Newark, NJ: LexisNexis.

Williams, F. P., III, & McShane, M. (1995, November). *Getting your kicks on cyberspace's Route 66: Erotica, the information highway, and constructed social problems.* Paper presented at the annual meeting of the American Society of Criminology, Boston, MA.

Williams, F. P., III, McShane, M. D., & Hsieh, M-L. (2007). Juveniles in cyberspace: Risk and perceptions of victimizations. In M. McShane & F. Williams (Eds.), *Youth violence and delinquency: Monsters and myths* (Vol. 1, pp. 145–158). Westport, CT: Praeger.

Williams, F. P., III, McShane, M. D., & Karson, L. (2007). Security in the evolution of the criminal justice curriculum. *Criminal Justice Studies: A Critical Journal of Crime, Law and Society, 20*(2), 161–173.

18 American Courts

Cassia Spohn

The past 50 years have witnessed significant changes in the structure of the American court system and the procedures that courts use to adjudicate criminal cases and sentence convicted offenders. Some of these changes resulted from Supreme Court decisions that interpreted constitutional provisions regarding right to counsel, selection of the jury, cruel and unusual punishment, due process of law, and equal protection under the law. Other changes resulted from legislative attempts to toughen criminal sentences and reduce sentence disparity, to provide alternatives to prison and probation, or to handle certain types of cases, such as drug offenses or cases involving mentally ill offenders, more efficiently and effectively. Considered together, these changes have revolutionized the way American courts do business.

The purpose of this chapter is to examine these changes and explore their policy implications. The chapter begins with an overview of Supreme Court decisions regarding right to counsel, selection of the jury, capital punishment, and the role of the jury in the sentencing process. The next section focuses on the sentencing reform movement of the past 30 years. The chapter ends with an examination of specialized or problem-solving courts.

Supreme Court Decisions and American Courts

The United States Supreme Court has played an important role in the development of the American court system, particularly with respect to such issues as right to counsel, jury selection, and sentencing. The decisions handed down by the Court in these areas have altered policy and practice and have led to fairer and less discriminatory court processing decisions.

The Right to Counsel

A series of court decisions broadened the interpretation of the Sixth Amendment's guarantee of the right to counsel and led to significant changes in requirements for provision of counsel for indigent defendants. The process began in 1932, when the Court ruled in *Powell v. Alabama* (287 U.S. 45 [1932]) that states must provide attorneys for indigent defendants charged with capital crimes. The Court's decision in a 1938 case, *Johnson v. Zerbst* (304 U.S. 458 [1938]), required the appointment of counsel for all indigent defendants in federal criminal cases, but the requirement was not extended to the states until *Gideon v. Wainwright* (372 U.S. 335 [1963]) was handed down in 1963. In subsequent decisions, the Court ruled that "no person may be imprisoned, for any offense, whether classified as petty, misdemeanor, or felony, unless he was represented by counsel"[1] and that the right to counsel is not limited to trial, but applies to all "critical stages" in the criminal justice process.[2] As a result of these rulings, states must provide most indigent defendants with counsel, from arrest and interrogation through sentencing and the appellate process.

States moved quickly to implement the constitutional requirement articulated in *Gideon* and the subsequent cases, either by establishing public defender systems or by appropriating money for court-appointed attorneys. In 1951, there were only 7 public defender organizations in the United States; in 1964, there were 136; by 1973, the total had risen to 573 (McIntyre, 1987). A national survey of indigent defense services among all U.S. prosecutorial districts found that 21% used a public defender program, 19% used an assigned counsel system, and 7% used a contract attorney system; the remaining districts (43%) reported that a combination of methods was used (Bureau of Justice Statistics, 2006). Although some critics have questioned the quality of legal services afforded indigent defendants (Casper, 1971; *Harvard Law Review*, 2000), particularly in capital cases where the stakes are obviously very high (Bright, 1994), the findings of a number of methodologically sophisticated studies suggest that case outcomes for defendants represented by public defenders are not significantly different from those for defendants represented by private attorneys (Hanson & Ostrom, 2004; Williams, 2002). These results suggest that poor defendants are no longer "without a voice" (Myrdal, 1944, p. 547) in courts throughout the United States.

Jury Selection

Supreme Court decisions also have placed important restrictions on the jury selection process. The Court has consistently ruled against racial and ethnic bias in the selection of the jury pool and has made it more difficult for prosecutors and defense attorneys to use their peremptory challenges to exclude black and Hispanic jurors. As the Court has repeatedly emphasized, the jury serves as "the criminal defendant's fundamental 'protection of life and liberty against race or color prejudice.'"[3] Reflecting this, in 1889 the Supreme Court ruled in the case of *Strauder v. West Virginia* (100 U.S. 303 [1880]) that a West Virginia statute limiting jury service to white males violated the equal protection clause of the Fourteenth Amendment and therefore was unconstitutional.

The Court's ruling in *Strauder* made it clear that states could not pass laws excluding blacks from jury service, but it did not prevent states, and particularly southern states, from developing techniques designed to preserve the all-white jury. In a series of decisions that began in the mid-1930s, the Supreme Court struck down these laws and practices, ruling, for example, that it was unconstitutional for a Georgia county to put the names of white potential jurors on white cards, the names of black potential jurors on yellow cards, and then "randomly" draw cards to determine who would be summoned for jury service (*Avery v. Georgia*, 345 U.S. 559 [1953], at 562). As the Court stated in this case, "the State may not draw up its jury lists pursuant to neutral procedures but then resort to discrimination at other stages in the selection process."

Critics contend that the Court's decisions regarding the peremptory challenge do, in fact, open the door to discrimination in jury selection (Kennedy, 1997; Serr & Maney, 1988). The Supreme Court's insistence that the jury be drawn from a representative cross-section of the community and that race is not a valid qualification for jury service applies only to the selection of the jury pool. It does not apply to the selection of individual jurors for a particular case. As the Court has repeatedly stated, a defendant is *not* entitled to a jury "composed in whole or in part of persons of his own race."[4] Thus, prosecutors and defense attorneys can use their peremptory challenges—"challenges without cause, without explanation, and without judicial scrutiny"[5]—as they see fit. Critics of the process contend that, decisions handed down by the Supreme Court notwithstanding, prosecutors and defense attorneys can use their peremptory challenges to produce juries that contain few, if any, racial minorities.

The Supreme Court's rulings regarding racial discrimination in the use of peremptory challenges have evolved over time. The Court initially ruled that, although the prosecutor's use of peremptory challenges to strike all of the black potential jurors in a jury pool did not violate the equal protection clause of the Constitution, a defendant could establish a prima facie case of purposeful racial discrimination by showing that the elimination of blacks from a particular jury was part of a *pattern of discrimination* in that jurisdiction (*Swain v. Alabama*, 380 U.S. 202 [1965]). The problem, of course, was that the defendants in *Swain*, and in the cases that followed, could not meet this stringent test. As Wishman (1986, p. 115) observed, "A defense lawyer almost never has the statistics to prove a pattern of discrimination, and the state under the *Swain* decision is not required to keep them." The ruling, therefore, provided no protection to the individual black or Hispanic defendant deprived of a jury of his peers by the prosecutor's use of racially discriminatory strikes.

It was not until 1986 that the Court, in *Batson v. Kentucky* (476 U.S. 79 [1986]), rejected *Swain*'s systematic exclusion requirement and ruled "that a defendant may establish a *prima facie* case of purposeful discrimination in selection of the petit jury solely on evidence concerning the prosecutor's exercise of peremptory challenges at the defendant's trial." The justices added that once the defendant makes a prima facie case of racial discrimination, the burden shifts to the state to provide a racially neutral explanation for excluding black jurors.

Although *Batson* seemed to offer hope that the goal of a representative jury was attainable, an examination of cases decided since 1986 suggests otherwise. State and federal appellate courts have ruled, for example, that leaving one or two blacks on the jury precludes any inference of purposeful racial discrimination on the part of the prosecutor,[6] and that striking only one or two jurors of the defendant's race does not constitute a "pattern" of strikes.[7] Trial and appellate courts have also been willing to accept virtually any explanation offered by the prosecutor to rebut the defendant's inference of purposeful discrimination (Serr & Maney, 1988, pp. 44–47). Decisions such as these led Kennedy (1997, p. 214) to characterize the peremptory challenge as "a creature of unbridled discretion that, in the hands of white prosecutors and white defendants, has often been used to sustain racial subordination in the courthouse." The Supreme Court's decisions notwithstanding, the peremptory challenge continues to be an obstacle to the creation of a racially neutral jury selection process.

Capital and Noncapital Sentencing

A third area that has been significantly reshaped by Supreme Court decisions is sentencing. The Court has handed down a series of important decisions on the capital sentencing process. Although the Court has never ruled that the death penalty per se is cruel and unusual punishment, it has said that the death penalty cannot be imposed on an offender convicted of the rape of an adult woman (*Coker v. Georgia*, 433 U.S. 584 [1977]) or child (*Kennedy v. Louisiana*, 554 U.S. ___[2008]) and that the death penalty can be imposed on an offender convicted of felony murder if the offender played a major role in the crime and displayed "reckless indifference to the value of human life" (*Tison v. Arizona*, 107 S.Ct. 1676; 481 U.S. 137 [1987], at 157). The Court also has ruled that the execution of someone who is mentally handicapped is cruel and unusual punishment in violation of the Eighth Amendment (*Atkins v. Virginia*, 536 U.S. 304 [2002]), that the Eighth and Fourteenth Amendments forbid the imposition of the death penalty on offenders who were younger than age 18 when their crimes were committed (*Roper v. Simmons*, 543 U.S. 551 [2005]), and that the Constitution does not prohibit the use of lethal injection (*Baze v. Rees*, 553 U.S. ___[2008]). With the exception of the felony murder and lethal injection rulings, these decisions all restrict the use of the death penalty by state and federal courts.

The Supreme Court also has addressed the issue of the role played by the jury at sentencing. The first case, *Apprendi v. New Jersey* (530 U.S. 466 [2000]), involved an offender, Charles Apprendi Jr., who fired several shots into the home of a black family; he made a number of statements, which he later retracted, suggesting that he had fired into the home because he did not want the family living in his neighborhood. Apprendi pled guilty to possession of a weapon for an unlawful purpose, a crime that carried a term of imprisonment of 5 to 10 years. The prosecutor then filed a motion for an enhanced sentence under the New Jersey hate-crime statute. The judge in the case found by a preponderance of the evidence that the shooting was racially motivated and sentenced Apprendi to 12 years in prison. Apprendi appealed, claiming that the due process clause of the Constitution required the state to prove the allegation of bias to the jury beyond a reasonable doubt. The Supreme Court ruled in Apprendi's favor, stating that any fact that increases the penalty for a crime beyond the prescribed statutory maximum, other than the fact of a prior conviction, must be submitted to a jury and proved beyond a reasonable doubt. In 2002, the justices similarly ruled that a jury—not a judge—must find the aggravating circumstances necessary for imposition of the death penalty (*Ring v. Arizona,* 536 U.S. 584 [2002]).

The Court reiterated this position in subsequent decisions involving defendants who were challenging sentences imposed under state and federal sentencing guidelines. In 2004, for example, the Court ruled in *Blakely v. Washington* (542 U.S. 296 [2004]) that the judge's decision to impose a sentence more severe than the statutory maximum allowed under the Washington sentencing guidelines violated the defendant's Sixth Amendment right to trial by jury. The Court revisited this issue 6 months later. This time, the issue was the power of federal judges to impose sentences more severe than called for under the United States sentencing guidelines. In *United States v. Booker* (543 U.S. 220 [2005]), the Court ruled, consistent with its decisions in Apprendi and Blakely, that the jury must determine beyond a reasonable doubt any fact that increases the defendant's sentence beyond the maximum sentence allowed under the sentencing guidelines.[8] The facts in this case were similar to those in Blakely. Booker was found guilty of a drug offense that, under the guidelines, carried a sentence of 210 to 262 months. At the sentencing hearing, however, the judge found additional facts that justified a harsher sentence; he sentenced Booker to 360 months in prison. The Court held that the 30-year sentence imposed by the judge violated the Sixth Amendment right to a jury trial and ordered the district court either to sentence Booker within the sentencing range supported by the jury's findings or to hold a separate sentencing hearing before a jury. The Court also ruled that the federal sentencing guidelines were advisory, not mandatory. In two cases decided in 2007,[9] the Court reiterated that the guidelines were advisory and ruled that the below-guidelines sentences imposed in each case were "reasonable" and that the judges who imposed the sentences had not abused their discretion. In the Gall decision, the Court noted that, although the guidelines are the starting point and initial benchmark, they are not the only factors to be taken into consideration.

The Supreme Court's decisions in these sentencing cases enhance the role played by the jury in both capital and noncapital cases. The decisions emphasize that the jury, not the judge, is to determine the facts in the case, that juries must determine the existence of aggravating factors that justify the imposition of the death penalty, and that sentences cannot exceed the maximum sentence based on the facts that were admitted in a guilty plea or found by the jury.

The Sentencing Reform Movement

In 1972, Marvin Frankel, U.S. district judge for the Southern District of New York, issued an influential call for reform of the sentencing process (Frankel, 1972). The focus of Judge Frankel's critique was the indeterminate sentence, in which the judge imposed a minimum and maximum sentence, but the parole board determined the date of release based on its assessment of whether the offender had been rehabilitated or had served enough time for the particular offense. Judge Frankel characterized the indeterminate sentencing system as "a bizarre 'nonsystem' of extravagant powers confided to variable and essentially unregulated judges, keepers, and parole officials" (Frankel, 1972, p. 1). Frankel, who maintained that the degree of discretion given to judges led to "lawlessness" in sentencing, called for legislative reforms designed to regulate "the unchecked powers of the untutored judge" (p. 41).

Judge Frankel's calls for reform did not go unheeded. Reformers from both sides of the political spectrum joined in the attack on indeterminate sentencing and pushed for reforms designed to curtail judicial discretion and eliminate arbitrariness and disparity in sentencing. In response, state legislatures and Congress enacted a series of incremental structured sentencing reforms. A number of jurisdictions experimented with voluntary or advisory sentencing guidelines. Other states adopted determinate sentencing policies and abolished release on parole. Still other jurisdictions created sentencing commissions authorized to promulgate presumptive sentencing guidelines. Most states and the federal government also enacted mandatory minimum sentences for certain types of offenses (especially drug and weapons offenses), "three-strikes-and-you're-out" laws that mandated long prison sentences for repeat offenders, and truth-in-sentencing statutes that required offenders to serve a larger portion of the sentence before being released.

This process of experimentation and reform revolutionized sentencing in the United States. Thirty years ago, every state and the federal government had an indeterminate sentencing system, and "the word 'sentencing' generally signified a slightly mysterious process which . . . involved individualized decisions that judges were uniquely qualified to make" (Tonry, 1996, p. 3). The situation today is much more complex. Sentencing policies and practices vary enormously on a number of dimensions, and there is no longer anything that can be described as the American approach.

A discussion of each of the major reforms enacted during the sentencing reform movement is beyond the scope of this chapter. Instead, the chapter focuses on the movement away from the indeterminate sentence and toward a more structured sentencing process.

Determinate Sentencing

In the mid- to late 1970s, several states abolished release on parole and replaced the indeterminate sentence with a fixed (i.e., determinate) sentence. Under this system, the state legislature established a presumptive range of confinement for various categories of offenses. The judge imposed a fixed number of years from within this range, and the offender would serve this term minus time off for good behavior. Determinate sentencing, which was first adopted in California, Illinois, Indiana, and Maine, was seen as a way to restrain judicial discretion and thus to reduce disparity and (at least in the minds of conservative reformers) preclude judges from imposing overly lenient sentences. However, the degree to which the reforms constrain discretion varies. The California Uniform Determinate Sentencing Law, which took effect on July 1, 1977, provides that judges are to choose one of three specified sentences for persons convicted of particular offenses. The judge is to impose the middle term unless there are aggravating or mitigating circumstances that justify imposing the higher or lower term. Judges have considerably more discretion under the Illinois Determinate Sentencing Statute. Felonies are divided into six classifications, and the range of penalties is wide, especially for the more serious offenses. Murder and Class X offenses are nonprobationable, but judges can impose prison terms of 20 to 60 years or life for murder and 6 to 30 years for Class X offenses. If there are aggravating circumstances, the sentence range for Class X felonies increases to 30 to 60 years.

Although judges in jurisdictions with determinate sentencing retain control over the critical probation or prison decision, their overall discretion is reduced, particularly in states like California. Evaluations of the impact of the California law showed that judges complied with the law and imposed the middle term in a majority of the cases (Cohen & Tonry, 1983). Despite predictions that discretion would shift to the prosecutor and that plea bargaining would consequently increase, there were no changes in the rate or timing of guilty pleas that could be attributed to the determinate sentencing law. On the other hand, there was some evidence that prosecutors were increasingly likely to use provisions regarding sentence enhancements and probation ineligibility as bargaining chips. One study, for example, found that the sentence enhancement for use of a weapon was dropped in 40% of robbery cases and that the enhancement for serious bodily injury was struck in 65% to 70% of these cases (Casper, Brereton & Neal, 1982). As Walker (1993, p. 129) noted, "The net effect of the law seems to have been to narrow and focus the exercise of plea-bargaining discretion. Given the very restricted options on sentence length, the importance of the various enhancements and disqualifiers increased."

Partly as a result of research showing that determinate sentencing laws did not significantly constrain the discretion of judges, the determinate sentencing movement lost steam and eventually sputtered out. With the exception of the District of Columbia, no jurisdiction has adopted determinate sentencing since 1983.

Presumptive Sentencing Guidelines

Since the late 1970s, presumptive sentencing guidelines developed by an independent sentencing commission have been the dominant approach to sentencing reform in the United States. About half of the states have adopted or are considering sentencing guidelines, and sentencing at the federal level has been structured by guidelines since 1987. In 1994, the American Bar Association (ABA) endorsed sentencing guidelines; it recommended that all jurisdictions create permanent sentencing commissions charged with drafting presumptive sentencing provisions that apply to both prison and nonprison sanctions and are tied to prison capacities (American Bar Association, 1994).

The guidelines systems adopted by Congress and by state legislatures have a number of common features (Stith & Cabranes, 1998). In each jurisdiction with presumptive guidelines, there is a permanent sentencing commission or committee composed of criminal justice officials and, sometimes, private citizens and legislators. The commission is charged with studying sentencing practices and formulating presumptive sentence recommendations. The commission is also authorized to monitor the implementation and impact of the guidelines and to recommend amendments. A second common feature is that the presumptive sentence is based primarily on two factors: the severity of the offense and the seriousness of the offender's prior criminal record. Typically, these two factors are arrayed on a two-dimensional grid; their intersection determines whether the offender should be sentenced to prison and, if so, for how long.

Jurisdictions with presumptive sentencing guidelines, as opposed to voluntary or advisory guidelines, require judges to follow them or provide reasons for failing to do so. Judges are allowed to depart from the guidelines and impose harsher or more lenient sentences if there are specified aggravating or mitigating circumstances. Some jurisdictions also list factors that should not be used to increase or decrease the presumptive sentence. For example, both the federal guidelines and the Minnesota guidelines state that the offender's race, gender, and employment status are not legitimate grounds for departure. In North Carolina, on the other hand, judges are allowed to consider the fact that the offender "has a positive employment history or is gainfully employed" (Bureau of Justice Assistance, 1996, pp. 79–80). In most states and in the federal system, a departure from the guidelines can be appealed to state appellate courts by either party. If, for example, the judge sentences the defendant to probation when the guidelines call for prison, the prosecuting attorney can appeal. If the judge imposes 60 months when the guidelines call for 36, the defendant can appeal.

The Impact of Sentencing Guidelines

A detailed discussion of the impact of sentencing guidelines would consume many pages; there have been literally dozens of studies focusing on compliance with the guidelines and attempting to determine whether the guidelines (and mandatory minimum sentences) resulted in more punitive sentences and reduced disparity and discrimination in the sentencing process. Although the evidence is somewhat mixed, it does appear that sentences are more punitive today than in the past (Austin & Irwin, 2001; Engen & Steen, 2000; Frase, 1997; Kramer & Lubitz, 1985; Marvel & Moody, 1995; Moore & Miethe, 1986; Spohn, 2000; United States Sentencing Commission, 1991a, 1991b, 2004). The movement away from indeterminate sentencing and the rehabilitative ideal to determinate sentencing and an emphasis on just deserts—coupled with laws mandating long prison terms—have resulted in harsher sentences. As a result of these changes in sentencing policy, offenders convicted of felonies in state and federal courts face a greater likelihood of incarceration and longer prison sentences than they did in the prereform era. These changes, in turn, have led to dramatic increases in the nation's prison population.[10]

The evidence regarding the question of whether sentences today are fairer or more equitable in the past also is mixed. Critics of sentencing reform contend that members of the courtroom workgroup have been able to circumvent—or even sabotage—the reforms enacted during the past 30 years; they argue that this makes it difficult to assess the impact of the reforms. Nonetheless, most studies of sentences imposed under federal and state guidelines conclude that guideline sentences are more uniform and less disparate (Anderson, Kling & Stith, 1999; Ashford & Mosbaek, 1991; Hofer, Blackwell, & Ruback, 1999; Knapp, 1987; Kramer & Lubitz, 1985; Stolzenberg & D'Alessio, 1994; United States Sentencing Commission, 1991a; Washington State Sentencing Guidelines Commission, 1992; Wright, 1998). There is less interjudge disparity in jurisdictions with sentencing guidelines, and sentences are more tightly linked to the seriousness of the offense and the offender's prior criminal record.

The evidence regarding the effect of legally irrelevant offender characteristics—race, gender, age, education, and employment status—is less inconsistent and, unfortunately, more negative. There is a lack of longitudinal research comparing the effect of offender characteristics on sentence outcomes before and after the implementation of guidelines; this makes it difficult to assess the degree to which the guidelines have reduced unwarranted disparities in sentencing. Nonetheless, the studies of sentences imposed in federal and state jurisdictions operating under sentencing guidelines showed that racial minorities and women were sentenced differently from whites and men (Albonetti, 1997, 2002; Demuth & Steffensmeier, 2004; Everett & Wojtkiewicz , 2002; Kramer

& Steffensmeier, 1993; Kramer & Ulmer, 1996; LaFrentz & Spohn, 2006; Mustard, 2001; Spohn, 2000; Spohn & Sample, forthcoming; Stacey & Spohn, 2006; Steen, Engen, & Gainey, 2005; Steffensmeier & Demuth, 2000, 2006; Steffensmeier & Hebert, 1999; Steffensmeier, Kramer, & Streifel, 1993; Steffensmeier, Ulmer, & Kramer, 1998). This suggests that attempts to constrain judicial discretion have not eliminated unwarranted disparities in sentencing. The guidelines notwithstanding, judges mete out harsher sentences to black and Hispanic offenders than to similarly situated white offenders. They impose more lenient sentences on females than on males, and the unemployed and less educated receive harsher sentences than their counterparts.

These conclusions apply to sentences imposed under the more restrictive federal sentencing guidelines as well as the looser guidelines at the state level. They imply that judges and prosecutors are reluctant to place offenders into cells of sentencing grids defined only by crime seriousness and prior criminal record and, thus, that statutorily irrelevant factors such as race, gender, age, employment status, and social class may be factually relevant to criminal justice officials' assessments of dangerousness, threat, and culpability. In sum, these conclusions attest to the validity of Tonry's (1996, p. 180) assertion, "There is, unfortunately, no way around the dilemma that sentencing is inherently discretionary and that discretion leads to disparities."

Specialized or Problem-Solving Courts: A Focus on Drug Courts

The last three decades have witnessed another important change in the American court system: the development of specialized or problem-solving courts. These are limited-jurisdiction courts specializing in certain crime problems, such as drugs, guns, and domestic violence. These courts are like traffic courts in that they address a specific problem, but several factors set them apart (Berman & Feinblatt, 2001). The typical specialized court focuses on case outcomes—for example, getting offenders off drugs or protecting women from further intimate partner abuse—rather than case processing, and judges closely supervise offenders and monitor their progress. Specialized courts also are characterized by collaboration among criminal justice and social service agencies, nontraditional roles for participants, and a focus on systemic change.

The Drug Court Movement

The development of specialized courts is best illustrated by the drug court movement. Increases in the number of drug offenders appearing in state and federal courts—coupled with mounting evidence of both the linkages between drug use and crime and the efficacy of drug treatment programs—led a number of jurisdictions "to rethink their approach to handling defendants charged with drug and drug-related offenses." (Drug Court Clearinghouse and Technical Assistance Project, 1999, p. 3). Some jurisdictions, such as Cook County (Chicago), Illinois, established specialized dockets designed to manage the drug caseload more efficiently and to alleviate stress on the felony court system (Inciardi, McBride, & Rivers, 1996). Other jurisdictions, such as Dade County (Miami), Florida, created "drug treatment courts," which incorporated intensive judicial supervision of drug offenders, mandatory drug treatment, and rehabilitation programs providing vocational, education, family, and medical services.

The drug treatment court concept spread rapidly during the 1990s. As of June 1999, 377 drug courts were operating, and an additional 217 drug courts were in the planning stages in 49 of the 50 states, the District of Columbia, Puerto Rico, Guam, several Native American tribal courts, and two federal district courts (Drug Court Clearinghouse and Technical Assistance Project, 1999, p. 1). By December 2007, there were 1,786 adult and juvenile drug courts operating in jurisdictions throughout the United States; another 284 courts were in the planning stages (Bureau of Justice Assistance, n.d.). A 2005 report by the National Drug Court Institute (Huddleston, Freeman-Wilson, Marlowe, & Roussell, 2005) estimated that, at any one time, more than 70,000 drug offenders were participating in drug courts throughout the United States and its territories.

Although the nature and characteristics of drug courts throughout the United States vary widely, they share several key elements (National Association of Drug Court Professionals, 1997):

- Integration of substance abuse treatment with justice system case processing;
- Use of a nonadversarial approach;
- Early identification and prompt placement of eligible participants;
- Access to a continuum of treatment, rehabilitation, and related services;
- Frequent testing for alcohol and illicit drugs;
- A coordinated strategy among judge, prosecutor, defense, and treatment providers to govern offender compliance;
- Ongoing judicial interaction with each participant.

In the typical preadjudication drug court, drug offenders who meet the eligibility criteria for the program are given a choice between participation in the drug court and traditional adjudication. Although the eligibility criteria vary, most programs exclude offenders who have prior convictions for violent offenses or whose current offense involved violence or use of a weapon. They target offenders whose involvement with the criminal justice system is due primarily to their substance abuse. The program may last 12 months, 18 months, or longer. Offenders who are accepted and agree to abide by the requirements of the program are immediately referred to a substance abuse treatment program for counseling, therapy, and education. They also are subject to random urinalysis and are required to appear frequently before the drug court judge. Offenders who do not show up for treatment sessions or drug court or who fail drug tests are subject to sanctions. Repeated violations may result in termination from the program and in adjudication and sentencing on the original charges. The charges against the offender are dismissed upon completion of the program.

The Effectiveness of Drug Courts

There is mounting evidence that drug courts reduce offender recidivism and prevent drug relapse. A report by the U.S. General Accounting Office (1997) summarized the results of 20 evaluations of 16 drug courts that had been completed by early 1997. The GAO report indicated that these early evaluations generally concluded that drug courts were effective in reducing drug use and criminal behavior. A later review by Belenko (1998) summarized the results of 30 evaluations of 24 drug courts that had been completed by May 1998. Belenko (1998, p. 29) observed that most of these evaluations concluded "that criminal behavior was substantially reduced during participation in the program." For example, an evaluation of a Ventura County, California, drug court, which tracked recidivism over an 8-month period, found that only 12% of the drug court participants were rearrested, compared with 32% of those in a comparison group. A Jackson County, Missouri, evaluation similarly revealed 6-month rearrest rates of 4% for program participants and 13% for nonparticipants.

Belenko's review also included studies that assessed the impact of drug court participation on postprogram recidivism. Eight of the nine evaluations reported lower recidivism rates for the drug court group, compared with a group of similarly situated offenders who did not participate in the drug court program. An evaluation of the Multnomah County, Oregon, drug court, for example, found statistically significant differences between drug court participants (0.59 new arrests) and drug-court-eligible nonparticipants (1.53 new arrests) over a 24-month tracking period. Belenko (1998, p. 18) concluded that "drug use and criminal behavior are substantially reduced while clients are participating in drug court, [and] criminal behavior is lower after program participation."

More recent and methodologically sophisticated studies also provide evidence that drug courts are effective in preventing recidivism. An evaluation of the Baltimore City Drug Treatment Court, for example, used an experimental design in which eligible offenders were randomly assigned either to the drug court or to traditional adjudication (Gottfredson & Exum, 2002). The results of the evaluation revealed that offenders assigned to the drug court were less likely than offenders placed in the traditional adjudication group to be rearrested during the 12-month follow-up period. A follow-up study using 3 years of recidivism data found similar results; this study also found that the positive effects of participation in the drug treatment court extended past the offenders' involvement in the drug court (Gottfredson, Najaka, Kearley, & Rocha, 2006).

Policy Implications

The American court system has undergone significant changes over the past three decades. Criminal procedure has been reformed as a result of Supreme Court decisions that broadened the rights of criminal defendants, established rules for the selection of juries and the use of peremptory challenges, and placed restrictions on judges' sentencing discretion. Sentencing policies and practices in state and federal jurisdictions have undergone important modifications, and specialized or problem-solving courts have spread throughout the United States.

The question, of course, is whether these changes have produced a fairer and more equitable court system. It seems clear that the Supreme Court's decisions broadening the right to counsel and restricting the use of race in the jury selection process have resulted in fairer treatment of poor defendants and defendants who are racial minorities, and that the Court's decisions limiting the use of the death penalty has made it more likely that capital punishment will be reserved for particularly heinous crimes. Less clear are the effects of the Court's decisions enhancing the role of the jury in sentencing and making the federal sentencing guidelines voluntary. Although these decisions, which place significant restrictions on judicial discretion, may produce less disparity in sentencing, it also is possible that discretion will simply shift downstream to prosecutors. In other words, the source of disparity, including unwarranted disparity, in the new regime may be prosecutors' charging and plea-bargaining decisions.

The impact of specialized or problem-solving courts is also less evident. Research evaluating these courts is limited, and the research that does exist suffers from a number of methodological problems (Belenko, 1998). Nonetheless, there is mounting evidence that drug courts, domestic violence courts, and other specialized courts do reduce recidivism rates, and there is some evidence that these courts also lead to improvements in offenders' education and employment status, physical and mental health, and cognitive functioning. As research on problem-solving courts accumulates, our conclusions regarding their effectiveness will become less tentative.

DISCUSSION QUESTIONS

1. How have the Supreme Court's decisions regarding the right to counsel changed the American court system? In your opinion, have these been positive or negative changes?

2. Why would critics of the public defender system argue that criminal defendants "get what they pay for"? What are the problems inherent in the public defender system?

3. Evidence suggesting that prosecutors continue to use their peremptory challenges to preserve all-white juries in cases involving African American or Hispanic defendants has led some commentators to call for the elimination of the peremptory challenge. What do you think is the strongest argument in favor of eliminating the peremptory challenge? In favor of retaining it? How would elimination of the peremptory challenge change the criminal trial?

4. What will be the impact of the Supreme Court's decision making the federal sentencing guidelines voluntary/advisory rather than mandatory? Will these decisions lead to less uniformity and more disparity in sentencing, or will they enable judges to individualize justice in appropriate ways?

5. An important goal of sentencing guidelines was to eliminate unwarranted disparity in sentencing. Given this, how would you explain the fact that research reveals that both the offender's race/ethnicity and the offender's sex influence sentences imposed under state and federal sentencing guidelines?

6. How do specialized or problem-solving courts differ from traditional courts? Why have these courts become so popular in the United States?

NOTES

1. *Argersinger v. Hamlin*, 407 U.S. 25 (1972), at 37.

2. A defendant is entitled to counsel at every stage "where substantial rights of the accused may be affected" that require the "guiding hand of counsel" (*Mempa v. Rhay*, 389 U.S. 128 [1967], at 134). These critical stages include arraignment, preliminary hearing, entry of a plea, trial, sentencing, and the first appeal.

3. *McCleskey v. Kemp* (481 U.S. 279 [1987], at 310), quoting *Strauder v. West Virginia*, 100 U.S. 303 (1880).

4. *Strauder v. West Virginia*, 100 U.S. 303 (1880) at 305; *Batson v. Kentucky*, 476 U.S. 79 (1986) at 85.

5. *Swain v. Alabama*, 380 U.S. 202, 212 (1965) at 380.

6. *United States v. Montgomery*, 819 F.2d at 851. The Eleventh Circuit, however, rejected this line of reasoning in *Fleming v. Kemp* (794 F.2d 1478 [11th Cir. 1986]) and *United States v. David* (803 F.2d 1567 [11th Cir. 1986]).

7. *United States v. Vaccaro*, 816 F.2d 443, 457 (9th Cir. 1987); *Fields v. People*, 732 P.2d 1145, 1158 n.20 (Colo. 1987).

8. Also decided at the same time, and with the same result, was *United States v. Fanfan* (125 S. Ct. 12 [2004]).

9. *Gall v. United States*, No. 06–7949, decided December 10, 2007. *Kimbrough v. United States*, No. 06–6330, decided December 10, 2007.

10. Most scholars contend that this punitiveness has not produced the predicted reduction in crime. Conservative advocates of harsh crime control policies claim that

locking up increasingly large numbers of felony offenders for increasingly long periods of time has caused the crime rate to fall; however, conceptual and methodological flaws in the "prison 'works'" argument call this conclusion into question. Critics suggest that a more careful examination of the evidence leads to the conclusion that increasing incarceration rates have little, if any, effect on crime rates (see, for example, Austin & Irwin, 2001; Tonry, 1995).

REFERENCES

Albonetti, C. A. (1997). Sentencing under the federal sentencing guidelines: Effects of defendant characteristics, guilty pleas, and departures on sentence outcomes for drug offenses, 1991–1992. *Law & Society Review, 31,* 789–822.

Albonetti, C. A. (2002). The joint conditioning effect of defendant's gender and ethnicity on length of imprisonment under the federal sentencing guidelines for drug trafficking/manufacturing offenders. *Journal of Gender, Race, and Justice, 6,* 39–60.

American Bar Association. (1994). *Standards for criminal justice—sentencing alternatives and procedures* (3rd ed.). Boston: Little, Brown.

Anderson, J. M., Kling, J. R., & Stith, K. (1999). Measuring interjudge sentencing disparity: Before and after the federal sentencing guidelines. *Journal of Law and Economics, XLII,* 271–307.

Ashford, K., & Mosbaek, C. (1991). *First year report on implementation of sentencing guidelines, November 19889 to January 1991.* Portland: Oregon Criminal Justice Council.

Austin, J., & Irwin, J. (2001). *It's about time: America's imprisonment binge* (3rd ed.). Belmont, CA: Wadsworth.

Belenko, S. (1998). Research on drug courts: A critical review. *National Drug Court Institute Review, 1,* 1–42.

Berman, G., & Feinblatt, J. (2001). *Problem-solving courts: A brief primer.* New York: Center for Court Innovation.

Bright, S. B. (1994). Counsel for the poor: The death sentence not for the worst crime but for the worst lawyer. *The Yale Law Journal, 103,* 1835–1883.

Bureau of Justice Assistance. (1996). *National assessment of structured sentencing.* Washington, DC: U.S. Department of Justice, Bureau of Justice Assistance.

Bureau of Justice Assistance Drug Court Clearinghouse Project at American University. (n.d.). Retrieved on October 21, 2009, from http://spa.american.edu/justice/documents/2343.pdf

Bureau of Justice Statistics. (2006). *State court organization, 2004.* Washington, DC: United States Department of Justice, Bureau of Justice Statistics.

Casper, J. D. (1971). Did you have a lawyer when you went to Court? No, I had a public defender. *Yale Review of Law and Social Action, 1,* 4–9.

Casper, J. D., Brereton, D., & Neal, D. (1982). *The implementation of the California determinate sentencing law: Executive summary.* Washington, DC: Government Printing Office.

Cohen, J., & Tonry, M. H. (1983). Sentencing reforms and their impacts. In A. Blumstein, J. Cohen, S. E. Martin, & M. H. Tonry (Eds.), *Research on sentencing: The search for reform, Vol. 1* (pp. 305–349). Washington, DC: National Academy Press.

Davis, K. C. (1969). *Discretionary justice: A preliminary inquiry.* Baton Rouge: Louisiana State University Press.

Demuth, S., & Steffensmeier, D. (2004). Ethnicity effects on sentencing outcomes in large urban courts: Comparisons among white, black, and Hispanic defendants. *Social Science Quarterly, 85,* 991–1011.

Drug Court Clearinghouse and Technical Assistance Project. (1999). *Looking at a decade of drug courts.* Washington, DC: U.S. Department of Justice.

Engen, R. L., & Steen, S. (2000). The power to punish: Discretion and sentencing reform in the war on drugs. *American Journal of Sociology, 105,* 1357–1395.

Everett, R. S., &Wojtkiewicz, R. A. (2002). Difference, disparity, and race/ethnic bias in federal sentencing. *Journal of Quantitative Criminology, 18,* 189–211.

Frankel, M. (1972). Lawlessness in sentencing. *University of Cincinnati Law Review, 41,* 1–54.

Frase, R. (1997). Prison population growing under Minnesota guidelines. In M. Tonry & K. Hatlestad (Eds.), *Sentencing reform in overcrowded times.* New York: Oxford University Press.

Gottfredson, D. C., & Exum, M. L. (2002). Baltimore City Drug Treatment Court: One-year results from a randomized study. *Journal of Research in Crime and Delinquency, 39,* 337–356.

Gottfredson, D. C., Najaka, S. S., Kearley, B. W., & Rocha, C. M. (2006). Long-term effects of participation in the Baltimore City Drug Treatment Court: Results from an experimental study. *Journal of Experimental Criminology, 2,* 67–98.

Hanson, R. A., & Ostrom, B. J. (2004). Indigent defenders get the job done and done well. In. G. F. Cole, M. G. Gertz, & A. Bunger, A. (eds.), *The criminal justice system: Law and politics.* Belmont, CA: Wadsworth.

Harvard Law Review. (2000). Gideon's promise unfulfilled: The need for litigated reform of indigent defense. *Harvard Law Review, 113,* 2062–2079.

Hofer, P. J., Blackwell, K. R., & Ruback, B. (1999). The effect of the federal sentencing guidelines on interjudge sentencing disparity. *The Journal of Criminal Law & Criminology, 90,* 239–321.

Huddleston, C.W., III, Freeman-Wilson, K., Marlowe, D. B., & Roussell, A. (2005). *Painting the current picture: A national report card on drug courts and other problem solving court programs in the United States.* Washington, DC: National Drug Court Institute.

Inciardi, J. A., McBride, D. C., & Rivers, J. E. (1996). *Drug control and the courts.* Thousand Oaks, CA: Sage.

Kennedy, R. (1997) *Race, crime, and the law.* New York: Vintage Books.

Knapp, K. A. (1987). Implementation of the Minnesota guidelines: Can the innovative spirit be preserved? In A. von Hirsch, K. A. Knapp, & M. Tonry (Eds.), *The sentencing commission and its guidelines* (pp. 127–141). Boston: Northeastern University Press.

Kramer, J. H., & Lubitz, R. L. (1985). Pennsylvania's sentencing reform: The impact of commission-established guidelines. *Crime & Delinquency, 31,* 481–500.

Kramer, J. H., & Steffensmeier, D. (1993). Race and imprisonment decisions. *The Sociological Quarterly, 34,* 357–376.

Kramer, J. H., & Ulmer, J. T. (1996). Sentencing disparity and departures from guidelines. *Justice Quarterly, 13,* 81–106.

LaFrentz, C., & Spohn, C. (2006). Who is punished more harshly? An examination of race/ethnicity, gender, age and employment status under the federal sentencing guidelines. *Justice Research & Policy, 8,* 25–56.

Martinson, R. (1974). What works? Questions and answers about prison reform. *Public Interest, 24,* 22–54.

Marvel, T. B., & Moody, C. E. (1995). The impact of enhanced prison terms for felonies committed with guns. *Criminology, 33,* 247–281.

McIntyre, L. (1987). *The public defender: The practice of law in the shadows of repute.* Chicago: University of Chicago Press.

Moore, C. A., & Miethe, T. D. (1986). Regulated and unregulated sentencing decisions: An analysis of first-year practices under Minnesota's felony sentencing guidelines. *Law & Society Review, 20,* 253–277.

Mustard, D. (2001). Racial, ethnic and gender disparities in sentencing: Evidence from the U.S. federal courts. *Journal of Law and Economics, 44,* 285–314.

Mydral, G. (1944). *An American dilemma: The Negro problem and modern democracy.* New York: Harper.

National Association of Drug Court Professionals. (1997). *Defining drug courts: The key components.* Washington, DC: Bureau of Justice Assistance, U.S. Department of Justice.

Serr, B. J., & Maney, M. (1988). Racism, peremptory challenges and the democratic jury: The jurisprudence of a delicate balance. *Journal of Criminal Law & Criminology, 79,* 1–65.

Spohn, C. (2000). *Thirty years of sentencing reform: The quest for a racially neutral sentencing process.* Washington, DC: U.S. Department of Justice.

Spohn, C., & Sample, L. (forthcoming). The dangerous drug offender in federal court: Stereotyping blacks and crack cocaine. *Crime and Delinquency.*

Stacey, A. M., & Spohn, C. (2006). Gender and the social costs of sentencing: An analysis of sentences imposed on male and female offenders in three U.S. District Courts. *Berkeley Journal of Criminal Law, 11,* 43–76.

Steen, S., Engen, R. L., & Gainey, R. R. (2005). Images of danger and culpability: Racial stereotyping, case processing, and criminal sentencing. *Criminology, 43,* 435–468.

Steffensmeier, D., & Demuth, S. (2000). Ethnicity and sentencing outcomes in U.S. federal courts: Who is punished more harshly? *American Sociological Review, 65,* 705–729.

Steffensmeier, D., & Demuth, S. (2006). Does gender modify the effects of race-ethnicity on criminal sanctioning? Sentences for male and female white, black, and Hispanic defendants. *Journal of Quantitative Criminology, 22,* 241–261.

Steffensmeier, D., & Hebert, C. (1999). Women and men policymakers: Does the judge's gender affect the sentencing of criminal defendants? *Social Forces, 77,* 1163–1196.

Steffensmeier, D., Kramer, J., & Streifel, C. (1993). Gender and imprisonment decisions. *Criminology, 31,* 411–446.

Steffensmeier, D., Ulmer, J., & Kramer, J. (1998). The interaction of race, gender, and age in criminal sentencing: The punishment cost of being young, black, and male. *Criminology, 36,* 763–797.

Stith, K., & Cabranes, J. A. (1998). *Fear of judging: Sentencing guidelines in the federal courts.* Chicago: University of Chicago Press.

Stolzenberg, L., & D'Alessio, S. J. (1994). Sentencing and unwarranted disparity: An empirical assessment of the long-term impact of sentencing guidelines in Minnesota. *Criminology, 32,* 301–310.

Tonry, M. (1995). *Malign neglect: Race, crime, and punishment in America.* New York: Oxford University Press.

Tonry, M. (1996). *Sentencing matters.* New York: Oxford University Press.

United States General Accounting Office. (1997). *Drug courts: Overview of growth, characteristics, and results.* Washington, DC: U.S. General Accounting Office.

United States Sentencing Commission. (1991a). *The federal sentencing guidelines: A report on the operation of the guidelines system and short-term impacts on disparity in sentencing, use of incarceration, and prosecutorial discretion and plea bargaining.* Washington, DC: U.S. Sentencing Commission.

United States Sentencing Commission. (1991b). *Special report to Congress: Mandatory minimum penalties in the federal criminal justice system.* Washington, DC: U.S. Sentencing Commission.

United States Sentencing Commission. (2004). *Fifteen years of guidelines sentencing: An assessment of how well the federal criminal justice system is achieving the goals of sentencing reform.* Washington, DC: Author.

van den Haag, E. (1975). *Punishing criminals: Confronting a very old and painful question.* New York: Basic Books.

von Hirsch, A. (1976). *Doing justice: The choice of punishments.* New York: Hill and Wang.

Walker, S. (1993). *Taming the system: The control of discretion in criminal justice, 1950–1990.* New York: Oxford University Press.

Washington State Sentencing Guidelines Commission. (1992). *A decade of sentencing reform: Washington and its guidelines, 1981–1991.* Olympia: Washington State Sentencing Guidelines Commission.

Williams, M. (2002). A comparison of sentencing outcomes for defendants with public defenders versus retained counsel in a Florida circuit court. *Justice Systems Journal, 23,* 249–257.

Wilson, J. Q. (1975). *Thinking about crime.* New York: Basic Books.

Wishman, S. (1986). *Anatomy of a jury: The system on trial.* New York: Penguin Books.

Wright, R. F. (1998). *Managing prison growth in North Carolina through structured sentencing.* National Institute of Justice, Program Focus Series. Washington, DC: U.S. Department of Justice, National Institute of Justice.

19

The Juvenile Justice System

Randall G. Shelden

This chapter focuses on the juvenile justice system. Founded in 1899 in Chicago and Denver, this new court promised that children's "best interest" would be served, as it was based upon the old English doctrine of *parens patriae* (for more detail, see Shelden, 2008, chapter 5). The new laws that defined delinquency and predelinquent behavior were broad in scope and quite vague, covering the following: (1) violations of laws also applicable to adults; (2) violations of local ordinances; (3) such catchalls as "vicious or immoral behavior," "incorrigibility," truancy, "profane or indecent behavior," "growing up in idleness," "living with any vicious or disreputable person," and many more. The third category would eventually be known as *status offenses.*

The juvenile court system rapidly spread throughout the country, following the lead of Chicago and Denver (both opened in 1899). Juvenile institutions, such as industrial and training schools and reform schools, continued to develop and expand. Until the 1960s, there were relatively few structural changes within the juvenile justice system. However, serious problems emerged from the very start, not the least of which was an obvious class, race, and gender bias. Indeed, the vast majority of youth brought into the juvenile court have been drawn from the ranks of the poor and racial and ethnic minorities (Shelden, 2008).

Although the most common disposition of cases processed through the juvenile court is probation, many young offenders end up placed somewhere other than within their own home. Most spend at least some time locked up in a secure facility, most commonly called a *detention center.* This subject is treated in the following section.

Juvenile corrections include several different types of out-of-home placements of which the courts can make use. Some of these institutions are public (i.e., run by state or local governments), and others are privately funded. They can be further subdivided into short-term confinement (usually ranging from a few days to a couple of months) and long-term confinement (ranging from 3 or 4 months to 1 or 2 years).

Detention Centers

Detention is the most common temporary holding facility for juveniles. Here is where youths are placed pending a court hearing to determine whether or not they should be released. Despite the reforms of the past half century, conditions in many of the nation's detention centers remain horrible. This is especially true for the growing numbers of youth with serious mental health problems. Several recent reports have documented this. For example, an investigation by the *Pittsburgh Post-Gazette* (Twedt, 2001) found that, in response to a survey, more than 40% of detention centers responded that "children with mental health problems stay in detention longer than others because placements can't be found for them" (para. 3). Further, of the 12 Pennsylvania detention centers responding to the survey, "[Eleven] cited a shortage of placement options as the reason that juveniles with mental health problems stay in detention longer" (para. 4). According to the report, Alex Wilson, the director of the Allegheny County's Shuman Juvenile Detention Center, began tracking emotionally ill children at his facility shortly after state officials closed a local state hospital's adolescent unit. The director noted that most juveniles stay an average of 11 days before placement, but among those with mental problems, the average is between 35 and 40 days. Further, he stated, "When they closed those big facilities and put them in the community, more and more children wound up in the juvenile justice system. A lot of times, it might not be that serious a charge, but they still end up in detention" (para. 7).

A report by the U.S. Senate's Governmental Affairs Committee concluded that "thousands of children with mental illnesses await needed community mental health services in juvenile detention centers across the country" (Bazelon Center for Mental Health Law, 2004, para. 1). One expert testified that "[j]uvenile detention facilities lack the resources and staff to confront this problem; yet, corrections is being forced to shoulder the burden of the nation's failure to properly diagnose and care for children with mental or emotional disorders" (para. 3). Another survey—commissioned by Representative Henry Waxman (D-CA) and Senator Susan Collins (R-ME) and conducted by the Special Investigations Division of the minority staff of the Government Reform Committee of the U.S. House of Representatives—came up with very disturbing findings similar to those in the Pennsylvania survey (Bazelon Center, 2004). This report concluded that, in 33 states, juveniles with mental health problems were being held with no charges against them. Over a 6-month period, about 15,000 youths spent time in a detention facility while waiting for mental health services, and on any given night about 2,000 are being held (representing about 7% of the total). Echoing the Pennsylvania survey, these youth spend an average of 23 days in detention compared to about 17 days for all detainees. About $100 million is spent each year to house kids waiting for mental health services (Bazelon Center, 2004).

Special Issues Facing the Juvenile Justice System _____

The juvenile justice system cannot be discussed honestly without reference to two glaring problems: gender and race.

Status Offenses and the Double Standard

Since the beginning of the juvenile court, one of the biggest issues has been the vagueness of status offenses. Much of this vagueness stems from the differential application of such offenses, especially the use of a double standard for males and females who are brought within the juvenile court jurisdiction (Chesney-Lind & Shelden, 2004). Today, status offenses involve such behaviors as truancy, violating curfew, running away from home, and "incorrigibility" (often called by other names, such as "beyond control" and "unmanageable"). The ambiguity of such statutes gives those in authority a tremendous amount of discretionary power, which often leads to arbitrary decisions based on subjective value judgments imbued with class, race, and (of course) sexual bias.

From the very start of the juvenile court, girls particularly were victimized by the ambiguity of status offenses and the resulting double standard of treatment. Studies of early family court activity reveal that almost all the girls who appeared in these courts were charged with immorality or waywardness (Chesney-Lind, 1971; Schlossman & Wallach, 1978; Shelden, 1981).

The sanctions for such misbehavior were extremely severe. For example, the Chicago family court sent half the girl delinquents but only a fifth of the boy delinquents to reformatories between 1899 and 1909. In Milwaukee, twice as many girls as boys were committed to training schools, while in Memphis, females were twice as likely as males to be committed to training schools (Schlossman & Wallach, 1978; Shelden, 1981). In Honolulu between 1929 and 1930, more than half the girls referred to juvenile court were charged with "immorality," which meant there was evidence of sexual intercourse; 30% were charged with "waywardness." Evidence of immorality was vigorously pursued by arresting officers and social workers alike through lengthy questioning of the girls and, if possible, of males with whom they were suspected of having sex. Girls were twice as likely as males to be detained for their offenses and spent five times as long in detention, on average, as their male counterparts. They were also nearly three times more likely to be sentenced to the training school. Well into the 1950s, half of those committed to training schools in Honolulu were girls (Chesney-Lind, 1971).

Subsequent studies of the juvenile justice system continued to find evidence of this double standard continuing throughout the 20th century and into the current century (for a complete review, see Chesney-Lind & Shelden, 2004). One recent study by Human Rights Watch documented what is done to girls within the juvenile penal system of New York State. Their report, which focused on two training schools for girls, concluded that "far too often, girls experience abusive physical restraints and other forms of abuse and neglect, and are denied the mental health, educational, and other rehabilitative services they need. Because of the facilities' remote locations, confined girls are isolated from their families and communities" (Human Rights Watch, para. 2). The report further notes that

> a disproportionate number of girls confined in New York are African-Americans from families who have lived in poverty for generations, with parents or other close relatives who themselves have been incarcerated. In many cases, these girls fall into juvenile facilities through vast holes in the social safety net, after child welfare institutions and schools have failed them. In the wake of legal reform in 1996, girls who commit "status offenses" such as disobedience and running away from home are no longer supposed to be placed in custody, but such offenses—and the related issue of involvement with child welfare agencies because of parental abuse and neglect—continue to function as gateways through which particularly vulnerable children are drawn into the juvenile justice system. (para. 5)

Race, the War on Drugs, and Referrals to Juvenile Court

It is impossible to talk about juvenile court processing without reference to race and, especially in recent years, drug offenses. Race often plays an indirect role in that it relates to offense, which in turn affects the police decision to arrest. Race may also relate to the *visibility* of the offense. This is especially the case with regard to drugs. There is abundant evidence that the War on Drugs has targeted African Americans on a scale unprecedented in U.S. history. As research by Jerome Miller (1996) has shown, young African American males have received the brunt of law enforcement efforts to "crack down on drugs." He notes that in Baltimore, for example, African Americans were arrested at a rate six times that of whites; more than 90% of the arrests were for possession (Currie, 1993; Miller, 1996, p. 8; Lockwood, Pottieger, & Inciardi, 1995; Tonry, 1995).

The juvenile arrest rate for both races for heroin and cocaine possession was virtually the same in 1965. By the 1970s, the gap had begun to widen;

by 1990, the arrest rate for African Americans stood at 766 per 100,000, compared to only 68 for whites. The national rate for all drug arrests was about the same for black and white juveniles in 1980. The arrest rate for whites dropped by one third in the early 1980s, while the rate for blacks remained about the same. As the War on Drugs expanded, the arrest rate for black youths rose from 683 in 1985 to 1,200 in 1989—five times the rate for whites. By 1991, the rate had risen to 1,415. An even more alarming study in Baltimore found that total arrests for black youths was around 86 in 1981 (versus 15 for whites); by 1991, that number had increased to 1,304 for blacks, compared to a mere 13 for white youths (Miller, 1996, p. 86).

Between 1987 and 1988, the number of whites brought into the juvenile court remained virtually the same (up 1%); the number of minorities referred to the court increased by 42% (Miller, 1996, pp. 84–86). In Miller's Baltimore study, only 15 white juveniles were arrested on drug charges in 1981, compared to 86 African Americans. In 1991, 13 whites were arrested; the number of African Americans arrested skyrocketed to 1,304—an increase of 1,416%. The ratio of African American youths to whites grew from about 6:1 to 100:1 (Miller, 1996, p. 86). According to 1999 national data, the drug referral rate for blacks was 11.3 per 1,000 juveniles, nearly twice the rate for whites (5.8) and 4 times the rate for youths of other races (2.7; Puzzanchera et al., 2003).

Regardless of whether race, class, or demeanor is statistically more relevant, one fact remains: Growing numbers of African American youths are finding themselves enmeshed in the juvenile justice system. They are more likely to be detained, more likely to have their cases petitioned to go before a judge, more likely to be waived to the adult system, and more likely to be institutionalized than their white counterparts (Walker, Spohn, & DeLone, 1996, p. 144). While some of this relates to the nature of the offense, as we have shown, the likelihood of one race being associated with a particular offense, especially drugs, cannot be denied.

Quite often the discrepancies are even starker when we look at individual cities. A recent study in Columbia, South Carolina, illustrates this point. In this city, although African Americans make up less than 20% of the total juvenile population, they constitute 60% of all juvenile arrests. In fact, between 1995 and 2003 the number of black youths arrested has increased, while the number of whites arrested has decreased. Whereas in 1996 the arrest figures were almost evenly split between whites and blacks (50% black, 49% white), in 2003 the arrest figures were 60% black and only 39% white. The police have concentrated their patrols in increasing numbers in the city's near west side, a 12-square-block area of mostly black residents. Not surprisingly, the detention rate for black youth is far greater than for whites (Moore, 2004).

Further evidence of racial bias is shown in a recent study by the Sentencing Project. This study examined drug arrest data for individual cities and found that in the largest cities in the country, "drug arrests for African Americans rose at three times the rate for whites from 1980 to 2003, 225% compared to 70%. This disparity is not explained by corresponding changes in rates of drug use" (King, 2008, p. 2). In 11 cities, the drug arrest rate for blacks increased by 500% in that same time period. Data for some cities are startling. For instance, in Tucson, Arizona, the black drug arrest rate rose by 1,184% between 1980 and 2003; in Buffalo, it rose by 930%; in Kansas City, Missouri, it increased by 881%. Although the study did not focus on juveniles, there is little doubt that such findings would be the same regardless of age (King, 2008).

Racial bias is cumulative, starting long before a youth is ever contacted by the police. More is said about racial differences in the rates of detention and institutionalization later in the chapter, but suffice it to say at this point that black youth are found in detention centers and juvenile correctional facilities at a rate four times that of whites. Such differences remain regardless of offense charged. Black youth are seven times more likely to be detained if charged with a drug offense and six times more likely to be committed on a drug charge.

While some may believe that the overrepresentation of minority youth is a result of their committing more crimes than whites, such is not the case, as indicated by self-report surveys and surveys on drug use (actually showing that whites are more likely than minorities to use illegal drugs). It may be the result of differential police policies (e.g., targeting low-income, mostly minority neighborhoods) or the location of some offenses in more visible places (especially drug use). Regardless of the reasons, studies have shown race to be a very important factor (Leonard, Pope, & Feyerherm, 1995).

Race and Detention

One of the most important decisions within the juvenile court is whether or not to detain a youth. Such decisions are usually based on written court policies. The three typical reasons for detention are (1) the youth may harm self or others or may be subject to injury by others if not detained; (2) the youth is homeless or a runaway, or has no parent, guardian, or other person able to provide adequate care and supervision; and (3) it is believed that, if not detained, the youth will leave the jurisdiction and not appear for court proceedings.

It could be argued that detention should be reserved for youth who are charged with serious crimes. This is not the case, however (Puzzanchera et al., 2003). The distribution according to offense is shown in Table 19.1. As shown here, only about one fifth of those detained are charged with a serious violent crime (19%), while the largest percentage are charged with a "technical violation" (violation of a court order or violation of probation or parole, which does not include a new offense, as these are the "most serious offenses").

Table 19.1 Juveniles in Detention, by Offense, Sex and Race (Percent Distribution), 2006

| Most serious offense | Detained | | | | | | | | |
| | Total | Sex | | Race/Ethnicity | | | | | |
		Male	Female	White	Black	Hispanic	American Indian	Asian	Other
Total	100%	100%	100%	100%	100%	100%	100%	100%	100%
Delinquency	97%	98%	93%	95%	97%	99%	91%	97%	91%
Person	31%	32%	27%	27%	35%	30%	24%	35%	31%
Violent Crime Index*	21%	23%	12%	15%	25%	22%	14%	28%	15%
Other Person	10%	9%	14%	12%	10%	8%	10%	7%	16%
Property	22%	23%	17%	24%	20%	21%	22%	28%	18%
Property Crime Index**	18%	19%	13%	20%	17%	17%	19%	25%	13%
Other Property	4%	4%	4%	5%	3%	5%	3%	3%	5%
Drug	8%	9%	6%	8%	9%	8%	6%	7%	7%
Public order	11%	11%	10%	9%	12%	11%	8%	8%	10%
Technical violation	25%	23%	33%	27%	21%	28%	30%	20%	25%
Status offense	3%	2%	7%	5%	3%	1%	9%	3%	9%

Source: Sickmund, M., Sladky, T. J., & Kang, W. (2008). From *Census of Juveniles in Residential Placement Databook*, by M. Sickmund, T. J. Sladky, & W. Kang, 2000.

Notes: *Includes criminal homicide, violent sexual assault, robbery, and aggravated assault.
**Includes burglary, theft, auto theft, and arson.

Race figures prominently in the decision to detain. The same data shown in Table 19.1 are presented in Table 19.2 but expressed as rate per 100,000 juveniles. Here, the racial discrepancies are clear. Regardless of offense, African American youths are far more likely to be detained than their white counterparts. Indeed, for all delinquent offenses, black youths are about four times more likely to be detained (a rate of 225 versus 52), while for personal crimes the ratio is just over 5:1; the differences are most pronounced for drug offenses, with black youths more than seven times more likely to be detained.

The most severe disposition is commitment to an institution. Once again, race appears to be a big factor. Regardless of the offense, both African

Table 19.2 Offense Profile of Detained Residents by Sex and Race/Ethnicity for United States, 2006 (Rate per 100,000 Juveniles)

Most serious offense	Detained							
		Sex		Race/Ethnicity				
	Total	Male	Female	White	Black	Hispanic	American Indian	Asian
Total	84	134	31	43	228	103	152	27
Delinquency	81	131	28	41	222	101	137	26
Person	26	43	8	11	80	31	36	9
Violent Crime Index*	18	31	4	6	58	23	21	7
Other Person	8	12	4	5	22	8	16	2
Property	18	31	5	10	47	22	34	7
Property Crime Index**	15	25	4	8	39	17	30	7
Other Property	3	6	1	2	8	5	4	1
Drug	7	12	2	3	20	9	9	2
Public order	9	14	3	4	26	11	12	2
Technical violation	21	31	10	12	49	29	46	5
Status offense	3	3	2	2	6	1	14	1

Source: Sickmund, M., Sladky, T. J., & Kang, W. (2008). From *Census of Juveniles in Residential Placement Databook*, by M. Sickmund, T. J. Sladky, & W. Kang, 2000.

Notes: * Includes criminal homicide, violent sexual assault, robbery, and aggravated assault.

**Includes burglary, theft, auto theft, and arson.

American and Hispanic youth have the highest rates of commitment. For all cases, the rate for black youths is four times that of whites; the same holds true for personal and property crimes. For drug offenses, the discrepancy is even greater, as black youth are more than six times more likely to be committed. Hispanic youth have the second-highest rate in all offense categories, just ahead of whites but far below blacks. In the 1960s, the following phrase surfaced: "If you're white, you're all right; if you're brown, stick around; if you're black, stay back." While this is true nationally, such is not the case in California. In the 12 most populous counties in the year 2000, whites accounted for 15% of the youths committed to the California Youth Authority, blacks were 35%, and Hispanic youth were 45% (Building Blocks for Youth, 2000).

This is not to suggest that everyone connected with the juvenile justice system is racist and practices discrimination, although stereotypes about youth from certain race or class backgrounds definitely exist. Part of the problem is institutional in that such negative stereotypes are deeply embedded in our culture. Juvenile courts and police departments are largely staffed by whites. The widespread poverty and joblessness affecting minority communities result in the lack of available resources (e.g., alternatives to formal court processing) to deal with crime-related issues and the general failure of schools.

Many studies have reported that prior record, instant offense, and previous sentences are among the most important factors in determining the final disposition (for a review, see Shelden, 2006). Other studies have noted the importance of race and other social factors (Peterson, 1998). Some data show that, statistically speaking, prior record is more important than race. However, these studies fail to consider that race can contribute to prior record because of cultural biases that affect police practices (especially drug cases) and the existence of various forms of racial profiling (Chambliss, 1995, 1999; Cole, 1999).

The Racial Composition of Juvenile Institutions

The percentage of incarcerated youth who are racial minorities has risen steadily over the years. The national percentage of minorities in training schools was 23% in 1950, 32% in 1960, 40% in 1970, 60% in 1989, and 66% in 1997. In contrast, the majority of youths confined in private facilities are white. This is no doubt because most of the costs are paid by family members, usually through their insurance (Walker, Spohn, & DeLone, 1996, pp. 223–224; U. S. Department of Commerce, 1975, p. 419).

Not surprisingly, the overall *rate* of incarceration was considerably higher for minorities. Table 19.3 reveals stark contrasts. The overall rate for blacks was 634, compared to a rate of 253 for Hispanics and 155 for whites. Even when the most serious offense charged is considered, commitment rates for minorities far exceeded those of whites. For example, the black rate for personal crimes was 231, compared to 89 for Hispanics and 50 for whites. For drug offenses, the black rate was 70, the Hispanic rate 25, and the white rate 11. For drug offenders, *the black incarceration rate was more than six times greater than for whites*. In every offense category, whites had the lowest rate, blacks had the highest, and Hispanics were in the middle.

Table 19.3 Offense Profile of Committed Residents by Sex and Race/Ethnicity for United States, 2006 (Rate per 100,000 Juveniles)

| Most serious offense | Committed | | | | | | | |
| | | Sex | | Race/Ethnicity | | | | |
	Total	Male	Female	White	Black	Hispanic	American Indian	Asian
Total	205	345	58	124	518	219	381	57
Delinquency	193	332	48	114	494	214	331	54
Person	73	126	17	41	202	76	116	19
Violent Crime Index*	50	91	7	27	142	55	71	15
Other Person	22	34	10	14	59	21	45	4
Property	54	93	13	34	126	61	100	16
Property Crime Index**	44	77	10	29	106	47	82	13
Other Property	10	16	3	6	21	13	18	3
Drug	18	31	5	10	50	20	25	4
Public order	22	38	5	13	52	25	39	8
Technical violation	27	44	9	16	63	32	51	7
Status offense	12	13	10	10	25	5	51	2

Source: Sickmund, M., Sladky, T. J., & Kang, W. (2008). From *Census of Juveniles in Residential Placement Databook,* by M. Sickmund, T. J. Sladky, & W. Kang, 2008.

Notes: *Includes criminal homicide, violent sexual assault, robbery, and aggravated assault.

**Includes burglary, theft, auto theft, and arson.

A Notorious Example: The California Youth Authority

The California Youth Authority (now called the Division of Juvenile Justice, which is part of the California Department of Corrections and Rehabilitation, CDCR) consists of 11 youth correctional institutions, 11 forestry camps, 59 detention facilities, and several dozen probation camps scattered all over the state. The CYA was the result of the passage of the Youth Corrections Authority Act of 1941. The law created a three-person commission and mandated the acceptance of all youths under the age of 23 who had been committed to various prisons and already existing youth facilities (CDCR, 2009). The youths sent to the CYA were referred to as *wards*—a term that has remained in use since. A year later, they established camps and a unit called Delinquency Prevention Services. In 1945, the Division of Parole was created. According to their mission statement, these institutions are supposed to "protect the public from criminal activity by providing education, training, and treatment services for youthful offenders committed by the courts" (CDCR, para. 1).

The reality, however, is far different, as revealed by recurring scandals within the CYA. A series of reports surfaced in the 1980s condemning practices within the CYA (DeMuro & DeMuro, 1988; Lerner, 1982, 1986). Each of these reports documented extreme brutality and the lack of meaningful treatment within these institutions. The third and final report found that the CYA institutions "are seriously overcrowded, offer minimal treatment value despite their high expense, and are ineffective in long-term protection of public safety" (DeMuro and DeMuro, 1988, p. 11).

Few improvements were made during the years following these reports. More recently, a report by the Legislative Analyst's Office stated,

> A significant amount of the educational program at various institutions is delivered in temporary buildings. These temporary buildings inherently have a rather limited useful life, and have functional deficiencies such as inadequate security and ineffective air conditioning at institutions located in warm climates. The location of some of these temporary buildings is also an issue because they are often located a distance from housing units, requiring intensive staff supervision of ward movements (California Legislative Analyst's Office, 2004).

In the fall of 2004, the CYA was once again in the news. A series of reports in the *Los Angeles Times* revealed cases of extreme brutality, suicides, horrible physical conditions, and the CYA's almost total failure to live up to its mission statement. One report quoted Dan Macallair, a 20-year veteran of juvenile justice work, who stated, "The California Youth Authority is a dinosaur" (Warren, 2004c, para. 3). A report in the *Los Angeles Times* (Leovy & Chong, 2004) noted that within several facilities within actual classrooms youths were placed in special cages called "secure program areas" (para. 6), ostensibly to protect both youth and teachers from violent acts. "The cages essentially are large boxes in which wards are supplied with a chair and desk, and teachers instruct them through a barrier of metal mesh or chain link" (para. 8). Still another news report, of two more deaths within a CYA institution (Bell & Stauring, 2004), revealed "excessive rates of violence; inadequate mental health care and educational services; overuse of isolation cells; and deplorable conditions, including feces spread all over some of the cells. Some boys were being forced to sit or stand in cages while attending classes, a 'normal' situation in the state's Kafkaesque system" (para. 3). The report further stated that "more than nine out of 10 CYA 'graduates' are back in trouble with the law within three years of their release. On top of that, the CYA system costs taxpayers a whopping $85,000 a year per youth. It seems likely that if the majority of CYA youths came from white, middle-class neighborhoods, the public would never stand for its failures and abuses" (para. 6).

Numerous additional reports appeared in the *Los Angeles Times* during 2004 (Warren, 2004a, 2004b; Warren, Leovy, & Zamichow, 2004). One of these (Warren 2004b) reported on a special senate hearing where state senator Gloria Romero (D-Los Angeles) said, after reviewing a report that was part of a class action suit filed by a group of CYA wards, called the conditions "chilling" where some inmates were kept in "steel-mesh cages not much bigger than phone booths" (para. 9). Romero said the CYA was "totally failing in its mission to rehabilitate youths" (para. 10). She called it a system "that is in chaos, ruled by fear and neglect," despite an expenditure of more than $80,000 annually on each young offender (para. 11).

On January 31, 2005, the State of California signed an agreement with juvenile justice advocates (who had brought the aforementioned lawsuit) and filed it in Alameda County Superior Court. The agreement puts "therapy and positive reinforcement at the heart of California's youth prison system, rejecting today's more punitive approaches in favor of models that have been successful in other states" (Warren, 2005, para. 1).

Unfortunately, the agreement did not go far enough. As noted in a 2005 report (Anderson, Macallair, & Ramirez, 2005), "What the agreement does not explicitly require, however, is that the CYA close any of its existing eight facilities as part of its new juvenile justice model for the state. These prison facilities are large, remote, outdated, dangerous, and cannot provide the right environment within which to conduct rehabilitative programming" (p. 1).

California is not the only state plagued by scandals, for virtually every state in the nation has had similar experiences. Texas, Ohio, Florida, South Dakota, Oklahoma, Indiana, Maryland, Hawaii, Arizona, and Mississippi are among those states in which scandals have erupted and lawsuits have been filed (Dexheimer, 2007).

The Future of the Juvenile Court

In the years since the Supreme Court began reviewing issues related to juvenile justice (e.g., *In re Gault*) there has been a great deal of discussion concerning the role of the juvenile court. Should it be abolished, should it adhere strictly to a legalistic framework (e.g., due process considerations), or should it focus more on its original *parens patriae* principles? Many have challenged as counterproductive the movement toward treating young offenders as adults (Feld, 1999); besides, certification has not had very many positive results, which is one reason its use has declined in recent years (Shelden, 2006, 341–344). The Supreme Court ruling in *Roper v. Simmons* demonstrated that young offenders need to be treated more leniently because there are significant differences between adolescent and adult reasoning processes (Shelden, 2006, 423–424).

There is no question that there should be a separate system for young offenders, but it should be one that would adhere to principles consistent with that of restorative justice. Restorative justice is based on the idea that the only way to rid oneself of hurt and anger is through forgiveness. The object is to cease further objectification of those who have been involved in the crime—the victim, the offender, the families connected to these two individuals, and the community at large (Sullivan & Tifft, 2000). My position is summed up nicely in one of the classic critiques of the juvenile court by Supreme Court justice Abe Fortas, when he wrote in *Kent v. United States* (383 U.S. 541, 1966) that "the child receives the worst of both world; that he gets neither the protection accorded to adults nor the solicitous care and regenerative treatment postulated for children" (quoted in Shelden, 2006, p. 316).[1] Let us have a Court that gives youth both the protection of the Bill of Rights *and* the care and treatment that should be available to all children.

DISCUSSION QUESTIONS

1. How do you explain the persistence of the double standard despite the many changes brought about by the women's movement of the past several decades?

2. Why do you think that race remains such a critical issue within the juvenile justice system?

3. Reports have consistently found little difference in drug usage among the different races, yet blacks continue to be vastly overrepresented within the juvenile justice system for drug offenses. Explain this.

4. What do you think accounts for the persistent abuse within such juvenile institutions as the California Youth Authority?

5. Do a Google search of other states, and find some examples of other scandals centering around juvenile detention centers and correctional institutions.

6. Do you agree with the author's recommendation concerning the future of the juvenile court? Why or why not?

NOTE

1. *Kent v. United States* was the first juvenile court case heard by the U.S. Supreme Court; a minor's waiver from the jurisdiction of a juvenile court to that of an adult court was reviewed. For more detailed discussion, see Shelden (2006, pp. 316–317).

REFERENCES

Anderson, C., Macallair, D., & Ramirez, C. (2005). *CYA warehouses: Failing kids, families, and public safety*. Oakland, CA: Books Not Bars. Retrieved on October 19, 2009, from http://www.prisonpolicy.org/scans/cya_warehouses.pdf

Bartollas, C., & Miller, S. J. (2001). *Juvenile justice in America* (3rd ed.). Upper Saddle River, NJ: Prentice Hall.

Bazelon Center for Mental Health Law (2004, July 7). *Thousands of children with mental illness warehoused in juvenile detention centers awaiting mental health services*. July 7. Retrieved on October 19, 2009, from http://bazelon.org/newsroom/archive/2004/7-7-04jjhearing.htm

Bell, J., & Stauring, J. (2004, May 2). Serious problems festering in juvenile justice system require serious reforms. *Los Angeles Times*. Retrieved on October 20, 2009, from http://articles.latimes.com/2004/may/02/opinion/oe-bel

Bortner, M. A. (1982). *Inside a juvenile court: The tarnished ideal of individualized justice*. New York: New York University Press.

Building Blocks for Youth. (2000, April). *And justice for some*. Retrieved from http://cjcj.org/jjic.race_jj.php

California Department of Corrections and Rehabilitation. (2009). *Department of Juvenile Justice: Mission and values*. Retrieved from http://www.cdcr.ca.gov/Juvenile_Justice/About_DJJ/index.html

California Legislative Analyst's Office (2004, May). *A review of the California Youth Authority's infrastructure*. Retrieved on October 20, 2009, from http://www.lao.ca.gov/2004/cya/052504

Center on Juvenile and Criminal Justice. (2004). *Race and juvenile justice*. Retrieved on October 20, 2009, from http://cjcj.org/jjic/race_jj.php

Chambliss, W. J. (1995). Crime control and ethnic minorities: Legitimizing racial oppression by creating moral panics. In D. F. Hawkins (Ed.), *Ethnicity, race, and crime* (pp. 14–27). Albany: State University of New York Press.

Chambliss, W. J. (1999). *Power, politics, and crime*. Boulder, CO: Westview Press.

Chesney-Lind, M. (1971). *Female juvenile delinquency in Hawaii*. Unpublished Master's thesis, University of Hawaii.

Chesney-Lind, M., & Shelden, R. G. (2004). *Girls, delinquency, and juvenile justice* (3rd ed.). Belmont, CA: Wadsworth.

Cole, D. (1999). *No equal justice: Race and class in the American criminal justice system*. New York: The New Press.

Currie, E. (1993). *Reckoning: Drugs, the cities, and the American future*. New York: Hill and Wang.

DeMuro, P., & DeMuro, A. (1988). *Reforming the California Youth Authority*. Bolinas, CA: Common Knowledge Press.

Dexheimer, E. (2007, April 29). "Scandal and reform: A familiar cycle in agencies that deal with juvenile delinquents." *Austin American-Statesman*. Retrieved on October 19, 2009, from http://www.statesman.com/news/content/region/legislature/stories/04/29/29states.html

Feld, B. C. (1999). *Bad kids: Race and the transformation of the juvenile court*. New York: Oxford University Press.

Fellner, J. (1996, October). Stark racial disparities found in Georgia drug law enforcement. *Overcrowded Times* 7, 5.

Human Rights Watch. (2006). *Custody and control conditions of confinement in New York's juvenile prisons for girls: Summary*. Retrieved on January 27, 2008, from http://hrw.org/reports/2006/us0906/

King, R. (2008, May). *Disparity by geography: The War on Drugs in America's cities*. Washington, DC: The Sentencing Project. Retrieved from http://www.sentencingproject.org/Admin/Documents/publications/dp_drugarrestreport.pdf

Leonard, K., Pope, C., & Feyerherm, W. (Eds.). (1995). *Minorities in juvenile justice*. Thousand Oaks, CA: Sage.

Leovy, J., & Chong, J. (2004, February 6). Youth authority to review use of cages. *Los Angeles Times*. Retrieved on October 20, 2009, from http://www.latimes.com/news/local/la-me-cage6feb06,1,5621030.story?coll=la-home-local

Lerner, S. (1982). *The CYA report: Conditions of life at the California Youth Authority*. Bolinas, CA: Common Knowledge Press.

Lerner, S. (1986). *Bodily harm: The pattern of fear and violence at the California Youth Authority*. Bolinas, CA: Common Knowledge Press.

Lockwood, D., Pottieger, A. E., & Inciardi, J. A. (1995). Crack use, crime by crack users, and ethnicity. In D. F. Hawkins (Ed.), *Ethnicity, race, and crime*. Albany: State University of New York Press.

McGarrell, E. (1993). Trends in racial disproportionality in juvenile court processing: 1985–1989. *Crime and Delinquency, 39*, 29–48.

Miller, J. G. (1996). *Search and destroy: African-American males in the criminal justice system*. New York: Cambridge University Press.

Mnookin, R. H. (1978). *Child, family and state: Problems and materials on children and the law*. Boston: Little, Brown.

Moore, D. (2004). As some U.S. cities make progress in lowering the number of blacks in juvenile detention, Columbia's numbers rise. *Columbia Tribune*. Retrieved on October 20, 2009, from http://archive.columbiatribune.com/2004/feb/20040208feat051.asp

Peterson, R. D. (1988). Youthful offender designations and sentencing in the New York criminal courts. *Social Problems, 35*(2), 111–130.

Puzzanchera, C., Stahl, A. L., Finnegan, T. A., Tierney, N., & Snyder, H. N. (2003). *Juvenile court statistics 1999*. Pittsburgh, PA: National Center for Juvenile Justice.

Schlossman, S., & Wallach, S. (1978). The crime of precocious sexuality: Female delinquency in the progressive era. *Harvard Educational Review, 8*, 65–94.

Shelden, R. G. (1981). Sex discrimination in the juvenile justice system: Memphis, Tennessee, 1900–1917. In M. Q. Warren (Ed.), *Comparing male and female offenders*. Newbury Park, CA: Sage.

Shelden, R. G. (2006). *Delinquency and juvenile justice in American society*. Long Grove, IL: Waveland Press.

Shelden, R. G. (2008). *Controlling the dangerous classes: A history of criminal justice in America* (2nd ed.). Boston: Allyn and Bacon.

Sickmund, M. (2004, June). *Juveniles in corrections*. Washington, DC: Office of Juvenile Justice and Delinquency Prevention. Retrieved on October 20, 2009, from http://www.ncjrs.org/html/ojjdp/202885/page14.html

Sickmund, M., Sladky, T. J., & Kang, W. (2004). *Census of juveniles in Residential Placement Databook*. Retrieved on October 20, 2009, from http://www.ojjdp.ncjrs.org/ojstatbb/cjrp/asp/Offense_Detained.asp?state=0&topic=Offense_Detained&year=2001&percent=rate

Sickmund, M., Sladky, T. J., & Kang, W. (2008). *Census of juveniles in Residential Placement Databook*. Retrieved on October 20, 2009, from http://www.ojjdp .ncjrs.gov/ojstatbb/cjrp/

Siegel, L. J. (2002). *Juvenile delinquency*. Belmont, CA: Wadsworth.

Sullivan, D., & Tifft, L. (2000). *Restorative justice as a transformative process*. Voorheesville, NY: Mutual Aid Press.

Thornberry, T. P. (1973). Race, socioeconomic status, and sentencing in the juvenile justice system. *Journal of Criminal Law and Criminology, 64*, 90–98.

Tonry, M. (1995). *Malign neglect: Race, crime, and punishment in America*. New York: Oxford University Press.

Twedt, S. (2001, July 15). U.S. detention centers becoming warehouses for mentally ill youth. *Pittsburgh Post-Gazette*. Retrieved on October 20, 2009, from http:// www.post-gazette.com/headlines/20010715surveyJP3.asp

U.S. Department of Commerce. (1975). *Statistical abstracts of the United States*. Washington, DC: U.S. Government Printing Office.

Walker, S., Spohn, C., & DeLone, M. (1996). *The color of justice: Race, ethnicity, and crime in America*. Belmont, CA: Wadsworth.

Warren, J. (2004a, February 3). Youth prison system unsafe, unhealthful, reports find. *Los Angeles Times*. Retrieved on October 20, 2009, from http://articles .latimes.com/2004/feb/03/local/me-youth3

Warren, J. (2004b, February 4). Disarray in juvenile prisons jolts capital. *Los Angeles Times*. Retrieved October 20, 2009, from   http://articles.latimes.com/2004/ feb/04/local/me-cya4

Warren, J. (2004c, September 22). Shut down state youth prisons, experts say. *Los Angeles Times*. Retrieved on October 20, 2009, from http://articles.latimes.com/ 2004/sep/22/local/me-cya22

Warren, J. (2005, February 1). For young offenders, a softer approach. *Los Angeles Times*. Retrieved on October 20, 2009, from http://articles/latimes.com/2005/ feb/01/local/me-cya1

Warren, J., Leovy, J., & Zamichow, N. (2004, February 17). A daily lesson in violence and despair. *Los Angeles Times*. Retrieved on October 20, 2009, from http://articles.latimes.com/2004/feb/17/local/me-cya17

PART V

Corrections and Societal Response

20 The Philosophical and Ideological Underpinnings of Corrections

Anthony Walsh and Ilhong Yun

What Is Corrections?

Corrections is a generic term covering a wide variety of functions carried out by government agencies (and, increasingly, by private ones) having to do with the punishment, treatment, supervision, and management of individuals who have been convicted of crime. These functions are implemented in prisons, jails, and other secure institutions, as well as in community-based agencies, such as probation and parole departments. As the term implies, the whole correctional enterprise exists to correct, amend, or put right the criminal behavior of its clientele. This is a difficult task because that which must be corrected has festered for many years, and offenders often have a psychological, emotional, or financial investment in their current lifestyles (Andrews & Bonta, 2007).

The Theoretical Underpinnings of Corrections

Ever since humans have devised rules of conduct, they have wanted to break them. Most of us conform to the rules of our social groups most of the time and feel shamed and guilty when we violate them, but traveling the straight and narrow road does not always come naturally. Control theorists tell us that the real question is not why some people commit crimes but rather why most of us do not. After all, crime affords immediate gratification of desires with little effort: "money without work, sex without courtship, revenge without court delays" (Gottfredson & Hirschi, 2002, p. 210). We must learn to curb our appetites for immediate gratification and learn self-control as the social emotions—guilt, shame, embarrassment—merge with lessons taught us to become our consciences.

In our earliest days, parents chastise us for doing things that we have an urge to do: throw temper tantrums, hit our siblings or steal their cookies, bite the cat's tail, and so on. Later on, teachers scold us, peers ostracize us, and employers fire us if we don't behave according to the rules. These chastisements are examples of informal social control used to achieve peace and predictability in our relationships with others. The more heavy-handed punishment handed out by the state is formal social control exercised against those who have not learned to behave well via informal control methods. In short, we have to learn to be good children and good citizens, and we learn that only when we realize that our wants and needs are inextricably bound up with the wants and needs of others and that they are best realized by cooperating with others who want the same things.

A Short History of Correctional Punishment

The earliest-known written code of punishment is the Code of Hammurabi, created about 1780 BC. This code expressed the concept of *lex talionis* (the law of equal retaliation, or "an eye for an eye, a tooth for a tooth"). These laws codified the natural inclination of individuals harmed by another to seek revenge, but they also recognize that personal revenge must be restrained if society is not to be fractured by a cycle of tit-for-tat blood feuds. To avoid this, the state took responsibility for punishing wrongdoers. Nevertheless, state-controlled punishment was typically as uncontrolled and vengeful as that which any grieving parent might inflict on the murderer of his or her child. Prior to the 18th century, human beings were considered born sinners because of the Christian legacy of original sin. Cruel tortures, used on criminals to literally "beat the devil out of them," were justified by the need to save sinners' souls.

The practice of brutal punishment began to wane in the late 18th century with the beginning of the Enlightenment, which was essentially a major shift in the way people viewed the world and their place in it. It was also marked by the narrowing of the mental and emotional distance between people. Enlightenment thinkers questioned traditional values and began to embrace humanism, rationalism, and science, values that ushered in the beginnings of a belief in the dignity and worth of all individuals. This view would eventually find expression in the law and in the treatment of criminal offenders.

The first person to apply Enlightenment thinking to crime and punishment was the English playwright and judge Henry Fielding (1707–1754). Fielding's book, *Inquiry into the Causes of the Late Increase of Robbers* (1751/1967) set forth his thoughts on the causes of robbery, called for a "safety net" for the poor (free housing and food) as a crime prevention strategy, and campaigned for alternative punishments to hanging. Many of his suggestions were implemented and were apparently successful (Sherman, 2005).

The Emergence of the Classical School

Enlightenment ideas led to a school of penology known as the *classical school*. More than a decade after Fielding's book, the Italian philosopher and politician Cesare Beccaria (1738–1794) published a manifesto for the reform of European judicial and penal systems titled *On Crimes and Punishment* (1764/1963). Beccaria did not question the need for punishment but believed that laws should be designed to preserve public order, not to avenge crime. Punishment should be proportionate to the harm done to society, should be identical for identical crimes, and should be applied without reference to the social status of offenders or victims. Punishment must be certain and swift to make a lasting impression on the criminal and to deter others. To ensure a rational and fair penal structure, punishments for specific crimes must be decreed by written criminal codes and the discretionary powers of judges curtailed.

Beccaria's work was so influential that many of his reforms were implemented in a number of European countries within his lifetime (Durant & Durant, 1967, p. 321). His reform ideas tapped into and broadened the scope of such emotions as sympathy and empathy among the intellectual elite of Europe. Alexis de Tocqueville (1838/1956, Book III, Chapter 1) noticed the diffusion of these emotions across the social classes, beginning in the Enlightenment with the spreading of egalitarian attitudes, and attributed the "mildness" of the American criminal justice system to the country's democratic spirit. We tend to feel empathy for those whom we view as being like us, and empathy often leads to sympathy, which may translate the vicarious experience of the pains of others into active concern for their welfare. With cognition and emotion blended into the Enlightenment ideal of the basic unity of humanity, justice became both more refined and more diffuse (Walsh & Hemmens, 2007).

Another prominent figure was the British lawyer and philosopher Jeremy Bentham (1748–1832). His major work, *Principles of Morals and Legislation* (1789/1948), is essentially a philosophy of social control based on the principle of utility, which prescribes "the greatest happiness for the greatest number." The proper function of the legislature is to promulgate laws aimed at maximizing the pleasure and minimizing the pain of the largest number in society. If legislators are to legislate according to this principle, they must understand human motivation, which for Bentham was easily summed up: "Nature has placed mankind under the governance of two sovereign masters, pain and pleasure. It is for them alone to point out what we ought to do, as well as to determine what we shall do" (1948, p. 125). This was the Enlightenment concept of human nature: hedonistic, rational, and endowed with free will. Classical explanation of criminal behavior and how to prevent it are derived from these three assumptions.

Bentham devoted a great deal of energy (and his own money) to arguing for the development of prisons as substitutes for torture, execution, or transportation. He designed a prison in the 1790s called the *panopticon* ("all-seeing"), which was to be a circular "inspection house" enabling guards to constantly see their charges, thus requiring fewer staff. Because prisoners could always be seen without seeing by whom or when they were being watched, the belief was that the perception of constant scrutiny would develop into self-monitoring. Bentham felt that prisoners could be put to useful work to acquire the habit of honest labor.

The Emergence of Positivism

Classical thinkers were armchair philosophers, whereas positivist thinkers took upon themselves the methods of empirical science, from which more "positive" conclusions could be drawn. Positivists believe that human actions have causes and that these causes are to be found in the uniformities that precede those actions. While early positivists were excessively deterministic, they slowly moved the criminal justice system away from a singular concentration on the criminal act as the sole determinant of punishment to an appraisal of the characteristics and circumstances of the offender as an additional determinant. Others such as Raffael Garofalo (1885/1968) believed that, because human action is determined, the only things that should be considered at sentencing was offenders' "peculiarities" and the danger they posed to society. Garofalo's proposed sentences ranged from execution for *extreme criminals* (psychopaths), to transportation to penal colonies for *impulsive* criminals, to simply changing the law to deal with *endemic criminals* (those who commit "victimless crimes").

The Function of Punishment

The desire to punish those who have harmed us or otherwise cheated on the social contract is as old as the species itself. Punishment aimed at discouraging cheats is observed in every social species of animals, which leads biologists to conclude that punishment of cheats is an evolutionarily stable strategy designed by natural selection for the emergence and maintenance of cooperative behavior (Fehr & Gachter, 2002). Indeed, neuroimaging studies using PET and fMRI scans provide hard evidence that positive feelings accompany the punishment of those who have wronged us, and that negative feelings evoked when we are wronged are reduced. These studies showed that, when subjects were able to punish cheats, they had significantly increased blood flow to areas of the brain that responded to reward, suggesting that punishing those who have wronged us provides emotional relief and reward for the punisher (de Quervain et al., 2004; Fehr & Gachter, 2002). Perhaps we are hardwired to "get even," as suggested by the popular saying "Vengeance is sweet."

Sociologist Emile Durkheim (1893/1964) also argued that crime and punishment are central to social life. Crime is socially useful, argued Durkheim, because by shocking the collective conscience it serves to clarify the boundaries of acceptable behavior, and punishing criminals maintains solidarity because the rituals of punishment reaffirm the justness of the social norms. Durkheim recognized the inborn nature of the punishment urge and that punishment serves an expiatory role, but he also recognized that we can temper the urge with sympathy. He observed that, over the course of social evolution, humankind had largely moved from retributive justice (characterized by cruel and vengeful punishments) to restitutive justice (characterized by reparation). Both forms of justice satisfy the human urge for social regularity by punishing those who violate the social contract, but repressive justice oversteps its adaptive usefulness and becomes socially destructive. Repressive justice is driven by the natural passion for punitive revenge that "ceases only when exhausted . . . only after it has destroyed" (Durkheim, 1964, p. 86). Durkheim goes on to claim that restitutive justice is driven by simple deterrence and is more humanistic and tolerant, although it is still "at least in part, a work of vengeance" since it is still "an expiation" (1964, pp. 88–89).

The Objectives of Corrections

The five major objectives or justifications for the practice of punishing criminals are described next.

Retribution

Retribution is a *just deserts model*, which demands that criminals' punishments match the degree of harm they have inflicted on their victims. This is the most honestly stated justification for punishment because it both taps into our most primal urges and posits no secondary purpose for it, such as the reform of the criminal. California is among the states that have explicitly embraced this justification in their criminal codes (California Penal Code Sec. 1170a): "The Legislature finds and declares that the purpose of imprisonment for a crime is punishment" (cited in Barker, 2006, p. 12). This model of punishment avers that it is right to punish criminals, regardless of any secondary purpose that punishment may serve, simply because justice demands it.

Some of us may consider retribution to be primitive revenge and therefore morally wrong, but retribution as presently conceived is constrained revenge, curbed by proportionality and imposed by neutral parties bound by laws mandating respect for the rights of individuals against whom it is imposed. Logan and Gaes (1993, p. 252) go so far as to claim that only retributive punishment "is an affirmation of the autonomy, responsibility, and dignity of the individual." By holding offenders responsible and blameworthy for their actions, we are treating them as free moral agents, not as mindless rag dolls blown around by the capricious winds of the environment.

Deterrence

Deterrence justifies punishment by assuming that it will prevent crime. The principle that people respond to incentives and are deterred by the threat of punishment is the philosophical foundation behind all systems of criminal law. Deterrence may be either specific or general.

Specific deterrence refers to the effect of punishment on the future behavior of people who experience the punishment. For specific deterrence to work, it is necessary that a person make a conscious connection between an intended criminal act and the punishment suffered as a result of similar acts committed in the past. If that person fails to make the connection, it is likely that he or she will continue to commit crimes. Committing further crimes after being punished is called *recidivism*, or "falling back" (into criminal behavior). Nationwide, about 33% of released prisoners recidivate within the first 6 months after release, 44% within the first year, 54% by the second year, and 67.5% by the third year (Robinson, 2005, p. 222).

The effect of punishment on future behavior depends on its certainty, celerity (swiftness), and severity. In other words, there must be a relatively high degree of certainty that punishment will follow a criminal act, the punishment must be administered soon after the act, and it must be harsh. Unfortunately, the wheels of justice grind excruciatingly slowly today, with many months passing between the criminal act and the imposition of punishment; so much for celerity. This leaves the law with severity as the only element it can realistically manipulate, but it is unfortunately the least effective element. Studies from the United States and the United Kingdom find substantial negative correlations (as one factor goes up, the other goes down) between the likelihood of conviction (a measure of certainty) and crime rates, but much weaker ones (albeit in the same direction) for the severity of punishment (Langan & Farrington, 1998).

The effect of punishment on future behavior also depends on the *contrast effect,* which is the distinction between the circumstances of the possible punishment and the usual life experience of the person who may be punished. For people with little or nothing to lose, an arrest may be perceived as little more than an inconvenient occupational hazard, but for those who enjoy a loving family and the security of a valued career, the prospect of incarceration is a nightmarish contrast. Like so many other things in life, deterrence works least for those who need it most.

General deterrence refers to the preventive effect of the threat of punishment on the general population; it is thus aimed at *potential* offenders. The punishments meted out to offenders serve as examples to the rest of us of what may happen if we violate the law. The existence of a system of punishment for law violators deters a large but unknown number of individuals who might commit crimes if no such system existed.

What is the bottom line? Are we putting too much faith in the ability of criminals and would-be criminals to calculate the cost/benefit ratio of engaging in crime? Although many violent crimes are committed in the heat of passion or under the influence of mind-altering substances, there is evidence underscoring the classical notions that individuals do (subconsciously at least) calculate the ratio of expected pleasures to possible pains when contemplating a course of action. Gary Becker (1997) dismisses the idea that criminals lack the foresight to take punitive probabilities into consideration when deciding whether or not to continue committing crimes. He says, "Interviews of young people in high crime areas who do engage in crime show an amazing understanding of what punishments are, what young people can get away with, how to behave when going before a judge" (p. 20).

Some reviews of deterrence research indicate that legal sanctions do have "substantial deterrent effect" (Nagin, 1998, p. 16), and some have claimed that increased incarceration rates account for about 25% of the variance in the decline in violent crime over the last decade or so (Spelman, 2000; Rosenfeld, 2000). Of course, this leaves 75% of the variance to be explained by other factors. Unfortunately, we cannot determine if we are witnessing a *deterrent* effect (Has violent crime declined because more would-be violent people have perceived a greater punitive threat?) or an *incapacitation* effect (Has violent crime declined because more violent people are behind bars and thus not at liberty to commit violent crimes on the outside?).

Incapacitation

Incapacitation refers to the inability of criminals, while incarcerated, to victimize people outside prison walls. Its rationale is aptly summarized in James Q. Wilson's (1975, p. 391) remark, "Wicked people exist. Nothing avails except to set them apart from innocent people." The incapacitation justification probably originated with Enrico Ferri's concept of social defense (1897/1917). To determine punishment, notions of culpability, moral responsibility, and intent were to be subordinate to an assessment of offenders' strength of resistance to criminal impulses, with the express purpose of averting future danger to society. Ferri reasoned that the characteristics of criminals prevented them from basing their behavior on rational principles, so they could be neither deterred nor rehabilitated, and therefore the only reasonable rationale for punishing offenders is to incapacitate them for as long as possible.

It goes without saying that incapacitation works, at least while criminals are incarcerated. Elliot Currie (1999) uses robbery rates to illustrate this point. He states that, in 1995, there were 135,000 inmates in state and federal institutions whose most serious crime was robbery, and that each robber on average commits five robberies per year. Had these robbers been left on the streets, they would have been responsible for an additional $135,000 \times 5$ or 675,000 robberies, on top of the 580,000 actual robberies reported to the police in 1995. Similarly, Wright (1999) estimated that imprisonment averted almost 7 million offenses in 1990.

Rehabilitation

To rehabilitate means to restore or return to constructive or healthy activity. Whereas deterrence and incapacitation are primarily justified philosophically on classical grounds, rehabilitation is primarily a positivist concept. The rehabilitative goal is to change offenders' attitudes so that they come to accept that their behavior was wrong, not to deter them by the threat of further punishment. The difficulty with rehabilitation is that it asks criminals to return to a state which many (obviously, not all) of them have never been in (habilitation). But we keep on trying to rehabilitate criminals because what helps the offender helps the community. As former U.S. Supreme Court chief justice Warren Burger noted, "To put people behind walls and bars and do little or nothing to change them is to win a battle but lose a war. It is wrong. It is expensive. It is stupid" (in Schmalleger, 2001, p. 439).

Correctional scholars are always mindful of the "nothing works" position of those who demand too much of rehabilitative efforts. Many correctional programs did not work in the past for a variety of reasons: They relied on nondirective methods that were inappropriate for offenders; they sought to change behaviors unrelated to crime; they used programs that were not intensive enough; and they used inadequately skilled staff to run them. Correctional scholars are somewhat more upbeat about rehabilitation today, given a range of new treatment modalities (Latessa, Cullen, & Gendreau, 2002; Walsh, 2006).

Reintegration

The goal of reintegration is to use the time criminals are under correctional supervision to prepare them to reenter the free community as well equipped as possible. In effect, reintegration is not much different from rehabilitation, but it is more pragmatic, focusing on concrete programs like job training rather than attitude change.

In 2004, 503,200 adult convicts entered American prisons, and 483,000 left them (Glaze & Palla, 2005), and one in five will leave with no postrelease supervision, rendering parole "more a legal status than a systematic process of reintegrating returning prisoners" (Travis, 2000, p. 1). With the exception of convicts who max out, then, prisoners will be released under the supervision of a parole officer who is charged with monitoring offenders' behavior and helping them to readjust to the free world. The longer people remain in prison, the more difficult it is for them to readjust to the outside world.

Table 20.1 is a summary of the key elements of the five punishment philosophies. Their common goal, of course, is the prevention of crime.

Table 20.1   Summary of Key Elements of Different Correctional Perspectives

	Retribution	*Deterrence*	*Incapacitation*	*Rehabilitation*	*Reintegration*
Justification	Moral; just deserts	Prevention of further crime	Risk control	Offenders have correctable deficiencies	Offenders have correctable deficiencies
Strategy	None; offenders simply deserve to be punished	Make punishment more certain, swift, and severe	Offenders cannot offend while in prison. Reduce opportunity	Treatment to reduce offenders' inclination to reoffend	Concrete programming to make for successful reentry into society
Focus of Perspective	The offense and just deserts	Actual and potential offenders	Actual offenders	Needs of offenders	Needs of offenders
Image of Offenders	Free agents whose humanity we affirm by holding them accountable	Rational beings who engage in cost/benefit calculations	Not to be trusted but to be constrained	Good people who have gone astray; will respond to treatment	Ordinary folk who require and will respond to concrete help

The Past, Present, and Future of Corrections _____

Many features of corrections' past still manifest themselves in the current correctional landscape, albeit in modified forms. Recent decades have seen an increase of a type of jail similar to Bentham's panopticon in terms of its design and efficiency (Tartaro, 2002). Frequently termed the "new generation jail," the podular architecture permits continual surveillance with a minimal number of guards. In new generation jails, individual housing units are placed around an open area where a guard is permanently located. Inmates are allowed to move freely throughout the unit, but continual supervision of the movement is imposed by the centrally located guard. To maximize efficiency by reducing unnecessary movement and costs, all needed services—meals, phones, visits, counseling, showers, laundry, etc.—are directly offered within the unit.

The call for prison labor by early reformers as a way to reform criminals shaped the history of American corrections significantly, although the original rehabilitative rationale has largely been replaced by profits. In the United States, the Auburn system eventually outlasted the rival Pennsylvania system, largely due to the greater profits generated by the former's adoption of the congregate labor system, under which prisoners are able to pay for their own keep (Hawkins & Alpert, 1989).

Although inmate labor has been a central feature of prisons, it was not until the 20th century that prison industries flourished. During this period, the emerging *contract labor system* was implemented in many prisons nationwide. In this system, prison administrators contract with private firms, offering inmate labor in exchange for profits. The operation of prison industries was actively pursued, with the implicit notion of prisoner reform through disciplined work habits. This system hit a major roadblock during the Great Depression. Fearing the competition of inmate labor, labor unions successfully lobbied the legislature to curtail prison industries, and many of these legislative restrictions are still in force today. However, renewed emphasis on the rehabilitative merits of labor has recently brought about some regulatory relaxation. At the present time, goods produced in prison are mostly sold to public agencies, such as mental institutions or schools. Prison industries restore millions of dollars to state economies and contribute to rehabilitative relief from the boredom of prison life.

Diverse views still exist concerning what corrections is expected to accomplish, but the prevailing views of the public often become the basis for determining correctional objectives. With the advent of the Great Depression, the focus on retribution gave way to the goal of rehabilitation. The Great Depression drove many otherwise respectable people to poverty, suicide, and crime, owing to factors beyond their control. The age-old explanation of criminal behavior as a violation of free will did not seem to hold true anymore, and the time was ripe to look to what the positivists had to say about crime causation. The new *medical model* began to view inmates as individuals in need of help and treatment rather than moral failures. The old chain gangs and striped uniforms yielded to psychological diagnosis and counseling. Proof of rehabilitation became the basis of inmate release, therefore indeterminate sentences and parole replaced determinate sentences.

Much to the dismay of supporters of the medical model, however, proof of rehabilitation was sparse. Instead, beginning in the tumultuous 1960s, the criminal justice landscape was painted by rising crime rates and unabated recidivism. Eventually, the public's disillusionment with the ideal of rehabilitation, and the general conservative mood of the 1980s, saw the return of the just deserts model. The public's mounting demand to "get tough" on criminals resulted in longer and mandatory sentences. Early releases through parole were increasingly supplanted by fixed sentences, and many institutions became "no-frills" prisons divested of TVs, recreational facilities, and educational and vocational opportunities (Finn, 1996). Chain gangs, lock-step marching, and striped uniforms reappeared in some localities. The dubious fame of the United States as the nation with the highest incarceration rate is the direct corollary of this correctional model.

SUMMARY

Corrections is designed to punish, supervise, deter, and rehabilitate criminals. It is also the study of these functions. Although it is natural to want to exact revenge when people wrong us, to allow individuals to pursue this goal is to invite a series of tit-for-tat feuds that may fracture a community. The state has thus taken over responsibility for punishment. Over time, the state has moved to forms of punishment that are more restitutive than retributive, which, while serving to assuage the community's moral outrage, temper it with sympathy.

Much of the credit for the shift away from retributive punishment must go to the great classical thinkers such as Fielding, Beccaria, and Bentham, all of whom were imbued with the humanistic spirit of the Enlightenment period. The view of human nature (hedonistic, rational, and possessing free will) held by these men led them to view punishment as primarily for deterrent purposes, that it should only just exceed the "pleasure" (gains) of crime.

Opposing the classical notions of punishment are those of the positivists, who rose to prominence during the 19th century and who were influenced by the spirit of science. Positivists rejected the classicists' philosophical stance regarding human nature and declared that punishment should fit the offender rather than the crime.

The objectives of punishment are retribution, deterrence, incapacitation, rehabilitation, and reintegration, all of which have come into and out of favor and back again over the years. Retribution is simply just deserts—getting the punishment you deserve, no other justification needed. Deterrence is the assumption that people are prevented from committing crimes by the threat of punishment. Incapacitation means that criminals cannot commit further crimes against the innocent while incarcerated. Rehabilitation centers around efforts to socialize offenders in prosocial directions while they are under correctional supervision so that they won't commit further crimes. Reintegration refers to efforts to provide offenders with concrete, usable skills that will provide them a stake in conformity.

From the pursuit of correctional administrative efficiency emerged the construction of new generation jails and the wide use of sophisticated electronic devices. Traditionally, prison administrators made extensive use of inmate labor for monetary gain. Due to the opposition of labor unions and regulations imposed by the legislature, however, prison industry has dwindled during the second half of the 20th century.

The rehabilitation-oriented medical model of corrections largely gave way to the justice model during the 1980s. Instead of treatment and rehabilitation, the justice model emphasizes just deserts and being tough on criminals.

DISCUSSION QUESTIONS

1. Discuss the implications for a society that decides to eliminate all sorts of punishment in favor of forgiveness.

2. Is it good or bad that we take pleasure in punishment, and what evolutionary purpose does it serve?

3. Discuss the assumptions about human nature held by the classical thinkers. Are we rational beings, seekers of pleasure, and free moral agents?

4. Discuss the assumptions underlying positivism in terms of the treatment of offenders.

REFERENCES

Andrews, D., & Bonta, J. (2007). *The psychology of criminal conduct* (5th ed.). Cincinnati, OH: Anderson.

Barker, V. (2006). The politics of punishing: Building a state governance theory of American imprisonment variation. *Punishment & Society, 8,* 5–32.

Beccaria, C. (1764/1963). *On crimes and punishment.* (H. Paulucci, Trans.). Indianapolis, IN: Bobbs-Merrill.

Becker, G. (1997). The economics of crime. In M. Fisch (Ed.), *Criminology 97/98,* pp. 15–20. Guilford, CT: Dusskin.

Bentham, J. (1789/1948). *A fragment on government and an introduction to the principles of morals and legislation.* (W. Harrison, Ed.). Oxford, UK: Basil Blackwell.

Currie, E. (1999). Reflections on crime and criminology at the millennium. *Western Criminology Review, 2*(1). [Online]. Retrieved on October 20, 2009, from http://wcr.sonoma.edu/v2n1/currie.html

de Quervain, D., Fischbacher, U., Valerie, T., Schellhammer, M., Schnyder, U., Buch, A., & Fehr, E. (2004). The neural basis of altruistic punishment. *Science, 305,* 1254–1259.

Durant, W., & Durant, A. (1967). *Rousseau and revolution.* New York: Simon and Schuster.

Durkheim, E. (1893/1964). *The division of labor in society.* New York: The Free Press.

Fehr, E., & Gachter, S. (2002). Altruistic punishment in humans. *Nature, 415,* 137–140.

Ferri, E. (1897/1917). *Criminal sociology.* Boston: Little, Brown.

Fielding, H. (1751/1967). *Inquiry into the causes of the late increase of robbers.* Oxford, UK: Oxford University Press.

Finn, P. (1996). No-frills prisons and jails: A movement in flux. *Federal Probation, 60*(3), 35–44.

Garofalo, R. (1885/1968). *Criminology.* Montclair, NJ: Patterson Smith.

Glaze, L., & Palla, S. (2005). Probation and parole in the United States, 2004. *Bureau of Justice Statistics Bulletin.* Washington, DC: U.S. Department of Justice.

Gottfredson, M., & Hirschi, T. (2002). The nature of criminality: Low self-control. In S. Cote (Ed.), *Criminological theories: Bridging the past to the future* (pp. 210–216). Thousand Oaks, CA: Sage.

Hawkins, R., & Alpert, G. (1989). *American prison systems: Punishment and justice.* Englewood Cliffs, NJ: Prentice Hall.

Langan, P., & Farrington, D. (1998). *Crime and justice in the United States and England and Wales, 1981–1996.* Washington, DC: Bureau of Justice Statistics.

Latessa, W., Cullen, F., & Gendreau, P. (2002). Beyond correctional quackery—Professionalism and the possibility of effective treatment. *Federal Probation, 66,* 43–50.

Logan, C., & Gaes, G. (1993). Meta-analysis and the rehabilitation of punishment. *Justice Quarterly, 10,* 245–263.

Nagin, D. (1998). Criminal deterrence research at the onset of the twenty-first century. *Crime and Justice: A Review of Research, 23,* 1–42.

Robinson, M. (2005). *Justice blind: Ideals and realities of American criminal justice.* Upper Saddle River, NJ: Prentice Hall.

Rosenfeld, R. (2000). Patterns in adult homicide. In A. Blumstein & J. Wallman (Eds.), *The crime drop in America* (pp. 130–163). Cambridge, UK: Cambridge University Press.

Schmalleger, F. (2001). *Criminal justice today* (6th ed.). Upper Saddle River, NJ: Prentice Hall.

Sherman, L. (2005). The use and usefulness of criminology, 1751–2005: Enlightened justice and its failures. *Annals of the American Academy of Political and Social Science, 600,* 115–135.

Spelman, W. (2000). The limited importance of prison expansion. In A. Blumstein & J. Wallman (Eds.), *The crime drop in America* (pp. 97–129). Cambridge, UK: Cambridge University Press.

Stinchcomb, J. (2005). *Corrections: Past, present, and future.* Lanham, MD: American Correctional Association.

Tartaro, C. (2002). Examining implementation issues with new generation jails. *Criminal Justice Policy Review, 13,* 219–237.

Tocqueville, de, A. (1838/1956). *Democracy in America.* (H. Hefner, Ed.). New York: Norton Books.

Travis, J. (2001, May). But they all come back: Rethinking prisoner reentry. *Sentencing and Corrections: Issues for the 21st Century.* Washington, DC: U.S. Department of Justice, National Institute of Justice.

Walsh, A. (2006). *Correctional assessment, casework, and counseling* (4th ed.). Upper Marlboro, MD: American Correctional Association.

Walsh, A., & Hemmens, C. (2007). *Law, justice, and society: A sociolegal approach.* New York: Oxford University Press.

Wilson, J. Q. (1975). *Thinking about crime.* New York: Basic Books.

Wright, R. (1999). The evidence in favor of prisons. In F. Scarpitti & A. Nielson (Eds.,) *Crime and criminals: Contemporary and classic readings in criminology,* pp. 483–493. Los Angeles: Roxbury.

21

Community Corrections, Rehabilitation, Reintegration, and Reentry

Marilyn D. McShane and Traqina Emeka

Introduction

Community corrections is undoubtedly the backbone of offender supervision in this country. Currently, the number of probationers and parolees in the United States exceeds 5 million. The use of community corrections sentences has increased over time and now represents almost 70% of all who are under the supervision of the criminal justice system (Glaze & Bonczar, 2007). While community sentencing once may have represented a progressive reform in our justice system and an alternative to incarceration, it is now the primary form of punishment. Regardless of whether it is the most appropriate sanction, it appears to be the only one we can afford, given our limited resources.

The structure of community corrections operations reflects the inherent conflicts in managing local programs with significant state and even federal influence. While much of the day-to-day supervision of offenders takes place in a decentralized environment, there is always the coercive umbrella of legislation, regulation, and funding initiatives. Changes in the activities and priorities of law enforcement, court personnel, and prison and jail authorities mean that community corrections programs will be impacted and perhaps even undermined.

Realistically, the success of community corrections is likely to be determined by the ideological versions of one's goals and outcomes. Those who support a deterrence model will look for decreases in both self- and official reports of the offender's criminal activity. Evidence of rehabilitation would include abstaining from drug and alcohol use, steady employment, and consistent payments toward supervision and services. Retributive orientations, on the other hand, would expect the offender to have suffered for his or her offenses and, as with deterrence, to take steps to avoid more punitive sanctions in the future.

The concept of community corrections includes a broad array of legal alternatives to incarceration. Although most forms have traditionally involved monitoring the offender who resides at home, program options also include halfway houses, residential treatment, electronic tracking, and cyber monitoring. Today, advances in technology have changed the way community corrections officers perform their jobs, permitting more flexibility and remote supervision. In addition, contemporary public administration models rely more on networking and coordinating funded projects with schools, law enforcement, and civic leaders in the area. Both juvenile and adult justice systems employ these measures, and some do so as part of deferred adjudication, in which participants' records will be erased or expunged if the term of service under community supervision is successfully completed. The most common forms of community corrections are probation and parole.

Probation is usually administered by a local court, through the county or city, although separate systems are most often maintained for juveniles and adults. A probated sentence is the setting aside of a comparable prison term under a contract that includes a set of constraints and conditions the offender must meet in order to avoid incarceration. Conditions may include working; attending school; participating in treatment; paying various fines, restitution and court costs; and avoiding high-risk people, places, and activities. Violations of the terms, as recorded by a supervising probation officer, may mean that the probation is revoked, and the offender will then serve the entire sentence in prison. Over the past few decades, almost two thirds of offenders have been arrested while on probation, although more than half will eventually complete their probation terms. However, recent efforts have created a continuum of punitive options as progressive or intermediate sanctions that might better control offenders' behavior on probation, reduce infractions, and perhaps eliminate the need to revoke probation of those who violate their terms and conditions.

Parole is a term used to mean a period of supervision in the community following early release from prison during which the state continues to monitor the behavior of the parolee until the complete expiration of the defendant's full-sentence term. Thus, if a person with a 10-year sentence is released after 7 years, he or she will remain on parole, at least theoretically, for the remaining 3 years. Any violations that occur during the 3 years of release subject the parolee to revocation, whereby he or she would complete the entire remaining 3 years behind bars. Like probation, the offender agrees to follow conditions and rules enforced by a parole officer and may be subject to curfews, drug tests, and unannounced visits by the assigned case supervisor. Although more states are limiting the number of paroles and reducing the number of cases eligible to go before the parole board or increasing the time between parole hearings, more offenders are being released on a variation of parole called *mandatory release* or *mandatory supervision*. This is a legal status that usually reflects that inmates have served actual time and have accrued good time credit, the full length of their sentences. Release is then required by law; offenders remain under the jurisdiction of the state until the time by which they would have served the entire sentence without good time credit. This means that if a person has served 2 years in prison and has accumulated 2 years of good time credit through good behavior, he or she may be released from a 4-year incarceration term. However, the offender will be supervised by a parole officer in the community until the remaining 2 years (the good time credit portion) has been served.

For newly released inmates, halfway houses are a popular option, as they provide a more gradual release from custody. This alternative allows offenders to remain in a more structured environment until their transition to independent living and working arrangements is functioning smoothly. Likewise, prerevocation facilities, relapse centers for drug addicts, and state jails may provide structured support and intensive monitoring to avoid the need to return offenders to the more costly prison environment in order to control their activities.

Probation: Progressive Reform and the Promise of Rehabilitation

While the concept of probation can be traced to the English corrections system, the term *probation* appears to have been coined by the American philanthropist John Augustus (Rothman, 1980). Augustus, who focused his efforts on helping the more undesirable elements of Boston society, created a system that allowed offenders, particularly alcoholics, to remain in the community under his strict supervision and to engage in work apprenticeships and mentoring. Probation as a sanction was also extended to juvenile offenders with the creation of the Juvenile Court in 1899.

The corruption of the original intent of this rehabilitative venture is seen in its widespread application to most offenders, not just those who appear motivated to reform. In addition, probation moved from providing a residential type of supervision to one that sends the offender back into a potentially high-risk environment. Today, only 40% of probationers have misdemeanor or petty offenses; the majority are convicted of felony crimes (Schloss & Alarid, 2007). What appear to be high failure rates may be explained by the attempt to make a very intensive sentence, constructed for a relatively select group, applicable to all at very low levels of programming.

It is not surprising that, in the process of moving more offenders toward community sanctions, and in our overreliance on the application of one-size-fits-all treatment programs, we grew more pessimistic about the effectiveness of a medical model in corrections. Martinson's controversial 1974 essay, "What Works?—Questions and Answers About Prison Reform" (better known as "Nothing Works"), reflected the public's concern that rehabilitation efforts were not effective enough and, consequently, resulted in the suspension of programming in favor of more conservative models of deterrence and harsh punishment. As a result, more offenders were released from prisons without any treatment, which undoubtedly diminished their prospects for success in society. Still, corrections officials persisted in finding ways to divert offenders and avoid building more prisons. In California, counties were offered state subsidies to keep fewer serious offenders within their jurisdictions. At local levels, corrections administrators struggled to find more effective community-based components and formulas that would prescribe how much treatment and supervision were needed at what point in time for each type of offender.

As part of the attempt to create new varieties of probation services, officials in the late 1970s and early 1980s experimented with shock probation. Offenders were sent to prisons for a short time, usually less than 180 days, and then judges would release them to a term of probation, believing that they had been "shocked" into good behavior by the harsh realities of prison, much like juveniles exposed to prisons in the *Scared Straight* programs. Intensive supervision efforts seemed to yield higher levels of revocation, perhaps because probationers were being watched so closely or because higher-risk offenders were selected for this program. Some research indicated that intensive levels of services were not even being implemented in many of these programs (McShane & Krause,1993). Only the drug war, with its increased spending on enforcement and convictions, would force the prison building explosion of the 1980s and 1990s, thus diverting resources from community interventions as more offenders faced mandatory prison terms. Today, more to ease the burden of overcrowding than to effect any psychological advantage, prisoners are given split sentences, in which they serve a term of prison followed by probation or parole in order to monitor their behavior and assist with reintegration and reentry into society.

Parole as Reward or Relief

The earliest forms of parole were viewed as an indication that the offender was not only contrite and remorseful but prepared to engage in productive citizenship. Inmates who best demonstrated literacy, discipline, job skills, and a deep appreciation of the habits of industry were carefully selected for the privilege of early release. This designation was not only a personal reward for conforming to American values but a lesson to other inmates about the benefits of the assimilation of mainstream values. The period of postincarcerative supervision was considered an opportunity to ensure, under the watchful eye of the state, that the offender made a successful transition into the community. Ironically, Rothman's (1980) assessment of the public's perception of parole in the early 1900s is still relevant today. Then, as now, parole is criticized for its appearance of leniency and performance outcomes, in part, perhaps, because of unrealistic expectations about the criminal population. As Rothman explains, "Parole became the whipping boy for the failures of law enforcement agencies to control or reduce crime. Whenever fears of a 'crime wave' swept through the country, or whenever a particularly senseless or tragic crime occurred, parole invariably bore the brunt of attack" (p. 159).

An example of the politics of parole can be seen in the California system, where the explosive growth of the corrections system over the past 40 years has been fueled by a reluctance to build prisons, more punitive sentencing, more mandatory sentencing, and such conflicting trends as harsher terms for probationers and parolees with less supervision and oversight. The 1993 murder of a small-town girl abducted from her home in Petaluma by a parolee (who had already violated the terms of several conviction releases) led to replacements in that system's organizational leadership, changes in the release and revocation process, and the notorious "three strikes" legislation. Public criticisms of parole were further heightened when it was revealed that, on any given day, more than 20,000 California parolees are unaccounted for (Schaber, n.d.). In 2008, California voters struck outright at the parole system when they passed the Victims' Bill of Rights Act, which decreased the frequency of parole hearings and restricted the review of subsequent parole hearings after a denial for up to 15 years beyond eligibility. The state has also implemented policies increasing the number of witnesses who speak on behalf of victims at parole hearings and limiting the witnesses who speak on behalf of offenders at these hearings.

Assessment and Prediction: Risk and Stakes

One key to successful community corrections programming is making sure that proper mechanisms are in place not only for the rehabilitation of the offender but also for control measures to ensure the safety of the public. The latter is done by accurately assessing the risk of each individual and assigning offenders to levels of supervision that correspond to their different reoffending probabilities. Part of the concept of risk is a realistic picture of the stakes involved in any one offender's release. These stakes represent the concept of harm: to the public, to the victims, and even to the supervising agency. For example, notorious offenders who have high public profiles seem to cause more political harm if they recidivate, as compared to lesser-known and less serious offenders, because of the widespread anger and fear created by the publicity. Understandably, their cases must be weighed in terms of those stakes as well as according to the normal concept of risk (Williams, McShane, & Dolny, 2000). Stakes also include losses that may occur as a result of serious reoffending that remains undetected by the justice system.

There are typically two formal categories of risk assessments: clinical and actuarial (Gottfredson & Moriarty, 2006). Traditionally, clinical risk assessments have been used to determine the probability of offending based on professional judgments in the form of classification and prediction. Clinical assessments are more subjective and more individualized and take longer to complete than actuarial versions. Actuarial assessments, because they standardize prediction, are typically best for estimating future criminality for large groups of offenders. They involve statistical models and risk factor tools that predict behavior based on how others have acted in similar situations and/or an individual's similarity to various factor groupings. With an actuarial tool, offenders' characteristics are inventoried, and risk is determined by the extent to which he or she possesses various risk factors associated with recidivism (Zinger, 2004).

Risk prediction is traditionally based on static and dynamic factors that contribute to crime. Static variables are those which do not change (i.e., prior offense history, age at first offense). Dynamic factors represent issues or characteristics that may change, such as job stability and living arrangements. The importance of using risk assessment instruments involves matching needs with services, allocating resources efficaciously, preventing chronic offending, and increasing public safety.

Worse Than Prison?

Public safety is a major concern any time offenders remain in the community. Conservative attacks by more punitive lawmakers often restrict the use of community supervision and narrow the potential pool served by these alternative sanctions. Truth-in-sentencing laws passed over the last decade have increased the proportion of actual sentences served in prison and have limited the accrual of good time credit toward early release. Realistically, however, the current capacity of prisons will not allow more significant portions of sentences to be served. This issue is often overlooked when more conservative, punitive laws are passed.

Underlying the fight against expanding the community corrections base is a perception that probation and parole are soft on criminals, easy to serve, and not painful enough to be a deterrent. However, studies now indicate that many offenders view longer and more intensive levels of community supervision as harsher than prison (Jones, 1996; Petersilia & Deschenes, 1994; Spelman, 1995). In *Profiles From Prison* (2003), Michael Santos describes an offender who returned to prison to serve his final year rather than have his family suffer through the impositions and intrusions of constant surveillance. In this case, the parolee had to call for a recorded message each day to see if he was scheduled for a urinalysis, even though he had no prior drug use history or offenses. He also had to regularly attend anger management classes, Alcoholics Anonymous, and Narcotics Anonymous for 90 minutes each per week. He had to pay a fee for these meetings as well as miss work to attend them, which resulted in lower earnings. In addition, the offender reported to his parole officer monthly and filled out detailed records of all his finances and activities, including purchases made by his wife and children. His supervising officer made surprise weekly visits to his workplace and his home, sometimes at 5:30 in the morning when the family was asleep. The offender, Billy, describes the strain that parole put on his family. Billy told Santos that, for him and his wife,

> . . . living under the parole officer's microscope for five years seemed worse than another six-to-twelve months of imprisonment . . . Our marriage was strong. But the stress associated with supervised release was

too much . . . The stress threatened to break us up. I just wanted out. And if that meant going back to prison for a while, that's what I was willing to do. It was the only way I could get my life back. (p. 53)

Reintegration and Reentry

Every year, more than 600,000 federal and state prisoners are released (Listwan, Jonson, Cullen, & Latessa, 2008), and another 9 million are released from jails (Yoon & Nickel, 2008). Although rates vary by state enforcement levels, caseloads, and revocation policies, close to one half will not complete their probation term, and two thirds will violate parole. These offenders will most likely be returned to prison within a relatively short period of time. Ironically, as conditions for community release become stricter and supervision becomes more punitive, revocations have increased and contributed to prison overcrowding. Thus, the mechanism used to relieve crowding becomes its major contributor. Fortunately, this is not inevitable; officials can reform and revise criteria to make success more probable through meaningful reentry programming. This is especially important, as some recent research has indicated that people who are granted a discretionary release from prison seem to have lower rates of recidivism than those who complete their entire term incarcerated and "max out" (Schlager & Robbins, 2008).

The goal of reentry programs is to rehabilitate offenders by equipping them with the necessary skills to become law-abiding, productive citizens. Officials agree, however, that high caseloads, limited resources, and the lack of specialized training on the part of criminal justice agents greatly impact the probability of a successful transition into society (Byrnes, Macallair, & Shorter, 2002). Adequately trained justice professionals are critical to ensuring that offenders in transition fully benefit from reentry programs. Offenders most likely to recidivate are those with low levels of education and a general lack of social support, including shelter, food, employment assistance, clothing, substance abuse, and mental health treatment. Because offenders exhibit mental health disabilities at a rate three times that of the general population, the demand for services often creates a strain on communities' already overburdened health-care systems (Skeem, Emke-Francis, & Louden, 2006).

Legislative barriers are also challenges that newly-released offenders face. Certain crimes, such as distribution of drugs, may restrict someone with a felony record from accessing certain government services otherwise available for the needy. Federal education grants, welfare, food stamps, public housing, and certain types of jobs (i.e. childcare, nursing, etc.) often exclude those with certain offense histories (Byrnes, Macallair, & Shorter, 2002). Likewise, supplemental security income (SSI) recipients may lose benefits if they violate certain parole conditions. Offenders may also be excluded from jobs that require them to be bonded and to obtain driver's licenses (Travis, 2002).

Today, the most common reentry programs are those funded in part by faith-based and nonprofit community organizations (Yoon & Nickel, 2008).

Civil liberties concerns about the potentially exclusive nature of religious programming and its implications for ideologic coercion have generated parallel programs that are more secular. Both types utilize volunteers, donations, and local services as well as opportunities to integrate the offender back into the community with both physical and psychological support, mentoring, and gradual progression toward independent living.

Factors Correlated With Community Supervision Success and Failure

There are several consistent correlates of community supervision success and failure, including offense history, substance use and abuse, age, marriage, employment status, and gender. Individuals with a history of criminality, particularly property offenders, have long been associated with probation failure (Morgan, 1994; Petersilia, Turner, Kahan, & Peterson, 1985; Roundtree, Edwards, & Parker, 1984; Sims & Jones, 1997; Whitehead, 1991). Alcohol and drug use also appear to be predictors of probation recidivism. In addition, alcohol and drug treatment that is initiated but not completed may also result in a high rate of probation recidivism. Alcohol and drug treatment that addresses the motivation for committing crimes seems more likely to result in community supervision success (Gottfredson, Najaka, & Kearley, 2003).

Age appears to be a consistent predictor of probation success or failure, as younger offenders and those who begin their criminal activity at a younger age appear to be at greater risk for recidivism (Clarke, Yuan-Huei, & Wallace, 1988; Irish, 1989; Williams, McShane & Dolny, 2000). The theoretical literature suggests that those more likely to reoffend typically have fewer social bonds than offenders who have more social bonds. Further, having a job and living with a spouse would influence criminality (Farrington, 1988). Carmichael, Gover, Koons-Witt, and Inabnit (2005) found that age, race, and the use of alcohol and drugs were predictors of parolee success in a sample of 503 female offenders. Also, whites and older females were most likely to complete their sentences successfully. Females who did not indicate a history of drug or alcohol use and those who successfully addressed such problems were more likely to succeed on supervision.

Overall, it appears that most community supervision revocations are the result of technical violations, as opposed to a new offense (Carmichael et al., 2005). According to Sims and Jones (1997), technical violations surpass both major and minor violations. Gray, Fields, and Maxwell (2001) examined offenders who received probation violations, reasons for probation violation, and the time to violation. The 30-month study of 1,500 probationers found that most technical probation violations occurred during the first 3 months of supervision.

One of the major difficulties in interpreting studies on community corrections outcomes is the different definitions of recidivism that are used. Events that trigger revocation vary in levels of seriousness or degrees of probability that a violation actually took place. Some researchers measure arrest, reconviction, incarceration, absconding, and any probation or parole violations, as well as probation suspension or revocation. While most use arrest, this is often a subjective outcome that depends to some extent on law enforcement resources, probation and parole supervision policies, and court workloads.

Research at both the macro and micro levels has indicated that stereotypes about race and dangerousness may lead to harsher sentences (those that do not include community supervision) as well as to higher rates of probation and parole revocations (Huebner & Bynum, 2008). Awareness of disproportionate minority confinement has directed attention toward minimizing discretion in the community corrections process that might introduce bias and discriminate against segments of society. The U.S. Sentencing Commission's recent decision to address crack/powder cocaine-sentencing disparities by revising the sentencing guidelines and making those revisions retroactive may mean that many minority defendants are now eligible for parole or release. The development of a number of ethnically and culturally based programming initiatives has also created opportunities to meet the needs of minority youth in the community.

A recent New Mexico study found that, although the law required all offenders to receive mandatory treatment for any DWI after the initial offense, few actually did. Findings indicated that, in many instances, judges were not putting the orders for treatment into sentences. Although some offenders may have been attending regular treatment, the system did not have the reporting mechanisms needed to track their progress (Woodall, 2008). This finding is consistent with research over the years indicating that the consistency with which mandated services are provided and the integrity of treatments offered explain much of the success and failure in community corrections programming.

Ongoing Debates and Policy Implications

Community corrections continues to be a controversial component of the justice system, perhaps because of its attempt to balance meaningful correctional measures with fair sentences, affordable policies and practices, and victims' rights. As we often see, sensationalized media accounts of some crimes feed panics that create assumptions about risk and violence that perpetuate harsher punishments. In some cases, youthful offenders are transferred from juvenile courts to adult criminal courts. As trends indicate, harsher sentencing strategies and more assertive victims' rights measures may make it more difficult for some offenders to be assigned community corrections options.

As the criminal justice system struggles to adapt to changing public views about appropriate conditions of supervision as well as the technologies available to enforce them, many questions are ultimately settled by the courts. As judges review cases, they continue to divide the priorities of the system into control and reform. Conditions in either category must be rationally related to a correctional goal and must be clear, reasonable, and constitutional. Recently, the courts have found that probationers could not be compelled to enroll in religiously oriented treatment programs like Alcoholics Anonymous (AA; *U.S. v. Myers*, 1994; *Warner v. Orange County Department of Probation*, 1994), nor can they be forced to participate in publicly humiliating displays of guilt (*People v. Hackler*, 1993). While there is agreement that a wider range of strategies must be available, authorities must be careful about the potentially damaging effects of any requirements.

In Texas, the 2006–2007 legislature specifically set aside $55.5 million for new diversion programs that would reduce the caseload sizes carried by officers and increase the amount of outpatient and residential treatment services offenders could access. The goal was to increase the number of early dismissals from supervision and to develop more progressive sanctions that would reduce the number of technical violations contributing to revocations (Texas Department of Criminal Justice, 2007).

The reality of the revolving door between community and prison led Congress to pass several pieces of legislation aimed at increasing success in local corrections programming. First, the 2003 Serious and Violent Offender Reentry Initiative directed funds to programs nationwide that would develop best practices for dealing with high-risk juvenile and adult offenders at release. Second, in 2007, a $300 million federal spending package was passed to increase resources for reentry programs across the country under the Second Chance Act (Burke & Tonry, 2006). Funding focused on continued aftercare for those released after undergoing mental health or substance abuse treatments in prison. Programs were also developed around work readiness, family reunification, and mentoring services (Listwan, Jonson, Cullen, & Latessa, 2008). Still, though these new experimental programs and services appear to have significantly lowered recidivism rates, they reach only a fraction of the offenders in need. Much remains to be done to convince offenders that a true second chance really does exist.

DISCUSSION QUESTIONS

1. What is the purpose of community corrections in this country today, and what are the strengths and weaknesses of the concept in general?

2. What changes would you make in the operation of community supervision programs in your area, and how, specifically, would you engage the community in this process?

3. What are some of the barriers faced by offenders who have recently been released from prison? How can we address them effectively?

4. Many people seem to want to lock up more and more people for longer periods of time. How do we select offenders for community supervision programs so that we stay within our current budgets?

5. How realistic is the argument some offenders make that community supervision is worse than prison?

REFERENCES

Burke, P., & Tonry, M. (2006). *Successful transition and reentry for safe communities*. Silver Spring, MD: Center for Effective Public Policy.

Byrnes, M., Macallair, D., & Shorter, A. (2002). *Aftercare as afterthought: Reentry and the California Youth Authority*. San Francisco: Center on Juvenile and Criminal Justice.

Carmichael, S., Gover, A., Koons-Witt, B., & Inabnit, B. (2005). The successful completion of probation and parole among female offenders. *Women & Criminal Justice, 17,* 75–97.

Clarke, S., Yuan-Huei, W. L., & Wallace, W. L. (1988). *Probationer recidivism in North Carolina*. Chapel Hill: University of North Carolina, Institute of Government.

Farrington, D. P. (1988). Studying changes within individuals: The causes of offending. In M. Rutter (Ed.), *Studies of psychosocial risk: The power of longitudinal data* (pp. 158–183). Cambridge, UK: Cambridge University Press.

Glaze, L. E., & Bonczar, T. P. (2007). *Probation and parole in the United States, 2006*. Washington, DC: Bureau of Justice Statistics.

Gottfredson, S., & Moriarty, L. (2006). Statistical risk assessment: Old problems and new applications. *Crime and Delinquency, 52,* 178–200.

Gottfredson, D., Najaka, S., & Kearley, B. (2003). Effectiveness of drug treatment courts: Evidence from a randomized trial. *Criminology and Public Policy, 2,* 171–196.

Gray, M., Fields, M., & Maxwell, S. (2001). Examining probation violations: Who, what, and when. *Crime and Delinquency, 47,* 537–557.

Huebner, B., & Bynum, T. (2008). The role of race and ethnicity in parole decisions. *Criminology, 46,* 907–937.

Irish, J. F. (1989). *Probation and recidivism: A study of probation adjustment and its relationship to post-probation outcome*. Mineola, NY: Nassau County Probation Department.

Jones, M. (1996). Voluntary revocations and the "elect-to-serve" option in North Carolina probation. *Crime and Delinquency, 42*(1), 36–49.

Listwan, S. J., Jonson, C. L., Cullen, F. T., & Latessa, E. (2008). Cracks in the penal harm movement: Evidence from the field. *Criminology and Public Policy, 7*(3): 423–465.

Martinson, R. (1974). What works?—Questions and answers about prison reform. *The Public Interest, 35,* 22–54.

McShane, M. D., & Krause, W. (1993). *Community corrections*. New York: Macmillan.

McShane, M. D., Williams, F. P., & Dolny, H. M. (2000). Developing a parole classification instrument for use as a management tool. *Corrections Management Quarterly, 4*(4), 45–59.

Morgan, K. D. (1994). Factors associated with probation outcome. *Journal of Criminal Justice, 22,* 341–353.

People v. Hackler, 13 Cal. App. 4th 1049 (1993).

Petersilia, J., & Deschenes, E. P. (1994). Perceptions of punishment: Inmates and staff rank the severity of prison versus intermediate sanctions. *The Prison Journal, 74*(3), 306–328.

Petersilia, J., Turner, S., Kahan, J., & Peterson, J. (1985). Executive summary of Rand's study, "Granting Felons Probation: Public Risks and Alternatives." *Crime and Delinquency, 31,* 379–392.

Rothman, D. (1980) *Conscience and convenience: The asylum and its alternatives in progressive America*. Boston: Little, Brown.

Roundtree, G., Edwards, D., & Parker, J. (1984). A study of the personal characteristics of probationers as related to recidivism. *Journal of Offender Counseling, Services & Rehabilitation, 8*, 53–61.

Santos, M. (2003). *Profiles from prison: Adjusting to life behind bars*. Westport, CT: Praeger.

Schaber, D. (n.d.). On the loose: Convicted sex offenders roaming loose, despite registry effort. *ABC News.com*. Retrieved from http://www.rentalresearch.com/OnTheLooseABCNews.pdf

Schlager, M. D., & Robbins, K. (2008). Does parole work?—Revisited. *The Prison Journal, 88*(2), 234–251.

Schloss, C. S., & Alarid, L. (2007). Standards in the privatization of probation services. *Criminal Justice Review, 32*(3), 233–245.

Sims, B., & Jones, M. (1997). Predicting success or failure on probation: Factors associated with felony probation outcomes. *Crime and Delinquency, 43*, 314–327.

Skeem, J. L., Emke-Francis, P., & Louden, J. (2006). Probation, mental health, and mandatory treatment. *Criminal Justice and Behavior, 33*, 158–184.

Spelman, W. (1995). The severity of intermediate sanctions. *Journal of Research in Crime and Delinquency, 32*(2), 107–135.

Texas Department of Criminal Justice. (2008). *Annual review 2007*. Retrieved on December 10, 2008, from http://www.tdcj.state.tx.us/mediasvc/annualreview2007/supervision/cjad.html

Travis, J. (2002). Invisible punishment: An instrument of social exclusion. In M. Mauer & M. Chesney-Lind (Eds.), *Invisible punishment: The collateral consequences of mass imprisonment*. New York: W. W. Norton.

U.S. v. Myers, 864 F. Supp 794 (1994).

Warner v. Orange County Department of Probation, 870 F. Supp 69 (1994).

Whitehead, J. T. (1991). The effectiveness of felony probation: Results from an eastern state. *Justice Quarterly, 8*, 523–543.

Williams, F. P., McShane, M. D., & Dolny, M. (2000). Developing a parole classification instrument for use as a management tool. *Corrections Management Quarterly, 4*(4), 45–56.

Woodall, G. (2008). *Treating DWI offenders*. Albuquerque: University of New Mexico Center of Alcoholism, Substance Abuse and Addictions.

Yoon, J., & Nickel, J. (2008). *Reentry partnerships: A guide for states and faith-based and community organizations*. New York: The Council of State Governments, Justice Center.

Zinger, I. (2004). Actuarial risk assessment and human rights: A commentary. *Canadian Journal of Criminology and Criminal Justice, 46*, 607–621.

22

Restorative Justice in Theory

Lois Presser

When we have been harmed by another, we typically seek justice. But what is justice? According to the restorative justice perspective, *justice* is repair of harms, with the offender as the main agent of repair. The harms requiring repair are considered both concretely and broadly. For example, restorative justice requires attention to the medical bills that an assault victim might have accumulated. But the victim's fears and self-doubt must also be addressed. Harm to *relationships* is taken especially seriously. Restorative justice stresses the victim's and the offender's relationships with each other and with other members of their communities. And so, in the restorative justice perspective, repair is seen as best facilitated by dialogue—key tool of human relationship that it is.

In practice, restorative justice is various things. Restorative justice programs include community service orders for offenders, school-based antibullying interventions, victim–offender dialogue, and meetings where Mothers Against Drunk Driving confront persons convicted of driving while intoxicated. Restorative justice clearly means different things to different people. The expression *restorative justice* gets pressed into the service of various goals, such as community-building, rehabilitation of offenders, and victim healing. The fact of wide interpretation is a boon if one's goal is to gain support for a restorative justice program. It is a problem, however, if one's goal is to design a *focused* program—one whose measures of performance are agreed upon by all stakeholders. The purpose of this chapter is to clarify what restorative justice is and how it is *supposed to* work—that is, to review theories of restorative justice. Along the way, I identify certain key controversies surrounding restorative justice in theory and in practice. These concern whether restorative justice should ever intentionally harm offenders, whether participants should be forced to participate, whether certain interpersonal crimes are inappropriate for restorative justice practices, and whether restorative justice reproduces societal inequalities.

What Is Restorative Justice?

So what are we actually here for today? Can I ask you?

—Father of a young offender during a victim–offender
mediation session concerning vandalism[1]

I define a *restorative justice program* as any organized practice in which people, especially laypeople, participate by talking with one another; that focuses on a specific (pattern of) harm; that stands opposed to harm; and that is based on an understanding of justice as harm reduction. According to Presser and Van Voorhis (2002), the core processes of restorative justice are dialogue, relationship building, and communication of moral values. A restorative justice program generally aims to facilitate all three processes.

Essential and Desirable Features

The term *restorative justice* was first applied in the 1970s to interventions with low-level property offenders that entailed encounters between the offender and her or his victim (Zehr, 1995). Restorative justice is still frequently associated with face-to-face dialogue, but the latter must not be overstated. Dialogue may not occur, or it may occur via letters—as between incarcerated offenders and their victims. Expressions of apology and forgiveness are generally associated with restorative justice, but they are not essential, even as such expressions, if genuine, can be uniquely helpful in rebuilding relationships in the aftermath of harm.

Correctional treatment programs are designed to change offenders. But the potential targets of restorative justice are *all* those affected by crime: victims, offenders, and communities, whom Bazemore (1997) refers to as the "three clients" of restorative justice (p. 43). The healing of victims and communities is at least as important as any correctional impact that the intervention might have on the offender.

Is restorative justice simply a more traditional, premodern kind of justice? Ancient responses to crime were focused on the harms caused (Zehr, 1995). Dialogue, relationship-building, and communication of moral values prevailed. Laypersons "ran the show": Governments had not yet codified and commandeered social conflicts (Christie, 1977; Weitekamp, 1999). Hence, restorative justice borrows from traditional responses to crime. However, restorative justice proponents are not necessarily opposed to state sponsorship of responses to crime. For example, Van Ness and Strong (2006) include in their vision of restorative justice a role for the state in ensuring order: It has "both the power and mandate" to do so (p. 47).

A Place for Retribution and Control?

Some ancient societies, although focused on harm and not law violation, nonetheless sought to *harm* the offender—to exact retribution—and the same is true for indigenous societies today (Daly, 2002). The intent to harm would seem inconsistent with today's restorative justice. But the in/compatibility of restorative justice and retribution has been contested.

Both restorative justice and retribution focus on harms due to crime. They share the same end—to achieve justice—as opposed to the crime control sought by other rationales of punishment (i.e., deterrence, incapacitation, and rehabilitation). Zehr (2002) observes, "Both retributive and restorative theories of justice acknowledge a basic moral intuition that a balance has been thrown off by a wrongdoing" (p. 59). Yet, whereas retributivists would correct the balance through imposition of pain, restorativists would correct it through acknowledgement and repair of harms. In addition, restorativists consider the harms that the offender has experienced, which may or may not have instigated the offending behavior.

Bazemore and Schiff (2001, pp. 64–65) frame the difference another way: Retribution has the offender taking responsibility, but passively and retrospectively, as it forces the offender to pay for harm done to the victim. Rather than the agent, the offender is a recipient of "just deserts." Restorative justice looks both backward and forward, holding the offender responsible for what she or he did but also encouraging the active, future responsibility to make amends.

Whether or not restorative justice in *practice* precludes infliction of harm remains controversial. Some scholars contend that restorative justice is not incompatible with retribution. Based on her own careful research, Daly (2002) writes,

> I have come to see that apparently contrary principles of retribution and reparation should be viewed as dependent on one another. Retributive censure should ideally occur before reparative gestures (or a victim's interest or movement to negotiate these) are possible in an ethical or psychological sense. Both censure and reparation may be experienced as "punishment" by offenders (even if this is not the intent of decision-makers), and both censure and reparation need to occur before a victim or community can "reintegrate" an offender into the community. (p. 60)

Duff (2002) likewise makes a case for "restoration through punishment." He writes, "The wrongdoer should be pained by the censure of his fellow citizens: if he is not pained, their censure has failed to achieve its intended result" (p. 96).

Restorative justice proponents specify that censure, however harsh, involves declarations that the offense *but not the offender* is bad (Barton, 2003, p. 23). The reasons for this principle mainly have to do with crime control and are discussed in the next section. At the same time, in the restorative justice ideal, victims are encouraged to express the full range of their thoughts and feelings. Thus, the "disciplining" of censure within restorative justice encounters is *potentially* at odds with its deference to victims. What victims might want to say does not always accord with restorative justice ideals or theories.

Arrigo and Schehr (1998) observe that the protocol and language of restorative justice constrain what participants can say: "[L]imiting potentially hostile outbursts from victims (and offenders) is essential to the reconciliation and restitution process" (p. 649). For Barton (2003), however, a high degree of structure during the victim–offender conference ensures that all participants speak (relatively) free of intimidation: He believes that structure ultimately empowers. Braithwaite (2002) observes that "at least compared to courtroom processes, restorative justice does better in terms of recognition and empowerment" (p. 133). To my mind, the disagreements over harm and control in restorative justice encounters reflect deep questions concerning the very nature of harm and control and whether these are even avoidable in human interaction. To what extent can social control be avoided in human encounter? What is harm, and can we avoid doing harm as we attempt to change harmful ways?

Restorative justice is *not* a return to ancient justice practices, because it orients to an *ideal* of nonharm and usually works with or within a government-justice system. It follows that restorative justice seeks order *and* peace, crime control *and* healing experience (Van Ness & Strong, 2006).

How Is Restorative Justice Supposed to Work?

> *Sometimes it is like you are getting picked at. Like they are picking away at you but it is for the good. . . . And then other times it is like I have a whole circle, a whole network of people that are willing to help me and volunteer their time to come and do this, and I appreciate it.*
>
> —Domestic violence offender concerning
> a sentencing circle in Minnesota[2]

I turn now to theories of restorative justice. The chapter focuses on theories that *explain* potential *effects* of restorative justice practice. However, theories, in general, do not merely explain; they also discern the nature of things (Abend, 2008). That is, a theory can outline what a thing *is*. Theories that speak to the nature of restorative justice include (but are not limited to) theories of justice and the state, social movements, dialogue and democracy, the nature of conflict, and the nature of power.

What is restorative justice supposed to accomplish, and how? In an earlier essay, I suggested that restorative justice works by being an experience of justice (Presser, 2004). It need not achieve some other thing. Still, when people ask if restorative justice "works," they are generally asking if it helps in reducing crime. The corresponding theoretical question is, How is restorative justice supposed to reduce crime? But equally important questions are, How is restorative justice supposed to help victims heal, and how is restorative justice supposed to help build communities?

These questions are equally important; as such, I depict the corresponding theories laterally and not hierarchically in Table 22.1. Yet, it is certainly the case that theories of crime reduction receive the lion's share of attention, so I begin with these.

Table 22.1 Theories of Restorative Justice Effects		
Theories of Crime Reduction	*Theories of Victim Healing*	*Theories of Community Building*

Theories of Crime Reduction

A restorative justice practice may reduce crime at either individual (micro) or societal (macro) levels. That is, individual participants might change in ways that reduce criminal behavior, *or* crime rates might fall because a restorative justice practice changes something about culture or social structure. What follows is a selective review of given explanations of how restorative justice practice might reduce crime. (See Chapter 4 in Braithwaite, 2002, for an excellent discussion).

John Braithwaite's (1989) reintegrative shaming theory is most often cited to explain how restorative justice practice might reduce reoffending. Reintegrative shaming involves affirming and insisting upon conventional standards of behavior by the (would-be) offender. *Reintegrative* refers to the mode of communication—the "shamed" person is treated as a member of the collective—and to the practical reintegration that may follow from the shaming, including, for example, help finding or keeping a job. The offense, not the (would-be) offender, is condemned. In this way, she or he gets a lesson on how to behave without being and feeling alienated from those giving the lesson.

Reintegrative shaming theory is a macro-, meso-, and micro-level theory of crime. On the macro level, cultures that do reintegrative shaming should have lower rates of crime. In other words, reintegrative shaming supposedly prevents crime. The same is said to hold true for groups (the meso level): Group members are influenced by others' experience of reintegrative shaming. On the micro level, offenders who are subjected to reintegrative shaming should change their wayward patterns of behavior. That is, reintegrative shaming supposedly reduces recidivism. Commonly used restorative justice practices, especially those that convene community members *and* victims *and* offenders, like family group conferencing and peacemaking circles, involve both practical and symbolic gestures of reintegrative shaming (Braithwaite 2002).

Closely related to reintegrative shaming theory are Lawrence Sherman's (1993) defiance theory and Tom Tyler's (2006) legitimacy theory. Generally stated, these two theories propose that people obey the law to the extent that they view the law and its enforcers as legitimate. Sherman (1993) further specifies that people's obedience to law is conditioned by bonds to its enforcers. To the extent that restorative justice practices involve affirmation of the law by persons whom the offender respects, then according to these theories we should expect greater conformity with law following such practices.

Barton (2003) proposes that restorative justice works by intervening in moral disengagement. In offending against another, individuals "will tend to silence their conscience by means of various internal mechanisms of moral disengagement" (p. 50). Of course, the assumption here is that offenders have a conscience or sense of morality that proscribes doing what they did, an assumption not inconsistent with the optimistic attitude restorative justice proponents tend to hold concerning human nature. Barton refers to Albert Bandura's four mechanisms of moral disengagement by which the perpetrator of a harmful deed silences her or his conscience: morally justifying the deed, reducing one's personal responsibility, denying the harmfulness of the deed, and derogating the victim. These mechanisms are roughly comparable to Sykes and Matza's (1957) techniques of neutralization, and interventions to disable their use among known offenders are already featured in cognitively oriented correctional interventions (Andrews & Bonta, 2001). Barton's thinking is that encountering victims—and seeing and hearing what the crime did to them—is *uniquely* disabling to these means of disengaging. He proposes, "When victims tell offenders face-to-face about the harm the offenders' actions have caused, offenders' internal mechanisms of disengagement are seriously challenged and, in most cases, reversed" (Barton, 2003, p. 50).

Barton's theory of crime reduction based on moral engagement pertains exclusively to restorative justice programs that convene victim–offender encounters. Theories that emphasize strain (Agnew, 1992) and deficient social control (Hirschi, 1969) as the causes of offending pertain to those restorative justice programs that do not involve encounter but address offender needs. For example, a restorative justice program might intervene in offending patterns to the extent that the program contributes to the development of "competencies" among offenders (see Bazemore, 1991). A community member might offer job training and a job to the participant who perpetrated a property crime. This participant may thus gain the social capital that can serve as a hedge against future offending.

Finally, restorative justice practices may reduce reoffending by helping the offender to tell a new story about her- or himself. The dialogue featured in many restorative justice practices invites a renarrating of the past and a redemptive script for the future, which Maruna (2001) has identified as conducive to desistance from crime. Theories of narrative—in the social sciences and in literary studies—suggest that "one's story" is actually a collaborative production and that we act based on our stories (Bruner, 1990). As Braithwaite (2006) writes, "In restorative justice conferences, after each individual has their stories listened to, new stories that allow new identities are coauthored by a plurality of stakeholders in the injustice" (p. 428).

Note that each of the foregoing theories engages with some or all of the concepts of the dominant criminological theories, such as strain, learning, control, and labeling theories. As suggested earlier in regard to strain and control theories, the dominant theories can thus also explain restorative justice effects on criminal behavior. In addition, restorative justice practices can be seen as reinforcing positive conduct (social learning theory) or undermining "criminal" labels (labeling theory). However, the theories previously reviewed (e.g., theories of reintegrative shaming or revised narratives) go beyond the mainline theories in explicitly assigning causal roles to dialogue, relationship building, and communication of moral values. In that sense, they are truer to the aims of restorative justice.

Theories of Victim Healing

Victim healing is central to restorative justice. The goals of crime reduction and control ought not overshadow the goal of healing (Presser, Gaarder, & Hesselton, 2007). It follows that theories of restorative justice must give pride of place to theories of victim healing.

How is restorative justice practice supposed to help victims heal? The answer depends on what healing is thought to consist in. In some cases, healing can be tangible, such as compensation for destroyed or stolen property, or recovery from broken bones sustained during a robbery. The restitution agreements made via a restorative justice practice, if kept, thus can help in healing. Restitution can be used to replace property or to pay medical bills.

Victims generally experience a need for *emotional* healing. This is as true for victims of many property crimes as it is for victims of violence (Deem, Nerenberg, & Titus, 2007). Restorative justice stands to promote victim healing far more than interventions associated with criminal justice, which are largely neglectful of victims (see Kelly & Erez, 1997) and may even revictimize them. Judith Herman (1997) squarely makes this argument: "If one set out by design to devise a system for provoking intrusive posttraumatic symptoms, one could do not better than a court of law" (p. 72). Some crime victims are especially ill-treated by police officers, prosecutors, and/or judges. These include victims of rape and battering—crimes that, by their threat, oppress all women. But Daly and Stubbs (2006) note that use of restorative justice practices to address such crimes might provide the offender with a forum for further manipulation or abuse, and possibly communicates that the crime is not serious enough to warrant such punishment as the formal system metes out. These scholars also consider the *potential* for restorative justice to give victims a voice and an opportunity for validation of harms, which formal justice systems, at their best, have not done.

Bracketing these contrasting potentialities, I turn again to theories. Several theories can be advanced as to how restorative justice might emotionally heal victims. I identify three, which concern communication of the victim's worth, social reintegration of victims, and communication about moral (dis)order.

With acknowledgment of the crime and its effects and assurances that it was wrong, restorative justice participants would convey the basic worth of the victim. According to the late philosopher Jean Hampton (1988), the essential degradation of criminal victimization lies in its implicit or explicit message that the victim is less than the offender. The positive promise of retribution, she finds, is that it degrades the offender and thus counters the message that the victim is less than the offender.

Hampton observes that punishment has come to signify the victim's worth to the punishing collective. But punishment need not be the signifier of the victim's worth. Instead of bringing the offender down to the level to which she or he has brought the victim, we could do something to raise the victim up. It need not be the "ticker-tape parade" that Hampton playfully suggests (p. 128), but we could do far more to communicate, emphatically and publicly, that the victim should not have been hurt as she or he was. That message is clearest if the offender expresses remorse and apologizes. But even hearing an offender's relative or a neighbor say, "That should not have happened to you" can be restorative. Hampton's philosophy of retribution thus works as a theory of victim healing via restorative justice, especially those restorative justice programs that invite community members to participate.

Trouble lies in the possibility that restorative justice participants do not convey a message of victim worth—a message that they did not deserve to experience what they did. Rather, encounters might provide the offender or community members with a forum for reaffirming disrespect toward the victim. Such a hazard gives us pause when we consider the circumstances under which victims should meet with offenders and their supporters. The generally accepted guideline for *voluntary* participation of both victims and offenders is geared toward avoiding that hazard. Other guidelines are relevant here as well, pertaining to the order of speech in encounter programs (Barton, 2003), the screening of offenders (Presser & Lowenkamp, 1999) and victims, and the exclusion of certain crimes (e.g., battering) in which disrespect is an entrenched feature of the victim–offender relationship. In my view, however, because honest dialogue cannot be scripted in advance, the risk that dialogue will cause further trauma cannot be *completely* eliminated.

Crime can leave victims feeling alone, and isolation can compound the experience of degradation (Herman, 1997). Restorative justice programs that bring community members together, such as family group conferences and community circles, can assist victims in reconnecting with other people. Barton (2003) has been explicit about the restorative justice goal of victim reintegration. The victim's experience of reintegration relies not merely on "getting together" with other people. It relies also on telling one's story and having one's story taken as truth, discussing one's needs and getting help in meeting them, and expressing emotions and having those emotions acknowledged. As Herman (1997) writes, "Recovery can take place only within the context of relationships; it cannot occur in isolation" (p. 133).

Finally, restorative justice programming may reaffirm a sense of moral order for the victim. Crime can undermine victims' erstwhile belief that the world makes sense and that they control what happens to them. As a result, many victims feel confused and helpless (Herman, 1997). A victim–offender conference, where one confronts and questions the wrongdoer (e.g., "Why me?"), can recover a sense of an orderly world and personal power in that world. Alternatively, the conference may reveal that one actually had and has limited control over one's experiences (e.g., the victim was randomly chosen), and *this* might be a source of comfort (i.e., the victim did nothing wrong) or even spiritual enlightenment (Zehr, 2001). As spiritual writer Eckhart Tolle (2005) explains, "[T]he irruption of disorder into a person's life, and the resultant collapse of a mentally defined meaning, can become the opening into a higher order" (p. 196).

Theories of Community Building

From some perspectives, the essence of restorative justice is in community building or change. The expression *restorative community justice* is common (e.g., Bazemore & Schiff, 2001; Young, 1995). Clear and Karp (1999) subsume their discussion of restorative justice under that of community justice. And Sullivan and Tifft (2005) call for a restorative justice that transforms unjust social structures.

In the short run, a restorative justice conference brings people together to address a problem of common concern. As Nils Christie (1977) is famous for noting, interpersonal conflicts are the stuff with which healthy interpersonal relationships are forged. When government agents deal with citizens' conflicts for them, as is the case in developed societies, communities are weakened (see also McKnight, 1995).

In the long run, the values of restorative justice might infuse our society culturally (Harris, 1991). The restorative justice emphasis on harms and needs might influence public policies, including but not limited to criminal justice policies. If injustice is tolerance of unmet needs, then courtrooms might take more seriously the injustice of, say, constricted economic choice that causes poverty and despair. Yet, some charge restorative justice with simply reproducing societal inequalities. How so? If a restorative justice program is an adjunct of the criminal justice system, it will usually take the state's designations of "victim" and "offender" as given and not question them (Presser & Hamilton, 2006). As discussed previously, an unimpeded restorative justice conference might provide a new forum for the offender to bully or to show disrespect toward the victim. Or, the scripting of restorative justice dialogue might adhere to institutionalized inequalities, as when young offenders must abase themselves before adult victims (Arrigo & Schehr, 1998).

Observing that generally held values may be oppressive and thus that "justice" often requires transformation and not just restoration, Hudson (2003) states that restorative justice encounters can "not only perform the norm-affirming expressive role of adversarial criminal justice; it can also perform an additional, norm-creating role" (p. 444). Hudson sees the potential for restorative justice dialogues as resembling Habermas's "'ideal speech situation,'" with all "participants expressing their viewpoints and needs" and being heard (ibid.). The restorative justice philosophy is compatible with Collins's (1981) view of social structures as aggregations of human encounters. Thus, restorative justice is indeed compatible with, and might further, change to societies.

CONCLUSION

This chapter examined the nature of restorative justice and theories of how restorative justice works. Studies of restorative justice are usually concerned with restorative justice as a means of reducing the reoffense rates of participating offenders. In fact, restorative justice sets its sights on far more than recidivism reduction, because it serves victims *and* community members *and* offenders. As we have seen, several theories explain how restorative justice might achieve its goals. The next step is many careful program evaluations, both to discover what programs are accomplishing, if anything, and to discover how.

DISCUSSION QUESTIONS

1. Why is dialogue important to restorative justice?

2. What theories explain how restorative justice might help victims to heal?

3. What theories explain how restorative justice might help reduce crime?

4. What theories explain how restorative justice might help build communities?

5. Why should restorative justice planners take care in planning victim–offender encounters?

6. Could harming offenders be compatible with doing restorative justice? Explain.

7. How could restorative justice practices reproduce societal inequalities?

8. How could restorative justice practices transform societies?

NOTES

1. This excerpt is taken from Presser and Hamilton's (2006) study of a victim-offender mediation program with young offenders, p. 332.
2. From Gaarder, 2008, p. 6.

REFERENCES

Abend, G. (2008). The meaning of "theory." *Sociological Theory, 26*(2), 173–199.
Agnew, R. (1992). Foundation for a general strain theory of crime and delinquency. *Criminology, 30*(1), 47–88.
Andrews, D. A., & Bonta, J. (2001). *The psychology of criminal conduct* (3rd ed.). Cincinnati, OH: Anderson.
Arrigo, B. A., & Schehr, R. C. (1998). Restoring justice for juveniles: A critical analysis of victim–offender mediation. *Justice Quarterly, 15*(4), 629–666.

Barton, C. K. B. (2003). *Restorative justice: The empowerment model*. Sydney, Australia: Hawkins Press.

Bazemore, G. (1991). New concepts and alternative practice in community supervision of juvenile offenders: Rediscovering work experience and competency development. *Journal of Crime and Justice, 14*(2), 27–52.

Bazemore, G. (1997). Evaluating community youth sanctioning models: Neighborhood dimensions and beyond. In *Crime and place: Plenary papers of the 1997 Conference on Criminal Justice Research and Evaluation* (pp. 23–49). National Institute of Justice (NIJ) Research Forum. Washington, DC: U.S. Department of Justice, NIJ.

Bazemore, G., & Schiff, M. (2001). *Restorative community justice: Repairing harms and transforming communities*. Cincinnati, OH: Anderson.

Braithwaite, J. (1989). *Crime, shame, and reintegration*. Cambridge, UK: Cambridge University Press.

Braithwaite, J. (2002). *Restorative justice and responsive regulation*. New York: Oxford University Press.

Braithwaite, J. (2006). Narrative and "compulsory compassion." *Law and Social Inquiry, 31*(2), 425–446.

Bruner, J. (1990). *Acts of meaning*. Cambridge, MA: Harvard University Press.

Christie, N. (1977). Conflicts as property. *The British Journal of Criminology, 17*(1), 1–15.

Clear, T. R., & Karp, D. R. (1999). *The community justice ideal: Preventing crime and achieving justice*. Boulder, CO: Westview Press.

Collins, R. (1981). On the microfoundations of macrosociology. *American Journal of Sociology, 86*(5), 984–1014.

Daly, K. (2002). Restorative justice: The real story. *Punishment and Society, 4*(1), 55–79.

Daly, K., & Stubbs, J. (2006). Feminist engagement with restorative justice. *Theoretical Criminology, 10*(1), 9–28.

Deem, D., Nerenberg, L., & Titus, R. (2007). Victims of financial crime. In R. C. Davis, A. J. Lurigio, & S. Herman (Eds.), *Victims of crime* (3rd ed., pp. 125–146). Thousand Oaks, CA: Sage.

Duff, R. A. (2002). Restorative punishment and punitive restoration. In L. Walgrave (Ed.), *Restorative justice and the law* (pp. 82–100). Devon, UK: Willan.

Gaarder, E. (2008, June 6). Sentencing circles and domestic violence: Examining a pilot project in Minnesota. Paper presented at the annual meeting of the Justice Studies Association, Fairfax, VA.

Hampton, J. (1988). The retributive idea. In J. G. Murphy & J. Hampton, *Forgiveness and Mercy* (pp. 111–161). Cambridge: Cambridge University Press.

Harris, M. K. (1991). Moving into the new millennium: Toward a feminist vision of justice. In H. E. Pepinsky & R. Quinney (Eds.), *Criminology as Peacemaking* (pp. 83–97). Bloomington: Indiana University Press.

Herman, J. L. (1997). *Trauma and recovery: The aftermath of violence—From domestic abuse to political terror* (2nd ed.). New York: Basic Books.

Hirschi, T. (1969). *Causes of delinquency*. Berkeley: University of California Press.

Hudson, B. (2003). Restorative justice: The challenge of sexual and racial violence. In G. Johnstone (Ed.), *A restorative justice reader: Texts, sources, context* (pp. 438–450). Devon, UK: Willan.

Kelly, D. P., & Erez, E. (1997). Victim participation in the criminal justice system. In R. C. Davis, A. J. Lurigio, & W. G. Skogan (Eds.), *Victims of crime* (2nd ed., pp. 231–244). Thousand Oaks, CA: Sage.

Maruna, S. (2001). *Making good: How ex-convicts reform and rebuild their lives.* Washington, DC: American Psychological Association.

McKnight, J. (1995). *The careless society: Community and its counterfeits.* New York: Basic Books.

Presser, L. (2004). Justice here and now: A personal reflection on the restorative and community justice paradigms. *Contemporary Justice Review, 7*(1), 101–106.

Presser, L., Gaarder, E., & Hesselton, D. (2007). Imagining restorative justice beyond recidivism. *Journal of Offender Rehabilitation, 46*(1/2), 163–176.

Presser, L., & Hamilton, C. A. (2006). The micro-politics of victim offender mediation. *Sociological Inquiry, 76*(3), 316–342.

Presser, L., & Lowenkamp, C. T. (1999). Restorative justice and offender screening. *Journal of Criminal Justice, 27*(4), 333–343.

Presser, L., & Van Voorhis, P. (2002). Values and evaluation: Assessing processes and outcomes of restorative justice programs. *Crime and Delinquency, 48*(1), 162–188.

Sherman, L. (1993). Defiance, deterrence, and irrelevance: A theory of the criminal sanction. *Journal of Research in Crime and Delinquency, 30,* 445–473.

Sullivan, D., & Tifft, L. (2005). *Restorative justice: Healing the foundations of our everyday lives* (2nd ed.). Monsey, NY: Willow Tree Press.

Sykes, G. M., & Matza, D. (1957). Techniques of neutralization: A theory of delinquency. *American Sociological Review, 22*(December), 664–670.

Tolle, E. (2005). *A new Earth: Awakening to your life's purpose.* New York: Plume.

Tyler, T. R. (2006). *Why people obey the law.* Princeton, NJ: Princeton University Press.

Umbreit, M. S., Coates, R. B., & Vos, B. (2007). Restorative justice dialogue: A multi-dimensional, evidence-based practice theory. *Contemporary Justice Review, 10*(1), 23–41.

Van Ness, D., & Strong, K. H. (2006). *Restoring justice: An introduction to restorative justice* (3rd ed.). Cincinnati, OH: LexisNexis/Anderson.

Walgrave, L., & Aertsen, I. (1996). Reintegrative shaming and restorative justice: Interchangeable, complementary or different? *European Journal on Criminal Policy and Research, 4*(4): 67–85.

Weitekamp, E. G. M. (1999). The history of restorative justice. In G. Bazemore & L. Walgrave (Eds.), *Restorative juvenile justice: Repairing the harm of youth crime* (pp. 75–102). Monsey, NY: Criminal Justice Press.

Young, M. A. (1995). *Restorative community justice: A call to action.* Washington, DC: National Organization for Victim Assistance.

Zehr, H. (1995). *Changing lenses: A new focus for crime and justice.* Scottdale, PA: Herald Press.

Zehr, H. (2001). *Transcending: Reflections of crime victims.* Intercourse, PA: Good Books.

Zehr, H. (2002). *The little book of restorative justice.* Intercourse, PA: Good Books.

23 Garbage In, Garbage Out?

Convict Criminology, the Convict Code, and Participatory Prison Reform[1]

Alan Mobley

The prison experience and its aftermath have been the subjects of much study and description. In different ways and with varying degrees of success, scholars (e.g., Clemmer, 1958; Jacobs, 1977; Johnson, 2002; Stern, 1998; and Sykes, 1958), journalists (e.g., Conover, 2000; Earley, 1992), and current and former prisoners (e.g., Abbott, 1981; Cleaver, 1968; Hassine, 1999; Irwin, 1970, 2005; and Jackson, 1970) have sought to chronicle the pain, degradation, and emotional devastation of incarceration. In spite of these efforts, the present authors are inclined to believe that much remains to be told. Although we hold confidence in the possibility that sensitive people can achieve a conceptual understanding of "doing time" without having to experience prison for themselves, we respectfully maintain that an intellectual understanding of prison is not enough.

Our task in this chapter is to provide some sense of the many intangibles implicit in a prisoner perspective on incarceration. Someday, humans may have the ability to download sensate experience directly, but until that day it seems that the best we can do for our readers is to analogize. Instead of laboring to induce empathy, we will try to convey some of the learning we have acquired as a result of occupying—indeed, embodying—the convict perspective. The named author has passed 10 years in prison and 5 more on parole. His collaborators tally decades more behind bars, and some remain there still. The analogy that presents itself as most like the psychological cesspool of prison is the locker room: a high school or college locker room for male athletes.

In your mind's eye, fill out the room, if you will, with damp and sweat, stench and soiled belongings. Now, put in place a large number—too large for the room—of opposing athletes. Watch some gamely strut and posture while others withdraw into the self-imposed isolation of daydreams and consuming, reflexive thought. Feel the hypermasculinity manifested in shouted expletives and grunting sexual innuendo. Observe the sophomoric humor and carelessly displayed bodily functions.

Think of those participating in the antics as World Wrestling performers. See their legendary menace and outrageous, provocative acts. Now consider, quite seriously, that they are not acting, that they see their individual performances as competitive, as vital to their integrity and personal safety. Consider that they view one another as lethal threats. Throw in one or two officials who are paid to keep an eye on things but who make going home safely every night their top priority. Now, finally, go ahead and step into the locker room yourself, and seal the door behind you. How do you feel? If you have conscientiously engaged in this exercise, you now have a reasonable approximation of prison. Enjoy your stay.

Mass Incarceration in America

From 1970 to 1988, the prison population in the United States tripled (Bureau of Justice Statistics, 1989). In the next 12 years, it tripled again, threatening to fill prisons faster than states could build them (Lynch, 2000). The incarceration business is said to employ 747,000 people and involve over $37 billion in expenditures (Jacobson, 2005, pp. 67–70). California now spends more on prisons than on the state university system. The electoral passage of Proposition 21 in California, which allows prosecutors to try accused criminal perpetrators 14 years old and above as adults, has at least symbolically impacted the state's prisons by bringing children—disproportionate numbers of minority children—into the adult justice system.

Advocates for the rights of racial minorities are alarmed at this new development, since overcrowding and racial segregation may worsen prevailing conditions both in prisons and in mostly minority neighborhoods. The life chances of African American and Latino males are already diminished by their frequent interaction with the criminal justice system (Miller, 1996; Western, 2007). Across the country, they are overrepresented in the new cohorts of specially selected penal detainees (Mauer, 1999; Mauer & King, 2007). Critics of the expanding prison-industrial complex complain that offender incapacitation is just the latest punitive twist in the continuing legacy of America's hot and cold running fascination with race-based social engineering (Clear, 2007; Gordon, 1999).

Criticisms of penal expansion and its variations are not new. Auerhahn (1999) convincingly shows that the underlying rationales supporting incapacitation have been repeatedly challenged on conceptual, ethical, and methodological grounds. Even the chief architect of selective incapacitation, the Rand

Corporation's Peter Greenwood (with colleague Susan Turner, 1987), later disputed the efficacy of profiling and targeting selected groups for incarceration.

Some proponents of penal incapacitation responded to criticism by crediting the policy with lowered crime rates in U.S. cities and towns. Officially compiled crime rates do show that some categories of major crimes are down 15% to 20% and more (Austin et al., 2009; Lichtblau, 1999). It is uncertain to what extent we can credit the decrease in crime to the increase in the number of the incarcerated.

The so-called War on Drugs has brought other groups into prison besides the traditionally oppressed minorities. Among them are the middle class. These convicts have had some impact on the prison system, and the system has deeply affected them. Some have gone on to make the study of prison their lifework. Most of these are reformers. Their energy, it is said, comes from the poignant observation that "you can take the man out of prison, but it's hard to take the prison out of the man." Some of these folks, mostly male, mostly of European American extraction, have grouped together under the banner of convict criminology.

Convict Criminology

It is fair to say that convict criminology was brought into being by the War on Drugs. Although the large majority of people swept into prisons by the wars on drugs and crime have been minority, poor, and poorly educated, another subgroup has been brought along, mostly for the ride, it seems. This group, mostly of European American extraction and middle class, found itself imported into a world of strange customs and moral codes. The prison experience itself, far from being routine and an accepted rite of passage, was bizarre. Some individuals within this group began to look upon the prison as an object of study and brought the culture of prison into their inquiry as well. They have become known, at least in their initial foray into research and publishing, as *convict criminologists*. The form and function of prisons in America was taken up as their first object of study.

Convict criminology began as an organizing effort to bring the human back into prison scholarship. In the mid-1990s, agitated by a curriculum void of any indication that those persons referred to as criminals, inmates, and offenders were also flesh-and-blood human beings, Chuck Terry and Alan Mobley—two University of California, Irvine, graduate students—met regularly to share strong coffee and even stronger opinions reflecting their convicted perspective.

Soon, Terry and Mobley realized that what they saw in their course materials as the dehumanization of justice system clients existed at an even more profound level at professional conferences. As intense immersions in the thought, politics, and personalities of a profession, these professional conferences were both repulsive and alienating for Terry and Mobley. From these intense experiences came the pair's desire to step beyond conventional criminology and make their own way. Mobley soon began to pursue social justice activism, prison reform, and fieldwork-based scholarship. Terry, however, sought out other academics who shared an incarcerated past. His research revealed several former prisoners teaching criminal justice and sociology at U.S. universities. As he began to share his misgivings over criminological study and practice, these new colleagues responded with a litany of their own concerns.

Sparked by the collective sentiment, Terry wanted change. Rather than continue to toil in relative isolation among the conventionally minded, he thought that the ex-con criminologists ought to take a tip from Narcotics Anonymous (a group to which he belonged) and form a mutual-aid support group. When one of his graduate school advisors suggested he organize a panel of ex-con academics for the upcoming American Society of Criminology (ASC) meeting, Terry did the legwork. As luck would have it, his advisor also happened to be on the conference organizing committee and could see to it that the panel was seated. So, out of frustration, comradeship, and with logistical help from a sympathetic insider, Convict Criminology was born (Terry, 2003).

Convict criminology was announced as a "new school" in a 2001 issue of the journal *Social Justice* (Richards & Ross, 2001). An edited volume titled *Convict Criminology* was released in 2003 (Ross & Richards, 2003). As defined, "Convict Criminology represents the work of convicts or ex-convicts, in possession of a Ph.D. or on their way to completing one, or enlightened academics and practitioners, who contribute to a new conversation about crime and corrections" (Ross & Richards, 2003, p. 6).

Several principles were declared as core to this new school. Among them were the failure of prisons, the value of taking an insider perspective, the centrality of ethnography, and the preeminence of noted penologist and ex-convict John Irwin.

Irwin is the author of several works of penology (Irwin, 1970; 1980; 1985; 2005; Irwin & Austin, 2000) that have achieved the status of classics in the field. His work combines social analysis with descriptive statistics and ethnography. For his latest book, *The Warehouse Prison,* Irwin gained access to California state prisons, where he assembled groups of convicts with whom he met over a 2-1/2-year period. Irwin credits them with contributing significantly to the book. The group "shared ideas, descriptions, and analyses of prisoner behavior and relationships. These 'experts' read and critiqued drafts of most of the book's chapters. They [10 prisoners] have served a total of 207 years in prison" (Irwin, 2005, p. ix).

Following Irwin's lead, convict criminologists offer an often blistering critique of U.S. penal justice and mainstream criminology. Often, the two are lumped into one lucrative, self-perpetuating machine (see Ross & Richards, 2003). Convict criminologists use their academic credentials to argue for their own analytical abilities, if not their objectivity, and burnish their pasts as further validation of the insights and recommendations they offer. They challenge the standard bearers of the mainstream to let them in and heed their words, and to an extent they have been successful. Since the first conference panel in 1997, Convict Criminology has grown tremendously. The group now boasts three very well-attended panels at criminology's flagship conference and other national and regional meetings, dozens of journal articles and books, a website (see: http://www.convictcriminology.org/index.html) that offers everything from consulting services to advice for prisoners wanting to attend college, and most importantly, many new cohort members. In short, Convict Criminology is productive and growing.

As might be expected, countercriticism has come from the criminological mainstream. *The New York Times* quoted one prominent criminologist as implying that convict criminologists lack objectivity, asking, "What convict criminologist is going to say people are in prison because they have low self-control and lower I.Q. scores?" (St. John, 2003, p. 7). The prominent mainstream criminologist goes on: "There's a tendency among convict criminologists to say, 'Because I've been there, I know and you don't.' Being there gives you access to some information, but not all the information. It illuminates and it distorts" (ibid.).

A more subtle form of critique is the exclusion of convict criminology from the discipline's leading journals. This does not surprise the convict criminologists, however, as they see their exclusion as further proof of scholarly complicity with a negligent (and perhaps malign) government in furthering a mutually beneficial prison-industrial complex (see Ross & Richards, 2003, pp. 18, 41, 349). John Irwin sets the tone in the preface to *Convict Criminology*, when he states the need for a convict perspective within the larger, ill-informed discipline: "Not only do we have to push, we have to guide them" (Ross & Richards, 2003, p. xviii).

The prison is one place where all agree that convict criminologists can serve as useful guides. In what follows, we discuss the legendary convict code and its more recent variation (for the traditional treatment of the "inmate code," see Sykes and Messinger, 1960).

The Convict Code

Modern American prisons are largely self-contained establishments operating behind barbed-wire-topped fences and razor wire rolls. Within the confines of penal institutions, prisoners live, work, and play, providing all manner of services necessary for the continued safety, security, and sanitation of their community. Off hours are passed in leisure activities not so different from the outside world's. Prisoners read; watch television; engage in sports, games, and hobbies; eat junk food; and sleep. A prisoner's incarcerated life is lived in a compressed, communal lifestyle, no doubt much altered from whatever manner of living the imprisoned knew when free (see Wacquant, 2001, and Anderson, 1998, for different views on the exclusivity of the prison experience).

Prior to the introduction of congregate-style prisons, prisoners passed their days in silence and solitude. Meals were taken, labor performed, and all activities carried out within each individual prisoner's cell. No particularly new mode of living was imparted to prisoners; they were simply expected to utilize the time their sentences allowed to make peace with themselves and with God. Reaching the goal of inner peace was more than some prisoners could manage, however, and methods of incarceration were implemented that were essentially like those used today.

Adapting to limited personal autonomy, enforced material and heterosexual deprivation, and the rigors of communal living among strangers necessitated the development of norms, rules, and roles appropriate to the peculiar world of the prison. Solitary confinement had made for peacefully running prisons, and the shift to prisoners working together to perform institutional tasks was rough. Congregate living did ease high rates of suicide and insanity among prisoners, but it replaced those hazards with violence. Frustrated convicts spent their rage upon one another, finally settling into regular patterns of transactions, exchanges, and interactions that permitted each prisoner an opportunity to survive according to his strength and cunning. Two rules in particular emerged as conducive to peaceful, individualized communal living: "Do your own time" and "Don't snitch."

Both these rules mainly concern the effects of prisoner actions on other prisoners. "Doing your own time" entails not bothering others, while "not snitching" means not involving officials or other convicts in one's private affairs. Our contention here is that these two behavioral guidelines are not only obsolete and in disuse but, through a lingering sense of their continuing validity, actually serve to undermine the ability of prisoners to rehabilitate themselves. A new basis for interaction between incarcerates, between prisoners and staff, and between prison society and the outside world can interrupt our prisons' current spiral toward stupefaction or anarchy and serve the best interests of all who participate in good faith.

Before explaining the fundamentals of a new convict code, however, we will review the original code, its current state, and some causes of its demise.

The Original Convict Code

The convict code is a short set of principles that serve as guidelines for interactions between convicts, convicts and jailers, and convicts and the outside world. The convict code recognizes that each prisoner has different goals and desires to fulfill within a highly circumscribed environment of scarce resources. The convict code also encourages each prisoner to acknowledge the commonality of circumstances all prisoners face. No matter what a prisoner chooses to do with his time, all are subjected to the same limitations that coerced, unisexual incarceration brings.

By explicitly identifying the predicaments of imprisonment as universal to all convicts, while simultaneously admitting the validity of diverse individual pursuits among the prisoner population, the convict code of conduct was intended to provide for peaceful, individualized, communal living.

Rule 1: Do Your Own Time

The vague but fundamental rule "Do your own time" typifies the code. "Do your own time" implies the uncomfortable fact that each convict is essentially alone. Each was judged alone, sentenced alone, admitted to prison alone, and will be released completely alone. The criminal justice system places other individuals in extremely close proximity and in remarkably similar circumstances to each convicted individual, but the salient point of imprisonment, time to be served, belongs/applies to each individual alone. Because of this simple fact, that each prisoner's sentence (or "time") is his to serve alone, each individual in prison is separate from the start. The question is not, How and when do we get out? It is, How can I get out?

Obtaining release appears to be a main goal of nearly all prisoners. The actions in which a convict chooses to engage can often either speed or delay the release process, however. Participation in activities that can prolong a prisoner's sentence, such as fights, killings, escape attempts, or drug use, is therefore a highly personal decision affecting the decision maker, his confederates, and possibly victims. Being drawn into such situations unexpectedly is a convict's worst nightmare. As defense against this possibility, a high degree of external awareness is advisable at all times.

"Doing your own time" means one should mind one's own business so as not to become involved in the potentially dangerous escapades of others. Strengthening oneself as a preventative measure against possible victimization is a second goal of this rule. When a convict follows the suggestion "Do your own time, don't let the time do you," he is careful not to let the deprivations of prison life get him down. When prisoners mope around in an attitude of self-pity, the chances of becoming entangled in confrontations with staff and other prisoners are greatly increased. A convict is a person who practices self-defense with the utmost vigilance. A convict can take a breather and relax when he goes home.

Safety

The issue of personal safety is the only issue that rivals obtaining release as a convict's priority. The convict code tries to restrict one's exposure to dangerous situations to those situations one willingly enters. For example, if a prisoner enters into a gang relationship for personal safety, drug accessibility, or any other reason, certain obligations are acquired. If a gang member is peacefully walking down a hallway and happens to see a fellow gang member being physically assaulted by one or more assailants, he is obligated to immediately enter the fray on the side of the compatriot. Such an action could result in injury or death immediately or in the future, or in an increased sentence should injury or death occur to another involved in the conflict. A prisoner knowingly assumes this sort of obligatory risk when voluntarily entering into a gang relationship. A prisoner who is unaffiliated with the gang, who walks by and witnesses the same incident, is under no obligation to put himself at risk. In fact, the convict code demands that bystanders be totally detached and not even look toward any event outside each one's immediate personal interest.

The prohibition against "rubbernecking," or looking at things or people beyond one's previously established parameters of legitimate interest, exists for two reasons. The first, essentially "What you don't know can't hurt you," alludes to the precariousness of witnessing any illegal act. If a passerby witnesses illegal or improper actions, that person can be seen as a possible informant and therefore threatens the perpetrators by his very existence. Strong feelings of mistrust born of personal or vicarious experience involving the treachery of informants, or "snitches," can build to the point of confrontations and preemptive violence. It is also standard procedure for the prison administration to segregate or "lock up" witnesses to serious events in order to interrogate them more effectively. If one fails to witness the activities of others, however, one bypasses exposure to such unpleasant involvements.

Privacy

A second reason why rubbernecking is derided, is simple privacy. Prisons are designed so that most every prisoner action occurs in a public, or at least a visible, space. There are windows in every door; lights never go completely off; and even the toilet stalls are open to view, the doors having been removed. In such a potentially degrading environment, where a total lack of privacy for inhabitants is institutionalized, prisoners must look to one another for whatever bits of privacy there are to be had. After all, usually only one or two officers patrol each living unit at any one time. Nearly every eye observing any prisoner's actions, therefore, belongs to a fellow convict. If prisoners have the consideration and discipline not to allow their eyes to wander into areas outside their immediate, legitimate concern, some vestige of personal privacy is possible for each individual. Not surprisingly, having a greater degree of privacy is often considered a more pleasant, dignified, and safer manner of living.

Personal Responsibility

Surviving the prison experience as comfortably as possible and allowing others to do the same is basic to the code. Each imprisoned individual is granted the right to say and do as he pleases. With this right comes the further implication that one's actions, because they are freely chosen, are representative of one's intentions. Prisoners' words and actions are assumed to demonstrate their thoughts, and others form judgments accordingly. Failure to defend one's words or actions when challenged sends a message that one is weak and can be exploited easily.

Exploitation

The nature of communal living, as well as the administration's perceived need to force all actions and interactions of prisoners into open spaces, guarantees tension over utilization of scarce resources. This tension is often prevented from becoming hostile and potentially dangerous competition by the implicit threat of retaliation against aggression. Retaliation against aggressors can be carried out by the offended party or by someone acting as his proxy. The possibility of retaliation by the state may be just as deterring as unsanctioned violence. If a prisoner is caught engaging in overt aggression by an officer or through the use of informants, privileges can be taken away and sentences lengthened. Prisoners acting aggressively to hoard resources or intimidate others are looked upon as intentionally challenging those chosen as victims. The convict code holds the aggressor responsible for his actions and thus liable to retaliation for encroachment on the rights of others. The code also provides for victims to rightfully seek revenge.

Actually, the convict code stipulates that those acting as aggressors must themselves be victimized by their victims. The manner of such retaliation should be disproportionately greater than the original offense. Those who fail to defend themselves, their speech, or their property violate the code. Compliant victims unwilling to retaliate against aggressors forfeit their "respect," that is, their right to expect others to treat them in accordance with the code. Victims who do not stand up for themselves are seen as both weak and failing to abide by the code's directions. In short, the convict code condones the exploitation of people who are unwilling or unable to defend themselves.

Opportunities to exploit others without fear of retaliation are rare in prison, so those who seek victims are drawn to individuals who have revealed a willingness to be victimized. If the degradation inflicted by "wolves" upon a "mark" becomes too great, the mark often seeks protection in the formal structure, either by requesting to be segregated (locked up) or by informing on victimizers so that they are segregated.

Rule 2: Don't Snitch

The use of informants by police agencies is responsible for a majority of arrests. In exchange for lesser sentences, money, or other considerations, individuals with knowledge of others' criminal culpability often provide incriminating evidence to police. Nearly all prisoners serving time in prison were convicted with the aid of informants, often former friends. As the conviction and incarceration experience is perceived to be the wellspring of a prisoner's troubles, individuals responsible for incarcerating others are particularly despised by convicts. Police officials and officers of the court are usually viewed quite unfavorably, but government informants, people ostensibly acting as criminals but actually helping law enforcement build cases against outlaws, are generally hated.

Many convicts presume that one small benefit of imprisonment is separation from informants. Everyone in close-custody prisons (fenced and guarded facilities) is there for conviction of a felony considered serious, a conviction most often made possible by the cooperation of an informant. Prisoners thus feel they should have some things in common: an identity as convicts, similar deprivations, and status as victims of informants. When a prisoner is identified as an informant, therefore, it causes a fissure in the social bond of prisoner society.

Life outside frequently permits individuals to let their guard down and be themselves. Prison life does not. With essentially no privacy and surrounded by mostly hostile or apathetic strangers, prisoners have no "back stage" in which to relax. The assumed presence of snitches within prisons influences convicts to cloak their acts with respect to how they may appear to others. Even if a prisoner is not doing anything significantly deviant, chances are he could be set up as another's "fall guy." Additionally, each prisoner knows that hardly a day goes by when he does not commit some sort of infraction of prison rules, and most prisoners have personal property in violation of known statutes. Even if the nature of one's deviance falls short of provoking severe official sanctions, such as segregation or additional time, just the prospect of being hassled by guards and having one's lifestyle disrupted is bothersome and threatening.

To illustrate this point, prisoners who possess items considered "serious" contraband—knives, syringes, tattoo guns, and so forth—usually do not store such things in their designated personal territory. Contraband is routinely tucked into hidden spots in public places, territory over which no single prisoner has responsibility or control. This sort of precaution against prosecution presupposes the eventuality of detection. Though snitches ensure that no one gets away with anything for long, if one avoids being caught red-handed with illicit goods, disciplinary action by the prison administration cannot usually be taken.

Prisoners who do not routinely engage in serious deviance still check their living areas for signs of tampering. Intrusion by guards, thieves, or set-up artists trying to plant evidence is not uncommon. In self-defense against loss of property or additional punishment, prisoners routinely police their primary personal territories. The fact that prisoners feel compelled to take precautions against theft or entrapment reveals the high level of mistrust present in captive society.

Thieves and snitches form an antisocial aggregate most responsible for the breakdown of community values in prison. Together, they create an atmosphere of defensiveness and suspicion that is perpetuated because each group feeds off the other. For example, thieves operate with near impunity because they know that snitches indirectly protect them. If a thief is caught by a prisoner and violence ensues, the victim of the theft will be punished by authorities as harshly as the thief. The convict code is supposed to protect the anonymity of both thieves and revenge-seeking victims of theft so that retribution against thievery can occur without official intervention. Snitches bring officials into privacy disputes and therefore undermine enforcement of the code.

Victims of thieves and snitches often see the wisdom of cutting their losses and simply writing off stolen articles and incidences of disrespect. Silent acceptance of ostensibly prohibited conduct has always occurred in prison. When, for example, the perpetrator of a proscribed act is an especially feared individual or one particularly well supported by a strong group, discretion on the victim's part becomes the wiser part of valor.

Snitches benefit from thieves in equal measure to the covert assistance given. When a rash of break-ins raises tensions, and the administration needs an arrest to quiet things, snitches provide the information. Those apprehended often avoid serious punishment because actual physical evidence of their guilt is rarely discovered. Snitches, however, still get credit from officials for cooperating at significant personal risk.

The existence of informants on the outside and snitches inside works to absolve individuals of a measure of responsibility for their own actions. Where dealings between individuals are based on at least some level of trust and expectation of mutual profit, activities involving bureaucratized structures revolve around procedures, laws, and regulations. Individual responsibility is replaced by systematized expediency where benefit accrues to the bureaucracy. Snitches bring third parties—police agents—into private affairs. The power relationship of any interaction between prisoners is fundamentally altered by including the bureaucracy. Involving the formal prison structure in informal private dealings takes the responsibility for and consequences of outcomes away from prisoners and places it in the hands of hostile administrators. Instead of trust and mutual benefit, prisoner interactions become forced, shaped by suspicion and fear.

Bringing the prospect of negative sanctions and lengthened incarceration to another's door is antithetical to the convict code. "Squealing" by prisoners compels officials to enter situations they could not otherwise involve themselves in. Since police agents dispense negative sanctions almost exclusively, little chance exists for prisoners to benefit from their inclusion in prisoner affairs. Snitching, squealing, and informing thus make a mockery of Rule 1, "Do your own time." For this fundamental reason, the proscription against snitching has always held a prominent position in the convict code. Snitching has traditionally been met with the most severe informal sanctions, including removal from the general population of prison society—one way or another.

Factors Undermining the
Convict Code/Formal Structure

As stated above, the two traditional premises underlying the convict code of conduct are "Don't squeal on other prisoners" and "Do your own time" (i.e., mind your own business). The second principle implies that it is forbidden to disturb anything other than oneself, one's relationships, and one's possessions. For example, bothering others by noisy or intrusive behavior is considered wrong. Listening in on, or "burglarizing," others' conversations or looking at what others are doing ("rubbernecking") are likewise inappropriate. Taking or in any way upsetting others' possessions or modes of lifestyle, called "routines," is forbidden as well.

Previous studies and anecdotal evidence suggest that belief in the validity of these elements of the informal convict code are fairly universal in U.S. prisons, especially higher-security prisons. Popular adherence to the code's dictates, however, has probably never been as consistent as hard-core convicts would like to believe. By and large, episodes of violence resulting from deviations from the code have kept alive the notion that the code is still a valid expression of prisoner ideals and a reliable guideline for prisoner action. The relative rarity of violent incidents in prison as compared with the generally high level of disrespectful behavior, however, illustrates how seldom the code is actually enforced.

Several factors have arisen in recent years to help break whatever real effectiveness the code once had. First, unprecedented growth in prison construction now enables authorities to more easily transfer prisoners between facilities and isolate prison leaders. Frequent transfers dilute prisoner solidarity, remove leaders from leadership positions, pacify prisoners by keeping them either farther from home or closer to it, and remove the threat of such negative social sanctions as ostracism and violent attacks, once the promised outcome of conduct code violations. Authorities now have the luxury of rewarding informants and punishing the rebellious through facility designation.

A second factor leading to the code's demise is the professionalization of correctional occupations. Authorities' unwillingness to allow prisoners to enforce informal codes and police themselves has removed an important ingredient of power from prisoner groups. Enforcement of informal rules through violence is no longer tacitly or implicitly permitted. Enforcers are now themselves harshly punished through additional time incarcerated and segregation from general population. Code enforcers are also transferred to other facilities as punishment for their informal roles. Their sacrifices for the common good are then unknown, unrecognized, and therefore unrewarded in unfamiliar, far-flung facilities.

The growing number of institutions in most prison systems has enhanced the trend toward professionalization of increasingly sought-after careers in corrections, as well as exposing the presence of individual code enforcers and informal leadership structures. Informants who reveal the secrets of captive society to officials can be protected by the anonymity of submergence in an ocean of inmates at one of any number of prisons. Bureaucratic tendencies to centralize expanding prison systems and staff institutions with better-trained personnel stem largely from the same causes that have boosted incidences of snitching. The criminalization of drug use and the prioritization of law enforcement resources against drugs criminals—known in recent years as the Drug War—is the central factor influencing the prison industry and the dissolution of the convict code itself.

Self-Concept

The rise of drug sales and consumption in the 1980s and 1990s led certain individuals into criminality who otherwise possessed mainstream sensibilities.

Stringent drug-law enforcement prompted by political pressures brought many of these users/dealers into contact with the criminal justice system. The experience of being taken from one's environment, stripped of possessions, separated from friends and family, and labeled a criminal often has a dramatic and apparently enlightening effect on offenders guilty of consensual crimes. Drug profiteers were often trying to reach approved societal goals but used inappropriate means to do so. (Criminology has long recognized this phenomenon. See Akers, 1997; Sykes & Messinger, 1960.) For individuals who have no real "outlaw" mentality, after feeling the power of negative social sanctions, the shift back to a more complete agreement with legal, socially approved norms is not difficult to envision.

Whether from upper-, middle-, or lower-class backgrounds, offenders without genuine criminal self-concepts typically adapt to the incarceration experience by throwing themselves upon the mercy of the criminal justice system and begging for release. Their common strategy is to prove to law enforcement officials that a terrible mistake has been made and a valuable lesson learned. The convict code, therefore, has little force or meaning for prisoners without criminal self-concepts. This self-styled "noncriminal" tries to impress officials by cooperating in every way. He works hard for nominal pay, keeps his living area up to prescribed standards, acts respectfully toward staff, withdraws from illicit elements of prison life, and informs, either baldly or surreptitiously, on other prisoners.

In medium- and lower-security institutions, these mostly Caucasian, noncriminal drug users and entrepreneurs comprise a substantial aggregate. The presence of such a large segment of prisoners disinterested in adherence to the convict code calls into question the code's relevance as a functioning normative system. Following the code's prescriptions once guaranteed prisoners' personal safety. In today's largely nonviolent medium- and lower-security institutions, however, adapting one's behavior to an existent prison subculture has become unnecessary. The threat to personal safety, and the subculture itself, have been invalidated by the introduction of relatively large numbers of uninitiated prisoners acting independently and unilaterally who are interested in only one thing: going home.

Gangbangers

Gangbangers are another large group of prisoners who fail to abide by the principles of the convict code. Interestingly, on the surface gangbangers are almost exact opposites of the mostly Caucasian, noncriminal drug user/entrepreneur. Gangbangers are primarily African Americans from homogeneous inner-city social environments. They appear to have completely assimilated criminal identities and consider doing time just another part of the criminal lifestyle. Like noncriminals, however, gangbangers have no use for the convict code. They care little what members of the general population think or do. Their alliances and allegiance are uniformly tied to outside gangs operating inside prison walls. So many young inner-city African American males are incarcerated that one's homeboys can be found in any penal institution. Young gangsters, therefore, need not trouble themselves to adapt their behavior to a prison subculture.

With their homeboys, gangsters comprise a distinct subculture themselves, whether on the streets or in prison. They "look out for," or protect, their own, live an almost familial lifestyle, and rarely so much as speak to prisoners outside their own set. No loyalties exist toward prisoners in general or to the ideal of a united convict society. Gang bangers "run with" their "dogs" from "the 'hood," meet up with each other in the joint, then plan to reunite again on home turf. No involvement with outsiders is needed or apparently desired.

This fragmentation of incarcerated African Americans into distinct gangs, whether Crips, Bloods, or others, mirrors a similar move made by Chicanos in the 1960s. Racial and ethnic minorities have long tended to congregate in large prison gangs (for reflections on a first-hand examination of racial tensions in California prisons, see Irwin, 1980). Neighborhood economic and protection associations merged with others of the same race in prison in order to provide a larger membership greater economic power and individual security. Particularly in large state prison systems, the formation of race-based groups led to strict voluntary racial segregation. Incidences of personal differences often escalated into tit-for-tat warfare, with a seemingly endless supply of gang "soldiers" ready to avenge attacks on "brothers." In self-defense, whites were forced to form similar associations, dropping in the name of survival the cliquishness typical of intra-Caucasian behavior.

Today, some state systems, such as California's, have had to adopt the extraordinary practice of designating certain prisons as the territory of certain gangs. Where once wings of particular prisons were segregated by race, now entire prisons are integrated racially but segregated according to gang affiliation. Internecine rivalries apparently arose around the struggle for control of prison groups. Leaders of smaller street gangs were reluctant to surrender their power and authority just because they were incarcerated. As more and more members of individual gangs were incarcerated, however, gang leaders saw less need to join larger, prison-based racial associations. Street gangs thus reformed within prison yards, with competition for traditional rackets soon flaring and then evolving into hostile and often violated truces.

Intraracial unity is no longer the norm in prison except in times of extreme interracial conflict. Prisoners brought into the penal system by increased law enforcement pressure on urban areas and mandatory prison terms for crack cocaine crimes look to alliances formed in neighborhoods for guidance, protection, and provision of material resources in prison.

The task of initiating prisoners into the prison subculture, once accomplished by means of a generalized code of conduct, is now successfully completed for a large number of prisoners by reliance on preprison affiliations. Whether they are Native Americans associating exclusively with members of their own tribe; voluntarily segregated gang members; old-timers; bank robbers, and dope fiends hanging out on the compound telling lies; or noncriminal drug entrepreneurs reverting to precriminal behavior patterns and beliefs, a majority of today's prisoners no longer need to feel accepted by a generalized inmate subculture. The convict code of conduct, therefore, which exists for the explicit purpose of initiating prison neophytes into captive society, is functionally obsolete.

A New Code

Today's convict would be well advised to admit several things and react accordingly. First, society has developed a habitual intolerance for deviance. Increased frustration with unsolved social problems has led politicians and the public to scapegoat societal out-groups as responsible. Political rhetoric that decried intolerance and punishment-laden responses to deviance born of inequality, although often heard during national election campaigns of past generations, has been dropped from public discourse. To pacify a frightened and worried public, policymakers continue to resort to higher levels of policing, criminalization of deviant behavior, and incarceration. Even though fiscal shortfalls will result in early releases for some prisoners and the elimination of parole supervision for others, this exercise in budgetary pragmatics should not be mistaken for a new, liberal wave in incarceration practices. In fact, reactionary measures and increased unpleasantness for prisoners should be anticipated. Budget cuts mean reduced programs and services for prisoners, and hard times tend to bequeath hard time.

Second, because policymakers have an apparent mandate to use whatever means are necessary to curb crime, factors contributing to the demise of the convict code will intensify in magnitude. More corrections infrastructure will be built, more professionalization of correctional occupations will occur, more noncriminal offenders and gang-oriented criminals will be incarcerated, and increased competition in overcrowded institutions for scarcer material resources will further splinter captive populations and promote the formation of antagonistic prison groups.

Third, due to these factors, prison officials now hold all the cards in their dealings with medium- and lower-security prisoners. Penal administrators will only be strengthened by prisoner uprisings. Any show of protest against social or penal policies will be met by harsher conditions, justified by the public's unwillingness to face and deal with social problems or the offspring of those problems. America's problem children are to be incarcerated for the foreseeable future because no one sees any long-term solutions.

Fourth, the high level of mistrust in prisons will intensify between prisoners themselves and between prisoners and politicians. Harsher sentencing and mandatory minimum prison terms for drug crimes have taken the carrot from government's traditional carrot-and-stick program. Prisoners of past years have had a glimmer of hope for early release through the parole mechanism. Even if apprehended, convicted, and sentenced, felons knew that, with good behavior, time incarcerated could be cut drastically. The pressure to inform on colleagues in order to avoid prison was there, but it was not nearly as strong as it is today, when little hope exists for meaningful sentence reduction.

The fate of prisoners and prison society depends partly on prisoners themselves. If convicts insist on perpetuating antagonism among themselves and toward prison staff, they play right into the hands of custody-oriented penal administrators. The structural antagonism between incarcerates and staff has reached its intended goal and serves only the interests of career bureaucrats, politicians, and corrections unions. Individual prisoners are not well served by prisons filled with tension and removed from mainstream culture; nor are their families, communities, or victims, and surely not the public. Convict criminology suggests that all groups can best be served if each is permitted a meaningful voice in the justice reform process. We hope that this chapter has provided some evidence for the value of the convict perspective.

DISCUSSION QUESTIONS

1. Why do you think incarceration rates have continued to climb in spite of falling crime rates? Is this a reasonable state of affairs?

2. What might you consider to be the pros and cons of convict criminologists in the classroom? What value do you place on experience in your own education?

3. What do you see as the appropriate role (if any) for prisons in a free society?

4. Many commentators take note of the distinct racial composition of U.S. prisons and jails. To what do you attribute the overrepresentation of racial minorities? What, if anything, should be done about it?

NOTE

1. This paper was prepared with the assistance of many current and former prisoners, particularly my friend and colleague, Chuck Terry. The collaborative nature of the project suggests to the named author that he honor his unnamed colleagues through the use of "we" throughout the narrative. We also acknowledge the patient assistance of Paul Jesilow, William Granados, Michael Braun, and the editors and peer reviewers of this volume in the preparation of this paper.

REFERENCES

Abbott, J. H. (1981). *In the belly of the beast: Letters from prison*. New York: Vintage Books.

Akers, R. (1997). *Criminological theories: Introduction and evaluation*. Los Angeles: Roxbury.

Anderson, E. (1998). *Code of the street: Decency, violence, and the moral life of the inner city*. New York: W.W. Norton.

Auerhahn, K. (1999). Selective incapacitation and the problem of prediction. *Criminology, 37*, 703–733.

Austin, J., Clear, T., Duster, T. Greenberg, D. F., Irwin, J., McCoy, C., et al. (2007). *Unlocking America: Why and how to reduce America's prison population*. Washington, DC: JFA Institute.

Bureau of Justice Statistics. (1989). *Prisoners in 1988*. Washington, DC: U.S. Government Printing Office.

Clear, T. (2007). *Imprisoning communities.* London: Oxford University Press.

Cleaver, E. (1968). *Soul on ice.* New York: McGraw-Hill.

Clemmer, D. (1958). *The prison community.* New York: Rinehart.

Conover, T. (2000). *Newjack: Guarding Sing Sing.* New York: Random House.

Earley, P. (1992). *The hot house: Life inside Leavenworth Prison.* New York: Bantam Books.

Gordon, A. F. (1999). Globalism and the prison industrial complex: An interview with Angela Davis. *Race and Class, 40,* 145–157.

Greenwood, P., & Turner, S. (1987). *Selective incapacitation revisited: Why the high-rate offenders are hard to predict.* Santa Monica, CA: Rand.

Hassine, V. (1999). *Life without parole: Living in prison today* (2nd ed.). Boston: Roxbury.

Irwin, J. (1970). *The felon.* Englewood Cliffs, NJ: Prentice Hall.

Irwin, J. (1980). *Prisons in turmoil.* Boston: Little, Brown.

Irwin, J. (1985). *The jail.* Berkeley: University of California Press.

Irwin, J. (2005). *The warehouse prison: Disposal of the new dangerous class.* Los Angeles: Roxbury.

Irwin, J., & Austin, J. (2000). *It's about time: America's imprisonment binge.* Belmont, CA: Wadsworth.

Jackson, G. (1970). *Soledad brother.* New York: Coward-McCann.

Jacobs, J. B. (1977). *Stateville.* Chicago: University of Chicago Press.

Jacobson, M. (2005). *Downsizing prisons: How to reduce crime and end mass incarceration.* New York: New York University Press.

Johnson, R. (2002). *Hard time: Understanding and reforming the prison.* Belmont, CA: Wadsworth.

Lichtblau, E. (1999, May 17). Crime rates continue record 7-year plunge. *Los Angeles Times,* p. A1.

Lynch, T. (2000, February 20). All locked up. *The Washington Post,* p. B07.

Mauer, M. (1999). *Race to Incarcerate.* New York: New Press.

Mauer, M., & King, R. (2007). *A 25-year quagmire: The "War on Drugs" and its impact on American society.* Washington, DC: The Sentencing Project.

Miller, J. (1996). *Search and destroy: African-American males in the criminal justice system.* Cambridge: Cambridge University Press.

Richards, S. C., & Ross, J. I. (2001). The new school of convict criminology. *Social Justice, 28*(1), 177–190.

Ross, J. I., & Richards, S. C. (2003). *Convict criminology.* Belmont, CA: Wadsworth.

Stern, V. (1998). *A sin against the future.* Boston: Northeastern University Press.

St. John, W. (2003, August 9). Professors with a past. *The New York Times,* p. 7. (Quoting University of Cincinnati criminal justice professor Francis Cullen).

Sykes, G. (1958). *The society of captives.* Princeton, NJ: Princeton University Press.

Sykes, G., & Messinger, S. (1960). The inmate social system. In R. Cloward et al. (Eds.), *Theoretical studies in social organization of the prison.* New York: Social Science Research Council.

Terry, C. M. (2003). From C-block to academia: You can't get there from here. In J. I. Ross & S. C. Richards (Eds.), *Convict criminology.* Belmont, CA: Wadsworth.

Wacquant, L. (2001). Deadly symbiosis. *Punishment and Society, 3*(1), 95–133.

Western, B. (2007). Mass imprisonment and economic inequality. *Social Research, 74*(2), 509–542.

Index _____

About the Editors _____

Mary Maguire is an assistant professor in the Division of Criminal Justice at California State University, Sacramento. She has published in the area of policing and is a recipient of an NIH pilot grant to study race and gender as it relates to police occupational stress. She has coauthored white papers for the State of California on sex offender management, and her current research focuses on moral panic and advocacy legislation related to sex offenders. Prior to her work as an assistant professor, Dr. Maguire had 15 years of clinical experience working with high-risk populations.

Dan Okada is an assistant professor in the Division of Criminal Justice at California State University, Sacramento. A Vietnam veteran, Dan earned his doctorate in criminology at the University of Maryland and has been on the faculties of California State University, Long Beach, and Marist College in Poughkeepsie, New York. He is currently editor-in-chief of *Contemporary Justice Review*. His research focuses on culture, crime, and intergenerational communication.

About the Contributors___

Janice Ahmad is an assistant professor in the Department of Criminal Justice at the University of Houston–Downtown, where she also serves as assistant chair. Dr. Ahmad's research interests include police management issues, citizen involvement in policing, women in policing, crime victims, and program evaluation. Dr. Ahmad earned her PhD in criminal justice at Sam Houston State University.

Michael Bachmann is an assistant professor of criminal justice at Texas Christian University. He received his PhD in sociology from the University of Central Florida in 2008 and his MA in social sciences from the University of Mannheim, Germany, in 2004. Dr. Bachmann specializes in the investigation of computer and high-tech crimes. His research focuses primarily on the social dimensions behind technology-driven crimes. He is the author of several book chapters and journal articles on cybercrime and cyber criminals.

Cyndi Banks is a professor of criminology and criminal justice at Northern Arizona University. She is known internationally for her work as a criminologist in the Asia/Pacific region and in Bangladesh, Sudan, East Timor, and Iraq, in the areas of international children's rights and juvenile justice legal reform, adult community corrections, justice policy, and integration. She has published widely on such topics as comparative and cultural criminology, international children's rights, professional women in the criminal justice system, gender and crime, indigenous women's incarceration, youth in juvenile institutions, and justice ethics. She is the author of six books and, most recently, a second edition of *Criminal Justice Ethics*.

Dimitri A. Bogazianos is an assistant professor of criminal justice at California State University, Sacramento. With a BA in philosophy, an MA in religious studies, and a PhD in criminology, law, and society, he has been involved with the exchange of ideas across disciplines for his entire intellectual trajectory. This diversity of perspectives, however, has been anchored by one fundamental focus: the context, form, function, and possibility of justice in its myriad expressions. And it is this diverse intellectual trajectory that continues to animate his approach to teaching as well as his primary research interests: the intersections of crime, culture, and the media industries. Currently, he is completing a book, to be published by New York University Press, that examines the merger of street crime and white-collar crime that has become the defining story of the rap music industry in the new millennium.

Meda Chesney-Lind is a professor of women's studies at the University of Hawaii at Manoa. Nationally recognized for her work on women and crime, her books include *Girls, Delinquency, and Juvenile Justice; The Female Offender: Girls, Women and Crime; Female Gangs in America; Invisible Punishment;* and *Girls, Women, and Crime.* She has just finished a book on trends in girls' violence, entitled *Beyond Bad Girls: Gender, Violence, and Hype,* published by Routledge.

Sharla J. "Kris" Cook is an adjunct instructor for criminal justice courses at California State University, Sacramento (CSUS). She earned master's degrees in logistics management from the Air Force Institute of Technology and in criminal justice from CSUS. Previously, she served as an active-duty U.S. Air Force officer and retired as a brigadier general. She has studied the topics of terrorism and counterterrorism at the National Defense University and CSUS. In 2008, she was named an academic fellow by the Foundation for Defense of Democracies (FDD), which included travel to Israel for a 10-day intensive course in terrorism and counterterrorism studies.

Christopher C. Cooper is a former officer with the Washington, D.C. (Metropolitan) Police and a former U.S. Marine sergeant; he served with the 2nd Reconnaissance Battalion and is an Iraq War veteran. Presently, he is a civil rights attorney based in Chicago. In 1987, he graduated from the City University of New York (John Jay College) Dispute Resolution Program. He is the author of approximately 36 publications, including books and peer-reviewed journal articles, most of which concern police training, the use of force, and conflict resolution processes. In 2009, he was awarded a Postdoctoral Fulbright Scholarship to study at the University of Akureyri, Iceland, on the Faculty of Law and Social Science. In 1996, he was a Postdoctoral Fulbright lecturer and researcher at the University of Copenhagen, Denmark, lecturing on and studying police conflict resolution processes. Dr. Cooper has taught at police academies and was an enlisted instructor of urban combat at The Basic School of the U.S. Marine Corps in Quantico, VA. He has been featured as a consultant on MSNBC, CNN, BBC, NPR, CBC, and other media outlets regarding police work and as a representative of the National Black Police Association. He can be contacted at cooperlaw3234@gmail.com.

John Crank is a professor and past director of the School of Criminal Justice and Criminology, University of Nebraska, Omaha. With 48 refereed publications and 5 books, he has published primarily in the area of the police and also has authored in the areas of counterterror issues, organizational theory, and philosophy of social science. His work *Imagining Justice* was chosen as the Academy of Criminal Justice Sciences' outstanding book in 2004.

Helen Taylor Greene is a professor and interim chair of the Department of Administration of Justice in the Barbara Jordan–Mickey Leland School of Public Affairs at Texas Southern University in Houston, Texas. She is the author, coauthor, and coeditor of numerous articles, book chapters, and books. Her recent publications include the *Encyclopedia of Race and Crime* (Sage, 2009), coedited with Shaun L. Gabbidon, and *Race and Crime* (2nd edition, Sage, 2009), coauthored with Shaun L. Gabbidon.

Dawn Irlbeck is an assistant professor of sociology at Creighton University. She received her PhD in criminology and criminal justice from the University of Nebraska at Omaha. She teaches courses on the criminal justice system, American cultural minorities, and social stratification, as well as other courses in sociology. Her primary research interests include racial profiling, policing and minority communities, Latino police officers, and ethnic identity formation. She has recently published on racial profiling and vehicle searches, as well as on variations in ethnic identity among Latino police officers.

Connie M. Koski earned her master's degree from Wayne State University and is currently a doctoral student in the School of Criminology and Criminal Justice at the University of Nebraska at Omaha. Her primary research interests include policing, hate crimes, and comparative criminal justice. Her work has appeared in such publications as *Policing: An International Journal of Police Strategies and Management* and *Police Practice and Research*.

Peter B. Kraska is a professor, Program of Distinction research fellow, and director of graduate studies in the College of Justice and Safety at Eastern Kentucky University. He is the author, coauthor, or editor of *Theorizing Criminal Justice: Eight Essential Orientations* (2010); *Criminal Justice and Criminology Research Methods* (2008; with W. Lawrence Neuman); *Drugs, Crime, and Justice* (with Larry K. Gaines); and *Militarizing the American Criminal Justice System: The Changing Role of the Armed Forces and the Police*. His numerous articles have been published in such journals as *Social Problems, Justice Quarterly*, and *Policing and Society*. His research on police militarization has been featured by print and television media outlets, including *60 Minutes, The Jim Lehrer News Hour, The Economist, The Washington Post, The New York Times*, and *the Los Angeles Times*.

Marilyn D. McShane is a professor of criminal justice at the University of Houston–Downtown. Her published work includes journal articles, monographs, encyclopedias, and books on a wide range of criminological and criminal justice subjects. Recent works she has authored or coauthored include *Prisons in America* (LFB Scholarly Publishing, 2008); *Criminological Theory*

(5th ed., Prentice Hall, 2009); *A Thesis Resource Guide for Criminology and Criminal Justice* (Prentice Hall, 2008); the coedited, three-volume set *Youth Violence and Delinquency: Monsters and Myths* (Praeger, 2008), and the *Encyclopedia of Juvenile Justice* (Sage, 2003).

Alan Mobley is an assistant professor of public affairs at San Diego State University. While in federal prison for the distribution of narcotics, he earned a bachelor's degree in economics and a master's degree in sociology. After release from prison, he earned a doctorate in criminology, law, and society from the University of California, Irvine. His research focuses on entrepreneurship, faith-based corrections, prison privatization, and substance abuse treatment.

Stephen L. Muzzatti is an associate professor of sociology at Ryerson University in Toronto, Canada, where he teaches courses in media, crime, and popular culture. He has written extensively on the news media's criminalization of youth culture, as well as on terrorism, crimes of globalization, crime and consumerism, motorcycle culture, and street racing. He is also an expert in arson and demolition. He has served as vice-chair of the American Society of Criminology's Division on Critical Criminology and as editor of *The Critical Criminologist*.

Johnny Nhan is an assistant professor of criminal justice at Texas Christian University. He obtained his PhD in criminology, law, and society from the University of California, Irvine. He has written on several areas of cybercrime, focusing largely on public and private policing of cyberspace. His research interests include network security, hacking, electronic piracy, and spam.

Thomas W. Nolan is an associate professor in criminal justice at Boston University, where he teaches courses in forensic behavioral analysis, policing and multiculturalism, crime and punishment, gender and justice, forensic criminal investigation, and the law and criminal procedure. A 27-year veteran (and former lieutenant) of the Boston Police Department, Nolan is consulted regularly by local, national, and international media outlets for his expertise in police procedures, the police subculture, gender issues in law enforcement, and crime trends and criminal behavior. Nolan's scholarly publications are in the areas of gender roles in policing and the influence of the popular culture on criminal justice processes.

David L. Parry is a professor of criminal justice at Endicott College in Beverly, Massachusetts. After receiving a BA in political science from UCLA, he earned his MA and PhD in the School of Criminal Justice at the University at Albany, State University of New York. The editor of *Essential Readings in Juvenile Justice* (Pearson Prentice Hall, 2005), he has directed research projects examining delinquent behavior; the operation of state and local juvenile justice systems; and the interaction of police, court, and correctional agencies with youth in numerous jurisdictions across the United States.

Lois Presser is an associate professor of sociology at the University of Tennessee. She holds a bachelor's degree in human development and family studies from Cornell University, an MBA from Yale University, and a doctoral degree in criminal justice/criminology from the University of Cincinnati. Dr. Presser is author of the book *Been a Heavy Life: Stories of Violent Men* (2008, University of Illinois Press), as well as articles in *Justice Quarterly, Signs, Social Justice,* and *Social Problems.* Currently she is developing a theory of harmful action.

Randall G. Shelden is a professor of criminal justice at the University of Nevada, Las Vegas, where he has been a faculty member since 1977. He is also a senior research fellow with the Center on Juvenile and Criminal Justice in San Francisco. He received a master's degree in sociology from Memphis State University and a PhD in sociology from Southern Illinois University. He is the author or coauthor of the following books: *Criminal Justice in America: A Sociological Approach; Girls, Delinquency and Juvenile Justice* (3rd ed., Cengage Publishers), with Meda Chesney-Lind (which received the Hindelang Award for outstanding contribution to Criminology in 1992); *Youth Gangs in American Society* (3rd ed., Cengage), with Sharon Tracy and William B. Brown; *Crime and Criminal Justice in American Society,* with William Brown, Karen Miller, and Randall Fritzler (Waveland Press); *Controlling the Dangerous Classes: The History of Criminal Justice* (2nd ed., Allyn and Bacon); *Delinquency and Juvenile Justice in American Society* (Waveland Press); and *Juvenile Justice in America: Problems and Prospects* (Waveland Press), coedited with Daniel Macallair. Dr. Shelden's next book is *Our Punitive Society,* to be published by Waveland Press. He is also the author of more than 50 journal articles and book chapters on the subject of crime and justice and has written more than 100 commentaries appearing in local and regional newspapers. He is coeditor of the online *Justice Policy Journal.* His website is www.sheldensays.com.

Cassia Spohn is a professor in the School of Criminology and Criminal Justice at Arizona State University, where she also serves as the director of graduate programs for the school. She is the coauthor of four books: *The Color of Justice: Race, Ethnicity, and Crime in America; How Do Judges Decide? The Search for Fairness and Justice in Punishment; Courts: A Text/Reader;* and *Rape Law Reform: A Grassroots Movement and Its Impact.* Dr. Spohn has published extensively on prosecutors' charging decisions in sexual assault cases, the effect of race/ethnicity and gender on sentencing decisions, sentencing of drug offenders, and the deterrent effect of imprisonment.

Craig D. Uchida is president of Justice & Security Strategies, Inc. (JSS), a consulting firm that specializes in issues related to criminal justice, homeland security, children and youth violence, public health, and public policy. Dr. Uchida was a senior executive with the Office of Community Oriented

Policing Services (COPS Office), U.S. Department of Justice. He was also director of criminal justice research at the National Institute of Justice. Dr. Uchida has published numerous journal articles, monographs, and book chapters on policing and evaluations of a variety of criminal justice programs. He is coeditor of two books on drug enforcement and police innovation. Dr. Uchida received his doctorate in criminal justice from the University at Albany, State University of New York, and holds two master's degrees, one in criminal justice and one in American history.

Anthony Walsh received his PhD in criminology from Bowling Green State University, Ohio, in 1983. He has field experience in both law enforcement and corrections and teaches criminology, law, and statistics at Boise State University, Idaho. He is the author, coauthor, or coeditor of 25 books and more than 100 journal articles. His latest book is *Biology and Criminology: The Biosocial Synthesis*; as the title suggests, his primary interest is in the integration of the biological and social sciences to develop a truly scientific criminology.

Frank P. Williams III is a professor of criminal justice at the University of Houston–Downtown and professor emeritus at California State University, San Bernardino. He has published a number of articles, research monographs, encyclopedias, and books in areas ranging from criminological theory to correctional management. His recent works include *Statistical Concepts for Criminal Justice and Criminology* (Prentice Hall, 2008) and *Imagining Criminology* (Taylor & Francis, 1999). He is coauthor of *Criminological Theory*, (5th ed., Prentice Hall, 2009), *A Thesis Resource Guide for Criminology and Criminal Justice* (Prentice Hall, 2008), and the three-volume, coedited set *Youth Violence and Delinquency: Monsters and Myths* (Praeger, 2008).

Ilhong Yun is an assistant professor in the Department of Criminal Justice at Boise State University. His research interests include victimology, biosocial criminology, and comparative criminal justice issues. His recent work has appeared in the *Asia Pacific Journal of Police and Criminal Justice*.

Supporting researchers for more than 40 years

Research methods have always been at the core of SAGE's publishing program. Founder Sara Miller McCune published SAGE's first methods book, *Public Policy Evaluation*, in 1970. Soon after, she launched the *Quantitative Applications in the Social Sciences* series—affectionately known as the "little green books."

Always at the forefront of developing and supporting new approaches in methods, SAGE published early groundbreaking texts and journals in the fields of qualitative methods and evaluation.

Today, more than 40 years and two million little green books later, SAGE continues to push the boundaries with a growing list of more than 1,200 research methods books, journals, and reference works across the social, behavioral, and health sciences. Its imprints—Pine Forge Press, home of innovative textbooks in sociology, and Corwin, publisher of PreK–12 resources for teachers and administrators—broaden SAGE's range of offerings in methods. SAGE further extended its impact in 2008 when it acquired CQ Press and its best-selling and highly respected political science research methods list.

From qualitative, quantitative, and mixed methods to evaluation, SAGE is the essential resource for academics and practitioners looking for the latest methods by leading scholars.

For more information, visit **www.sagepub.com**.